ISRAEL
Is Real

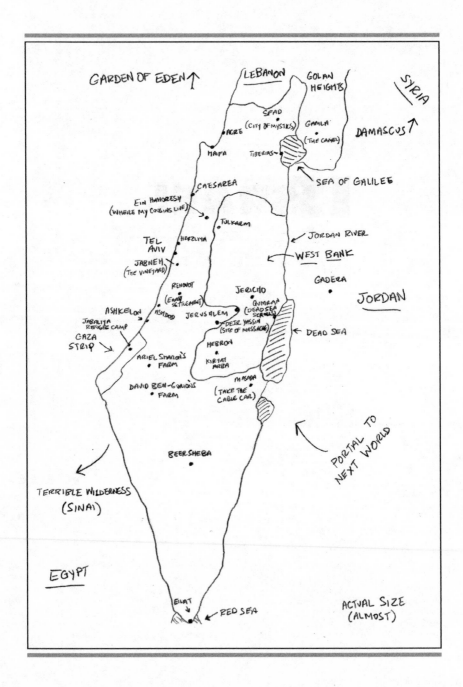

RICH COHEN

FARRAR, STRAUS AND GIROUX

New York

FARRAR, STRAUS AND GIROUX
18 West 18th Street, New York 10011

Copyright © 2009 by Rich Cohen
All rights reserved
Distributed in Canada by Douglas & McIntyre Ltd.
Printed in the United States of America
First edition, 2009

Library of Congress Cataloging-in-Publication Data
Cohen, Rich.
   Israel is real / Rich Cohen.—1st ed.
      p.   cm.
   Includes bibliographical references and index.
   ISBN-13: 978-0-374-17778-2 (hardcover : alk. paper)
   ISBN-10: 0-374-17778-3 (hardcover : alk. paper)
   1. Jews—History. 2. Cohen, Rich—Travel—Israel. 3. Israel—
Description and travel.   I. Title.

DS117.C64 2009
956.94—dc22

                                             2008049223

Designed by Cassandra J. Pappas

www.fsgbooks.com

1   3   5   7   9   10   8   6   4   2

For Jessica

Men of various nations had an identical dream. They saw a woman running at night through an unknown city; she was seen from behind, with long hair, and she was naked. They dreamed of pursuing her. As they twisted and turned, each of them lost her. After the dream they set out in search of that city; they never found it, but they found one another; they decided to build a city like the one in the dream.

—ITALO CALVINO, *Invisible Cities*

It is better to dwell in the wilderness, than with a contentious and angry woman.

—PROVERBS

Contents

ISRAEL
Is Real

June 1967

A wild euphoria swept the country. Israel had defeated the armies of Egypt, Syria, and Jordan, conquering the Sinai Desert, the Golan Heights, the West Bank of the Jordan River, and East Jerusalem, with its Old City and holy places, which Jews had not been allowed to visit in twenty years. Israelis stood in the street in front of the Western Wall, the holiest place in the world for Jews, weeping and praying. It's as if the images minted in the war—tanks wedged in the alleys of the Arab market, jets blazing across the sky, soldiers storming the Temple Mount—were too much. Even atheists felt the press of God.

There is a condition suffered by tourists who visit Israel. It's called the Jerusalem Syndrome. It's contracted mostly by Christians, who, touched by the light of the city and its ancient names (Gethsemane, Calvary) lose their minds, claim they are not the person on the

passport but a figure from the Bible, sometimes a major figure such as
Solomon or John the Baptist, sometimes a minor figure such as Boaz
or Enoch. They say they have come with a mission, a purpose: to
ready the people, to clear the way for the end-time. Their eyes glow.
They shout fearful warnings. There are around a hundred cases a
year. The symptoms usually disappear when the sufferer leaves the
country. One thing always confused me about the Jerusalem Syndrome: Why do Jews rarely get it? What makes them immune? Then,
one day, as I was walking around the Jewish Quarter of the Old City,
looking at the Israeli soldiers in their Kevlar, with their machine guns
and aviator sunglasses, and at the Hasids praying in the cave beside
the Western Wall, it dawned on me: they don't get it because they already have it. In 1967, with the triumph of the biblically named Six-
Day War, a strange, haunted quality entered the Jewish soul. Nearly
every Jew in the world has since evidenced symptoms of the Jerusalem
Syndrome.

There were two million Jews living in Israel in 1967. In the week following the war, five hundred thousand of them visited East Jerusalem. They wanted to see the old places, touch the old stones. They
went through the city, then out into the West Bank, a desert that runs
from Jerusalem to the Jordan River. This was once Judea, the heartland of ancient Israel, with its capital in Hebron. For the first seven
years of his reign, King David ruled from Hebron. It's where the Ark
of the Covenant was kept in its tabernacle, where, according to Genesis, the Hebrew patriarchs are buried: Abraham, Isaac, Jacob. It was
home to half a million Palestinian Arabs, whose towns and cities had
suddenly come under Israeli control. Jews crowded the markets of
Bethlehem and Tulkarm and Nablus. They haggled with Arab merchants and dug in the fields, looking for artifacts, shards of pottery,
anything that might connect them to the past.

Ariel Sharon was then thirty-nine years old. He had led a column
of tanks through the Sinai Desert, taken prisoners, defeated armies.

He was one of the heroes of the war. Everywhere he went, Israelis shouted, "Arik, King of the Jews!" He toured Jerusalem and the West Bank with his wife, Lily, and son Gur. Lily was his second wife, the younger sister of his first wife—Gur's mother—who had been killed in a car crash. "The roads were choked with people," he wrote.

> And every place we stopped we were met by an outpouring of love and affection. I had never seen people in such a state of excitement, visiting Jericho, the old cemetery on the Mount of Olives, the Western Wall, all the holiest sites that had been closed to Jews throughout the Jordanian occupation . . . [Nothing could] dampen the euphoria. It was as if the country was celebrating the most joyful period of its existence. Certainly it was the happiest time I had known, there was a feeling that we had finally broken free from the noose that had been around our necks . . . Once again we were able to go to all these places, these old places that were so much a part of our identity.

A friend gave Sharon's son Gur an antique gun found in the Judean hills, a front-loading rifle that had not been fired in perhaps a hundred years. It was a weapon you might see a Bedouin carrying in a daguerreotype, cresting a hill in white robes. In October, on the eve of Rosh Hashanah, Sharon was in his bedroom at home when Gur came in as if he wanted to say something, then, seeing his father on the phone, saluted—"the gesture of a boy who had grown up around the army," Sharon wrote—then went outside. A moment later, Sharon heard a shot. He ran to the yard, where he found Gur on his back, the antique rifle at his side, and a hole in his eye. Gur's little brothers, Gilad and Omri, were a few feet away, in their playpen. Sharon rushed to the hospital with the boy on his lap breathing heavily. "Ages seemed to pass as we raced to the hospital," he wrote, "and as we did, he died in my arms."

This was a personal tragedy for Sharon and his family, but it's also the story of Israel and the Jews. Like a story in the Bible, it can be read both literally and symbolically. Here is Ariel Sharon, the war hero, greeted everywhere by cries of "Arik, King of the Jews!" Here is the rifle, a relic waiting all those years in the hills, which is the ancient world of the Hebrews. Here is the man who goes into the hills and comes back with the artifact, the old gun presumed harmless. Here is the boy, the oldest son of the general, at play on a warm afternoon, his baby brothers looking on. Here is the bullet that comes from the past and kills the boy who was to inherit the kingdom.

I n AD 70, when the Second Temple was destroyed, a group of rabbis saved Judaism by reinventing it—by taking what had been a national religion, identified with a particular territory, as most religions were in the ancient world, and, amazingly, detaching it from its nation. The Temple and the sacrifices and practices associated with it were replaced by prayer. The capital, Jerusalem, was replaced by the image of an ideal or heavenly city, where people would gather at the end of time. Jews would no longer need Jerusalem in order to be Jews, not the physical Jerusalem. Whenever a Jew prayed, or studied the Torah, he would be in Jerusalem. In this way, the rabbis turned a real city into a city in the mind; in this way, they turned the Temple into a book. Which is why Judaism survived. You can burn a city, but you cannot sack an idea, or kill a book. But in our own time, Zionists have turned the book back into a temple. (Modern Israel is itself the Third Temple.) Temple into book back into temple. And unlike an idea, a temple can be destroyed. By making the faith physical, by locating it in a particular place at a particular time, Zionists have made Jews vulnerable in a way they have not been since the fall of the Second Temple. The fact that Judaism survived that calamity was a miracle, but would it survive it again? In this way, modern Israel, meant to protect Jews, may have put them in greater danger than they have known in two thousand years.

ONE

The Fire

Most great cities have a reason for being where they are, and doing what they do. Either they sit at the confluence of great rivers, at the head of a mountain pass, on the shore of a canal, on a trade route or a railroad crossing or a superhighway, but Jerusalem, as far as anyone can tell, has no reason for being where it is—at the edge of the desert, on a hill surrounded by identical hills, guarding nothing but itself, doing nothing but being Jerusalem.

Is it the oldest city in the world?

No. Jericho is older. But it's in that same league, from the same place in time. Always at issue. Always changing hands, filling and emptying. Stained with the blood of its citizens. Claimed by people who do not live there—nor did their parents, nor did their grandparents—but who still consider it their own. It exists in the past, as the capital of a lost civilization. It exists in the future, as the portal to the next world. It exists everywhere but in the present. It's where the past and the future overwhelm the present.

Jerusalem is first mentioned in Egyptian writings circa 1900 BC, where it's called Aushamen, a city on a hill on the far side of the desert. It turns up later, in the literature of Acadia and Assyria, as Urushalima, city of the deity Shalem. It was then a Canaanite city, holy to the priests of Ba'al. In the Torah, in which it's mentioned just once, it's called Salem. It's where Abraham, on his way home from battle, is given sustenance by the stranger "Melchizedek, the king of Salem," who, according to Genesis, "brought forth bread and wine: and he was the priest of the most high God. And he blessed [Abraham], and said, 'Blessed be Abram of the most high God, possessor of heaven and earth.' "

Melchizedek is the spirit of the Canaanite city blessing and forgiving its future usurpers: this story is like a mural in which Pocahontas kisses John Smith. To Christians, Melchizedek prefigures Christ, hints at Christ's coming, or is Christ Himself, the founder of a clerical line that will be fulfilled in the Church. That's why he blesses Abraham with bread and wine, the meal of the last supper and the Catholic Mass. In the New Testament, Melchizedek is called a "priest forever," an eternal priest who was never born and never dies, who always existed and always will, as the holy city always existed and always will.

Jerusalem entered history in 1000 BC, when it was conquered by David, the warlord who became king of the Hebrews.* David, who was in the process of uniting the scattered Hebrew tribes, picked Jerusalem as his capital because it was on neutral ground, located between the northern and southern kingdoms (Judea and Samaria) but had no special meaning to either. (It was chosen in the way Washington, D.C., was chosen.) It had already been hallowed by hundreds of years of Canaanite sacrifices to their gods Ba'al and Ashera,† deities who ap-

---

*The word *Jew* began to refer to the people as a whole—as opposed to merely the members of the tribe of Judah—around 700 BC, following the destruction of the nation's northern kingdom (Israel) by Assyria.

†Ba'al was worshipped in Jerusalem even after the Temple was built. During times of backsliding, altars to the Canaanite god sat beside altars to Yahweh. In the reign of Josiah, while the Temple was being renovated, a lost scroll was found between the walls. Josiah studied the scroll (probably Deuteronomy), read it to his priests, rent his garments, and went into mourning. The next day, all statues and altars to Ba'al were dragged off Mount Moriah and burned.

pear in the Bible as examples of the defunct order. In other words, Jerusalem was holy to Jews because it had been holy to Canaanites. Holy because it always had been, always had been because it always was.

David moved the Ark of the Covenant to his new capital. It was kept in a tent on a hill in the center of the city. When Solomon became king, he built a house for the Ark, thus a house for the Lord. The Temple of Solomon lingers in Jewish imagination as the center of the world when the world was whole. This move from tabernacle to temple represents the evolution of the Jews from tent-dwelling Bedouins to book-reading urbanites. The hill, which flattened out on top, had been used as a threshing floor by the Canaanites and was later identified as the Mountain of God—where the first man was made of clay, where Abraham bound Isaac. "Get thee into the land of Moriah, and offer him there for a burnt offering." It's unclear if everything happened on this mountain or if, when something enormous does happen, you are somehow back on the mountain, the navel of the world.

By moving the Ark to Jerusalem, David made his capital the center of political and religious power. Over time, it became something more: a symbol, a metaphor. It was the city as civilization, sacred as all cities are sacred. As Paris is sacred. As New York is sacred. But more so. The most famous story associated with Jerusalem is that of David and Bathsheba. The king looks out from the roof of his palace and sees Bathsheba washing herself. Sends for her. The rest is tragedy. The collapse of the United Kingdom of Israel. What is of interest here are the logistics: the fact that by looking from his roof David can see a woman bathing. This happens only in a city. In a sense, the downfall of the Jews results from the temptation and sin that come from life in a city—its concentration and compression, all those windows stacked on top of one another.

Jerusalem came to have a spiritual power not warranted by its size. It's a model for all great cities. When plans were drawn for Moscow in the seventh century, one proposal (not executed) based the city on the layout of Jerusalem, as depicted in the Book of Ezekiel. When Lalibela, the king of Ethiopia, returned from exile in Jerusalem (or maybe the idea came in a vision or dream; no one is really sure) he rebuilt his capital as a copy of the holy city, with churches and buildings carved from African sandstone. Jerusalem became a prize, a treasure to be taken and dominated. The list of its conquerors is the story of the world: Hebrews, Babylonians, Persians, Greeks, Romans, Arabs, Turks, Britons, Zionists. It entered the orbit of Rome in AD 66. The legions came at the invitation of Jews, who wanted them to establish order at a time of civil unrest. There had long been tension in the city between Hellenized Jews, who behaved like Greeks, and those who followed the ascetic faith of the desert.

The Romans restored order, then stayed, which is how Israel became a vassal, then a province. We know what this Jerusalem looked like. From letters, documents, books. It was dust colored and sat on a hill. It was a confusion of walls and streets. There were markets, mansions, slums. There was an Upper City and a Lower City. There was a trash dump in a valley called Gehenna, where pagans practiced human sacrifice. There was an underground spring, tunnels, chambers where food was stored in case of a siege. As you approached from the west, you would first see the Temple, then the walls. There was a sharp line between city and country, a black line, where wilderness ended and civilization began. One moment you were in the desert, the next you were swallowed up in the noise and chaos of town.

Y ou could not live under the Roman emperor and practice as a Jew. Not really. Roman officials looted the treasury and abused the priests. Roman soldiers sacrificed to pagan gods on the Temple Mount. To the Romans, every holy place offered access to the eternal, as in our time every money card works at every ATM. In AD 39, when Caligula declared himself a living god and gave orders to raise his statue in the Temple, the Jews rioted. These two cultures, occupying the same land, ground against each other. The particularity of the Jews—the fact that they recognized no god but their own—was a constant irritation to Rome. Why wouldn't the Jews, these tax-paying vassals, accept what was plain to the conquerors? That the Hebrew God was inferior to the gods of the Imperium.

This refusal alone was reason to hate the Jews—a hatred widespread even in the ancient world. Without saying so, the Jews seemed to insist that only their belief was true. In *The Decline and Fall of the Roman Empire*, Edward Gibbon calls Jews the "single people [who] refused to join in . . . the common intercourse of mankind. The sullen obstinacy with which they maintained their peculiar rites and unsocial manners seemed to mark them out as a distinct species of men, who boldly professed or faintly disguised their implacable hatred to the rest of humankind."

Rebellion was inevitable. In the event of rebellion, Roman victory was inevitable. In this way, the destruction of Jerusalem was also inevitable. The city was created to be destroyed. Is created and re-created to be destroyed again and again. The story of Jerusalem is not complete if it is not destroyed. As the story of Rome is not complete if it does not destroy. Rome destroys, Jerusalem gets destroyed. Flesh and spirit, reason and faith. Jerusalem needs Rome as Jesus needs Judas: to be sacrificed into a symbol. By being destroyed, Jerusalem sheds its skin, its alleys and markets and tortured history, and becomes immortal.

The last days of the ancient kingdom were rank with false messiahs and premonitions. The Book of Daniel, the Book of Revelation. *The seven angels came out of the Temple, having seven plagues, clothed in pure white linen.* When Jesus told Mark, "Seest thou these great buildings? There shall not be left one stone upon another, that shall not be thrown down," he was working less as a prophet than as a poet, amplifying the mood of his time. How should a Jew live? How should a Jew face occupation? These were the questions of the day. There were moderates who said Jews should find a way to exist in the Roman world. There were Essenes who, in their practice, seemed to say the only way to survive as a Jew was to leave Jerusalem. There were Zealots who said to be a Jew in a Roman world is to fight and die. When Christ said, "Render unto Caesar," he was, in a way, responding to the Zealots, giving the people permission to live.

It was a golden age of building. A boom. Projects paid for by Rome in hopes of winning the consent of the ruled. Herod, who had been

made the king of Judea by the occupier, restored the walls of Jerusalem, built hippodromes and theaters, littered the countryside with
palaces. He rebuilt the Temple, restoring it to a glory it had not known
since the age of Solomon. (The First Temple had been destroyed by
the Babylonians in 586 BC.) When people think of the Jewish Temple,
it's this building they have in mind: stark, white, glowing in the sun.
Herod followed the plan described in the Book of Kings—God was
the architect, Herod his contractor—60 cubits by 20 cubits by 40 cubits; 162 columns; reached by fourteen steps; entered through 9 gates,
each with a double door plated in bronze and silver. There were royal
chambers, porches, pedestals for the shofar blowers. (The ram's horn,
perhaps the most ancient wind instrument in the world, was blown on
the Temple Mount to announce new moons, feast days, jubilees, etc.;
today it is heard in the synagogue on Rosh Hashanah and Yom Kippur.) There was a courtyard for men and a courtyard for women and
a courtyard for Gentiles. At the gate to the inner court a sign warned,
in Latin and Greek, NO FOREIGNER MAY PASS WITHIN THE LATTICE
AND WALL AROUND THE SANCTUARY. WHOEVER IS CAUGHT, THE
GUILT FOR HIS DEATH WILL BE HIS OWN. Gardens and cloisters and
chambers, and chambers within chambers, all centered around an
outer court, centered around an inner court, centered around the holy
of holies, a black room, twenty cubits by twenty cubits, where, once a
year, the high priest stood alone in the dark and whispered the secret
name of God.

It took eighty years to finish the Temple. Here's how Josephus, the
Jewish general who became a citizen of Rome, described it in his
history:

> Viewed from without, the sanctuary had everything that could amaze
> either mind or eye. Overlaid all around with stout plates of gold, in
> the first rays of the sun it reflected so fierce a blaze of fire that those
> who endeavored to look at it were forced to turn away as if they had
> looked straight at the sun. To strangers as they approached, it seemed
> in the distance like a mountain covered with snow; for any part that
> was not covered with gold was dazzling white.

Historians cite various proximate causes for the first Jewish revolt, which did not come until after a century of Roman rule. In AD 66, for example, in Caesarea, a mixed town of Greeks and Jews on the Mediterranean, Greeks, as part of a pagan ceremony, sacrificed birds at the doors of a Hebrew shrine, which Jews understood as a sacrilege and a threat (in the nature of finding a cross burning on one's lawn). When Jewish leaders asked for protection, the Romans refused, saying they wanted no part in sectarian strife. Word of this refusal swept through the community. By the time it reached Jerusalem, people were in a rage. The Zealots, a radical religious party, said there could be no peace with Rome. It was God or Caesar. They set upon the occupiers, sacked the garrisons, burned the barracks, stormed the forts, most spectacularly the mountaintop stronghold of Masada, which had been built as a palace by Herod.

Meanwhile, a debate was taking place between the Zealots and a group later known as the Peace Party: accommodation or war? What if the Zealots had lost this argument? What if the Temple had survived? Would people still speak of "the Jewish character"? Perhaps this speculation is pointless. If the Germans don't invade Russia, they're not the Germans. If the American colonists don't throw off the British, they're not the Americans. If the Jews don't rebel against Rome, they're not the Jews.

The Romans assembled a small army in Antioch; to Rome, this was still a minor disturbance, easily repressed. The Twelfth Legion, serving under General Cestius Gallus, invaded from the north. They marched in columns, the road stretching away behind them. They wore black metal chest-and-backplates held together by leather straps; iron helmets; neck guards; hobnail boots that laced to the calf; and metal belts that holstered a knife, a double-edged sword, and a javelin. They raised their shields as they went into battle, making a canopy of leather, each shield decorated with the symbol of its legion: tiger, serpent, eagle. They were met outside each town by fanatics, Zealots in flowing robes, head scarves, sandals. In the folds of their coats, the Zealots carried little knives, which they wielded in the manner of the Tongs, the Chinese gangs of New York. This army was led by a priest named John. Before each battle, the Jews cleaned their bodies, said their prayers. They did not fear death, and so fought with an abandon that terrified the professional soldiers of Rome. They hid in caves, then attacked as if out of nowhere. The Roman legion was destroyed, the bodies of its soldiers left to rot in the sun.

There were celebrations in the walled cities of Judea. The Temple was filled with worshippers. Coins were struck depicting a victorious Jewish soldier standing over the body of a defeated Roman.

This was a moment when Rome could have lost its empire. There were rebellions in several provinces. Judea would serve as the example. In AD 67, Vespasian, considered the greatest soldier in Rome, led sixty thousand men—a huge army for the time—into the Galilee. His method was massacre. Burn everything. The first battle was fought in a town called Gadera.

Here's how Josephus described it in *The Jewish War*:

> Vespasian descended on Gadera, and finding it almost without defenders took it at the first assault. He marched into the town and put to the sword all except small children, the Romans showing mercy to neither young nor old through hatred of the nation and the memory of the way they had treated Cestius. He burnt down not only the town but all the hamlets and villages around the town. Some of these he found completely abandoned; from others he carried off all the occupants as slaves.

Vespasian made his headquarters in Caesarea, where he was joined by his son Titus. I've seen busts of Vespasian. He had a weak chin, narrow eyes set far apart—on opposite sides of his head, like a hawk—and scanty strands of hair. After Vespasian defeated a Jewish town, the Greeks of Caesarea honored him with a twenty-day party. At first Vespasian waged war exclusively in the north, the most radical part of the country. If the Jews were defeated in the north, he said, the rest of the nation might fall without a fight. One after another, the ancient towns were surrounded, starved, conquered. If the defenders surrendered, the men were killed, the women sold into slavery. If the defenders did not surrender and were quickly defeated, the men were killed, the women were killed, and the children were sold into slavery. If the defenders fought with limited success, the men were killed, the women were killed, the children were killed, and the babies were sold into slavery. If the defenders fought with great success, the men were killed, the women were killed, the children were killed, the babies were killed, and the town was burned.

In the course of the war, the Galilee was depopulated; six thousand young Jews were sent to work on the isthmus of Corinth, twelve hundred old Jews were killed, and the rest, more than thirty thousand people, were sold into slavery.*

The war in the north culminated in Gamla. To get there from Tiberias, which is the largest town in northern Israel and, not coincidentally, the only town spared by Vespasian—the entire population surrendered before a javelin was thrown—you take Road 92, which hugs the Galilee. In the summer, the sea is a luminous blue eye. On the eastern shore, the hills rise from the beach to the black folds of Syria. At the first intersection, you turn onto Road 869, which follows switchbacks into the Golan Heights. The road narrows as you climb, the air turns wintry. This is territory Israel captured in 1967. Before that, Syria used it as a base, with reconnaissance posts and missile sites. When Israel captured it, they built posts and sites of their own. Along the way, you see cannons built into the rock, then reach a plateau that comes like a crescendo at the end of a symphony. Grasslands ringed by mountains. Birds of prey. Pine needles. The country is beautiful because it's terrible and old.

Gamla is one of the great archeological sites of the Jewish Revolt,

---

*See *The Jewish Encyclopedia.*

a place where the Zealots made a dramatic stand, where the old Israel with its warrior Jew passed into lore. Yet, unlike Masada, it never became a holy place for Zionists—partly because it's so hard to reach, with no bus service or cable car; partly because it was not excavated until after the Six-Day War, by which time Israelis no longer needed a shrine to Jewish heroism. In other words, Gamla missed its moment. It's like an actress who would have been perfect in silent movies but was discovered after *The Jazz Singer*.

It was a two-hour walk from the parking lot, most of it along a treacherous path. The town itself is perched on a peak that rises from the valley floor. It's a geological oddity, a city on an island in a sea without water. On either side, the path drops into a green abyss. Hawks turn above. That day, the sky was filled with the type of clouds that meteorologists call "fair weather cumulus," flat bottoms and cottony peaks. The sun came through in search beams, Jacob's ladders, which, according to Genesis, are "ramps set against the ground with tops reaching the Heavens, with messengers of God going up and coming down." I could see hills in the distance. Some were one kind of green, some were another kind. The path grew steeper. I had to scramble. The peaks around the town loomed and leaned and towered ominously ahead, peaks that rise in humps and give the town its name: *Gamla* derives from "camel."

The town itself was a snug piece of work, with houses and storerooms and ritual baths and terraces squeezed inside a wall sitting on a cliff. There was a lower city and an upper city, with a gate between. If the walls of the lower city fell, the people could retreat to the upper city. Like a ship, in which, in case of a breach, you seal off the lower galley and move to the upper decks. The windows of the town stood hundreds of feet above the valley. Above these were towers that commanded a view of the country for miles.

All this made Gamla easy to protect, and almost impossible to conquer. No matter where a defender stood, he stood on high ground. An invading army would have to make its charge up a steep grade over an abyss. The Romans did not attack until the second year of the war. By then, most of the big towns of the Galilee had fallen. The most radical Zealots, those who had survived, had gone to Gamla, where they would make a final stand. Pacing in the ruins, I had no trouble imagining a legion appearing suddenly in the pass at the foot of the valley, twenty thousand men dragging slaves and siege engines behind them.

The Zealots stood on the ramparts watching the Romans assemble their equipment. Like watching the hangman prepare the scaffold. The first assault came before it was expected. Roman soldiers climbed the cliffs in the dead of night, slipped past the sentries, and rushed into the lower town. Vespasian was with them. Many of the Jews, caught by surprise, fought half-dressed, wildly. The Romans used swords. The Jews used stones, clubs. They were routed, but able to slip into the upper city and close the gate behind them. They disappeared, then reappeared on the walls, throwing rocks and spears.

The Romans climbed onto the rooftops, from where they could reach the upper city. Their uniforms were leather and steel, covered in knives and spears. More climbed onto the roofs, a carpet of squares, a sea of soldiers, mountains all around. The roofs sagged beneath the weight, then buckled. When the first house collapsed, it took down the adjoining one, which took down the next. They went like dominoes. Within seconds, the entire lower town had slid over the precipice, with hundreds of Roman soldiers clinging to rubble.

This image—the Romans, heaped together, screaming as they fell—is so clear in my mind I feel I must have seen it somewhere. In a painting, maybe. I've spent hours searching museums for just the right shade of light, just the right concentration of men and equipment. What kind of sound did it make? Jews stood at the windows in the upper town, exhilarated because their pursuers had been swept away, God had made their city clean. Several thousand Romans died. An entire division went over, along with half the town architecture. Survivors fought in the rubble. Vespasian was seen with his sword. The Romans retreated, then cordoned off Gamla. They would starve the Zealots into submission. The Romans patrolled the hills for Jews who, as food grew scarce, came out to forage.

The siege lasted a year, by which time the Jews, half mad with hunger and fear, had begun to turn on one another. This was, in fact, the situation throughout Judea. Orthodox Jews will tell you that it was not the Romans who destroyed the kingdom. It was the civil war that pitted pragmatists against absolutists. In the end, Vespasian dragged his siege engines up the hill and battered his way into Gamla. He knocked down wall after wall, invaded room after room. Many of the Zealots gathered in the tower that loomed over the valley. It was called the Citadel. There was a staircase. The defenders fought as they went up, like going to heaven. Now and then, a Roman lost his balance and fell screaming. The sky darkened and a storm blew into the valley, thunderheads pouring out of darker clouds, light glowing within. The rain came down in stinging lashes.

Josephus:

> [The Jews] were struck full in the face by a miraculous tempest, which carried the Roman shafts up to them but checked their own and turned them aside. So violent was the blast they could neither keep their feet on the narrow ledges, having no proper foothold, nor see the approaching enemy. Up came the Romans and hemmed them in: whether they resisted or tried to surrender, their fate was the same, for the Romans boiled with rage against them all when they remembered those who had perished in the first onslaught.

In this way, God Himself, grown tired of the rebellion, flicked the Jews off their perch. After all, who could defeat the chosen of God but God Himself?

Rather than face capture, the last defenders leapt into the abyss, throwing their children and wives before them. According to Josephus, five thousand died in this way, more than were killed in the battle itself.

Much of this history was written by Josephus, the most notorious traitor in the epic of Israel, a Jewish general who defected to the Imperium, serving as an advisor to Vespasian, then to Titus. After the war, he settled in Rome, where he changed his name from Joseph ben

Matthias to Flavius Josephus. He was given a pension and a villa and spent the rest of his life writing about the fall of the kingdom.

His first book was *The Jewish War*, which tells the story of the rebellion and his part in it. He sent copies to Vespasian, Titus, and Agrippa, the king of Antioch. He wanted their approval. All his books were written with Roman power in mind. The victors come off as heroic, the defeated as fanatics. He plays up his own importance—described in third person—and justifies his treason. For this reason, many historians question the accuracy of the book, which, they say, should be regarded as one would regard a commissioned portrait of a monarch. Josephus went on to write many more books, including a twenty-volume history of the Jews, *Antiquitates Judaicae* (*Jewish Antiquities*), in which he tells the stories of the Bible in the voice of the Greeks. (Tacitus was his model.) He starts with Adam and ends with Josephus.

These books were not preserved by Jews—they had enough history already—but by Romans, then by Christians, for whom they were the only picture of the world at the time of Jesus. In Christian homes in Europe in the eighteenth and nineteenth centuries, the works of Josephus often sat on the shelf next to the King James Bible. Near the end of his life, Josephus was challenged by Justus ben Pistus, a rival from Tiberias, who said Josephus had exaggerated his role in the rebellion. Josephus responded in a memoir, *Vita*, meant to clear his name. But this was entirely unnecessary: Justus ben Pistus remained a part of the Jewish world, which had been defeated and was about to leave history, whereas Josephus had attached himself to Rome, and so would live on forever.*

It is the clearest example I know of history being written by the winners. Because Josephus defected, it's his story we tell two thousand years later. He was the first writer of the Exile—the first to realize that for a stateless Jew, power comes only by making yourself useful to the goyim. The only Jewish voices to survive from that generation—a generation of lunatics and visionaries, perhaps the most important generation in Jewish history—are those of Josephus and Jesus, a general who went over to Rome and a rabbi who said, in essence, "Give the

---

*In fact, we know of Justus ben Pistus only because Josephus wrote about him.

Romans what they want as their power is here and our power is elsewhere."

It's easy to feel conflicted about Josephus: his treason hurt his
people, but it also put him in a position to tell their story. Our entire
knowledge of the Jewish Revolt, what happened in Gamla, but also
what happened at Masada and Jerusalem, comes from Josephus.

He was born in AD 37 in the Galilee. His family traced its lineage
to the Hasmonean kings, who ruled Judea before the Roman occupation. He was a Cohen, a priest. At fourteen he was recognized as a
prodigy. He could read the land as if it were a book. He walked its
hills, slept in its caves. If you looked into his eyes, you would see the entire kingdom reflected there—the walled cities of the north, the Zealot
strongholds and merchant towns of the south. The land was the body
of the people, with Jerusalem its great beating heart.

He studied with every sect and still could not decide which was
closer to the truth. He spent three years meditating in the desert, then
went to see the world: Antioch, Alexandria, Rome. A wealthy young
man from the provinces. According to the Roman busts, he was pointy
faced, with a crooked nose, curly hair, and a turned-down mouth. He
spent several years in the capital, learned its languages, read its epics.
Maybe he wished he had been born Roman. Maybe he wished he
could straighten his nose, change his name, marry a shiksa, and retreat
to a villa overlooking the sea.

When he returned to Jerusalem in AD 66, the air was filled with talk
of rebellion. Josephus had been to Rome, seen its river crowded with
ships, its parade grounds filled with soldiers. He knew its power. He
said that revolt would only bring disaster. He joined the Peace Party.
At such times, a reasonable voice can sound treasonous. An order was
issued for his arrest. He took sanctuary in the Temple and stayed there
for weeks, until the Zealots had won the argument and the Romans
had been driven from their garrisons. After that, Josephus was no
longer a threat. The warrant was rescinded. He joined the leaders of
the nation as they prepared for war. The Sanhedrin, the council that
ruled Judea, made him governor of the Galilee. He would control towns
and cities and an army of a hundred thousand.

Josephus believed he could save the north by keeping his soldiers out of the fight. He ignored Roman legions as they marched by his towns. To the Zealots, he had always been perfidious. They tried to remove him from office, then tried to kill him. He did not send men into battle until the second year of the Revolt, when a division of Roman soldiers massacred the inhabitants of a Jewish town. He proved a master of asymmetrical warfare. His army was smaller than that of Rome, yet he always fought with a numerical advantage. He attacked the enemy's weak point. His soldiers would strike, disappear, strike again. They came from the direction least expected, the sun at their backs, under the cover of fog. He was a riddle to the professional generals of Rome. He did not follow the rules, did not adhere to the patterns, yet won again and again.

The end came in the third year of the Revolt, in a valley north of Hebron, where Josephus was surprised by a large Roman force. His soldiers broke under fire and ran in search of shelter. They made it to Jotapata, and threw the gates closed behind them.

Jotapata was a fortified town. There were tunnels beneath it, buried rivers and wells. Even in the time of Josephus, it was considered ancient, its walls built by Joshua.* It probably looked like Arab towns you see in the north today, picturesque from afar, squalid and impoverished up close. Vespasian settled in for a long siege, surrounding Jotapata with soldiers and choking off its supplies. Every day, the Romans launched rocks into the town and pummeled its gates with battering rams. Zealots lined the walls, throwing back the invaders.

In his history, Josephus singles out a soldier—it's a last fleeting image of the ancient warrior Jew.

In the struggle, one of the Jews distinguished himself in a way that calls for special mention. His father's name was Zamias, and his birthplace was Saba in the Galilee. This man raised a huge stone and flung it from the wall at a battering ram with such tremendous force that he broke off its head. Then he leapt down and seizing the head under

---

*The Jewish Encyclopedia: "The site of Jotapata has been identified with the modern town of Tell Jafat, north of Sepphoris."

the noses of the enemy carried it back to the wall without turning a hair. A target now for all his foes and with no armor to protect his body from the rain of missiles, he was pierced by five shafts but paying not the slightest regard to them he climbed the wall and stood there for all to admire his daring; then, writhing with the pain of his wounds, he fell to the ground with the head of the ram still in his grip.

Jotapata was besieged for forty-seven days. It would have held out longer were it not betrayed by a deserter who met with Vespasian and told him of the desperate, fatigued state of the defenders. The next morning, at dawn, the Romans scaled the walls and slipped into the town. (Vespasian's son, Titus, was the first man on the ladders.) Roman soldiers were everywhere before the Jews knew the walls had been breached. A few men had time to get their weapons, but most fought with their hands. As Jews came out of their houses—and many, seeing what was happening, did not come out, but said their prayers, killed their families, then killed themselves—they were swept up in a tide of retreat.

It had rained the night before, which I mention because it was a factor, another detail in the tragedy. When the Jews turned to fight, their feet gave way on the slick stones. Many were killed on the ground. The Romans pushed the others down the hill like herd animals. In Josephus's description, you see the white fog that enveloped the town, the Romans driving the women and children before them. Bodies lay in the streets. Thousands were massacred. More killed themselves. This fact of suicide is often mentioned to demonstrate the fanaticism of the Jews, but it probably says less about the Jews than about how terrible it was to be taken prisoner by Rome. When the Romans won a war—and they won wars all the time—it was due to their organization, their training, their roads, but also to their willingness to be more brutal than anyone else. Civilization had not made them more gentle—it had perfected their brutality.

Josephus wandered the ruins, waiting to be captured or killed. A survivor of the massacre led him to a chamber beyond the walls of town, where Jewish leaders were hiding. These men spent days in this basement, speaking in whispers as the Roman soldiers combed the rubble above. Each night, some Jews sneaked out in search of food. One of these foragers was spotted and followed back to the basement. Romans ordered the Jews hiding there to surrender. It's not clear what happened next; the only testimony comes from Josephus, who claimed there was an argument. He wanted to surrender, but others wanted to take their own lives instead. He quotes one of the men scolding him, saying, "Are you so in love with your life, Josephus, that you can bear to live as a slave?"

Josephus argued for existence, or, as the traitor himself wrote in the third person, "Josephus, in this critical situation, began to philosophize.

"'Why, my friends, are we so anxious to commit suicide? Why should we make those best of friends, body and soul, part company?'"

There was a vote: the majority chose death. Lots were drawn. Each man would kill his neighbor. The holder of the short straw would kill the next-to-last man, then himself. Josephus drew short.* When it was his turn to kill, he convinced the next-to-last man they should surrender and live.

Josephus represents all those who, by trick or compromise, survive the fall. He is everyone who lives through the end and keeps on living. How much easier defeat would be if you actually died of heartbreak.

Not dying is the problem.

Josephus was offered terms. He would be made a slave in name only: neither humiliated nor transported out of the country nor forced to work. "Josephus's prowess made him admired rather than hated," Josephus wrote, "and the [Roman] commander was anxious to bring him out, not for punishment but because he preferred to save so excellent a man."†

Still, there was protocol. Josephus had to walk between Roman soldiers through the ruins of town; had to stand in the door of Vespasian's tent with head bowed; had to kneel before the general. Romans fastened leather bands around his ankle and wrist, marking him as a slave. He was told to rise. Vespasian looked him over, poured

*Of course!

†Remember, this is Josephus on Josephus.

a glass of wine. Then gave him dinner and a place to sleep. The next evening, the men talked: about the battle, about the culture of the Jews, about morale, and about what direction the war might take.

Josephus became an advisor to Vespasian. He explained the Jewish world and helped the general devise strategy. Vespasian was told that Josephus was a priest and could interpret dreams. Josephus said he had foreseen the defeat of the Jews in a vision, towns on fire and rivers boiling. He cast himself in the tradition of his namesake Joseph, the favorite son of Jacob, who, sold into slavery, won power through the interpretation of dreams.* (The relationship between Josephus and Vespasian echoes the relationship between Joseph and Pharaoh.) Josephus told Vespasian about a dream he had had. It was filled with symbols and numbers and signs that might mean nothing to a common man, but to Josephus the meaning was plain: Vespasian would soon be made emperor of Rome.

Josephus asked to say a word in private. Vespasian ordered everyone but his son Titus and two friends to withdraw, and Josephus began thus: You suppose sir, that in capturing me you have merely secured a prisoner, but I come as a messenger of the greatness that awaits you.

---

*"Pharaoh spoke to Joseph: 'In my dream, behold, I was standing on the bank of the Nile; and behold, seven cows, fat and sleek came up out of the Nile, and they grazed in the marsh grass. Lo, seven other cows came up after them, poor and very ugly and gaunt, such as I had never seen for ugliness in all the land of Egypt; and the lean and ugly cows ate up the first seven fat cows. Yet when they had devoured them, it could not be detected that they had devoured them, for they were just as ugly as before. Then I awoke . . .' Joseph said to the Pharaoh, '. . . The seven good cows are seven years . . . The seven lean and ugly cows that came up after them are seven years . . . God has shown to Pharaoh what He is about to do. Behold, seven years of great abundance are coming in all the land of Egypt; and after them seven years of famine will come, and all the abundance will be forgotten in the land of Egypt, and the famine will ravage the land. So the abundance will be unknown in the land because of that subsequent famine; for it will be very severe . . . Now let Pharaoh look for a man discerning and wise, and set him over the land of Egypt.' . . . Pharaoh said to Joseph, 'Since God has informed you of all this, there is no one so discerning and wise as you are. You shall be over my house, and according to your command all my people shall do homage; only in the throne I will be greater than you.' . . . Pharaoh took off his signet ring from his hand and put it on Joseph's hand, and clothed him in garments of fine linen and put the gold necklace around his neck" (Genesis 41:14–42). (I have tried to quote from the King James Bible throughout, varying only where there is a specific purpose.) Dreams and the interpretation of dreams have played a long, mysterious role in Jewish history, as anyone who has looked at the scriptures knows— God appears in dreams before battle, and the ability to interpret dreams is a way to salvation. (Is it any wonder that a book that helped make the name of Sigmund Freud, whom Isaac Bashevis Singer called "that latter-day prophet," was *On the Interpretation of Dreams*?)

Had I not been sent by God himself, I knew the Jewish law and how a General ought to die. Are you sending me to Nero? How so? Will Nero and those who succeed him on the throne before your turn comes remain on the throne? You, Vespasian, are Caesar and Emperor, you and your son here. So load me with your heaviest chains and keep me for yourself; for you are master not only of me, Caesar, but of land and sea and all the human race; and I ask to be kept in closer confinement as my penalty, if I am taking the name of God in vain.*

A few months later, Vespasian was ordered back to Rome. A civil war had broken out there. Josephus accompanied the general as far as Alexandria, where they crossed paths with Titus, who, having gone to the capital not long before, was returning to Judea. Josephus went along to advise Titus during the siege of Jerusalem. Titus and Josephus were camped outside the city when word came from the capital: Vespasian had put down the rebellion and been made emperor; the prophecy had been fulfilled. Vespasian freed Josephus in acknowledgment, and made him a citizen of Rome.

Jerusalem was besieged for three years. You could not enter or leave the city without being stopped and searched by Roman soldiers. Imagine what it looked like from a military camp across the valley. The city was already ancient, older than time. Like Rome, it represented something. It was the antipodes of Rome, which was reason and plumbing and progress and power. Jerusalem was spirit and faith and no plumbing and desert. In choking Jerusalem, Rome was the brain come to stop its own heart, the body come to kill its own soul. In movies, when they want to show a city in the ancient world, they put actors in sandals and stand them before a blue screen, which is then filled in by animators. The result is supposed to be super real but always looks like a cartoon. And maybe that's right. There is something cartoonish about

*The Jewish War, Josephus.

these Ur-cities, fantastic literary settlements on which our world was
built. A fantasy conjured on a screen. From a distance, the city looks as
if it's made of earth, as if God fashioned Adam out of clay, then made
him a city, then filled it with breath. There are dusty stone roofs. There
are alleys. There are domes and arches. There's an outer wall and an
inner wall, a box in a box, with a passage between. If the outer wall
fell, the defenders would retreat behind the inner wall. The Romans
had thrown up yet another wall, a siege wall made of wood and stone.
Much is made of the fence Israel is now building between itself and
the Palestinians on the West Bank. Looking back, you realize that the
history of the city is nothing but walls.

The Romans put up the blockade during a holy week, when the
city was filled with pilgrims. These people were trapped inside, with
neither enough food nor beds nor water. The situation deteriorated.
There was a struggle for control of the streets, which was won, after a
violent clash, by the Zealots. They were led by John of Giscala, who
came to Jerusalem following the destruction of his own village in the
south. John is a familiar type in Jewish lore, the man from the fringe,
the extremist who takes control in extremis, then steers the ship onto
the rocks. He is Captain Ahab. He is Meir Kahane. He is the fanatic
who believes there is just one way.

Josephus:

> John set his heart on one-man rule, and, not content to be on equality
> with any of his fellows, gradually built a following of the worst types.
> He issued orders like a lord. Some gave way through fear; some were
> genuine adherents.

John enforced a strict version of religious law in the city, driving
moderates underground, or killing them. He was less concerned with
the Romans outside the walls than with the Jews inside. If he could
bring the Jews into alignment with God, then God would take care of
the Romans.

In *The Jewish War*, Josephus seems most keenly interested in what
he calls "the Zealots' unholy acts." He details the massacre of the

Peace Party, the killing of scholars and priests. "With these out of the way," he writes, "the Zealots fell upon the remaining population and butchered them like a herd of unclean animals." Josephus explains how the Zealots barricaded themselves inside the Temple, then used it as a base, drinking the holy water. He calls the Zealots "a pack of rogues" and describes them as you might describe the Barbary pirates:

> Their passion for looting was insatiable. They ransacked rich men's houses, murdered men and violated women for sport: through sheer boredom they shamelessly gave themselves up to effeminate practices, adorning their hair and putting on women's clothes, steeping themselves in scent and painting under their eyes to make themselves attractive. They copied not merely the dress but also the passions of women, and in their utter filthiness invented unlawful pleasures; they wallowed in slime, turning the whole city into a brothel and polluting it with the foulest practices. Yet though they had the faces of women, they had the hands of murderers.

Jerusalem was not destroyed by the Romans, says Josephus, but by the Zealots. (Like John, he does not believe it is in the power of Rome to end the city of God.) Josephus and John are, in a sense, engaged in an argument: What will bring the Jews to ruin? Being too stubborn and too literal, or straying and acting like the Romans? Resisting, or failing to resist?

The Zealots forbade Jews from leaving the city. Those caught trying were killed, their bodies thrown over the wall into a trench. "A stream of deserters eluded the Zealots," writes Josephus, "but flight was difficult as every exit was guarded and anyone caught was assumed to be on his way to the Romans and [was thus] dispatched." Some escaped through the water tunnels, then turned up starving at the gates of the Roman camp. They were questioned and set free. According to Josephus, a few Jews swallowed their money before they fled: coins. A mercenary saw a prisoner picking metal out of his own excrement. "The rumor [then] ran around the camps that the deserters were arriving stuffed with gold," writes Josephus. "The Arab unit and the Syrians cut open the refugees and ransacked their bellies. In a single night two thousand were ripped up."

Oh Josephus! What did you feel like in those awful last days, when you slept among the Romans as your people were starving behind the wall? Was your slave girl a comfort? Did you wake in the dead of night, with the desert all around, and think, *What have I done?*

A few days before the final attack, Titus sent Josephus to walk beneath the city walls and call the Jews to surrender. *You cannot win*, said Josephus. *You're on the wrong side of history. The war will destroy the city you love! Come! Render unto Caesar!* Josephus was hated in Jerusalem; among the Zealots, he might have been the most hated man in the world. If the Jews had prevailed over the Romans, if Judaism had prevailed over Christianity, Josephus would be Judas. As he was shouting, a Zealot threw a rock that caught Josephus in the head and dropped him. He lay motionless. Romans crowded around. The city turned above. It was made of pink stone. There was blood on the stone and beneath it was the older stone of older civilizations. The Jews watched as Josephus was carried back to the Roman camp. A cheer went through the city. *The apostate is silenced! The dog is dead!* There were prayers of thanks. But a few days later, he was back, head wrapped in a bandage, eyes glassy, using a cane. An old Jew on the docks of Smyrna, or walking on Collins Avenue in North Miami Beach. "You obdurate fools!" he shouted, "Throw away your weapons! Take pity on your birthplace at this moment plunging into ruin. Turn around and gaze at the beauty of what you are betraying!"

The return of Josephus was a blow to the Zealots. It was like the dream in which you slay the beast, and the beast rises again. The Romans launched their invasion the next day. First came the archers, who showered the city with arrows. Then came the siege towers and battering rams, rolled into position on great wooden wheels. Zealots dashed out to sabotage the towers and fight the Romans in the trenches. They wore sandals and skullcaps and robes belted with swords; they were bearded, with the large, luminous eyes of the emaciated. They shouted the name of God as they went into battle. Here is what they sounded like: *Ahhhhh! Ka! Ka! Ka!* They were fearless, driven for glory. "They were concerned only with what they could inflict, death had no terror for them if it fell on one of the enemy too," writes Josephus. In his last throes, a Zealot would turn to look at the Temple, which gave him comfort. He was seeing a reflection of the kingdom he was about to enter.

In the chaos of battle, thousands of Jews escaped the city. During the siege, the Romans released those who escaped and had been captured. During the battle, they assumed every Jew was an enemy. Thousands of Jewish prisoners were crucified beside the walls of Jerusalem. "The soldiers nailed up their victims in various attitudes as a grim joke," writes Josephus. Crosses were planted everywhere, fields of crucified Jews dying in agony. They rotted, their faces came apart, hawks pecked out their eyes. These corpses, visible from the ramparts, were meant to demoralize those who fought on.

What a finale!

Jerusalem expires in an orgy of crucifixion. Not three crosses on Calvary but a forest of crosses, each a tree, each tree heavy with fruit. It's like a painting by Jan Van Eyck: Jerusalem on its hill, behind its walls, beneath its lucent blue sky. The foreground is a sea of dying men, each drawn in outlandish detail, the population of the defeated kingdom. In building these crosses, the Romans used trees from the surrounding hills; the same trees they had long used to make crosses in Judea; the same trees they had used to make the cross for Jesus. In the final weeks of the war, trees were felled in such terrific numbers—to make crosses, but also to make battering rams and siege engines—that the hills were stripped. In this way, the landscape of Judea came to mimic the interior desolation of the Jews. What had once been a green carpet of fig and pine was now made desolate and black. "The countryside was a pitiful sight, for where once there had been a vista of woods and parks there was nothing but desert and stumps of trees," wrote Josephus. "No one—not even a foreigner—who had seen the old Judea and the glorious suburbs of the city and now set eyes on her present desolation, could have helped sighing and groaning at so terrible a change; every trace of beauty had been blotted out by war, and nobody recognized the place."

Israel was ruined, desiccated. Which is how it was still being described into the modern age. From its beginning, a core project of political Zionism was to replant the hills and recover the wastes of Judea, "make the desert bloom." In the early twentieth century, when a young Jew from Poland was preparing to emigrate to Palestine, he was given lessons in self-defense (because of the Arabs) and lessons in agriculture (because of the waste). Since the Jews and the land died together, they must be revived together. That's what they believed.*

The Romans battered through the outer walls, through the inner walls, then were on the streets of the city. The Zealots fought with abandon. Behind them was the Temple. The Romans went up its stairs, through its courtyards and into the sanctuary. Smoke poured out of its windows, flames danced in its doorways. There was much argument later about how the Temple caught fire. It had been called a wonder of the world, and its destruction was considered a crime. Titus said he had given his men specific orders to protect the Temple.

Josephus, perhaps seeking the favor of the conquerors, explained the fire as a failure to follow commands: "Then one of the soldiers, without waiting for orders and without a qualm for the terrible consequences of his action, but urged on by some unseen force, snatched a blazing piece of wood and climbing on another soldier's back hurled the brand through a golden aperture giving access on the north side to the chambers built round the sanctuary."

"Urged on by some unseen force"—meaning that God, outraged by the sacrilege of the Zealots, had gotten involved, as only God can destroy the house of God.

The Zealots believed Titus destroyed the Temple because he knew the Temple was not just a building. It was the house of the Lord and a place of pilgrimage. It's where you went to sacrifice to God, who was everywhere but was most at home in Jerusalem. Judaism was obliga-

---

*Planting a tree in Jerusalem was therefore considered a holy act. American Jews sometimes receive bonds issued by the Jewish National Funds for their bar mitzvahs that are decorated with pictures of the trees the bonds will fund in Israel. You can actually see these trees in a forest east of Jerusalem—there is a line where the desert ends and the woods begin.

tions, many of which could not be fulfilled without the Temple, especially animal sacrifice, the center of the faith. When Moses said to Pharaoh, "Let my people go," it was partly so they could go into the wilderness and kill animals. The Temple was ancient even to the ancients. It was the house Solomon built when God quit the country for town. It was a symbol even while it was standing. It was the universe collapsed to a point, and it was on fire. "As the flames shot into the air, Jews sent up a cry that matched the calamity and dashed to the rescue, with no thought of saving their own lives or husbanding their strength," writes Josephus. The Zealots attacked blindly through the smoke and the fire and died in great numbers.

Josephus:

Around the altar, the heap of corpses grew higher and higher, while down the sanctuary steps poured a river of blood and the bodies of those killed at the top slithered to the bottom. Such were the height of the hill and the vastness of the blazing edifice that the entire city seemed to be on fire, while as for noise, nothing could be imagined more shattering or more horrifying. There was the war cry of the Roman legions as they converged; the yells of the partisans encircled by fire and sword; the panic flight of the people cut off above into the arms of the enemy, and their shrieks as the end approached.

The marble walls of the Temple heaved. The columns went down in a shower of sparks—watch those sparks, because each is a holy emanation that will have to be gathered together before the world can be made complete. The Zealots raced for the inner chambers, where they were swallowed by flames. The cedars of Lebanon were burning, the icons melting. Then the roof fell in and the holy of holies was lost. Huge pieces of stone tumbled from the Mount and into the street far below. Hitting the ground, these must have sounded like F-16s breaking the sound barrier. The debris piled high. It smoked and glowed for months. These were like the ruins of the World Trade Center had they been left forever. The pile was eventually built over and forgotten. In the twentieth century, archeologists removed layers of sediment and found the debris just as it had been left two thousand years earlier: masonry where it had broken off the Temple Mount, letters marking the place for the shofar blowers, stones singed with fire.

When the last support fell, the fight went out of the Zealots. They dropped their weapons and wandered without purpose. Some killed themselves, some let themselves be killed.*

According to tradition, the Temple was destroyed on the ninth day of the Hebrew month of Av. (It usually falls in August.) The Ninth of Av is probably the most somber day on the Jewish calendar. Men rend their garments and read from the Book of Lamentations. According to another tradition, the Temple of Solomon was also destroyed on the Ninth of Av. It's also the day the Jews of the Warsaw Ghetto were deported to the camps. Other terrible things have happened on the Ninth of Av. I was once given a list of them by an old Hasidic rabbi on a Friday morning in the plaza before the Western Wall. He had blue eyes and his beard stuck out when he pursed his lips. He told me the Jews had been expelled from Spain on the Ninth of Av. He told me World War I began on the Ninth of Av. He told me the Jews were killed in the Polish town of Kielce on the Ninth of Av. This coincidence of bad things impressed me. It's as if God keeps hitting the same note to make the same point. But I wonder if all these events really did happen on the same day, or if the Ninth of Av instead describes a kind of day the Jews have experienced again and again. It's the day when the voice tells you, "Flee! All is lost!" For the Jews, every disaster is the same disaster, and it's always the Ninth of Av.

The Second Temple stood for 639 years and 45 days—since the Persian monarch Cyrus let the Jews return from exile to rebuild it. Except for the brief sojourn in Babylon, there had been, according to tradition, a Jewish temple on Mount Moriah for 1,130 years.

---

*In the course of the war, an estimated 1.2 million Jews died.

When news of the fire went through Israel, the Jews simply surrendered. The only holdouts were on Masada, the fortress commandeered by the Zealots early in the war. From a distance, Masada looks like a mountain among mountains, a finger rising in the middle of a wasteland. It had been a retreat of King Herod, then a Roman base. It was flat on top, a complex of buildings, turrets, walls. It was self-sustaining, fed by an ingenious network of cisterns that captured rainwater and dew. The only approach was up a steep trail known as the Snake Path, which climbed in switchbacks below the fortress, making it vulnerable to attack. The Romans made several attempts, but each time were driven back down the hill. In the end, they simply built a ramp and walked up to the gates. Once inside, they found nothing but dead bodies. The Zealots had killed themselves rather than be taken as slaves. Two women escaped and made their way to the Roman camp, where they talked to Josephus, which is how we know the story.

Historians question the accuracy of this account,* but its veracity seems less important than what political Zionists later made of it: the legend of the last stand, the glory of the fighting death. Better to die on your feet than to live on your knees. In his book, Josephus included a speech given by the Zealot leader Eliezer Ben Yair as the Romans battered down the walls.

> Since we long ago resolved never to be servants to the Romans, nor to any other than God Himself, Who alone is the true and just Lord of mankind, the time is come that obliges us to make that resolution true in practice. We were the first that revolted, and we are the last to fight against them; and I cannot but esteem it as a favor that God has granted us, that it is still in our power to die bravely, in a state of freedom.

Masada, the location of which had been lost, forgotten because not needed, was rediscovered in 1838 by E. Smith and Edward Robinson,

---

*The witnesses seem a tad too convenient, they say, so were probably an invention of Josephus.

American travelers who came across it while hiking in the desert. The ruins were taken up by Zionists, to whom they offered a picture of the fighting Jew in his death agony. These Zionists seemed to say, "See those dark-coated, slump-shouldered hordes in Galicia? That's not us. This is us, over here, in the desert, going down in a blaze." In the 1920s, the Hebrew writer Isaac Lamdan wrote a poem called "Masada," which began the process of bringing the story to the center of a modern Jewish narrative. Some say it was this poem that inspired the uprising in the Warsaw Ghetto. (I don't believe them. I think it was the Nazis who inspired the uprising in the Warsaw Ghetto.)

Masada is a holy site of Zionism, a Sinai towering over the wilderness. Its ruins were finally excavated in the 1960s by Yigael Yadin, an Israeli archeologist and general. Yadin published a book called *Masada: Herod's Fortress and the Zealots' Last Stand*, in which he includes pictures of the ruins, the excavation, and a modern Israeli tank crew being sworn in to the army while standing on the cliffs. This was Yadin's idea. He believed all Israeli recruits should be inducted on the Zealots' mountain. He ran the ceremony himself, arriving by helicopter, descending, like Yahweh, in a storm of dust.

Masada became a place of pilgrimage for American Jews. Youth groups sleep in its shadow, wake as Orion enters Jupiter, make their ascent up the Snake Path, cresting the hill in Jelly sandals as the sun rises over the desert. (Fat, wheezy kids take the cable car.) You stand on the peaks, squint in the glare. You look at the Dead Sea and the remains of the Roman siege wall, a necklace of stones. The guide says the mountain emerged from the mists, like Brigadoon; had been hiding all these years, waiting for a new generation of messianic nationalists to pump it full of air.* The seeds of fig trees were found in the storerooms. Two thousand years old, remnants of the forest that once carpeted the Jordan Valley. Biologists planted a few of them. And they

---

*The high-water mark of Masada worship came in 1981, with the release of the miniseries *Masada*, based on Ernest Gann's bestselling novel *The Antagonists*. Shot on location in Israel, it starred Peter O'Toole as the Roman commander and Peter Strauss as the leader of the Zealots. (In biblical epics, British actors play the Romans, Americans play the Jews or Christians.) Here's what Peter O'Toole says after the battle: "A victory? What have we won? We've won a rock in the middle of a wasteland, on the shores of a poisoned sea."

sprouted! It was a miracle: these ancient seeds giving birth to shoots, a symbol of the modern nation itself! Left for dead at Masada, reborn after two millennia of tortured sleep, the plants grew quickly—then, just as quickly, they withered and died. They had used all their energy to stay alive. Planting them killed them.

The Romans razed every building in Jerusalem, then set the ruins on fire. In the end, the city was wind in dead trees, blood on old stone. It was like Berlin after World War II. Rubble, as all cities will be rubble in the end—hidden in the architecture of every town is the image of its desolation. When the sun rose, it rose on ruins. When the sun set, it set on ruins. It rained on ruins, and it snowed on ruins. The Romans built a base in the ruins, converting holy Jerusalem into a garrison town. They wanted to cut the wires that connected the city to God. They built a shrine to Jupiter on the Temple Mount, hung flags and banners, erected statues of emperors, but did not touch the remains of the Temple itself, which were left for centuries, first as a reminder of what happens when you defy Rome, then, after Constantine, as a reminder of what became of those who killed God.

In the final hours of battle, a handful of Zealots went into the tunnels beneath the city. They hid there for weeks, some wanting to survive, some wanting to survive only long enough to die fighting. After the Temple burned, they emerged in white robes, their faces chalky with dust. They looked like ghouls and fought wildly, but were quickly cut down. To me, these men, the last defenders of Jerusalem, foreshadow the Jewish partisans of Vilna and Warsaw who took to the sewers as their cities were destroyed. This is how it's always been for Jews: no matter how high you climb, you end up in the caves beneath the town.

The Romans sifted the ruins of the Temple for treasures. These were more than physical objects—they were the history of the people, described with great precision in the Bible. ("And thou shalt make a candlestick of pure gold: of beaten work shall the candlestick be made: his shaft, and his branches, his bowls, his knops, and his flowers, shall be of the same"—Exodus 25:31.)

Josephus named the treasures taken by the Romans. The list reads like a newspaper report on the estate sale that marks the end of a storied old family.

> Two lamp stands resembling those kept in the sanctuary, as well as tables, basins and cups, all of solid gold and very heavy . . . the vestments of the high priests with the precious stones, and many other articles required for the temple services . . . tunics and girdles of the priests and a large supply of purple and scarlet kept in store for repairing the great curtain, together with cinnamon in bulk, cassia, and quantities of other spices, which were blended and daily burnt as incense to God . . .

These spoils were sent to Rome, where they were carried in a parade that celebrated the victory in Judea. Titus rode at the head of this parade; followed by soldiers; then by officers; then by noblemen, who carried the treasures; then came prisoners of war, including dozens of Zealots. Only the most physically impressive had been brought for the parade—the old and infirm were killed, the rest sent to slavery in Egypt.* The parade ended in the Coliseum, where a scale replica of Jerusalem had been built—like a Broadway set. The Jewish prisoners stood in the abbreviated windows and turrets and reenacted the destruction of their city. The treasures were put on display in the "Temple of Peace" in the Forum, where they remained from AD 75 to around AD 400. They vanished in the first years of Christian rule.

The disappearance of the Temple treasures is one of those mysteries that people, many of them slightly crazed, spend their lives trying to solve. If they find the treasures, they believe, they will prove the legend true—that it happened, even the part where God spoke from the pillar of fire. It's a strange thing about a religion based not merely on timeless truths but also on historical events: the slavery of the Jews, the crucifixion of Christ. If your faith is historical, its truth, it seems, can be proved (or disproved) by what you find (or don't find) in the ground.

*John, the leader of the Zealots in Jerusalem, died in slavery in Alexandria.

Some say the treasures are still in Rome—in a locked room beneath the Vatican. There have been official requests from Israel to search these chambers. (Some say the Ark is down there too, mislabeled.) Others say the treasures have been carried around the world. *In God's Gold: A Quest for the Lost Temple Treasures of Jerusalem*, the British historian Sean Kingsley claims the treasures were removed from Rome in AD 455, following the sack of the city by the Vandals. Kingsley says the Vandals moved the treasures by ship, first to Carthage, then to Hippo, in modern Algeria, where they were captured again, this time by Eastern Christians, who took them to Constantinople, where they remained until the sixth century AD, when the Christians, threatened by siege, moved them back to Judea, where, writes Kingsley, they are currently buried under a monastery south of Bethlehem.*

After the war, the Romans built the Arch of Titus—it rises over the Via Sacra, near the Forum in Rome—to memorialize their victory. Its columns are covered in sculpted crowns, and each side is decorated with a bas-relief. One shows Titus on a chariot being led by a woman, who is said to personify the Empire. Another shows him riding on the back of an eagle. Another shows Roman soldiers carrying the treasures out of the Temple as it burns: the seven-branched candelabrum, the golden table of the divine presence, the sacred silver trumpets.† Josephus, in exchange for services rendered, was given first choice of the treasures. He asked only for a few sacred books. In choosing the books, however, he was choosing the story, which he knew was the only thing that would last.

---

*Sean Kingsley, *God's Gold*: "The Temple treasure remains a deadly political tool in the volatile Arab-Israeli conflict centered on the Temple Mount . . . The treasure's final hiding place—in the modern West Bank . . . deep in Hamas territory—will rock world religions."

†During the Second World War, the British fielded a battalion of Jews from Palestine. After the war, these soldiers were stationed in Rome, where some of them were caught trying to blow up the Arch of Titus.

TWO

The Vineyard

Jonathan ben Zakkai saved the Jews from oblivion after the Second Temple was destroyed. In *Zakhor: Jewish History and Jewish Memory*, the historian Yosef Hayim Yerushalmi calls the school that ben Zakkai founded "a fortress against oblivion." This is a description I love because it suggests that all that stands between the people and the abyss are books, and stories, and words.

Ben Zakkai was raised in Judea in the last years of the kingdom. In a sense, his life mirrors the life of Josephus. Both had one foot in the old world, one foot in the Exile. Both straddle eras, like men astride tectonic plates. But ben Zakkai offers a counter-model—a different answer to the same question: How do you live as a Jew after the fall of Judea? For Josephus, the answer was to become a Roman. For ben Zakkai, the answer was to be a Jew in a new way.

According to folklore, ben Zakkai grew up in the Galilee. At twenty—this was around AD 35, soon after the crucifixion of Jesus— he traveled to Jerusalem, where he fell in with the circle around Rabbi Hillel, the last of the great men who lived and died before the disaster.

Hillel is one of those names, like Chabad or Maimonides, that you might know from the Haggadah* or from Hebrew school, names buried so deeply in the dust that they're almost impossible to read. They are intoned as the name of your great-grandfather from Plotsk is intoned, the learned man, the decent man, who walked to town on Sabbath. To me, Hillel is like that odd personage in the family photo, with the white beard and the black eyes and the dark hat and the dark clothes. The past, the ancient Jewy past. It was only recently that I came to see him as he probably saw himself, a link in a chain that stretches clear back to Sinai.

Most of what we know about Hillel comes from the oral tradition, which was preserved and collected in the manner of the Greek epics and Norse sagas. His actions and sayings were told and retold until they grew into stories (because stories are how you remember) that hundreds of years later were written down in books. These stories are set in Jerusalem, in the courtyards of the Temple, in the shade of the fig trees, on the green hills outside the city walls, with the golden roof in the distance. It makes me think of the flashbacks you see in martial arts movies, where you get a glimpse of the world before everything fell into violence: a dreamy, light-soaked vision of the past. You see the hero as a boy among boys, at the feet of a teacher, who holds out his hands, palms up, and talks of the wisdom hidden even from kings, the secrets God taught Adam in the Garden, which were forgotten and remembered again and again.

Hillel descended from Jews carried into slavery when the First Temple was destroyed. He was raised in Babylon, in a magnificent house with a magnificent garden, but rejected the wealth of his parents and set off for Jerusalem with nothing but a traveler's sack. He was like Siddhārtha, forsaking his father's house in search of enlightenment. He was a beggar. To him, poverty was holy. He studied sacred books in search of clues. We remember him for a few precious sayings:

---

*The Haggadah is a prayer book that contains the liturgy for the Jewish Passover Seder. In many editions, Hillel is credited with inventing the sandwich a thousand years before John Montagu, the Fourth Earl of Sandwich. It happened during a Passover Seder, when the old rabbi took various items from the Seder plate (parsley, Paschal Lamb, bitter herbs) and wrapped them in matzoth.

If I am not for myself, who will be for me?
And if I am only for myself, what am I?

If not now, when?

No one knows exactly what he said, as opposed to what was said later in his name. It does not matter. His enlightenment was like that of Buddha—it's not important that he said it, only that it was said. Hillel chafed at legalisms and sought the truth in its simplest form. He said love is at the heart of every teaching. You might not get this from reading the Torah, but by saying it, Hillel made it true. He was, in fact, inventing a new religion. In him, you see the evolution away from the monotheism of the desert. Christianity was being formed at the same time; Hillel and Jesus were responding to the Roman occupation in the same way, both stripping the faith to its golden rule, which is in the Jewish Bible, only surrounded by so many other rules you might miss it.

There's a story. It's been worn smooth by the telling, but behind it you intuit the presence of a real person. A traveler came to see Hillel. He said he was thinking of converting to Judaism, but would do so only if the rabbi could summarize the entire faith while standing on one foot. (You sense this man was mocking the rabbi, pulling his beard.) While standing on one foot, Hillel said, "What is hateful to you, do not do to your fellow: this is the whole Law; the rest is the commentary."

This is the Golden Rule* expressed in the negative. For Christians, it's "Do unto others." For Jews, it's "Do not do unto others." It's a difference that gets at the character of the Jews: they do not proselytize; for the most part, they just want to leave alone and be left alone.

---

*The Jewish Encyclopedia on the Golden Rule: "By this name is designated the saying of Jesus (Matt. vii. 12): 'All things therefore whatsoever ye would that men should do unto you, even so do ye also unto them.' In James ii. 8, it is called 'the royal law.' It has been held to be the fundamental canon of morality. In making this announcement, Jesus is claimed to have transcended the limitations of Jewish law and life. The fact is, however, that this fundamental principle, like almost if not quite all the 'logia' attributed to Jesus in the Sermon on the Mount, had been proclaimed authoritatively in Israel. In the instructions given by Tobit to his son Tobias, after admonishing him to love his brethren, the father proceeds to urge upon the son to have heed of all his doings and to show himself of good breeding in all his conduct. 'And what is displeasing to thyself, that do not unto any other' (verse 15)."

The Vineyard

Rabbi Hillel trained his students for a world he would not live see, a world without a temple, and so without a center. His favorite student was the youngest: Jonathan ben Zakkai, whom Hillel designated his successor, "the father of coming generations." Ben Zakkai's story picks up where Hillel's leaves off. Ben Zakkai's life, as described in the oral history (Mishna) unfolded like a drama, in three acts. In act 1 he is a merchant, buying and selling and concerned with money. In act 2 he is a student, sitting at the feet of Rabbi Hillel. In act 3 he is a teacher, explaining what he learned in acts 1 and 2.

Ben Zakkai founded a school. It had no official name, but people called it the Great House. (A reference to a school mentioned in the Book of Kings.) He sat on the Sanhedrin, the body that governed the Hebrew nation. He was famous as a teacher, as a scholar, as a holy man. In the oral history, his accomplishments are catalogued in the way accomplishments are catalogued in a blues song:

> *He never spoke an idle word;*
> *he did not go four yards without*
> *reflecting on the Torah and without*
> *the phylacteries;*
> *no one ever preceded him*
> *in entering the bet ha-Midrash;**
> *he never slept in the bet ha-Midrash, and*
> *was always the last to leave;*
> *no one ever found him engaged in*
> *anything but study.†*

Now ain't that a man?

Because these were the last years of the old Jerusalem, the stories about ben Zakkai linger on the physical details of city life. The crowds

*This is a house of study, a place where students gather to discuss the law and read the Midrash, biblical commentaries that attempt to probe the deeper meaning of the ancient stories.

†This comes from the Midrash, as does much of the information in this section. There is an excellent essay on Rabbi Hillel and ben Zakkai by Solomon Schechter in *The Jewish Encyclopedia*. Schechter, a founder of the Conservative Jewish movement in America, was a president of the Jewish Theological Seminary.

rushing through the narrow streets on Friday afternoon. The animals sacrificed in the courtyards. The hush of the sanctuary on a holy day, the priest in his garments, in his turban, with his ephod.* These stories are riddled with nostalgia, but a nostalgia of a special kind. It's an ache for a city that you have never seen, that does not exist and has not existed for thousands of years. It's nostalgia for someone else's nostalgia. It's the second cousin of nostalgia twice removed. Like the best stories, it's motivated by a single, overwhelming need: to get back what's been lost. There's a tone in these stories—the old man recalling his youth—that would become the tone of all Jews talking about their lost capital.

Next year in Jerusalem.

In its last years, Jerusalem was visited by portents of destruction. (Some were recorded by Josephus.) In the autumn before the First Revolt, for example, a comet appeared over the city, fiery orange and trailed by sparks. It lingered in the sky for weeks, like the finger of God. It pointed at the city, it pointed at the people, it said, "There they are, right there."

The Jews are the Chosen of God, but chosen for what? ("What is hateful to you, do not do to your fellow"—that is the Jews pleading with God.)

During the Passover feast, a flash illuminated the nighttime sky. It was a pop, like a flashbulb going off, Yahweh taking a picture of his home before he leaves it forever. For a moment, it was as bright as day, the houses and streets of the city appearing suddenly, as if caught by surprise, in awkward, magnified detail, then vanishing back into the dark.

Was it a symbol? Was it a warning?

Would Jerusalem itself be lit up, then gone?

On Pentecost, the feast of the harvest, during which farmers from across the country made pilgrimage to the Temple, an image appeared in the clouds: a chariot on fire, a rider crossing the heavens in a panic.

---

*The ephod, mentioned several times in the Torah, was an object worn in the Temple by the priests and used as a kind of divining rod, to soothsay or prophesy. It played a mysterious role in the ancient ritual.

Was the chariot the city itself?

One day a beggar came to the Temple Mount. He was dressed in rags. He screamed: "A voice from the East, a voice from the West, a voice from the four winds, a voice against Jerusalem and the sanctuary, a voice against bridegrooms and brides, a voice against the whole people."

According to Josephus, this man screamed for seven years and five days, then stopped screaming.

A cow brought to the Temple for sacrifice gave birth to a lamb.

Years later, in the schools of the Diaspora, the following story was being told about Jonathan ben Zakkai: the teacher was sitting in the courtyard of the Temple on a warm, still day when a strange, cold wind suddenly blew open the golden doors of the sanctuary. Ben Zakkai sang, "O Temple, Temple, why dost thou frighten thyself? I know of thee that thou shall be destroyed; Zechariah the son of Iddo, has already prophesized concerning thee: 'Open thy doors, O Lebanon,* so that the fire may devour thy cedars.'"

Do I believe in signs of the coming end?

Well, not really. I mean, no, not at all. Yet I report them as if I believe them. As if they mean something. Well, they do mean something. A surfeit of omens suggests a town on the edge of hysteria, about to go off its rocker. I like the idea put forward by theologians who, faced with a lack of clear signs, the fact that the world where we live is so different from the world of the patriarchs—how easy to believe if God walked in a garden?—say that the world itself has changed: there was a time for prophecy, but it's over. The universe itself has grown old. God has mellowed, or stopped caring, or become distracted, or walked away. As it says in Deuteronomy, "Since then, no prophet has risen in Israel like Moses, whom the Lord knew face to face." In other words, there was the age when God talked to man; there was the age when God talked through prophets; there was the age when God talked through portents. Then there is our age, where the prophets are lunatics and the portents are explained by science.

*Lebanon is the Temple, as the Temple was made from the cedar trees of Lebanon.

When the rebellion began, ben Zakkai joined the Peace Party. His pacifism resulted less from idealism than from common sense. He knew the nation had been built by David as a military power—that Moses himself sat on a hill giving orders as the Hebrews battled the Amalekites. But the age of military power, like the age of prophecy, was over: it had been the adolescence of the Jews, suffered and endured and done. Meeting the Romans on the battlefield was suicidal. Besides, the Roman legions were merely a physical expression of a system of values. The way to defeat that system was not with force, but with another system. Overturn the system, its soldiers will vanish—or better yet, will become your soldiers.

This was ben Zakkai's strategy. He spent the rest of his life implementing it. The obvious victory came not to Judaism but to Christianity—Judaism without Jews. Jesus and Paul conquered Rome with values that grew out of the occupation (tactics used to survive Rome): "Turn the other cheek," "Render unto Caesar . . ."

Ben Zakkai was a critic of the rebellion, which made him a threat to the Zealots. When the war began, he was confined to the Temple, and so was stuck in Jerusalem during the siege. He watched as the holy buildings were defiled and the streets filled with corpses. He asked permission to leave the city, and was denied. He tried to flee, was caught, brought back. Not killed but not released. Tormented. If the Zealots had to die, they would bring the world down with them. Only when the world ended, would the redemption begin, at which point the Zealots would be restored and all would be revealed. They hated ben Zakkai because in him they recognized the man who would live on to judge them. His followers saw the same: he was not merely a teacher; he was a key to survival, "the father of the coming generations."

One morning ben Zakkai said his prayers, took a last look at the Temple, then, with the help of his students, climbed into a burial shroud and was placed in a wooden box, the kind used to transfer the dead to the graveyard. Students carried ben Zakkai in this coffin through the streets of Jerusalem. Others followed, members of a funeral procession. The students strained under the weight of their teacher, murmuring prayers as they went toward the Golden Gate. What was ben Zakkai thinking in his shroud, with his eyes closed, hands crossed over his chest? He was the germ of the new nation, the new religion. Everything depended on his survival. He was the Jews passing through the eye of a needle. Could he tell where he was? Even in the shroud? Did he know the city that well? Or was the city already a metaphor?

The gate was guarded by sentries who had been told to let no one leave the city alive. It was early morning. You can almost see them in the cold, fingering their swords, exhaling great clouds of steam, their blue beards stiff with frost, their eyes shining.

And who has died?

Jonathan ben Zakkai.

Ben Zakkai's in there?

Yes, dead.

How dead?

Dead dead.

The sentries wanted to run the coffin through with their swords to be certain—there was a moment when everything was in balance—but the students convinced them it would be a sin to mutilate the body. So the sentries let them pass with the coffin, as did the Romans—as did everyone watching the funeral procession wind along the road, into the valley, then up the other side.

It was a Houdini-like escape, and should be one of the most famous moments in Jewish history, though it's not. It should be the subject of novels and operas and Chinese poems:

Teacher here
Teacher gone.

It was the moment the spark escaped from the ash heap, letting the holy fire burn on. It makes me think of the last shot in *Star Wars*, when the Death Star explodes and you see the escape craft slipping from the inferno—the ship that carries Darth Vader, and so allows for some satisfying (some not so satisfying) sequels; or of the last page of *Moby-Dick*, when the *Pequod* is dashed but Ishmael, alive, floats above the wreckage in a coffin. Ben Zakkai spirited out of the city in a shroud—it's a perfect symbol for the Jews, taken for dead, carried away for their funeral.

The students brought the coffin to Vespasian's tent. It was cut open; ben Zakkai crawled out. He was led to the general. You see Vespasian in the uniform of the legion, surrounded by officers, standing over a map, a stately eminence, talking of Rome. *If Nero goes over, there will be blood in the streets!* He studied ben Zakkai. Vespasian had great interest in the folkways of the conquered people. Was Josephus already at his side, whispering in his ear?

Jonathan ben Zakkai, sir. A great priest and scholar.

The rabbi spoke first: "Vive domine, Imperator!" (Live, O Lord Emperor!)

According to Pierre Vidal-Naquet, the author of *The Jews: History, Memory, and the Present*, this was the moment when the Jews accepted where they had power (the spiritual world) and where they did not (everywhere else).

Vespasian asked about the morale of the people in the city. Ben Zakkai, like Josephus, then prophesied the crowning of Vespasian as emperor. When Vespasian asked the source of this prophecy, ben Zakkai quoted the Book of Isaiah: "Lebanon shall fall by a mighty one."

Lebanon is the Temple, explained ben Zakkai. It's in the process of falling to Vespasian, which means Vespasian is the mighty one. Since no earthly king can be greater than the mighty one of Isaiah, Vespasian must rule the entire land.

Vespasian bowed.

He asked if ben Zakkai wanted any favors done.

Yes, said ben Zakkai. He wanted permission to open a school in Jabneh, a town on the Mediterranean, where he would teach Jewish law. Ben Zakkai described the school in the humblest terms: unimportant, a diversion for his dotage. But it was this school that would miraculously transport the faith from the ruins of the Temple to the new age.

Jabneh was north of modern Tel Aviv. It's mentioned in the Bible, in Chronicles, in a list of towns captured by Uzziah, the boy king of

Judea: "Uzziah went to war against the Philistines and broke down the walls of Gath, Jabneh and Ashdod." Over the centuries, Jabneh had been conquered and reconquered, passing from sovereignty to sovereignty, though most of its people had always been Hebrews. In 50 BC, Judah Maccabee, among the most famous warriors of Jewish lore, took it from the Assyrians. He set its buildings on fire, purified its temples, smashed its pagan idols. (In Leviticus, such idols are called "Goat Demons.") Smoke from the battle could be seen as far away as Jerusalem.* In the Judean mind, Jabneh was therefore associated with the glory of the Maccabees. It was captured by Pompey around 63 BC, and had been ruled by the Romans ever since.

According to tradition, ben Zakkai built his school in a vineyard, a description most scholars consider symbolic. A vineyard in that it was a fertile place of harvest. In my mind, the school hums like a laboratory, a room on the other side of the war, far from the siege choking Jerusalem—a building in a garden, not a symbolic garden, but a garden garden, that steams and stinks in the morning and is cool at night, with moonlight dappling its paths in shadow. This is where ben Zakkai learned that the Temple had been destroyed. He tore his clothes and wept. He was in exile from that moment, the first Jew to dream of return.

How to free yourself of this gloom, how to clean your people of this terrible sin?

In an earlier time, ben Zakkai would have slaughtered a ram and thrown its blood against the altar, but such a ritual could be performed only in the Temple. Prayer, sacrifice, festivals—they all depended on the Temple. Without the Temple, there was no way to worship, no way to be clean, no way to rid people of their guilt. For that, you needed God. And God lived (or used to) in the Temple. Before that, God lived in the tabernacle. But where does God live now? Where did He go when the Temple was destroyed? Is God in exile? How can you worship an exile from exile? How can you be a Jew without Jerusalem?

These were the problems ben Zakkai was determined to solve. In doing so, he would free Judaism from its physical home—from sanctu-

*See the Book of Maccabees.

aries and courtyards and altars—so it could live in the air, where it could never again be plundered. It was ben Zakkai who turned the Temple into a book.*

After the war, ben Zakkai moved the surviving members of the Sanhedrin to Jabneh, from where they continued to rule. This was a government in exile in the way the government that Polish democrats set up in London during World War II was a government in exile—a body that kept minutes, took notes, wrote laws, but all of this activity unanchored and symbolic, rulings in a void, a brain signaling a body that's been blown to pieces.

The Sanhedrin continued to govern for several hundred years, moving from city to city. It was finally driven out of existence in the fourth century AD (it last met in Tiberias) by the Christian rulers of Rome. By then, generations of rabbis had been trained and sent into the Diaspora, where they carried on in ever smaller groups, ever farther from the old dead center.

The mere functioning of the Sanhedrin was the message: it told the Jews that all was not lost, that some lights still burned. In this way, ben Zakkai showed the people their nation could function even without the Temple; that God could be worshipped in exile. In explaining this, he referred to the precedent of Babylon, where a Jewish community flourished after the destruction of the First Temple. He quoted the prophet Jeremiah, who said it's good to worship in Babylon, as God is in Babylon, too.

If God is in Babylon, said ben Zakkai, God is in Jabneh.

If God is in Jabneh, God is in Vilna.

If God is in Vilna, God is in New York.

That's the story of the Diaspora.

In the past, the shofar, the ram's horn blown to call the faithful to feast and atonement, could be sounded only on the Temple Mount.

---

*It's as if the idea of being an American were to survive the destruction of America itself; as if, a thousand years after the fall of the nation, a few million people carried on as Americans in exile, their historical home turned into a concept—an ideal, sought after but never achieved; as if the towns and cities and words and documents were turned into holy abstractions: Washington, D.C., the "pursuit of happiness," the Bill of Rights, "Next year in Illinois."

The Sanhedrin changed that law, saying that it now could be blown in Jabneh. This meant Israel could have a center other than Jerusalem. It could have many centers, in fact; or many cities could be Jerusalem. In this way, too, Judaism was freed from Judea.

Jabneh replaced Jerusalem as the city where the priests determined the crucial details: the moment of sunrise and sunset, the phase of the moon. In the old world, setting the time, which determined the schedule of sacrifice and prayer, was a task of great importance. It suggested a special relationship between Jabneh and the divine, and made the city important in the way keeping the time for Britain made Greenwich important. (In Joseph Conrad's book *The Secret Agent*, anarchists plot to blow up the observatory in Greenwich with the idea that destroying the clock will rattle the Empire.) It's not that ben Zakkai made Jabneh holy; it's that he showed that worship could continue without a holy city. The fact that this was not Hebron, or Bethlehem, only underscored the point. If Jabneh can be holy, any place can be holy.

Judaism became portable in these years, a religion that could live out of a suitcase. This was accomplished (in part) by creating the canon—by collecting the various books and scriptures into the single book we know as the Jewish Bible. Which meant that all Jews, no matter where they lived, would read the same words and tell the same stories. In the process of choosing what to include, ben Zakkai and his followers reshaped what it meant to be a Jew.

There had been earlier canons; the first such collection dates back hundreds of years before Christ. After all, Solomon is a star of the Bible, but he was also a Jew who prayed in the Temple, so what did he read? (Not stories about Solomon.) Well, probably the first five books of the Bible—which include the stories of creation, Adam and Eve, the Flood, Abraham and Isaac, Jacob wrestling with the angel, Joseph in his coat of many colors, the skinny cows and fat cows, the Pharaoh, the golden calf, the pillar of fire and the pillar of smoke, the teachings on Sinai—known together as the Torah, which according to tradition was written by Moses himself. Scholars say this collection was assembled around 600 BC in the time of David; the process itself is described in the Book of Nehemiah.

Other books were added to the canon: books by prophets, books on leaders, such as 1 and 2 Samuel and the Book of Kings, which tell the stories of the nation, its evolution from theocracy to monarchy, the rise and fall of David (which reads like the rise and fall of the small-time gangster played by James Cagney in *The Roaring Twenties*).

These later books were rejected by some—most famously the Samaritans, who believe that only the first five books of the Bible are legitimate, the rest hokum.* (The Samaritans broke from the Judeans around 400 BC.) Ben Zakkai was troubled by several newer (to him) books, specifically the Hagiographa, a collection of poems and prophecies that chronicled the triumphs of battle. Dozens of these were circulating before the Revolt. The most lurid glorified martyrdom and war. If ben Zakkai could discredit these books, he could control the narrative, even determine what was held in greater value: fighting or surviving.

In other words, creating the canon was a matter less of putting in than of leaving out. Ben Zakkai left out the Book of Maccabees, for example, which told the story of the brothers who retook Jerusalem from the Greeks. The Maccabees were too much like the Zealots, and it was the Zealots, with their pride and notions of purity, that had led the nation to ruin. For ben Zakkai, such war stories taught lessons that could only result in disaster. He left out some and glossed over others, such as the story in which God orders King Saul to kill the Amalekites to the last woman and child, and emphasized abstract principles and universal commands, such as "Love Thy Brother as Thyself," instead. He found new meaning in some of the oldest stories. He said even the war stories were only about war at one level; at another, they were about struggle, the trials of the man who walks in the path of the righteous. He said that the other meanings had always been in the scriptures but had been overlooked, as the people had not been mature

---

*The Samaritans said the Temple of Solomon had been built in the wrong place—the mountain of God was not Moriah but Gerizim, in the wastes near the biblical city of Schechem, which is where they built their temple: built, destroyed, rebuilt, destroyed. Gerizim is probably what Yasser Arafat had in mind in 2000 when, as things fell apart between the Israelis and the Palestinians, he said there had never been a Jewish temple in Jerusalem.

enough to understand them. In Exodus, for example, when God tells Moses how to build the place of worship, He says there must be no iron used in the altar. In this, ben Zakkai discovered a hidden message: as iron is the tool of war, and the altar is the place of worship, God was actually telling Moses that there must be no war in worship, no worship of war.

Ben Zakkai wanted to diminish the role of the Messiah and the Apocalypse. He wanted to remake the story of the Hebrews as an epic without an ending—an ending it was not our business to know. In the thirst for end-times, he recognized the symptoms of a disease. He wanted to free the people from their visions. He wanted to move the religion from the stony and physical to the lofty and abstract. Here's an expression for which he is famous: "If you have a sapling in your hand and they say to you, 'The Messiah has come,' finish planting the sapling, then receive him."

Most important, he wanted to replace the Temple as the center of worship. To do this, he had to find a way for Jews to serve God without the animal sacrifice, which had been the core of their belief, a primary obligation of the people.

How important was sacrifice in the worship of the Jews?

The covenant between the Hebrews and God begins in Genesis, when the Almighty calls on Abraham to sacrifice Isaac—the son of his old age, who is to be the first of the nation God has promised—on Mount Moriah. Abraham saddles his mule, sits the boy behind him, and, without question, seemingly without thought, rides into the wilderness to kill and burn his boy. The mute complicity of Abraham is said to be the model of faith, but seems more like a terrifying demonstration of the nature of God: who he is, what he requires. Is this what binds the Jews to their Lord? This willingness to participate in murder? It ties the Jews to God as co-conspirators are tied together after a crime.

The journey took three days. When Abraham reached Moriah, he left his servants below and took the boy into the hills. Much has been written about what Isaac might have been thinking as Abraham led him into the mountains. Because Isaac is a zero in the Bible, with no life of his own, known only in relation to stronger characters, as the son to be sacrificed, then as the blind old father who is fooled into giving his blessing to his younger child, Jacob, the heel-clutcher. In the Bible, there is only this sad exchange between Abraham and Isaac.

"Father?"

"Yes, my son?"

"The fire and wood are here, but where is the lamb for the burnt offering?"

"God himself will provide the lamb for the burnt offering, my son."

Søren Kierkegaard's *Fear and Trembling** is a meditation on Abraham and Isaac. The philosopher, in an effort to understand God, reimagines the story, but is so bewildered ("the older he became the more his thoughts turned to that tale and yet less and less could he understand it") he is left only with his idea of the leap of faith: that is, you should believe in God precisely because belief in God is impossible. At one point, Kierkegaard imagines Abraham telling Isaac that it's his, Abraham's, desire, not that of God, to kill the boy, because Abraham loves Isaac and does not want him to know the terrible nature of God. "He caught Isaac by the chest, and threw him to the ground and said, 'Foolish boy. Do you believe I am your father? I am an idolater. Do you believe this is God's command? No, it's my own desire!'"

Hearing this story, the binding of Isaac, at a young age, say, in Hebrew school, is traumatic: first, there is what you're supposed to learn, which is the unquestioning nature of faith; then there is what you actually learn, which is the true nature of our grandfathers, just what those monstrous, psychotic, voice-hearing killers were capable of. (If you lived in the time of animal sacrifice, this story would have sounded different: you would have understood, without having to be told, that the ram you killed on the Temple Mount was being slaughtered in

---

*This book was published under the pseudonym Johannes de Silencio (John of Silence), himself something of a tortured literary character.

place of your son, as your father slaughtered a ram in your place; that the life of each man was redeemed from God by slaughter.)

Abraham built a pyre in the hills and bound Isaac with a rope and laid him on the wood and unsheathed his knife, which was made of iron. He drew back the blade and then—

> . . . the angel of the LORD called unto him out of heaven, and said, Abraham, Abraham: and he said, Here am I.
>
> And he said, Lay not thine hand upon the lad, neither do thou any thing unto him: for now I know that thou fearest God, seeing thou hast not withheld thy son, thine only son from me.
>
> And Abraham lifted up his eyes, and looked, and beheld behind him a ram caught in a thicket by his horns: and Abraham went and took the ram, and offered him up for a burnt offering in the stead of his son (Genesis 22:11–13).

Everything in Judaism is a repetition of this scene. Every animal sacrificed on the mountain is the ram in the thicket. Every prayer, every feast, every circumcision is another staging of the drama in which a crazy old man is ready to kill his son to earn the blessing of the Lord: "By myself have I sworn, saith the Lord, for because thou hast done this thing, and has not withheld thy son, thine only son: that in blessing I will bless thee, and in multiplying I will multiply thy seed as the stars of the heaven, and as the sand which is upon the sea shore."

In other words, the Jews earned their blessing by Abraham's willingness to kill his son. The animal on the pyre is an illusion—it's always the boy in the flames. This explains the terror instilled in Jews by the worship of Moloch, an ancient, sacrifice-demanding pagan god, which broke out like a plague in the time of the First Temple, in a moment of crisis and war, when Jews sacrificed their young to an iron bull set up in the Valley of Hinnom, below the Temple Mount, where the tiny bodies were burned on great fires—because everything is given to the man who gives his son. The bodies were piled in Gehenna, which is why it became a synonym for Hell.

Moloch is a symbol of everything life-devouring and evil. The cities of Cain, the City of Salt, the cities of man, the great whore of Babylon, the abomination of abominations. If you're a certain kind of visionary, the modern metropolis is Moloch, steely and smoke-spewing, devouring its young.

Here's Allen Ginsberg in *Howl*:

> *Moloch whose mind is pure machinery! Moloch whose blood is running money!*
> *Moloch whose fingers are ten armies! Moloch whose breast is a cannibal*
> *dynamo! Moloch whose ear is a smoking tomb!*
> *Moloch whose eyes are a thousand blind windows! Moloch whose skyscrapers*
> *stand in the long streets like endless Jehovas! Moloch whose factories dream*
> *and croak in the fog! Moloch whose smokestacks and antennae crown cities!*

Moloch is feared not because child sacrifice is alien to Israel, but because it's the center of the faith.

> *God said to Abraham kill me a son . . .*
> *Abe said where you want this killing done?**

In the end, the Hebrew slaves won their freedom from Pharaoh only by an orgy of human sacrifice—the death of the firstborn of Egypt, not just the human sons but the firstborn of the flocks and herds. This is the massacre memorialized on Passover, when Jews marked their doorposts with lamb's blood—the blood of the ram slaughtered in place of Isaac—so the angel of death (Moloch) knew to pass over the Hebrew homes and visit only the homes of Egyptians. For Christians, the story of Isaac culminates in the ultimate sacrifice: the crucifixion of the son of God, which solved the problem of animal sacrifice faced by early Christians, as well as Jews, when the Temple was destroyed. Christ himself is the final offering after which no more sacrifice would be necessary.

If you lived in Jerusalem in the time of the Temple, animal sacri-

---

*Bob Dylan, "Highway 61 Revisited."

fice was at the heart of everything. No matter what the problem, no matter how severe the guilt, it could be taken care of with an animal sacrifice. Think of it in the language of the film *Goodfellas* (in which the speaker is Yahweh): "You slept with a married woman? Kill me a lamb. You ate pork? Smite me a cow. You got down on your knees and kissed the Golden Calf? Burn me a red heifer. You came into the Temple with dirty hands and dirty feet, vile in dirtiness? Roast me a sheep." A vast architecture had grown up around the ritual—with money-changers in booths at the foot of the Temple, with butchers on the Temple Mount to slaughter the animals, with drains to collect or carry away the blood, with priests in vestments to say the prayers, with fires where the carcasses roasted (the smoke and smell of burning fat hung over the city)—a tremendous machinery of slaughter ("Moloch whose factories dream and croak in the fog!"), the only residue of which is the shank bone that, each spring, washes up on the Seder plate like debris from a ship that went down centuries ago.

In the wake of the First Revolt, with the Temple in ruins and Jerusalem serving as a Roman garrison, the physical act of sacrifice was impossible. It could not be done. If the faith were to survive, ben Zakkai would have to reinvent the ritual. It could no longer be about animals. It could no longer pantomime the work of the shepherd or the farmer, in which God is given the choice sheep or the first fruits in the way the prized portion of a meal is saved for the father. Sacrifice would be remade as a mental task, the act of an intellectual. Meditation and prayer. Things you give the Lord. The subject would be different. Neither rams nor sheep nor goats nor pigeons. The object would be the same.*

On those occasions when sacrifice was absolutely necessary, such as Yom Kippur, which in the Bible is called the "time of affliction," slaughter would be replaced by fasting. The rabbis justified this change with an elegant turn of logic: God wants me to sacrifice animals, which I cannot do, as there is no Temple, but what's an animal but

---

*Simon Goldhill, *The Temple of Jerusalem*: "The Temple service cannot be performed so it is recalled in creative poetry; this poetry itself becomes the new ritual. The ceremony here is a ritual performance of a myth about a ritual performance: a Temple service of the imagination."

flesh, and what do I lose if I don't eat? Flesh. So this is what I give the Lord. Not the flesh of the ram, but the flesh of my own body.

Here's a story from the Talmud:*

> When Rev Sheshet was engaged in a fast, he spoke thus after praying: "Master of the Universe, it is revealed before You that at the time when the Holy Temple stood a person who sinned would offer a sacrifice, and he would offer from it only its fat and blood, and that alone would atone for him. And now, when there is no Temple, I have engaged in fasting and my own fat and blood have been diminished. May it be Your will that my fat and blood that are diminished be regarded as if I had offered them before You on the Altar, and may You do me favor."

Ben Zakkai and his followers found ways to express the architecture of the Temple and its structure symbolically. Why is the bema (the altar) elevated in the synagogues of the Diaspora? Because it represents the heights of Moriah. Whenever you go to the bema, you are going up to the Temple. If you are called to read before the congregation, you are said to make aliyah, to go up, as the ancients went up to the sanctuary. In our time, when a Jew in the Diaspora moves to Israel, he is said to have made aliyah, ascended, as the entire nation is now the Temple Mount—only, without God.

I think the destruction of the Temple saved Judaism: it freed the Jews from architecture; it freed them from animal sacrifice; it freed them from the ho-hum life of nations; it forced their thought to become symbolic and abstract.

Ben Zakkai did not write down his teachings. His lessons were preserved in the manner of the lessons of Aristotle. He taught his students, who remembered his sayings and passed them on to other students, who gathered them in books with the sayings of other teachers—all of it accumulating into a literature that, over several centuries,

---

*A vast collection of oral history, Jewish law, and Jewish stories. To the devout, the Talmud ranks in importance with the Bible.

first in schools in Palestine, then in schools in Babylon, was collected as the Talmud and the Midrash, compendiums that include stories from the Bible and the oral history, and commentaries on those stories, and commentaries on the commentaries.

These books swelled until they were as intricate and vast and holy as the holy city itself. In this way, the Book replaced the city. In this way, the Temple became a book. In this way, study of the Book became as holy as worship in the Temple. In this way, the exterior Jerusalem of hills and valleys was replaced by an interior Jerusalem. In this way, Jews became lost in a book. In this way, the city became a dream and only the words were real. In this way, the destruction of the Temple freed the Jews from mundane concerns of statehood and let them drift in an orbit where they could contemplate God. In this way, the faith advanced from the particular, where it had been destroyed, to the universal, where it could never be destroyed.

The realities of life in a state and worship in a temple were replaced by prayers about that life and stories about that worship. It's not God you read about in the Bible, but the story of the Jews in conversation with God. It's not God whom Jews worship in the Diaspora but the story of the Jews worshipping God. In this way, the Jews came to live at a remove from everyday life, outside the glass, watching themselves worship, worshipping themselves worshipping. In this way, the Jews came to live inside a story instead of inside a temple. In this way, the Jews ceased to believe in the present: there was only the past of the stories and the future of the Messiah.

The Temple burned but had not been destroyed. It had instead broken into millions of tiny temples, each the size of the frontal lobe. It had metastasized. Everywhere and nowhere. The nation had been destroyed, but the Jews continued to be its citizens. What had started with ben Zakkai in Jabneh ended hundreds of years later with a new faith.

Take, for example, the Yom Kippur service:

In the days of the Temple, you would afflict yourself for your sins. You would go to the courtyard and slaughter an animal, then go into the sanctuary, where the priest would sacrifice a bull to cleanse the people. After that, a goat would be loaded with the sin of the nation and sent out through the doors of the Temple and into wilderness to wander and die, bearing away the shame. The height of the ceremony came when the priest went into the holy of holies and whispered the secret name of God, referred to only by the Greek term, the tetragrammaton, the word of four letters.

In the days after the Temple, you would go to a synagogue in a little town in Illinois, say, where you would hear stories about the Temple and sing songs about the days of the Temple, say prayers, stand when the Ark was opened, sit when it was closed—the Ark itself being raised on a bema said to represent the Mountain of God, the people going to read from the Torah making aliyah, ascending as the Jews once ascended the steps to the Mount to kill a ram or a sheep; you would hear a sermon about the state of the environment, or big tobacco, then go home, being careful not to eat till sundown.

I came across the below passage in a review by Charles Taylor* of *Radical Hope: Ethics in the Face of Cultural Devastation*, in which Jonathan Lear writes about the last Crow Indians and their practice of counting coups, in which a warrior would heave a spear into the ground, beyond which his enemy, if he advanced, would be killed, a practice that had no meaning after the buffalo were dead and the Indians forced onto reservations.

> As Lear explains, "Counting coups makes sense only in the context of a world of intertribal warfare; and once that world breaks down, *nothing* can count as counting coups." Lear imagines someone going to a restaurant to order a buffalo hamburger. He is told he can't have it because the last buffalo has been killed. Very different would be the predicament if we were transported to a future where restaurants no longer existed, and words like "ordering" no longer had any meaning. The first case is one of de facto impossibility; the second shows a radical impossibility.

A culture's disappearing means that a people's situation is so changed that the actions that had crucial significance are no longer possible in that radical sense. It is not just that you may be forbidden to try them and may be severely punished for attempting to do so; but worse, you can no longer even try them. You can't draw lines or die while trying to defend them. You find yourself in a circumstance where, as Lear puts it, "the very acts themselves have ceased to make sense."

Replace *buffalo* with *Temple* and *counting coups* with *sacrifice* and this is just what happened to the Jews. They had been massacred. The objects and places of their worship had been destroyed. They could neither pray in their sanctuary nor burn offerings on their mountain—the rituals that formed their identity. But the rabbis saved the people—this is the miracle—by reimagining the old rituals. They kept the buffalo and coup stick, but turned them into something spiritual, unreal— unreal in the way that you can kill the buffalo, but you cannot kill the idea of a buffalo unless you kill everyone who has that idea.

Judaism was like an old house that had burned. Ben Zakkai and his followers gutted and rebuilt the inside but left the ancient facade. The religion Jews practice today is nothing like the religion practiced in the Kingdom of Judea—the names are the same, but all the meanings have changed.

When he was old, Jonathan ben Zakkai left his school to his students, gave away his property, and traveled. Everywhere he went, he was followed by young men. To them, each word he said was holy, every sentence a prayer. I picture him in the way of Renaissance painters, who always painted sacred scenes as if they happened in their own countries, their own time, because if it's not happening here, now, it has no meaning. I see ben Zakkai wandering through Glencoe, Illinois, where I grew up, stopping to talk to people in the pharmacy and the video store, having a hot dog at Big Al's. I see him speaking to the parents sitting in their cars in front of Central School, on Elm

Street, listening to talk radio as their tailpipes send up plumes of smoke. My friend Jamie lives across the street from the school. He sees ben Zakkai and catches just a few words, but it's enough to occupy him for life.

Ben Zakkai was trying to fathom the secret teaching: what God whispered to Moses on Sinai. He searched the scriptures for hints and codes. He said heaven is the body of God; it goes on forever. As he went from town to town, he seemed less a man than a symbol of a man without a country. He was consumed by stories of the First Temple and its destruction. "Why was Israel exiled to Babylon?" he asked. He died far from Jerusalem, but it's not known where and it does not matter, as the Temple had been rebuilt in his head.

These were his last words: "Put the vessels out of the house, that they may not become unclean, and prepare a throne for Hezekiah, the King of Judah is coming."

These are beautiful words, and if I weren't so wound up in this story, I might end here, with this sentence as a coda, because our bodies dissolve and our spirits flee but our words live on, but I cannot help but point out a contradiction: here, in his last moment, is the man who worked so hard to free his people of their crazed suicidal end-of-the-worldism ("Finish planting the sapling, then receive him"), returning to the Jewish impulse to meet the Messiah and prepare for the end. Ben Zakkai lived as the greatest enabler of the Exile and the Diaspora, but he died as a Zionist.

THREE

The Son of the Star

In the decades following the Revolt, the Jewish community stirred back to life. Generations lived, had children, held their children in their laps, said, "In the time of the Temple . . . ," kept the commandments and awaited the Messiah. Jerusalem had been partially rebuilt. Jews were again living on streets below Mount Moriah, the top of which was buried in rubble, as if the people were worshipping their own ruin.

Hadrian became emperor of Rome in AD 117, thirty-seven years after the Temple was destroyed. When you come across busts of Roman rulers, you are often surprised by how small and unimpressive these men look. How human. They have fat faces, chubby cheeks, weak chins, crooked noses, or seem abbreviated, with half-formed features and bullet-shaped heads. Some look angry, even in stone. But Hadrian looks like you want him to: like Kirk Douglas or Rock Hudson. A Roman emperor in a movie. With curly hair and a long nose. He's considered among the greatest rulers of the Empire, and governed in an age of prosperity. He had a mission. He wanted to forge the far-flung tribes into a single people. If you are a Jew in modern America, you are probably less of a Judean than a Roman. The words and deeds of Hadrian would have you nodding in agreement. Rome was the march of civilization. Judea was tribal and strange, a people apart, clinging to a vindictive, invisible God.

Hadrian traveled to Jerusalem in AD 130, on a tour of the provinces. He was the first emperor to visit in peacetime. He came with an entourage of diplomats and architects. He talked to politicians and rabbis. He was fascinated by local customs and asked the Jews about their legends, which, to him, sounded no less colorful than the legends of the Britons.

Among the Jews who met Hadrian was Rabbi Akiba, the leader of the Jewish community. Akiba had a long white beard, like Merlin, and was famous for his faith and prodigious memory. He was thirty years old when the Temple was destroyed, and was eighty when Hadrian visited. He had seen the flames and smelled the smoke. He made the melancholy trek to Jabneh, where he had studied with ben Zakkai. Akiba was not interested in scripture until he turned forty. This age, forty, is often mentioned in regard to Akiba. He came to faith late, in a time of crisis, when he could first discern the contours of his own death. It gives his scholarship the feel of a midlife crisis.

There's a legend concerning the moment Akiba became a student.*

Akiba was walking in the hills with his flock. The hills were like waves in a summer sea and the sheep were soft and white. The sun was the finger of God pointing at Akiba. He led his flock through the hills to a river. The sheep stood on the bank, drinking. A stone tumbled off a hill into the water with a splash. Ripples spread across the river and washed onto the shore. The sheep looked up. Akiba was transfixed. Mesmerized. Seeing for the first time. If the effect of the rock can be seen, heard and felt even after the rock itself is gone, what about the emanations of God? Doesn't everything connect to everything? The rock caused the ripple and the ripple caused the wave and the wave

---

*This is a paraphrase. For the original, see the oral history, or Midrash.

moved the sheep. But what caused the rock? What is the first cause? Akiba then saw a stone worn down by the water. "If these drippings can, by continuous action, penetrate solid stone," he asked, "how much more can the persistent word of God penetrate the pliant, fleshly human heart?"

Akiba met Hadrian in a palace in Caesarea every morning for weeks, the old man in robes, the young man in imperial uniform. They talked about history, God, wisdom, infinity.* They talked about the afterlife and circumcision, a custom Hadrian considered barbaric. They talked about Judea, which was in ruin. Hadrian said he wanted to build a modern capital on the rubble of Jerusalem. This would be a gift for the Jews. It would win their appreciation and secure their loyalty. He would clear Mount Moriah and build a temple grander even than the Temple of Herod. Akiba asked which gods would be worshipped in this temple.

All gods, said Hadrian, as every god is a manifestation of the same divine.

Hadrian then said, "Jupiter is Jehovah."

There is only one God, said Akiba. These others are not a manifestation of the first—they are an illusion, a figment, or worse. "Moloch whose fingers are ten armies!" Only one God can be worshipped on the Temple Mount because there is only one God. Only God is God. Hadrian said something, Akiba said something else. By the end of this

*The conversations between Hadrian and the rabbis are described in the Midrash. Here is an example: "The Emperor Hadrian asked Rabbi Yehoshua, 'Does the world have a master?' 'Certainly,' replied Rabbi Yehoshua. 'Did you think the world exists without an owner?' 'Who then is the master?' asked Hadrian. 'The Almighty is the Creator of heaven and earth,' responded Rabbi Yehoshua. Hadrian persisted, 'If this is true, why doesn't He reveal Himself a few times a year so that people should fear Him?' 'That would be impossible,' replied Rabbi Yehoshua, 'for it says (Exodus 33:20), "No man can see Me and live." 'I don't believe that!' responded Hadrian angrily. 'No one can be so great that it is impossible even to look at him.' Rabbi Yehoshua left. Later, at noontime, Rabbi Yehoshua returned and asked the Emperor to step outside. 'I am ready to show you the Almighty!' he announced. Curious, Hadrian followed him to the palace garden. 'Look straight up into the sun. There you will discover God!' exclaimed Rabbi Yehoshua. 'What?' retorted Hadrian, bewildered. 'Do you know what you are saying? Everyone knows that it is impossible to look directly into the sun at noon!' Rabbi Yehoshua smiled. 'Note your own statement! You admit that no one can gaze at the sun's full strength when it is at its zenith. The sun is only one of the Almighty's servants, and its glory is only one millionth of a fraction of God's splendor. How then do you expect people to be able to look at Him?'"

discussion, the emperor had come to see Akiba as a backward, arrogant, small-minded Jew.

Hadrian left the country in a rage. He went on to Egypt, but left behind his architects with orders to clear the Temple Mount and build a new temple. To this, the Roman governor added the following edict: No more circumcision among the Jews. Did Hadrian understand the significance of this order? To Jews, circumcision is the first sign of the covenant.* Without it, there can be no proper worship of God.

Riots broke out. Firebrands called for the overthrow of the Empire. To the citizens of Rome, it must have come from out of nowhere. (You turn on the TV and there are a million people in Teheran chanting, "Death to America.")† The crowd coalesced around a young man from a Judean town called Chezib. His name was Simeon, but he was called Bar-Koziba: the son of Koziba, which scholars believe derives from the name of his hometown. Simeon Bar-Koziba comes without a back story. Even in the Midrash, he appears full grown, from nowhere, as if he was following the stage directions in the Shakespeare play: Enter Jew. Exit Jew.

No one knows what he looked like, but he was charismatic enough to convince even cynical old men that he was the leader they had been waiting for. His plan was the same as the plan of the Maccabees and Zealots and Meir Kahane. He would drive out the Romans, retake the city, become the power, and enforce the law. He trained a Jewish army, which was fanatical, desirous of war. Each soldier, to show his commitment and valor, was ordered to cut off a finger on his left hand.‡ The

---

*"And God said unto Abraham, This is my covenant, which ye shall keep, between me and you and thy seed after thee; Every man child among you shall be circumcised. And ye shall circumcise the flesh of your foreskin; and it shall be a token of the covenant betwixt me and you. And he that is eight days old shall be circumcised among you, every man child in your generations, he that is born in the house, or bought with money of any stranger, which is not of thy seed. He that is born in thy house, and he that is bought with thy money, must needs be circumcised: and my covenant shall be in your flesh for an everlasting covenant. And the uncircumcised man child whose flesh of his foreskin is not circumcised, that soul shall be cut off from his people; he hath broken my covenant" (Genesis: 17:9–14).

†The Jewish riots have been attributed to other causes as well, including the rape of a Hebrew girl by a Roman soldier, a plan to build a temple to Jupiter on the Mount, and the corrupt rule of the Roman governor, Tinnius Rufus, but the ban on circumcision was clearly at the center of the struggle.

‡See *The Jewish Encyclopedia*.

men set off at Bar-Koziba's order, attacking outposts and garrisons. The rabbis of Jabneh, those who had studied under ben Zakkai, vehemently opposed this Second Revolt. To them, Bar-Koziba was a Zealot, and the Zealot way had already been tried. Bar-Koziba appealed directly to Rabbi Akiba. Akiba came out of this meeting convinced, satisfied. He went into the streets.

He said, *The time is here!*

He said, *Bar-Koziba is the one!*

He said, *Resist! Hit back! Fight!*

He said, *Get behind this man, because this is not any man but the promised one, the Messiah.*

Akiba did not mean Messiah in the Christian way, as the son of God. He was speaking in the spirit of the Hebrew scriptures—Messiah as the anointed one,* the leader who will restore the kingdom, but who will grow old and die. He said Bar-Koziba would return the people to glory, as prophesied in the Book of Numbers: "There shall come a star [Kokba] out of Jacob who shall smite the corners of Moab and destroy all the children of Seth." In saying this, Akiba gave Bar-Koziba the name for which he is still known: Bar-Kokba, son of the star.

According to the rabbis, Akiba misread the moment and so forgot the first teaching of ben Zakkai: "If you have a sapling in your hand and they say, 'The Messiah has come,' finish planting the sapling, then receive him." Here's the judgment of Jabneh, as recorded in the Midrash: "Akiba, grass will grow in your cheeks and your Messiah will still not have come."

There were five hundred thousand men in Bar-Kokba's army. They quickly pushed the Romans out of Judea. Hadrian responded by sending the famed Tenth Legion. He traveled with them—it was the only war of his otherwise peaceful reign. The Romans met the Jews in battle. The Jews were fanatics, lit by faith. Their God was insane.

---

*This refers to the ancient ritual in which the new king of Israel was literally anointed with oil. It was a ceremony just as the inauguration of the American president is a ceremony. The Messiah is simply the king who will finally restore the kingdom that split into pieces a generation after David. The Jews await him as Americans await another Abraham Lincoln.

Thousands of Romans were killed. The survivors fled to Assyria. In his report to the Senate, Hadrian dispensed with the ritual greeting: "The emperor and the army are well." (They were not.)

Bar-Kokba entered Jerusalem through the Golden Gate. Much is made of how a redeemer enters the holy city. Jerusalem has been redeemed so many times that the manner of entrance, which is a question of style, constitutes a sub-genre of the historical literature. David came in dancing before the Ark. Jesus came in on a donkey. Omar, who conquered Jerusalem for Islam in AD 638, came in on a red camel, which, according to Edward Gibbon, "carried, besides his person, a bag of corn, a bag of dates, a wooden dish, and a leathern bottle of water." Bar-Kokba came in on a stallion. Coins were struck to mark the occasion. These showed Jerusalem on its hill over the words "For the Freedom of Israel."

How did Hadrian react?

Like an optimist who has run into reality. Like a man whose gift has been rejected. (The most devastating wars are often started by good men who realize, too late, that their goodness has not been appreciated.) Hadrian told the Senate it was not enough to suppress the rebellion. He wanted to destroy the Jewish nation.

He put the army under Julius Servius, the general who had defeated the Britons. Jews could see the Romans as they approached. Their army darkened the plain. The soldiers were methodical. Burned everything, killed everyone. Nazareth fell. Hebron fell. Jerusalem fell. Bar-Kokba retreated to a town called Bethar, where the people closed themselves behind siege walls. To this day, no one is sure where it was. It's gone the way Eden is gone, a garden from which the Jews were banished, with a sword turning before its locked door. Bar-Kokba hid in caves beneath the city. Without food or water. Out of his mind, dreaming, seeing his childhood home in the Galilee, the sea, the fields, cut grass and wheat, the days of conquest, Jerusalem, the Romans fleeing, the crowds chanting his name: *Bar-Kokba! Bar-Kokba!*

He issued orders, which were written on scrolls and carried by couriers to soldiers across Judea. In the end, he was betrayed by a

Samaritan who led the Romans to the hidden entrance of his cave. There was a battle at the bottom of a warren, in the center of the earth, at the entrance to Sheol, abode of the dead. Hundreds died fighting. Others were sealed in the tunnels—an army starved to death, the men seated in rank, as if awaiting orders that would never come.

Here's how it's reported in the Midrash:*

The Romans found him in a cave. There was a battle. He was killed. His head was cut off and carried by its hair, eyes open, green and glassy. It was brought to Hadrian's tent. The emperor studied the head, then asked,

"Who killed him?"

A soldier said, "I killed him."

Hadrian said, "Bring me the body."

The soldier went back to the cave. A snake was coiled around Bar-Kokba's torso. When the soldier reported this, Hadrian said, "If his God had not slain him, who could have?"

The Romans destroyed Bethar and massacred its people.[†]

Rabbi Jonathan (from the Midrash): "The brains of three hundred children were dashed on one stone."

Rabbi Gamaliel (from the Midrash): "There were five hundred schools in Bethar, and the smallest had no less than three hundred children. They used to say: 'If the enemy comes in against us, with these styluses we will go out and stab them.' But when the people's sins did cause the enemy to come, the enemy wrapped each pupil in his book and burnt him."

News of Bar-Kokba's death spread across the country. There were cries of disbelief. *The Messiah has been killed!* Then mourning. But the people were not mourning Bar-Kokba; they were mourning themselves. They had followed a false god. They had not listened to ben Zakkai. They did not plant the sapling but ran after the Messiah. They

---

*The following is my paraphrase.

†According to tradition, Bethar fell on the Ninth of Av.

were ashamed. With the death of Bar-Kokba, the example of the Jewish warrior was (nearly) discredited forever. If people had to speak of
him, it was no longer as Bar-Kokba but Bar-Koziba, the son of falsity,
the deceiver, the lie.

The Romans shackled Akiba and took him to Rome, where he was
tortured. Shot full of arrows and eaten by lions and put on a rack and
hanged from a cross. For the Jews, Bar-Kokba was the Son of Falsity
after the fall, but Akiba remained Akiba, a martyr and saint. According to Yehuda Halevi, the great poet of Jewish Spain, "Akiba reached
a degree so near to prophecy he held intercourse with the spiritual
world. He was as worthy of associating with the Shekhinah* as Moses,
but the period was not propitious."

Akiba was reciting the Shema when he died. This is really the first
prayer of Judaism: "Hear O Israel, the Lord our God, the Lord is
One." It gave Akiba strength and showed his loyalty to God. It was an
act of defiance, in that the Shema is a pure expression of the philosophy that infuriated the Romans, for whom God was not one, but
many. Akiba's last spoken word, according to the Mishna, was *One*.†

The Second Revolt lasted five years. It was damaging for Rome,
worse for the Jews. According to the Roman historian Dio Cassius,
580,000 Jews were killed. According to the Midrash, in which the Revolt is called the Final Polemos (*polemos* is Greek for "war"), 90 percent
of Judea's population died as a result of the illness and famine that followed.‡ Israel never recovered. The community that emerged in the
coming centuries was meek, defeated, battle-shy. Gone was the ancient veneration of holy war, gone was the longing for a tribal king,
gone was the belief that justice could be had by the sword. The Revolt
ended with the death of the nation and the birth of the Jew as we

---

*The spirit of God. To associate with the Shekhinah is, in essence, to speak to God face-to-face.

†Books are filled with stories of Akiba's death. In one, his corpse is cut to pieces and strung up and
sold in a butcher's stall in Rome. In another, it's borne away by the prophet Elijah, and carried on
a night journey to Caesarea.

‡Gershom Gorenberg said the Second Jewish Revolt was, aside from the Nazi Holocaust, the worst
tragedy ever to befall the Jews as a people. Since the Revolt ended the Old Kingdom, and the Nazi
Holocaust made possible its rebirth, you can almost say the nation died in holocaust and was reborn in holocaust.

know him. "Indescribable misery spread over Palestine," wrote Solomon Schechter. "The land became a desert. It must have been regarded as an evil omen that the pillar of Solomon in Jerusalem fell of itself. Indeed, the end of the Jewish nation had come."

The fighting was followed by an even darker period, which the rabbis called the Age of Persecution, during which the Romans passed laws meant to end the problem of Jewish uniqueness forever: laws meant to break the tie between the people and their city, between the city and its God. Jews were forbidden to live within ten miles of Jerusalem. (This was the Expulsion.) They were allowed to enter the city just once a year, on the Ninth of Av, to recall the destruction of their Temple. They would come on pilgrimage, stand beneath the mountain, and weep. St. Jerome described them in the fifth century: "You see a sad people coming, decrepit little women and old men encumbered with rags and years, exhibiting in their bodies and their dress the wrath of the Lord."

A generation after Bar-Kokba, there were hardly any Jews in Judea. They had migrated to the Galilee, or settled in towns along the trade roads, Alexandria, Cairo, Rome. Jews were not allowed back into Jerusalem until the mid-600s, when the city was conquered by Muslims. The relationship that Rome established between the Jews and their holy capital—that of ghosts haunting their old life—continued into modern times, when the Jews of Jerusalem were depicted as a dark-coated swarm, as homeless wanderers.

Roman workers knocked down and carted away what was left of the city. In its place, a modern capital was built. It was called Aelia Capitolina, after Hadrian's family name, Aelius. It was laid out like every other city in the Empire, on a grid, with a boulevard, the Cardo Maximus, running beneath arches. There was a covered market, shops, parks. There were statues of generals. There was a shrine to Venus and another to Hadrian, who, in the wake of the war, had declared himself a god. The new city was crowded with theaters, forums, and public baths. There was a temple to Asclepius, the god of medicine and healing, and another to Aphrodite, the goddess of beauty and sexual rapture. As Hadrian promised, a temple to Jupiter stood on the Mount. (It was there until Rome accepted Christ.) Aelia Capitolina was a hygienic, flavorless town laid on the twisted ruins of the old world, municipal planning on a grand scale, the life work of architects and masons. The victors were trying to drag Jerusalem into the light of Rome. Because the tribalism of the Jews had become a nuisance to the leaders of the Imperium.*

Judea disappeared from maps. The country was like a Russian man who made an inappropriate joke about Stalin, then vanished, from the present but also from the past. It was now called Palestine, after the Philistines, a tribe that, according to the Bible, lived in Canaan before the Hebrew Exodus.

For Zionists—adherents of the modern political movement that called for the reestablishment of a Jewish state in Palestine—the Second Revolt represented the last legitimate act in the history of the people. Everything after it was a mistake. The last true Israelis died beneath Bethar. In working to remake the Jews, the Zionists wanted to go back and pick up where Bar-Kokba left off. They wanted to edit the story so it cut directly from Bethar to the birth of Zionism. Everything between, all those centuries in all those nations, existed within historical parentheses. They did not matter, were not real. The Zionists vowed to turn away from the ideal of the brainy Jew that began with ben Zakkai in Jabneh. When an early Zionist club was founded in Berlin in 1898, it was called Bar-Kokba. Later, when Zionists began training the Jewish youth of Eastern Europe, these groups were called Bethar, the last stronghold, from the ruins of which a new Jew would emerge.

---

*Aelia Capitolina stood for less than two hundred years, from AD 135 to AD 326.

FOUR

A City in a Mirror

A fter the Expulsion, many Jews stopped concerning themselves with the contemporary world. The rabbis instead turned their attention to the centuries of experience their people had already accumulated. That is, the stories of the Bible. Because the Bible consists of stories of the glorious past and visions of the glorious future, the Jews came to live in the past and in the future—everywhere but in the present. Which did not exist. Because the old world had died and the new world had not yet been born. In this way, the Jews, who had been exiled from their land by Rome, exiled themselves from the present tense. In this way, the Jews came unstuck from time.

In this way, the Jews left history.

They were pushed first into the outskirts of the Old Kingdom, then into Jewish colonies in the Diaspora. This process of dispersion accelerated with the triumph of Christianity in the fourth century. When the Romans became Christians, the Jews were exiled from even the edges of the Old Kingdom—some converted, some were killed, many went east, into Arabia, where Jewish communities remained into our own time. The school at Jabneh shut down at the order of the Church and relocated to Mesopotamia, which is why you have two Talmuds: the Palestinian Talmud, written in Jabneh and surrounding towns, and the Babylonian Talmud, written in the East after the rise of the Church but before the rise of Muhammad.

With the triumph of the Roman Church, the Jews were seemingly rendered ancient, irrelevant: because the new faith claimed to super-sede the old; because the new faith was the desert religion cleansed of legalism; because the new faith was the only way to heaven; because the new faith was so much easier, without fasting or circumcision or animal sacrifice—as the ultimate sacrifice had already been made by God, who had given his son as even Abraham had not been required to do. All of which made the religion of the Jews seem out of date, its followers deluded. They were like the crew of a lost steamship. A flood had burst through the banks of the river, changing the river's course, turning the bend where the ship lay anchored into an oxbow, pinched off at either end. At night, you hear the foghorn, which is the blast of the shofar, as the crew, standing on the prow, which is the bema, searches for a way back to the mainstream.

To Christians, Christianity was Judaism fulfilled. To Jews, Chris-tianity was Judaism plus paganism minus Jews. You feel it in museums when you look at religious pictures done in the Renaissance, Jesus in Gethsemane, Christ at Golgotha, in which the intense young rabbi from Capernaum—you just know he had dark curly hair and murky green eyes—is replaced by a Norse warrior.

This was the new model.

What happens to the old model when the new model is released?

With the ascension of Jesus, there was no longer a need for Jews. Their continued existence was a theological problem. They should have converted, or else disappeared. Hundreds of nations have been wiped out, which is why the old books are filled with the names of civilizations so long gone they sound folkloric—Antioch, Edom—kingdoms of the deep past. Only the Jews refused to follow the worn path into oblivion. That they did not vanish and would not die is their mystery, a riddle that philosophers can go mad trying to solve: Maybe the Jews survived to be converted. Maybe the Jews survived so that when Jesus returns, He won't ask, "Hey, where are all my Jews?" Maybe the Jews survived so they can be punished, again and again, until Kingdom come.

Out of such beliefs grew one of the most uncanny myths of the Middle Ages, the story of the Wandering Jew, in which Jesus, as he carried his cross to Calvary, was taunted by a Hebrew cobbler. Jesus cursed the man, saying, "Go forever until I return." This man, according to the myth, has been roaming the world ever since. Two thousand years. Longing for death. He has been seen in every nation, working in every profession, wearing every kind of uniform. He is the last living witness of the murder of God. This story was first published as a pamphlet in a small town near Prague in the early 1600s. Within a decade, it had been translated into every language of Europe. New versions appeared, each adding scenes and details. In some, the villain was called the "Wandering Jew." In some, he was called the "Eternal Jew" or the "Immortal Jew." Plays and poems were written about him. Many people thought the story was true. The Wandering Jew was suddenly discovered in ancient texts—the mysterious onlooker, the character with no name.

He was seen in the modern world, too, in markets and churches where the story was popular. He wore a long black coat and carried a traveling case and a prayer shawl. His eyes were brown and his hair was black and he had purple lips and pale skin—and I don't have to tell you about his nose. You would see him and forget you saw him, then see him again in a dream at night, in which he was counting money and calculating terms of interest. He moved like the plague. He was spotted in Hamburg in 1547, in Spain in 1575, in Lübeck in 1603, in Bavaria in 1604, in Leipzig in 1642, in Paris in 1644, in Stamford, England, in 1658, in Astrakhan in 1672, in Frankfurt in 1676, in Munich in 1721, in Altbach in 1766, in Brussels in 1774, in Newcastle in 1790. The last recorded sighting was in America in 1868, where he was seen in the Arizona Territory, by a Mormon named Tom O'Grady. This was reported on September 23, 1868, in a periodical called *Desert News*.

The Eternal Jew is a stand-in for the Jews at large: who can be killed and be killed and still not die; because they do not deserve death; because wandering is their punishment.

W hy did the Jews leave history?
Because they had had enough history. Because they had been wounded by reality. Because Jerusalem had been destroyed. Because there was a temple to Jupiter on the Mountain of God. Because you could spend an eternity trying to understand what had already happened and still not come to the end of it.*

In this way, the Jews became a meta-people. They lived not in the world, but in their stories about the world. They lived in a text. In this way, they turned the Temple into a book. It began in Jabneh, where the rabbis collected the biblical canon, then compiled the Mishna, which means something like "the teaching." This is the oral history of Israel that grew over the centuries, a hodgepodge of legends and prophecies and poems that were written down in the first years of exile. It was constructed in the manner of the old Gothic cathedrals, slowly and meticulously, the effort going on and on. Never being finished was part of its function. It gave the rabbis a task. They worked on it as they once worked on their city. They vanished into it as they once vanished into their city. It was a city of the mind, a frontier between the actual, which is perishable, and the visionary, which never dies.

The Jews carried the Mishna with them in exile. It was the memory of the people. It was the nation on wheels. When they were driven out of Jabneh, they brought it to the Galilee, then to Babylon, where it was finished four hundred years after the Temple was destroyed. It had been worked on by several generations. (In this way, the rabbis of one era collaborated with the rabbis of another.) Though it had been sealed, the work continued, with rabbis writing new commentaries

*Yosef Yerushalmi, *Zakhor*: "If the rabbis, wise men who had inherited a powerful historical tradition, were no longer interested in mundane history, then this indicates nothing more than that they felt no need to cultivate it. Perhaps they already knew of history what they needed to know."

about the stories in the Bible and the Mishna, which were themselves collected in a work called the Gemara. In other words, instead of new books filled with new stories, the Jews had old books filled with old stories (the Bible, the Mishna) and new books filled with commentaries on the stories in the old books (Gemara). It's as if Hollywood stopped making movies in 1945 but the newspapers kept churning out reviews—reviews of old movies and reviews of other reviews. The Mishna and the Gemara were bound in a single volume—as big as the world, a book that includes everything, then comments on it—called the Talmud.

The Talmud became a center of the faith, second in importance only to the Torah itself. From it, the rabbis extracted many of the principles and laws you must follow to be a Jew. Together these laws were called the Halakah, which means "the way." As in, "The righteous walks in the way of the Lord." As in, "Straight is the path, narrow the way." To a Jew, Halaka means the way as Tao means the way to a Buddhist. At a certain point, the beliefs of all the religions converge, because when you strip away the local attributes, the angel wings and the silver hair and the flying horse, you see that each God is the same God talking in the voice of a particular time.

The status of the Talmud and the Torah in the Jewish world (everything in them is sacred, everything not in them is profane) led to the sort of close reading that will break down even the most straightforward text. (As when you repeat a familiar word—*Jew, Jew, Jew, Jew, Jew*—until it sounds strange.) The Jew is a traveler on a fifteen-hundred-year flight with just these books. He's read them so many times that he's come to see patterns in them, secret meanings, eerie coincidences, signals and clues.

The books have made him batty.

From this comes the discipline that probably best expresses the nature of the Exile: Jewish mysticism, which blossomed a few hundred years after the destruction of the Second Temple, and continues among Kabbalists and the followers of Rebbe Schneerson, the presently deceased Brooklyn-based Hasidic holy man who some believe is the Messiah.* When you see a Jew in a long dark coat with side curls, you might think of your grandfather with his sharp immigrant mind, but, in fact, the brain of the Hasid is filled with butterflies.

There are mystics in every faith—Buddhist, Hindu, Muslim, Christian—but there is something peculiar about the mysticism of Jews, and the way it's tangled up with the pain of exile.

I'm not very smart, and read but don't always understand—or do understand, then forget—so the hidden things remain hidden from me, but here is a rough idea of what Jewish mystics came to believe in the Diaspora: that there was a secret teaching given by God to Adam, then by God to Moses; that it was lost; that if the Jews recover it, they will understand the reason for their exile, or that there really is no exile; that the misery of the world is an illusion.

To the mystic, the Torah is not a national history. It's a metaphysical document, filled with esoteric meanings. He searches it for signs, patterns, and sequences. He dwells on the first pages of Genesis, as these describe the world before the Fall. He is fixated on the story of Enoch, as Enoch was the only man in the book who did not die. He puzzles over the Nephilim, those heavenly watchers, as they suggest an age when the gods dwelled on earth. Each of these stories has an obvious meaning, but behind it are thousands of secret meanings, our Torah being just a sliver of a hidden Torah. There are twenty-seven letters in the Hebrew alphabet, but the mystic says there is a secret twenty-eighth letter that, when it's revealed, will change the meaning of everything. Creation has passed through many dispensations, he says, each lasting a thousand years, culminating in the jubilee. In each new dispensation, the Torah will be read in a different way and only the name of God will remain the same.

As life in the Diaspora deteriorated, the system of the mystics grew more arcane and complex. The progression went like this: the rabbis of Jabneh turned the Temple into a book; the early mystics read this book as if it were a map of creation; the later mystics expanded the map un-

*Hence presently deceased.

til its symbols filled the entire world—until the world itself became a text that could be read like a book, literally, allegorically, or symbolically.

A novel written by Jehovah.

In this way, the things of the world became symbols, clues to a deeper message. The yew tree is eternity. The rose is mortality. Being a clue does not make a thing less real. On the Seder plate, the bitter herbs are both bitter herbs and a symbol of the bitterness of history; the shank bone is both a shank bone and a symbol of the sacrifice made in the wilderness.

There's a passage in the Joseph Mitchell book *Joe Gould's Secret* that perfectly captures the mind of the mystic:

> The old man sees meanings behind meanings, or thinks he does, and tries his best to tell what things "stand for." "Pomegranates are about the size and shape of large oranges or small grapefruits, only their skins are red," he says, cupping his hands in the air and speaking with such exactitude that it is obvious he has had firsthand knowledge of pomegranates long ago in the South. "They're filled with fat little seeds, and those fat little seeds are filled with juice as red as blood. When they get ripe, they're so swollen with those juicy red seeds that they gap open and some of the seeds spill out. And now I'll tell you what pomegranates stand for. They stand for the resurrection. The resurrection of the Lord and Savior Jesus Christ and your resurrection and my resurrection. Resurrection in particular and resurrection in general. All seeds stand for resurrection. The Easter egg stands for resurrection. So do the eggs in the English Sparrow's nest under the eaves in the 'L' station. So does the egg you have for breakfast. So does the caviar the rich people eat. So does shad roe."

Here's Gershom Scholem in *Major Trends in Jewish Mysticism*:*

> The thing which becomes a symbol retains its original form and its original content. It does not become an empty shell into which an-

---

*This is a great book, part of the modern Jewish canon, and was an important source.

other content is poured; it is itself, and through its own existence, it makes another reality transparent which cannot appear in any other form . . . the mystical symbol is an expressible representation of something which lies beyond the sphere of expression and communication, something which comes from a sphere whose face is turned away from us. A hidden and inexpressible reality finds its expression in the symbol.

Scholem then writes, "The infinite shines through the finite and makes it more not less real."

The most important symbol in the world is the Jew himself. The entire theology of mysticism was created around just this fact, which made the terror of exile easier to bear. The Jew is not a member of a defeated, scattered nation. Or not only. He is a symbol that reminds mankind of its own exile, the exile of the soul in the body. He is a symbol that tells you something has gone wrong, the world is fallen. It explains everything: the reason for the Exile and why people hate the Jews. Because they fear God. Because they flee from God, but He reaches out to them through the Jews. The Gentiles kill the Jews for the same reason Oedipus plucks out his own eyes.

Because the truth is too terrible to see.

If you were a Jew in the Middle Ages, it would have been consoling for you to believe the world was unreal, just a purgatory beyond which things would be clear, simple, just. (In the next world, only the name of God would be the same.) This was a feeling shared throughout the Diaspora, throughout time: that there had been an accident, as a result of which the Jew was in a place that was never supposed to exist. I went to sleep in my bed but woke in what looks like my bed but is actually another bed in another room, and I can't find my way back.

This is what Gimpel the Fool means at the end of the great story by Isaac Bashevis Singer:

No doubt the world is an entirely imaginary world, but it is only once removed from the true world. At the door of the hovel where I live, there stands the plank on which the dead are taken away. The gravedigger Jew has his spade ready. The grave waits and the worms are hungry; the shrouds are prepared—I carry them in my beggar's sack. Another schnorrer is waiting to inherit my bed of straw. When the time comes I will go joyfully. Whatever may be there, it will be real, without complication, without ridicule, without deception. God be praised: there even Gimpel cannot be deceived.*

Of course, mystics believe you can find your way back; that's the whole point of mysticism. To regain the old wisdom, to touch the hem of God's garment. You don't need a temple or a priest but can teach yourself to see the holy in the everyday—the presence of God, which is love—as you can teach yourself to see the pattern in a carpet. Abraham Heschel, who taught mysticism at the Jewish Theological Seminary in New York, spoke of training himself to see through the distraction, of learning to glimpse the eternal in the temporal. With a focused mind, a mystic can push aside the planets and stars to reveal the hidden machinery. Heschel said the universe is just God reaching out to man. (His most famous book is called *God in Search of Man*.) To him, the world is like the forest Pinocchio races through in the Disney movie, in which the branches of the trees become fingers, pulling at your clothes; every breeze shouts your name; every sign points to God.

To the mystics, there are two Jerusalems. The earthly city was smashed. But what was smashed? A city in a mirror. The real city lives on, untouched and untouchable. You can go there. You can pierce the veil. With prayer. This kind of prayer is less like the ritual you know from synagogue or church, where you say the words as if they were words in a magic spell, than like Buddhist meditation, in which the content is less important than the mere act of repetition, which focuses

*According to some mystics, whatever exists in this world must have a counterpart in the next. Whatever you see here is a reflection of what is happening there. If there is a tragedy here, there must have been an even greater tragedy there, the emanations of which wash up on our world as waves wash up on the beach when a ship sinks beyond the horizon. The fall of Jerusalem must therefore have echoed a metaphysical calamity.

the mind. The mystic chants, his eyes closed, he sweats like Charlie
Parker hitting the high notes, his breath comes fast and shallow, then
he sees.

The early mystics were called Merkabah mystics, after a verse in the
Book of Ezekiel that describes the chariot of God. These men would
emerge from a trance to give detailed descriptions of what they had
seen, descriptions preserved in the Apocrypha (the books left out of the
canon), such as the Testament of Abraham and the Book of Enoch:

They spoke of fountains and gardens and olive trees and fig bushes
and angels. They spoke of marble chambers and gold columns and
high roofs crossed by cedar beams. They spoke of stairs, a ziggurat ascending. They spoke of patterns. They spoke of numbers. They spoke
of immanence and transcendence. They spoke of outer courts and inner courts, of outer rooms and inner rooms, of the fantastic architecture of heaven. "The traveler in search of God, like the visitor at court,
must pass through endless magnificent halls and chambers," Gershom
Scholem writes. Heaven is structured like a video game, in which you
climb from level to level until, on the last screen, you see the chariot of
God, His throne, but never the first cause, which remains hidden.

In describing their visions, Merkabah mystics often referred to the
Book of Kings, in which the prophet Elijah makes a similar flight:
"Behold, there appeared a chariot of fire, and horses of fire, and Elijah went up by a whirlwind into heaven." The mystics believed in the
utter reality of these journeys, and, on their return, reported each
wonder—the seven heavens spread out like a plain, the chamber and
holy throne—like foreign correspondents just back from Istanbul or
Marrakech. These men were called Yorede Merkabah, "those that go
up in the chariot." Their stories were told with detailed exactitude,
and the elements of each vision were strikingly similar. Each mystic
described the same landscape of courtyards and sanctuaries. These
remind me of Italian paintings that illustrate the corporate hierarchy
of heaven: cloudy upper reaches, confused middle ground, violent un-
derworld. From such consistency, you can conclude either (1) the mystics
were conspiring in a lie, a vast hoax, the benefit of which it is impossible
to discern; (2) the souls of the mystics were in fact being regularly trans-

ported to heaven, which they were allowed to visit the way you visit a college campus before you make your choice; or (3) the mystics were caught in a collective hallucination, brought on, even willed into being, by the same experience, the same despair, and the same hope.

You can probably guess which I believe. (I left off number four, in which all the trances were conjured by a demigod to lead the faithful astray.) I think the Jewish mystics were undergoing a kind of mass hallucination, dreaming the same dream. Because when you read their testimonies alongside the Bible and the works of Josephus, you realize that the city they're describing is Jerusalem, the palace they're ascending to is the Second Temple. Their mystical descriptions of the next world perfectly match the worldly descriptions of the Jewish past as recorded in the Torah, the Mishna, and the Roman histories. By destroying the Temple, the Romans had freed its ghost, which lingered above the corporeal city. The Jerusalem of the mystics is not the real Jerusalem—it's the city idealized in the memory of its people, rebuilt in the brain of each believer. Christians make much of the resurrection of Jesus, but in the Jewish world, an entire city was crucified and resurrected.

For the peculiar speculative genius which discovers in the Torah layer upon layer of hidden meaning, there is in principle no limit. In the last resort, the whole of the Torah, as is often stressed by the author [of the Zohar], is nothing but the one great holy name of God.

—GERSHOM SCHOLEM

I saac Luria was educated in Jerusalem by his father, a scholar driven out of Europe during the Spanish expulsion of 1492. That Luria was brought up in the aftermath of another exile may explain his fascination with hidden things, secret teachings that explain the suffering of his people. He was recognized as a prodigy, known for his passion for codes and clues. He spent many years in silence, during which he studied the

Kabbalah, a range of esoteric works including the Zohar, probably the most influential text of Jewish mysticism.* In certain circles, a man is not allowed to read from the Zohar before age forty, as it is believed that premature exposure to such rapturous mysteries can drive a person insane.

Luria settled in Safed, in the Galilee, a refuge for Jews after the expulsion. In these years, because of Luria, Safed became the center of mysticism. Its heroes were holy men, sitting crosslegged beneath a blue sky, palms up, the energy of creation concentrated in their concentrating minds. The town sits on a hill. From its lower houses you see its upper houses. From its upper houses you see the valley. In the morning the streets are bloated with light the way a sponge is bloated with water. The mystics said this light is God pressing on your shoulders and warming your face. (Some said Adam was not a man, but a ray of light, the first emanation sent into the primordial darkness.) Even now, as tour buses groan uphill into the town, as tourists search the galleries for cheap prints of Jerusalem, as Hasids rush about preparing for a feast, Safed still feels holy—holy in the way of faded capitals (Alexandria, Trieste) in which something great happened long ago: raised up by an eminence, damaged when set back down.

Luria believed in the transmigration of souls. In the next life, he said, your spirit might be trapped in a donkey. He therefore never killed anything, not even a worm. He said anger is the most destructive force in the universe. He called for calm even in the face of assault. "Love all creatures," he said, "even non-Jews."† In this way, Luria turned the realities forced on the Jews by exile into virtues. People who

---

*The Zohar was said to be an ancient book of secret teachings, but Gershom Scholem basically proved it a fabrication written by a contemporary of Luria's. It's a collection of books that read like a commentary on the Torah. In it, fictitious writers unlock a code or secret teaching in the Bible. Like a work by Borges, it refers to and quotes texts that were themselves invented. Telling to Scholem were the descriptions of Judea in the Zohar, which resemble the actual Judea as the backgrounds in old Dutch paintings of the crucifixion resemble the actual Jerusalem. (Based on these descriptions, says Scholem, it seemed the author of the Zohar was familiar with rural Spain.) Interesting in that this shows how, by the early Middle Ages, the dream of Jerusalem had already replaced the real Jerusalem in the Hebrew mind. Scholem: "The Palestine which is described in all its parts [of the Zohar] is not the real country as it exists or existed, but an imaginary one . . . its descriptions of the mountains of Palestine are of the most romantic kind and accord far better with the reality of Castile than with that of Galilee."

†!

had no means to resist were told that resistance was a sin. Taken together, his teachings constituted a new religion,* a faith that consoled the Jews after the Spanish expulsion as Zionism consoled the Jews after the Nazi Holocaust. (The tenets of this religion made sacred the suffering of the Jews.) Luria's religion had its own rules and rites, even its own creation story, which is a metaphorical reading of Genesis.†

In the beginning, before God created heaven and the earth, God was everywhere and everything. Which left no place in creation for the world. Therefore, before God could create the world, He first had to remove Himself to make room for His creation. Luria called this an act of divine withdrawal, in which God goes out like the tide, Tsimtsum. Before God created the world, He created the void. (The world is the only place God is not.) He then poured His holy light into the void, as an artist pours paint onto a canvas, and the light grew into heaven and earth.

However, at the moment of creation, as the first dab of paint was squeezed from the tube, there was a disaster—in the nature of a spill. As a result, man became aware of his nakedness. As a result, death came into the world. This is the grand allegory of the Kabbalah, "The Breaking of the Vessels."

As God poured His infinite light into the void, He caught the excess in ten holy vessels, which the mystics call the Sefirot, but these vessels were not strong enough to hold the light, and so shattered. The light spilled into the void, where it mixed with the darkness—the infinite mixed with the finite; the good mixed with the evil. Which explains

---

*To Gershom Scholem, this new religion was a symptom of exile—the Jew, deprived of the wide world, turned his creative energy on the opaque. "The Kabalistic Aggadah reflects a narrow and circumscribed life which sought, nay, was compelled to seek inspiration from hidden worlds as the real world turned into the world of the Ghetto," he writes. "The depth of the penetration into the hidden worlds which can be encountered here at every step stands in direct proportion to the sinking perimeter of [the Jew's] historical experience."

†This passage and the one that follows are my paraphrased summaries.

the suffering of the Jew, who, in his exile, stands for the light trapped in the darkness and for God in exile from the world.*

According to Luria, the mission of the Jew is to gather the light and return it to the vessels. This is done through prayer and good deeds. The process is called *Tikkun olam*, to heal the breach. When all the light is recovered, the world will be redeemed and the Jews will return to the kingdom. We are hazmat workers, in other words, heavy with gear, combing the oil out of Prudhoe Bay.

---

*Gershom Scholem: "The event is traced back to technical flaws in the structure of the Sefirotic atom-cosmos from which the 'accident' follows with necessity."

FIVE

Messiahs:
True or False?

If you're an Orthodox Jew saying your prayers properly, you say "Jerusalem" ten times a day. Ten times a day you conjure up the image of the city. Throughout the Exile, it was this image that kept the nation from disappearing. In every other case, a nation in the position of the Jews assimilated, melted away. In fact, those Jews who went to China or India did vanish, leaving behind only the random temple, or scroll, or legend. Otherwise, they're as gone as the Incas. Of course, it was not just Jerusalem that preserved the people, but its image stood behind everything; it was the background against which every scene was played. The ritual, the worship, the faith—all of it is just Jerusalem in another way. The shank bone on the Seder plate is Jerusalem. The bema in the synagogue is Jerusalem. The language in the liturgy is Jerusalem. (The prayer shawl is Jerusalem, the yarmulke is Jerusalem, the menorah is Jerusalem.) In the Diaspora, everything is Jerusalem except

Jerusalem itself, which is a ruin, a mathematical remainder—what's left over when the soul of the town is raptured to heaven.

Everywhere you look, you see another picture of Jerusalem: in paintings, in poems, in books, in a billion minds—in each of which it's the capital of a different nation, populated by a different people. In the matchbook, in the keychain, in the lithograph, in the Hollywood epic, in the View-Master viewer. On medieval maps, the Garden of Eden was shown as an actual place. It was at the top of the world, at a latitude no explorer had yet reached. It was green and gold, and out of it flowed the four rivers that watered the earth. Columbus thought he found it on his second voyage, when he sighted the lush coast of Brazil. In letters to Queen Isabella, he described the deltas and rivers, which he said ascended as they went inland, rising to the garden. On the same maps, Jerusalem was pictured in the same way, as fantastic and attainable, a myth that happened to be true. The city, its name surrounded by a golden halo, was drawn at the center of the world, at its navel, where it mirrored and anchored the Garden of Eden. It's the great misfortune of Jerusalem to be both wholly imaginary and wholly real.

Saul Bellow, in *To Jerusalem and Back*: "I too feel the light of Jerusalem has purifying powers and filters the blood and the thoughts; I don't forbid myself the reflection that light may be the outer garment of God."

Here's something that always bothered me: If Jerusalem was at the center of Jewish worship; if Jerusalem was the overwhelming preoccupation of the Jewish mind; if every Passover Seder ended with the words "Next year in Jerusalem"; if Jerusalem was the object of every dream of redemption and it also happened to be real and not very far away, why didn't the community, at some point during all those centuries of oppression, just get up and go back? Why didn't they stand in a group and walk out of Minsk like they had walked out of Egypt? Why did we have to wait two thousand years, until our own time, for the rise of Zionism?

Besides various political factors—what was happening in Canaan from age to age; what was happening in the Diaspora, where sometimes Jews were not allowed to travel, and sometimes were not allowed to stop traveling—there were limitations that Jews put on themselves. Most simply did not consider return a possibility. It was as if all the bridges behind them had been burned; as if there were no roads back; as if the city, in becoming a symbol, had ceased to exist on terra firma.

What's more, during the years of dispersion, exile had been invested with religious meaning: it was where the Jews would expiate their sins; where the Jews would serve as witnesses; where the Jews would heal the breach. But if the exile could be ended by an act of human will, then all that Talmudic reasoning collapsed, leaving nothing but suffering without meaning—a prospect even more terrifying than the Exile itself. For this reason, those Jews who did speak of return were seen as heretics. They threatened the mission of the people. If God has a plan, part of that plan is the Exile. Any attempt to end that exile by what the Zionists would later call "auto-emancipation," was therefore an effort to thwart God's plan. Such men were said to be "Forcing the hand of the Almighty."

The roots for such thinking can be found in Jabneh, where the rabbis, sensibly, saw a great danger in any attempt to reestablish the kingdom. A third revolt would surely mean the final disappearance of the Jews. For this reason, the rabbis turned the ancient dream into a taboo: never to be spoken of, never to be attempted. (They did this as you might tell a dry drunk that the whiskey is poisoned.) Survival depended, as far as the rabbis were concerned, on Jews accommodating themselves to the realities of the Roman world. To accomplish this, they elevated the political necessities of exile—being meek, being invisible—into religious virtues. Over time, these virtues were confused with laws, so that to act in the spirit of an earlier tradition, the tradition of the warrior Jew, was to break the law. There is a remnant of Jews who still follow this rabbinical reasoning: you might have seen them on TV a few years ago, meeting with the president of Iran, denouncing Israel, and refusing to recognize its right to exist. It's not the state of the nation these men were concerned with, but the survival of the Jews, who persist merely to be punished and to worship God.

Jews internalized the edict of Rome, according to which a Jew was allowed to visit Jerusalem just once a year, on the anniversary of its destruction. People originally followed this rule so they would not be arrested or killed, but then refashioned it as a kind of unwritten commandment, so it could be followed without shame. In this way, they developed a mental barrier that distanced them from their capital and made return impossible. Jerusalem became a city behind a veil, close but unknowable. (Though the mind might be filled with it, the body could never go there.) There were always some Jews in Jerusalem, of course, or almost always, and Jewish merchants traveled there, but for the vast majority it grew as distant as Eden. The mere thought of going there, approaching it, was terrifying.*

Consider the Baal Shem Tov, who founded Hasidism in the eighteenth century. He never spent a day without longing for Jerusalem, which he tried and failed to reach on several occasions; the breach was simply too wide. He was born in Poland. And orphaned. And grew up in a shul. He was so simple and true he was recognized as holy even when he was taken for a fool. He received his revelation in a town in the Carpathian Mountains. (I have never been to the Carpathians, but in my mind they exist as one of the few wholly real and wholly imagined places left.) He read books all day, but at night he had visions in which he was visited by the ancients, who revealed secret teachings and hidden things.

Men gathered around him, sat at his feet, listened. It was in these years that people began calling him the Baal Shem Tov, which means master of the good name, and is a title like Holy Roman Emperor. He was an Idiot King, uneducated but wise. His followers were known as Hasids, "the righteous." They considered him a prophet, even the Messiah. They did what he did, dressed as he dressed, in black coats and black hats. They rocked as they prayed. When they looked up, their eyes were wet with tears. According to the Kabbalists, the world is just an emanation of God. According to the Baal Shem Tov, the

---

*In his book *On Zion*, Martin Buber writes of the astonishment a group of Jews felt, years later, in another age, when they traveled to the Holy Land. Before they reached Palestine, says Buber, "they had been quite unable to realize that the land of Israel really exists in the world. From everything they had read about its holiness in books they had imagined that it was in a completely different world. But when they came there they saw that the land really does exist and in its outward appearance is not different in kind from other countries from which they had come—its dust is like the dust of the whole world. And yet the land is entirely holy. It is as with the true Zaddik [holy man], who likewise looks exactly like other men. In truth, however, the land is separate from other lands in every respect and even the sky above it is different from the sky elsewhere. It is as with the Zaddik: only the man who believes in holiness recognizes and receives it."

world is not just an emanation of God; the world *is* God. We live inside God. Because there is nothing but God. We inhale God and we exhale God. We speak God's name with God's mouth. You can experience this directly, said the Baal Shem Tov, through prayer and meditation. "The ideal of man is to be a revelation himself," he told his followers, "to recognize himself as a manifestation of God."

According to legend, the Baal Shem Tov first tried to reach Jerusalem when he was young, perhaps still a boy. He had fallen in with the louts who frequented the local tavern. He would advise them and settle their disputes. In return, they offered to take him to Palestine via a network of underground tunnels. This is mythology, but it gets at a poetic truth: the upper world is connected through the lower, and the holy city, which is transcendence, is just beyond the next threshold. They left at dawn, making their way to the center of Earth, under the oceans, then up toward Jerusalem. But when they reached the final gate, the path was blocked by a sword turning slowly in the air, the city closed to the Baal Shem Tov as the Garden of Eden has been closed to all mankind.*

He tried again some years later. "He is said to have reached Istanbul," Martin Buber writes. "Here he was either warned in a dream and bidden to return, or else embarked with his family but was driven back by a great storm at sea."

Note how the details change—now it's a voice in a dream, now it's a tempest at sea—but the crucial fact remains the same: the Baal Shem Tov does not reach the holy city. To the believer, such failures evidence the working of the Almighty, but to the modern man they seem symptoms of neurosis. The sword is a Freudian symbol (ditto the voice, ditto the tempest) of the nameless force (Rome) that turns the Jew away from his goal. It's not that he cannot cross the threshold; it's that, at some level, he is scared to take his fate into his own hands.

In the Jewish psyche, the ancient capital is lit by the same charge that lit the Ark of the Covenant. It's a high-voltage wire: touch it, you die. In the third century, Emperor Constantine, who converted Rome to Chris-

---

*Here's how the legend was described by Martin Buber: "Just as he was about to cross a deep bog on the way, the revolving sword of the Cherubs appeared to him and he had to turn back."

tianity, was succeeded by Julian, a pagan, who, not thinking the religion proper for a great warrior nation, attempted to curb the influence of the Church. As part of this effort, he wanted to elevate the status of the Jews. He promised to restore their ancient capital and rebuild the Jewish Temple.* Julian believed the restoration of the Temple would undercut the Catholic bishops and expose their teaching as a lie, as the ruin of the Temple was said to be a fulfillment of Christian prophecy.

Julian made these promises in a letter written to the Jewish community of Rome in AD 363, shortly before he led his armies into battle in Persia.

Work began that same year.† Masons cleared the rubble and fortified the ancient foundations. Then, one day, as the crews hefted and hauled, and the blue eye of heaven stared down, the ground beneath them shook and fire blasted out of the holy mountain and debris went into the sky and fell down like rain.

Edward Gibbon, *The Decline and Fall of the Roman Empire*:

[As the architect] urged with vigor and diligence the execution of the work, horrible balls of fire breaking out near the foundations, with frequent reiterate attacks, rendered the place, from time to time, inaccessible to the scorched and blasted workmen . . . An earthquake, a whirlwind, and a fiery eruption, which overturned and scattered the new foundations of the temple, are attested, with some variations, by contemporary and respectable evidence . . . This public event is described by Ambrose, bishop of Milan, in an epistle to the emperor Theodosius, which must provoke the severe animadversion of the Jews.

No details were recorded, no numbers, no descriptions, so you are left with just this mysterious event, which speaks like a voice from the flames, saying this Third Temple was destroyed either because (Chris-

---

*Edward Gibbon, *The Decline and Fall*: "[Julian] resolved to erect without delay, on the commanding eminence of Mount Moriah, a stately Temple, which might eclipse the splendor of the Church of the Resurrection on the adjacent hill of Calvary."

†According to Christian sources: some historians suggest ground may never have been broken.

tian version) God no longer recognized the Jews as his people, or because (Jewish version) God did not want the Chosen in Jerusalem until their work in the wilderness was complete.

The project was abandoned in AD 364, when Julian died with his
troops in battle.

W hy didn't the Jews try to go back?
Why, after one of the countless massacres or pogroms, did they
not just get up and start walking? Well, the fact is, despite all the obsta-
cles and fears I've just described, despite the swords and tempests and
earthquakes, they did try to go back. They never stopped trying. It was
not just ritual and faith that preserved the Jews in the wilderness; it was
their longing for Jerusalem. Gibbon recognizes it as the defining char-
acteristic of the Hebrews: "The desire of rebuilding the Temple has, in
every age, been the ruling passion of the children of Israel."

For a Jew, a real Jew, a person with what Bernard Malamud called
a Jewish soul, or what my Grandma Esther called a *Yiddische kupp*,
the Exile was always a fleeting condition. Home while you can't go
home—because there has been a fire. The feeling of temporariness,
out-of-place-ness, which resulted from the physical reality of exile, is
a source of mystical belief. The Kabbalistic certainty that this world
is not the real world, but a reflection, begins with the dispersion. First
we had a nation. Then our nation was destroyed and we were exiled.
Then our destroyed nation became the object of our prayers, so was
turned into a symbol. The nation ceased to exist as an actual place, but
the feeling of exile from it persisted. In this way, exile became exile not
from a nation but from the past, from an idea.

Here is the meaning of the Exile: No matter how successful you become, no matter how grand your mansion, there remains something
uncanny about your life. It's not real because it's not Zion. The success
of a Jew in fourteenth-century Spain, say, was akin to the social success
you might have had as a boy at summer camp; it was nice, but it did

not count. As it was not your real home and these were not your real friends. It was a summer world, a tiny kingdom in the woods.

Hasdai ibn Shaprut had the worst case of exile longing I know. His soul was the Jew soul, his brain was the Jew brain. (Though he lived long ago, his worries and dreams are entirely familiar.) For several years in the tenth century, he served as the foreign minister of Andalusia, then the greatest nation in the world. He rose to this position quickly, from nowhere. His life went from success to success, and still he was not happy. (Is a Jew ever happy? Abraham, Moses—are these people you would describe as happy?) He was born in AD 910 in Cordoba, the intellectual capital of Muslim Spain. In its library were forty thousand volumes, including the masterworks of Greece and Rome. What can't be recorded by statistics are the city's conversations, its tumult and crowds. Though it leaves no evidence in stone, energy is the whole point of such a town. Hasdai was a human expression of this energy, its culmination. The purpose of Cordoba, its lives and generations, was to give us Hasdai ibn Shaprut.

You can never know what such a man looked like. In old encyclopedias he is pictured in a vague sketch, in a turban and fluffy pirate pants. In other words, you have to imagine. In my mind, he looks like the family doctor, a trusted presence, yet mysterious, as he keeps his feelings to himself. His story is as old as Jericho and as new as Scarsdale. He was the son of a Jewish doctor. His parents told him he could accomplish everything, so he was disappointed when he realized this was only mostly true. In school he mastered medicine, math, economy, philosophy, and astrology. He became known for his tremendous knowledge—first in his household, then in his city, finally in his country. He was a sought-after physician, famous for his miraculous cures. Patients left for dead, in fevers, in swellings and spots, emerged from their stupors to walk through the narrow streets of Cordoba. He was summoned by the caliph, Abdel al-Rahman, who made him the official doctor of the royal court.

See how it is with a Jew? He gets into the corporation, then takes over the whole place. You can't stop him from climbing. It's his nature. Though he began as a physician—and what was a physician then but a witch doctor, with a divining rod and leeches?—Hasdai was soon running entire departments, serving first as the minister of finance, then as the minister of academies. By thirty, he had been named foreign minister, the second highest office in the land, with only the caliph to answer to. As the caliph was dreamy and distracted, Hasdai was, in many ways, running Andalusia. This is the story of Rothschild or Kissinger, the Jew who has not been elected, cannot be elected, yet still has a hand on the switch. Foreign minister was, in fact, an office often held by Jews, as it dealt with lands beyond the kingdom, which Jews, as foreigners, were thought well equipped to understand—the Jews seemed a natural bridge between the Muslim and Christian worlds.

Did Hasdai live a life of material comfort?

Of course.

Did Hasdai have secretaries and advisors?

Of course.

Statesmen visited his office, with its grand views of the domed capital. He negotiated treaties and studied maps. He was the top Jew in the top country in a golden moment of exile, had climbed as high as a Jew could climb, and still was not happy. *Do you want to be caliph, Hasdai ibn Shaprut?* Yes, but it's more than that. Jerusalem's place in his imagination made every other place, even Andalusia, seem less important, less real.

In the course of his work, he hosted merchants from across the world. He met them in his office, listened to their proposals. He asked them to describe their capitals and what they had seen. It was in this way that he first heard about the Khazars. I imagine the scene, a sticky interior in medieval Spain, a fly making a lazy circuit around the room. Hasdai tries to follow the diplomats' talk of exchange rates and border crossings, but his eyes are heavy and the room is hot and his mind drifts . . .

Then: *Thwack!*

Something hits him. He's bolt upright in his chair, alert.

What was that? he asks.

What?

What you said? Say it again.

What? About the Khazars?

Yes. Who are the Khazars?

In the East, there's a kingdom ruled by a Jewish tribe called the Khazars.

Hasdai interrogated the man closely, then dismissed his talk as gossip. If there were a land where Jewish kings administered Jewish law, he would have heard about it long ago. But the rumors kept coming: that there was a country in the East called Khazaria, where Muslims and Christians paid tribute to Jews.

Hasdai questioned every traveler who visited the court. Finally, he sent a mission to find Khazaria, or dispel the rumors of it. The report written by this mission survives. In it, the people of the Jewish kingdom are carefully described. They live "north of the inhabited earth, toward the 7th clime, having over their heads the constellation of the Plough. Their land is cold and wet. Accordingly their complexions are white, their eyes blue, their hair flowing and predominantly reddish, their bodies large and their natures cold. Their general aspect is wild."

Khazaria was in Central Asia, beyond Byzantium, on the Caspian Sea, in what is now Azerbaijan. During the decades of Arab expansion, it served as a bulwark, thwarting invasion after invasion, protecting Byzantium and Europe. Hasdai became obsessed with it, sent ambassadors,* sent letters. These were addressed to the king of the Khazars, the khagan, who was named Joseph. In his first letter, Hasdai asked Joseph a series of questions. He wanted to know, among other things, the history of the Khazars and from which of the twelve tribes of Israel they descended. It was the start of a lengthy correspon-

---

*Here is how they were described in a report by an Arab traveler named Ahmad ibn Fadlan: "The Khazars and their King are all Jews. The Bulgars and all their neighbors are subject to him. They treat him with worshipful obedience. Some are of the opinion that Gog and Magog are the Khazars."

dence—written in Hebrew, these letters were carried back and forth by messenger between AD 954 and AD 961.

According to modern anthropologists, the Khazars were not Jews by blood, but Turks, a tribe of nomadic horsemen who migrated from the Asian steppes in the fifth century as part of Attila's horde. (The term *Khazar* comes from the Turkish root *gaz*, which means "to wander.") Joseph said his people descended from Japheth, the third son of Noah, whose grandson Togarma, according to lore, is the father of all Turkish tribes. "We have found in the family registers of our fathers that Togarma had ten sons," wrote Joseph, "and the names of their offspring are as follows: Uigur, Dursu, Avars, Huns, Basilli, Tarnikiakh, Khazar, Zagora, Bulgars, Sabir. We are the sons of Khazar, the seventh."

The tribe was converted from paganism in AD 740 by Joseph's grandfather, Khagan Bulan. Joseph describes Bulan as "a great conqueror who drove the sorcerers and idolaters from his land." According to the story, Bulan was told to convert the people in a vision, a dream in which he was visited by a white angel, who said, "Khagan, Thine intention is good, but not the manner in which thou servest God." The angel made a promise to Bulan not dissimilar to the promise Yahweh made to Abraham: if Bulan and his people followed God, they would be blessed for generations.

As the angel was not specific as to the form this worship should take, the khagan summoned a representative of each of the great monotheistic faiths.

Bulan asked the priest: Do you accept the Jewish teaching?

The priest said: Yes, but it's incomplete.

Bulan then asked: Do you accept the Muslim teaching?

No, said the priest, it's heresy.

Bulan asked the imam: Do you accept the Jewish teaching?

The imam said: Yes, but it's incomplete.

Bulan then asked: Do you accept the Christian teaching?

No, said the imam, it's heresy.

Bulan asked the rabbi: Do you accept the Christian teaching?

The rabbi said, No, it's heresy.

Bulan then asked: Do you accept the Muslim teaching?

No, said the rabbi. It, too, is heresy.

In other words, the only teaching accepted by all three clergymen was the Jewish. Which, according to Joseph, is why the Khazars became Jews.

According to Muslims—specifically, to a story in *The Book of Roads and Kingdoms* by al-Masudi, published in AD 1327—the khagan chose Judaism only because the imam missed the meeting—due to the treachery of the rabbi.

Historians say the Khazar conversion probably had less to do with faith than with politics. The tribe was powerful. Its members wanted to become monotheists the way, in the 1990s, the citizens of Eastern Europe wanted to become democrats—it was the future. Yet the khagan did not want to give up any power. If he became Christian, he would put himself under the control of the Pope. If he become Muslim, he would put himself under the control of the caliph. But the Jews were weak and scattered, with no central authority and no earthly capital. By becoming a Jew, the khagan became a monotheist but remained independent.

In his letters, Joseph chronicled the military accomplishments of his nation. Hasdai took a kind of preening pleasure in the prowess of these far-flung, red-haired Turkish Jews. He spoke with pride of their victories over the Byzantines, over the Arabs, over the (early) Russians, even over the Vikings, who sailed into the Caspian Sea in long wooden ships. The Khazars fought with ferocity. In battle scenes, you always notice their red hair and pale skin and translucent eyes. For the Jews of Spain, which was then the capital of the Jewish world, the picture of the Khazars, a powerful tribe ruling with the Torah, performed a role not dissimilar from the role performed in my house by the book *Great Jews in Sports*. The exploits of the Khazars were evidence that a Jew could be all things, even a horseman, even a warrior, strong and silent and not blown here and there, but rooted like a tree to a particular piece of the earth.*

*Leon Wieseltier, *The New York Review of Books* ("You Don't Have to be a Khazarian"): "In some instances Khazaria seems to have done for Jewish self-esteem in the Diaspora what Israel does for that same fluctuating quality today."

Hasdai's last letters to the khagan were wistful. (Hasdai died in AD 962.) As his world dimmed, he wondered what his life might have been like in a place where a Jew could express himself in every way, not just as a doctor, a rabbi, a money man. "I feel the urge to know the truth, whether there is really a place on this earth where harassed Israel can rule itself, where it is subject to nobody," he wrote. "If I were to know this is indeed the case, I would not hesitate to forsake all honors, to re-sign my high office, to abandon my family, and to travel over moun-tains and plains, over land and water, until I arrived at the place where my Lord, the King rules."

In these letters, I hear a portent of modern Zionism: Hasdai was a bird blown far ahead of its flock, turning up many seasons too early, in the dead of winter, alighting on the beach, dying of exposure. "Dis-honored and humiliated in our dispersion," Hasdai went on, "we have to listen in silence to those who say: 'every nation has its own land and you alone possess not even a shadow of a country on this earth.'" I say a portent of modern Zionism because Hasdai was not praying for a messiah, but dreaming of political freedom. What made Khazaria special was not its chosen-ness, nor its glory, but simply this: in Kha-zaria, being a Jew was nothing special, so in Khazaria, a Jew could stop being Jewish.

The kingdom, pressed on every side by enemies, weakened in the glacial way of empires. Decisive defeat came in AD 965, when it was beaten on land and sea by tribes from Russia. The destruction of Khazaria was a blow for Jews in exile; for those who knew about it, anyway. It had served as a beacon, the only place on earth where Jews had worldly power. When this last lantern was put out, the suffocating night of the Middle Ages settled on the Jews and the long, hellish slumber began. By AD 1200, every trace of Khazaria was gone. Within a hundred years, the stories of its exploits had come to seem more fan-ciful than real, a memory you're not so sure of: maybe it happened, maybe you saw it in a dream. The Khazars themselves became a myth, the legend of the red-haired mountain Jews. Only in our own time was the story rediscovered and explored as a clue to the mystery of exile.

The legend of the Khazars found its most poetic expression in the
work of Yehuda Halevi, whom many considered the greatest Jewish
writer of Muslim Spain and perhaps the greatest since the writers of the
Bible.* He was the leader of the Hebrew Renaissance, a literary movement that bloomed in the Iberian Peninsula in the eleventh century. He
was born in Toledo, in 1080, when it was under Islamic rule. His father
sent him to Grenada to study medicine, but he fell in with poets. He
spent six years at school. During his absence, Toledo was conquered by
Christian armies, its synagogues and mosques turned into churches.

The Christian conquest meant terrible suffering for the Jews of
Spain: it was the beginning of the era of racial laws and forced conversions that would culminate two centuries later with expulsion.
(Christians attempting to purify the peninsula after its occupation by
infidels.) The suffering that washed over the Jewish community confused Halevi, who had been raised in luxury and taught that more was
always possible. Here's what he kept asking himself: How can this oppressed people be the Chosen of God? One resulting poem is probably the greatest hymn of Jewish self-hate ever written:

> I have delighted in the wrath of my enemies; let them be, let them torment the one
> whom You tormented. It was from You that they learned their wrath, and I love
> them, for they hound the wounded one whom You struck down. Ever since You
> despised me, I have despised myself, I will not honor what You despise.

The war between Muslims and Christians was being fought all
across the Iberian Peninsula, everywhere turning, for the Christians,
into a battle for purity. There was a riot in Toledo. Gangs rampaged
through the streets. Smoke hung over the hills. Hundreds of Jews were
killed, the rest driven out. Halevi moved to Andalusia, which was still

---

*In an introduction to his collected work, the translator H. Slonimsky calls him "the greatest poet
and one of the profoundest thinkers Judaism has had since the closing of the canon."

under Muslim rule. He lived an exile dream in that city framed by distant hills—a dream because it was unreal and forever threatening to turn into a nightmare. He married, had children, wrote poetry, became famous. But the greater his success, the more his thoughts turned to the ancient past. It was not deprivation that drove him to Zion; it was acclaim. The more he accumulated, the less relevant his accumulation seemed. It was a dream, as I've said, but just a dream.

Then he was old. His hair was white and his body was frail and his eyes were black pools. His writing turned melancholy. He cared about just one thing: the land of Israel (Eretz Yisrael). As if his computer had just one key: Return.

> *My heart is in the East, and I am at the edge of the West;*
> *Then how can I taste what I eat, how can I enjoy it?*
> *How can I fulfill my pledges and vows, while*
> *Zion is in the domain of Edom, and I am in the bounds of Arabia?*
> *It would be easy for me to leave behind all the good things of Spain;*
> *It would be glorious to see the dust of the Ruined Shrine.* *

He was obsessed with the Khazars, as they were the only known example of Jews living not in the Book but in the world, here and now. In his work, Khazaria became an ideal. It was Atlantis, Utopia. It argued for a national Jewish life. He read and reread the letters that passed between Hasdai and the khagan, then, between AD 1130 and 1140, he turned these letters into a prose poem called *The Kuzari*, which many consider the great Jewish book of its time.

It was written in Andalusia as Muslim Spain fell. The streets beneath Halevi's window were filled with preachers and mystics, holy men calculating the number of days left till the end. It's a poem in defense of his faith on the eve of one of its great tragedies.† The book

---

*This is Halevi's poem "My Heart Is in the East." He wrote many on this same subject, in the same tone.

†In an article in *The New York Review of Books*, Harold Bloom described *The Kuzari* as "an aggressive argument for Judaism's truth . . . Heroic, tense, more relevant today than ever, *The Kuzari* seems to me the great book of the Hebrew Renaissance of Spain, which it totally repudiates as an immoral error."

appeared amid the turbulence that would culminate in the Spanish expulsion as Theodor Herzl's book (*The Jewish State*) appeared amid the turbulence that would culminate in the Nazi Holocaust. Halevi and Herzl: human seismographs, picking up the faint rumblings of the coming quake.

Halevi's wife died. His children grew and left. He sold his house and gave away his property. He said goodbye to his students. He traded his fine clothes for shirts and pants made of wool, more appropriate for the highway. Around 1100 he left Spain in hope of reaching the Holy Land, then ruled by the Frankish Crusaders.

O sleeper, whose heart is awake, burning and raging, now wake and go forth, and walk in the light of My Presence. Ride, and ride on! A star has come forth for you, and he who has lain in the pit will go up to the top of Sinai.

He traveled by ship to Africa, then continued on foot. He was on the road for three years. In his travels, Halevi's life itself became a kind of poem, a dramatization of the Jews' never-ending attempt to return. People met him at the gates of each town. He blessed their congregations, slept in their houses, in their fields, the wheat spiky against the setting sun.

The Jews of Alexandria begged him to stay. They said the trip to Palestine was dangerous and the country itself had fallen into the hands of killers. The last sighting puts him in the port of Alexandria, where he wandered among fisherman hauling in their nets. He boarded a ship for Acre, from where he would continue on to Jerusalem. It's believed this ship went down in a storm—that is, he went all the way to the final threshold, but was stopped by the cherub and the turning sword.

In one of his poems, Halevi seemed to foresee his own end:

Deceitfully, the sea covers the ship,
as though it had taken it by theft.
The sea is in turmoil, but my soul is full of joy,
for she is drawing near to the temple of her God.

Over the years, the story of Halevi's journey—the man who gives up a life of comfort for a glimpse of the old stones—was worked up into a legend. In later tellings, Halevi actually makes it to Palestine. He follows the road along the coast, then heads east to Judea. He sees Jerusalem in the distance. He goes through the Golden Gate. He is followed by animals and children. Every atom in his body is as pure as the first atom, which was a ray of light. He walks up the steps onto the Temple Mount. He stands before the Dome of the Rock, which, this being during the Crusades, is topped by a bronze cross. He falls to his knees, weeps, says a prayer in Ladino (Judeo-Spanish): the Shema. In that moment, with the words still in his mouth ("Hear O Israel,") a desert Arab dashes up the stairs on a white horse and tramples him to death.*

W hy didn't the Jews try to go back?
    Why, after one of the many massacres, forced conversions, pogroms, edicts, expulsions, revolutions, counterrevolutions, raids, betrayals, accusations, attacks, didn't they just pick up and start walking? Away. Back to Canaan, where the girls giggle at the wells and the sun stands still in the sky. Back to the land of ancient stories, where it's no crime to be a Jew.

Well, as I've said, they did try to go back. Again and again. Kept banging their heads against that same door. If not with their bodies, then in their dreams and in their prayers.

The centuries following the collapse of Muslim Spain, which was a dark time for the Jews, was, in fact, an age of false messiahs, each one calling the Jews to return. Every generation, starting in the Middle Ages, another visionary would rise, gather crowds, give speeches, proclaim the end. As proof of their mission, these men would cite the suffering of the Jews—as the more we suffer, the closer we must be.

*Note how this legend replicates the legend of the Baal Shem Tov, where merely approaching Jerusalem invites divine punishment. (According to *Jewish Post-Biblical History Through Great Personalities*, by Adele Bildersee, Halevi probably died in AD 1146.)

Behind each of these prophets was the same impulse: solve the problem; end the misery; write a chapter that will remake all the other chapters. It's called redemption: an ending that changes the meaning of the entire book.

They wanted to be Moses, every one of them. They wanted to cross the wasteland with a staff. They wanted to be looked at and followed. They did not want to live the small, timid, oppressed lives of their fathers. Were they insane? Of course. To live in that world and still think it worth doing something grand, you had to be insane. Lucidly insane.

Think of David Alroy, one of the many false messiahs that stud Jewish history. He was crazy every day, from the moment he got up to the moment he lay down, but it was the kind of crazy that is captivating, convincing. He was born in Amadia, a Muslim garrison town in what is now Kurdistan. His given name was Menahem, but he renamed himself David around 1160, when he began to prophesy: *Follow me to Jerusalem; redemption is at hand.* He went from town to town, synagogue to synagogue, spreading the news. His words were electric; they made people as drunk as wine. Men gave away their possessions and joined him.

Of course, anyone can call himself messiah and announce the end of time, and many do. In fact, as I sit in my apartment on Broadway, on the West Side of Manhattan, a man walks in the street below calling for me and the other people in my building to cast aside our jobs and follow him, because the end is now. We call this man Broadway Jesus, because that is what he yells: "Broadway *Jesus*, Broadway *Jesus*." He's in the street every day. And though he's persistent, I do not follow him: because I am busy and he is crazy. What makes a false messiah notable, after all, is not the false part (they've all been false, as far as I'm concerned) but the messiah part. To be a false messiah, you must be a real messiah first. You must be even more charismatic than a real messiah, who is with God; whereas a false messiah is alone. You must convince people you have the answer, that there is an urgency in what you say. Your words and your manner must carry me out of my life against my better judgment. This is what turns the run-of-the-mill Broadway Jesus into a messiah. And it's precisely this quality that cannot be captured in written accounts, which is why stories about people like David Alroy, who one day was alone and the next day was surrounded by men who had forsaken everything, are so hard to understand. The missing piece is the only piece that matters: that wild spark or gleam that people follow as the Hebrews followed the column of fire through the desert.

Alroy sent long, intricate letters to the leaders of the Jewish communities in Baghdad and Mosul in which he urged them to take up arms, to cross the wastes, to join him. Thousands came. They called him the King of the Jews. According to *The Jewish Encyclopedia*, "Alroy's intimate knowledge of the magic arts is said to have convinced many of the truth of his pretensions."

We don't know what he looked like. He lived in a Muslim world where image making was a sin. This is thought to be an obstacle, but I think it's a boon. A picture is a moment in a sea of moments, so it distorts as much as it reveals. Attila the Hun is more vivid without a picture, as is King David, as is Crazy Horse. In a picture, David Alroy would be a stiff figure in period costume. Without it, he is wild-haired, with happy eyes and dressed in a suit pulled from a Dumpster on skid row. He stands in the street screaming, "Your fathers whored after goat demons!"

He said he would attack the garrison in Amadia, drive out the Arabs, and purify the town, then lead his ragged army to Palestine. In old books, his story builds until the tension is unbearable. Then, soon after he sounds the battle cry, his army is gone, he is gone. It's a story without a finish. According to most scholars, this probably means the rebellion was crushed, and Alroy executed.

Over the years, myths were invented to explain what might have happened, or should have. In other words, people wrote their own endings. In some, Alroy is killed. In some, he is captured. In some, he flees to Jerusalem. In some, he wanders the streets weeping and crying, "Absalom, O Absalom." In some, he vanishes into the hills. In some, he falls in with a group of highwaymen. In some, he falls in love but his love is unrequited. In some, he survives and gets married and realizes too late that he has married the wrong woman. In some, he is a glutton and grows fat and tells his story but no one believes it's him. In some, he gives up his destiny for a happy life of not worrying about the Jews.

Alroy became a fantastic figure in the imagination of his people. Dozens of stories have been written, including Benjamin Disraeli's *The Wondrous Tale of Alroy*, but the most terrific was recorded by Benjamin Tudela, a Jewish merchant who kept a diary during his travels in the East. (He is sometimes called the Jewish Marco Polo.)

Tudela was in Kurdistan soon after the disappearance of Alroy and heard the story everywhere. In the most frequent telling, Alroy, at the height of his fame, is summoned to Damascus by the caliph. He is made to stand as the caliph, swimming in silk robes, sunken deep in silk pillows, smokes a hookah, exhaling great streams of cool white smoke.

Through half-closed eyes, the caliph asks: "Are you the King of the Jews?"

"It is as you say," says Alroy.*

The caliph calls a guard, who shackles Alroy and locks him in a cage.

The next day, while the caliph is meeting his advisors, discussing what should be done with the heretic, Alroy himself appears in the room. He has broken free of his chains and walked through the bars. He is Harry Houdini. (Or Harry Houdini, a Jew from Appleton, Wisconsin, whose real name was Eric Weisz, was an echo of David Alroy, the mercurial Jew in possession of the dark knowledge.) The caliph orders his guards to seize Alroy, but Alroy disappears. He is seen again, hours later, on the outskirts of Damascus. He is chased by a soldier. When Alory reaches the river, and is seemingly trapped, he turns his prayer shawl into a raft and sails away to freedom. That evening, he

---

*This is a repetition of the gospel story (Luke 23:3) in which Jesus is interviewed by Pontius Pilate. Pilate asks, "Are you the King of the Jews?" Jesus replies, "You said so." Then: "It is as you say." All of these stories, that of Jesus included, are stories of a defeated people.

miraculously turns up in Amadia, a ten-day ride from Damascus. He speaks with his followers, asking each of them, "Do you know me?" Then vanishes. The caliph, hearing this, threatens to kill every Jew in Arabia if Alroy is not turned over. The mayor of Amadia bribes Alroy's father-in-law, who kills the messiah in his sleep.

David Alroy was the first superhero. He was a caped crusader, only his cape was a prayer shawl and his crusade (like that of the Frankish Crusaders) was Zion. He was a prototype of the Jewish cultural heroes of later generations, the Jewish sports star and Jewish gangster. He offered a picture of strength to a people lousy with weakness. He was a model (consciously or not) for Superman, created in 1938, another dark age for the Jews, by Jerry Siegel and Joe Shuster, Jewish teenagers from Cleveland, Ohio. Superman is a writer; Superman is brainy in his glasses; Superman is in exile from an ancient nation destroyed by fire; Superman has two names, a fake Waspy name (Clark Kent) and a secret name in an ancient tongue, Kal-El, Hebrew for "strength"; Superman, whose cape is a tallis; Superman, whose logo, the *S* emblazoned on his chest, marks him as a freakish stranger as the yellow Star of David marks the Ghetto Jew.

Messiahs are the great export of the Hebrew nation, a product line that began with Moses and includes Jesus, David Alroy, and Superman.

Why do we create so many messiahs?

Because we need them.

M ore messiahs:
There was Abraham Abulafia, who lived in Sicily in the thirteenth century, a master of Kabbalah who read the signs and came up with the following: *I'm the One!* He hinted at this in the way of Rebbe Schneerson of Crown Heights, Brooklyn:

Are you the Messiah?

Who said I am?

I'm asking: Are you the Messiah?

Do you think I'm the Messiah?

Are you the Messiah?

You said it, not me.

Abulafia revealed himself in Messina around 1281. He quoted holy passages and mentioned dates and numbers. He said he was the long-awaited messenger: the age had begun. He gathered followers, gave sermons, broke rules. First the Sabbath, then everything else. This is something most messiahs have in common: they defy the law, publicly, with glee. Since their coming marks the dawn of a new era, the old rules do not apply. The mere fact of breaking the rules—that he can do so without being smote—proves a messiah's claims. Only a messiah could behave in such a way and live. The disciples around a false messiah often throw themselves into an orgy of kinky multi-partner sex.

Abulafia was excommunicated by rabbis, who, since the time of Bar-Kokba, have been wary of charismatic leaders. He left Messina, went north. He settled on Comino, an island near Malta, where he was forgotten. Did Abulafia really believe himself the Messiah? Was there a moment when he stopped believing? When he came to see himself as ordinary, as living a life no different from the millions of others that have been lived and forgotten since the Expulsion?

There was Asher Lemmlein, who announced himself as the Messiah in Istria in 1502. He said the new dispensation would begin if the Jews fasted, sunup till sundown, for one year. He called this the "year of penitence." Lemmlein traveled from town to town, making his way to Venice, where he stood in the synagogue talking of the last days. He attracted as many Christians as Jews. In him, they recognized the spirit of an ancient prophet. At the end of a year, thousands of followers gathered in a village to greet the new age. Lemmlein stood before them in a black coat. His face was black and his eyes were black. He said, When the new age comes, God will descend from heaven in a column of smoke and fire and the faithful will follow the column to Jerusalem. The people prayed as the sun went down, as the sky filled with stars, many of which were surrounded by planets with their own leaders and holy books and madmen. The stars cycled through their positions, the sky turned pale in the East, but the column did not descend. Lemmlein wandered off in the dawn and was never seen again.

There was Jacob Frank, a false messiah and a follower of false messiahs, a man Gershom Scholem describes as having "a demonic grandeur."* People described Frank as people later described Rasputin: a hypnotist magician, tall and lean, with delicate fingers. He was born in Poldovia, Poland, in 1726. He studied the Bible, the Talmud, the Kabbalah. He said there were no false messiahs—all messiahs are true and all messiahs preach the same sermon. Moses, David, Elijah, Jesus, Muhammad, Alroy—it was the same soul, again and again, showing the same trapped man the way out of the smoky towers. The fate of the Messiah varies in each incarnation. In some, he is not listened to. In some, he is not believed. In some, his message is lost. In some, he is executed. In some, he writes novels. In some, he is a Gentile. In some, he is a Jew. In some, he is terrified by his thoughts and dies with the message still coiled like a fetus in his brain.

Standing before his congregation, Frank said he was now in possession of the ancient redeemer soul. He was the Messiah. The rabbis excommunicated him, then chased him from Poldovia. He went away, preached. In 1759 he returned to tell his followers to convert to Christianity, as he had done in Warsaw. He said a Jew should consider himself a Jew even after he has converted. In other words, he was calling for false conversions, which, said Frank, was a way for the Jew to descend to the depths of error, where his work was most needed. He called this "redemption through sin." Which is why, early in the sixteenth century, thousands of Polish Jews were baptized in Christ. When the content of Frank's sermons was made known to the Church, he was arrested, and spent the rest of his life behind bars.

In some incarnations, the Messiah dies in prison.

There was Solomon Molko, a Spanish Marrano (a Christian whose Jewish parents had been forced to convert) who found himself, was circumcised, returned to Judaism, received a prophecy, predicted famines and floods, declared himself the Messiah, and was arrested, tried, and burned.

There was "The Prophetess" from Herara, a province in western

*Major Trends in Jewish Mysticism.

Spain, the only known lady messiah, who suffered hallucinations in which she saw herself leading the people through the wastes to Jerusalem. (Arrested, tried, burned.)

General principles regarding false messiahs: they tend to be charismatic and strange; they appear like waves, in sets, clustered in ages of upheaval, many in the 1400s, when Jews were being driven out of Spain, more in the 1500s, when Jewish villages were being flattened by Cossack raiders in Poland. Prophecy is catchy, with revelation leading to revelation; an age can grow rank with false messiahs. (In the years after Jesus, Judea became so filled with prophecy the Church elders declared the era of revelation finished; they blocked the heavenly frequency.) False messiahs are maddeningly specific when it comes to fixing a date. Years picked for Armageddon include: 440, 471, 1290, 1295, 1568, 1693, 1931, 1944, 1968, 1977, 2001. False messiahs are feared by clerics because they encourage lawlessness, undermine authority, and raise hopes, that, when dashed, can lead to a loss of faith. When you strip away the specifics of each prophecy, the core teaching is always the same: return, rebuild, redeem.

The greatest false messiah was born in Smyrna in 1626.* His name was Sabbatai Zevi. No one had to teach him. He was born strange. He would disappear into the woods for weeks at a time. He talked to himself constantly. His lips moved when he was thinking, his eyes flashed, his hair was towering and wild. He first read the Kabbalah when he was fifteen. He fell into it like the boy fell into the well. He was gone. Everything he needed was in its pages. From then till his death, he never spent a moment without demons. The Kabbalah is filled with expectation—every moment is the moment before the Messiah strides on stage. It stabbed Zevi like a finger, pressed him forward, saying: You, the Book is talking about you!

He heard the call of God in the evening sounds: crickets in the grass, horses in the stalls, a coyote howling like a shofar. Sometimes he was exhilarated. His eyes blazed, and people gathered because he spoke in riddles and in poems. In these moments, it was said the spirit

*On July 23, the Ninth of Av.

of God had descended upon him. Other times, he was listless and dull and so down he did not want to talk or look or be seen. In these moments, it was said the spirit of God had left him. In modern studies, Zevi is often described as a manic-depressive. In such tellings, the finger of God is the chemicals shifting in his brain.

Adele Bildersee, *Post-Biblical History*:

> A reverent band of followers gathered about him, and to them he would speak of the mysteries of the Kabbalah and the glories of the kingdom to come. He dominated them with the asceticism of his life, the noble spiritual beauty of his face, the majesty of his tall figure, and the solemn music of his voice.

Did Sabbatai Zevi tell the people he was their messiah?

No. He instead had the secret need of all prophets. He wanted the people to tell him who he was. If the voices in his head came from within or without. If he was crazy or righteous. He went to the Near East to find the answers. He spoke to crowds. He dazzled with his learning. Now and then, he was arrested. He spent time in jail. He reached Palestine in the middle of the seventeenth century. The country was ruled by the Ottoman Turks. He visited towns he had read about in the holy books. Being in this land, amid all these sacred names, was too much. It drove him mad. He went around asking, "Do you know who I am? Do you know why I'm here?"

He met a student who would later be called Nathan of Gaza, the first priest of the new faith. They stood together by the sea.

"Who am I?" asked Zevi.

"You are the Messiah," said Nathan.

Historians have come to believe Nathan was the man behind the movement—he was like St. Paul, gathering, building, turning a story into a system. He arranged sermons and spread the word. Zevi was the Messiah, and Nathan his prophet. The relationship was like that between Elvis Presley and Colonel Tom Parker. Without the Colonel, Elvis would still be Elvis, but with the Colonel, Elvis was an industry. Nathan sent Zevi to synagogues across the Jewish world. Men stood in line to hear him. He was extraordinarily handsome—that helped. He spoke of an age in which the Jews would defend their own nation and live with respect and dignity.

Adele Bildersee:

> His kingly presence, his persuasive voice, his fasting and praying won him adherents. Constantinople acclaimed him; so did Salonica, where he gained a great following, but where his mystic rites so shocked the rabbis that they banished him from the city. He went to Jerusalem, hoping, perhaps, that in the sacred city a miracle would take place to confirm him as the Messiah.

This was the age of the Chmielnitzki persecutions in Poland, when thousands of Jews were killed in pogroms. A Jewish girl hid in a convent during one of these raids. She converted to Catholicism and was ordained as a nun. One night, as she lay in the dormitory, surrounded by the sisters, she heard the voice of her father, who had been killed. "You will be the wife of the Messiah, who has appeared in the East." She slipped out of the convent and went in search of her husband. Nathan of Gaza heard the story and sent for her. She was married to Zevi in a public ceremony. According to Bildersee, "her queenly beauty gained him thousands of new followers."

Jewish leaders in Egypt sent a man named Samuel Gandor to meet Sabbatai Zevi in Jerusalem, observe and question him, and write a report:*

> It is said of Sebetai Zevi that for fifteen years he has been bowed down by the following affliction: he is pursued by a sense of depression which leaves him no quiet moment and does not even permit him to read, without his being able to say what is the nature of this sadness which has come upon him. Thus he endures it until the depression departs from the spirit, when he returns with great joy to his studies.

*This was written in 1665.

And for many years already he has suffered from this illness, and no doctor has found a remedy for it, but it is one of the sufferings which are inflicted by Heaven.

Zevi revealed his identity in the grand temple of Smyrna. The scene had been staged by Nathan of Gaza. It was the start of a political campaign, in which a candidate goes home to announce. He stood on the bema, with arms raised. He said the secret four-letter name of God, which only the high priest is allowed to say, in the holy of holies, on the holiest day. Supposedly, it had not been spoken since the destruction of the Temple, sixteen hundred years before. According to the Kabbalah, it must not be spoken until the start of the messianic age. Zevi whispered it, said it, then sang it. The ram's horn blew. People wept. He tossed back his head and screamed:

> *I am the Messiah!*
> *I am the Messiah!*
> *I have come!*
> *I have come!*
> *I have come!*

He was banished from Smyrna. He did not care. The age of the law was over. A new age had begun. The news was carried by merchants from town to town. If it had come ten years earlier or ten years later, if he had been shorter or taller—who knows? But this was just the right messenger with just the right message at just the right moment. Thousands were swept up. According to contemporary accounts, as much as 10 percent of the Jews of Europe left their homes to join him. Anyone who expressed doubt was attacked by the crowds. Hysteria bred hysteria until hysteria itself became the overwhelming fact.*

Zevi traveled to Constantinople, where he said the royal crown would be taken from the sultan and placed on his own head. He en-

---

*This, for example, is what is meant by the phrase "fifty million Elvis fans can't be wrong."

tered through the main gate of the city. Everything was like a scene in a drama, as if it had been written long ago. He spoke to a crowd, sat in the shade, had a meal, was arrested. A huge crowd gathered in front of the jail. People stood silently. (There is nothing more unsettling than the silence made by a crowd.) These people wanted to glimpse the Messiah. His cell became a throne room. He was visited by dignitaries. His talk was filled with prophecy. Even the imams believed him to be the king of the Jews.

This was a problem for the sultan: If Zevi were released, he would march on Jerusalem. If he were executed, he would become a martyr for the Jews.

The sultan summoned Zevi to his chamber.

"You will be stripped and shot full of arrows," he said. "Because you are the Messiah, these arrows will not pierce your skin. If these arrows do pierce your skin but do not kill you, then you will be tortured and killed because you have lied. But if you are not the Messiah, you can save your life now," he added, "you can repent and convert."

On September 15, 1666, the King of the Jews became a Muslim.

The spirit of God left Zevi. It would never return. He spent his remaining years in gloom. He wore a turban and refused to see his followers. He settled in a town high in the mountains of Albania. He died in 1676, a decade after his meeting with the sultan.

As for the thousands who had given away their property to follow him: most went home and continued as if nothing had happened; some denounced him; some lost faith in all religion; and some emulated his example. The Messiah, they said, is trying to tell us something with his apostasy. They talked about what this could be, and what it represented. In the end, they built a new theology around "the Sabbatian heresy." They said that what appeared to be an act of treachery was, in fact, the ultimate act of sacrifice—the anointed one throwing himself into the abyss to illuminate the path to redemption. (Zevi's followers called it the "heroic plunge.") The basis for such reasoning, writes Gershom Scholem, is in the Kabbalah, which speaks of doing good by doing evil, of "descending into darkness in search of divine sparks."

Across the Muslim world, Jews converted to Islam.* Descendants of these converts still worship in Istanbul. The Turks call them the Donmeh, the apostates. Heresy is their creed, an apostate is their savior.

Zevi's conversion marked the end of an era. Prophecy had failed. Entire communities had followed a mental patient over a cliff. His story became a warning: of the danger of poetry, the danger of visions, the danger of amateurism, the danger of zealotry, the danger of forcing the end. If return was ever to be accomplished, it would have to come in another age, under another creed. It would have to wait for secularism, in fact, for engineers and scientists, for Jews who could make their own miracles.

---

*In Poland, where this was not an option, several thousand more converted to Catholicism.

SIX

The Ghetto Jew

And upon them that are left alive of you I will send a faintness into their hearts in the lands of their enemies; and the sound of a shaken leaf shall chase them; and they shall flee, as fleeing from a sword; and they shall fall when none pursueth. And they shall fall one upon another, as it were before a sword, when none pursueth: and ye shall have no power to stand before your enemies. And ye shall perish among the heathen, and the land of your enemies shall eat you up. And they that are left of you shall pine away in their iniquity in your enemies' lands.

—LEVITICUS 26:36–39

T he first ghetto was built in Venice in 1518. It consisted of a few streets enclosed by a high wall, inside which Jews were locked from sundown to sunup, a people quarantined so as not to infect the general population.* It was constructed on the grounds of a

---

*This was an age of Pope-enacted edicts that curtailed Jewish freedom—edicts meant to demonstrate the fate of the people who had killed the Lord. In 1179, for example, the church passed a law by which any Christian "who presumes to live with [Jews] will be excommunicated." In 1215, Pope In-

dilapidated iron factory where many Jews were employed. In Italian, *gheto* means foundry.[†] That is, the misery of the Jews bequeaths us one of the worst words in the language, still used centuries later to describe the bleakest sections of cities, concrete cages from which escape is almost impossible. The system was so successful—it kept Jews out of society, yet close enough to fulfill necessary functions as tax collectors, moneylenders, and so on—that it was copied across Europe. In London, it was called the Jewry. In Frankfurt, it was called the *Judengasse*. By the end of the sixteenth century, the majority of European Jews were living in ghettos—this had much to do with the religious wars and the spread of Christianity. These ghettos became self-contained little worlds. Everything was inside their walls: homes, butchers, cobblers, and shuls, stuffy, prayer-filled cellars where life was characterized by insularity, proximity, and fear.

Over the centuries, the Jewish character was, according to some, remade in the image of the ghetto. The Jew is afraid to fight because the odds were against him in the ghetto. The Jew is estranged from nature because he could see the forest only through a crack in the ghetto wall. The Jew is afraid to be out after dark because the ghetto gate was locked at sundown. In short, every adjective that people came to associate with Jews (submissive, cunning, neurotic, sneaky, weak) derives from life behind the walls.

Moses Mendelssohn:

The Jew had gone into the ghetto refined in manner, scrupulously careful in all details of dress and personal cleanliness, precise and cultured in speech. It took three centuries of the ghetto's plague to make him indifferent to his appearance, careless in his speech.

---

nocent III ordered Jews to wear a badge to distinguish them from Christians. Jews were forbidden to farm, hold office, or own property, and were excluded from working in dozens of trades, forcing them into the kind of jobs, such as moneylender and tax collector, that came to define them as rootless, cosmopolitan manipulators. Rootless because they did not own land; cosmopolitan because they lived in town; manipulators because they charged interest. Yuri Slezkine described them as "useful strangers." Forced to perform tasks no one else wanted, the Jews became identified with those tasks.

[†]The authors of *The Jewish Encyclopedia* dispute this derivation, but offer no real alternative.

It's the ghetto that makes Woody Allen stammer; it's the ghetto that makes Richard Perle gin up war; it's the ghetto that makes Jerry Seinfeld funny; it's the ghetto that makes Albert Einstein calculate; it's the ghetto that makes Karl Marx foam. It is the prison the prisoner has come to need—the prison that the prisoner has forgotten is a prison. The desire of the paroled to return to his penitentiary is the mentality of the ghetto Jew in a nutshell.

There are no new characters in Jewish history. The actors are new, and the costumes are new, and new sets are built and hammered into place, and the desert background is rolled away, and the freshly painted background shows a city street receding under arc lights, and the scene at the well has been restaged in a village square, where Shylock is haggling for ducats, but the script and the characters never change. It's always the Jew and the tormenter of the Jew. You might not recognize this at first, but over time, as the plot unfolds, you realize it's the familiar scene from the Bible acted before a new crowd. This is what it means to live in a book: every disaster is an echo of the original disaster, and every enemy is the eternal foe, the prehistoric, blunt-nosed, Jew-eating shark, sometimes called caliph, sometimes called czar. He can come as a lord of war or as a messenger of peace, but he is always the same man backed by the same mob.*

In the nineteenth century, he came as a liberator named Napoleon. He was Corsican and championed the ideals of the French Enlightenment: liberty, equality, fraternity. He marched the most powerful army in the world from capital to capital, deposing monarchs, replacing them with a law administered by bureaucrats. He rode a white horse.

*According to Yosef Yerushalmi this sense of repetition is merely another defense mechanism developed by Jews in the Diaspora: "There is a pronounced tendency to subsume even major new events to familiar archetypes," he writes, "for even the most terrible events are somehow less terrifying when viewed within old patterns rather than in their bewildering specificity. Thus the latest oppressor is Haman, and the court Jew who tries to avoid disaster is Mordecai. Christendom is 'Edom' or 'Esau,' and Islam is 'Ishmael.' Geographical names are blithely lifted from the Bible and affixed to places the Bible never knew, and so Spain is 'Sefarad,' France is 'Zarefat,' Germany is 'Ashkenaz.'"

He was short. He was one of those uncanny figures who turns up now and then without explanation, foreshadowed in a run of numbers in the Talmud.

I saw a Picasso painting at the Centre Pompidou in Paris. It showed Napoleon standing next to his horse, hand under his lapel, a romantic look in his eyes. He is only half painted in this picture. Part of his jacket and face are filled with color, but the rest has been left in outline, a charcoal sketch, which gets at the truth about Napoleon. He was the most influential figure of his time, yet he remains mysterious. Even if you add up all the details—father owned a store, career in the military, won a battle in Egypt—they do not equal the wizard who struck fear in the rulers of his age, who redrew the map of the world, who declared himself emperor, who painted himself in whiteface, who conquered Austria and Prussia and burned Moscow and emancipated the Jews.

Remember the old movies in which, to demonstrate the progress of war, you were shown the boots of marching soldiers, galloping horses, and women waving flags on balconies? Well, it was just like that. Napoleon marched his army from the Adriatic to the Baltic Sea, outflanked, outmaneuvered, counterattacked. The arrival of the Grand Army electrified the young and the outcast. Napoleon promised to feed the poor, punish the corrupt, overturn everything. First would be last, last first: it was secular religion, millennial Christian dreams fulfilled by the godless values of the Enlightenment. In each conquered city, the walls of the ghetto were torn down. This had been an aim of the French Revolution from the start. In 1780 Claremont-Tonnerre, a leader of the Assembly, demanded that Jews be given equal rights. Napoleon was merely fulfilling those promises. He wanted to bring the Jews into the modern world, cure them of their decrepitude and sadness, return them to the present tense. He would end the Exile, not by shipping Jews east, but by making them citizens.

The Ghetto of Turin was opened in 1815. The ghetto of Nice was opened in 1816. The Ghetto of Venice was opened in 1817. Walls came down in Berlin, in Frankfurt, in Munich. Imagine it. You've grown up in the Vilna Ghetto. It's a world alike in every way to the world of your father, your grandfather, your great grandfather . . . who knows how far back it goes? Everything is small and particular, in its place. Everything makes sense. There are shops and merchants and horses and sacks of feed. There is a rabbi, a coffin maker, a gravedigger, and a cart that carries away the dead. The squares are crowded with narrow buildings, each as familiar as a familiar face. They lean together like derelicts. There is a shul where the men pray, and when ten pray together there is Jerusalem, with its towers and its Temple in the air. The streets twist and turn, as if in argument with themselves, but they always end at the same wall, beyond which is the goyische town, with its churches and pig butchers, then the goyische countryside, with its stony hills and forests through which a Jew is hurrying to reach the gate before sundown.

Then one day the countryside is black with soldiers. The valleys echo with cannon shot. The hills glow with fire. Napoleon has broken through. In the morning, no one comes to guard the ghetto gate. In the afternoon, a French officer gallops up on a gray horse. He has a mustache, his coat is blue, his boots muddy. He dismounts, walks to the synagogue, hammers a notice on the door. The Ghetto of Vilna has been opened by order of the emperor.

The rabbis urged the people to stay in the ghetto. They said freedom was a trick, a step on the way to disappearance. They said the world beyond the gate was dangerous and mean. A chimera, an illusion. If you wade in, you will get turned around and lost. You will become the dreamer so lost he forgets there is a waking world. The rabbis recognized the criticism buried in French theories that urged the faithful to "behave as a man abroad and a Jew at home."

Does that mean it's impossible to be a Jew and also be a man?

To the rabbis, it seemed the French did not merely want to emancipate the Jews; they wanted to cure them of being Jewish.*

Moses Mendelssohn was typical of the modern intellectuals who argued with the rabbis. A German-born philosopher, he was an early champion of "the Jewish Enlightenment," a movement that sought to free people from superstition and pointless worship of the past. He

*See "Bialik's Hint," by Cynthia Ozick, *Commentary Magazine*, 1983.

urged his co-religionists to seize freedom. There need be no struggle between faith and reason, he explained, nor between faith and nation. A Jew born in England should think of himself as entirely English and entirely Jewish. Mendelssohn gave young people permission to shave their beards and take up the challenge of the modern age. He invented a new way of being Jewish. (He is responsible for both Ariel Sharon and Gene Simmons.) He said the Jews must leave the ghetto— not just the streets behind the walls, but also the cage in their own minds.

The rabbis could block the gates, but the allure of the world was too great. The young men slipped away at night, first in dribs and drabs, then in a torrent. By the late 1800s, the ghettos had become ruins, monuments, empty windows amid desolate streets.

Isaiah Berlin:

> Once the enlightenment—secular learning and the possibility of a freer mode of life—began at first to seep, then flood into the Jewish townlets and villages of the Pale, that generation grew up no longer content to sit by the waters of Babylon and sing the songs of Zion in exile.

In 1840 there were close to four million Jews living in Europe.* Some were laborers, some were intellectuals, some were farmers, some were soldiers, some were rich. It was in these years that the great Jewish banking families were founded, each tracing its roots back to the patriarch who left a ghetto—no further, because that's when time began. Mayer Rothschild was freed from the Frankfurt Ghetto in 1810. He sent five sons to five cities, where each founded a bank. He made his first fortune while living on Judengasse, in a brick house fronted by the red shield that gave the family its name. Moses Warburg was freed from the Bremen Ghetto in 1812. He had six children and many more grandchildren and great-grandchildren, several of whom made terrific fortunes. One Warburg was German and signed the treaty that ended World War I, for which he was blamed by Hitler. Another was

---

*The given names database, operated by the Israeli professor G. L. Esterson, puts the number more precisely at 3,950,000.

American and helped found the Federal Reserve Bank in Washington, D.C.

For every fortune, thousands of families discovered, in being freed, how they had lost everything: the ghetto was gone, yet the new world did not accept these people. They were a wounded generation. They had been lied to, led out, left. Free? Yes, but free to do what? Europe, which had been a hodgepodge of religious communities and principalities, was being organized into nation-states defined by blood. As there is no ritual that turns a Jew into an ethnic Pole, or ethnic Slav, there was no place for a Jew in modern Europe.* In Christian Europe, the Jew had a role. Maybe he was Shylock, but at least there was a part to play. No Jew, no drama. It protected him from annihilation. But in this new Europe, in which the Christian Gospel was replaced by the national epic, there was no part to play. The Jew's presence suddenly seemed mysterious, unnecessary, threatening. The Jew, who had already been exiled from the present, was being exiled from the past, as the past was being reimagined ethnically, as the mystical birthplace of the nation, in which the Jew played no part. No present plus no past equals no future.

The reality behind all this was quite simple: though the Jews had been freed, they were still hated. Hatred was the engine of the age, the key to everything. It's why we have Israel, it's why we love Israel, it's why we hate Israel, it's why we could lose Israel. It's like the white noise astrologers find when they probe the reaches of the universe. It's so entirely everywhere you don't even hear it.

In *Semites and Anti-Semites*, Bernard Lewis says the Jews began to be hated, as Jews, at the start of the Christian age: "From the time the Roman emperor Constantine embraced the new faith and Christians obtained control of the apparatus of the state, there were few periods during which the Jews were not being persecuted in one or another part of the Christian world."

But such hatred predates the crucifixion by at least a thousand years. There were riots against Jews in the ancient world, in cities on

---

*Walter Laqueur: "The Romantic Age put heavy emphasis on faith and mystery and the *volksgeist*; how could one belong to the German people without sharing also in its religious experience?"

the Nile, in cities in Asia Minor, wherever Hebrews lived in colonies. Philo of Alexandria, a Jewish philosopher, wrote of a massacre in his town in AD 38 in which thousands of Jews were killed. Particular reasons are given for each of these riots, as particular reasons are given for riots in every age, but such reasoning fails. Though the causes vary, the effect remains the same: dead Jews. In fact, the existence of too many reasons tells you the experts are confused. They can't explain it because it's not science; it's faith. Hating Jews is a religion. (As with any religion, you either believe or don't; either feel or don't; either know or don't.) It might go away, but it always comes back. Nation succeeds nation, era succeeds era, but one thing does not change: people hate the Jews.

Why?

I would like to stand in front of the blackboard and write out some reasons:

The Jews are manipulators.

The Jews corner every market.

The Jews undermined the communists.

The Jews undermined the capitalists.

The Jews own the factory.

The Jews run the union.

The Jews are reactionary.

The Jews are liberal.

The Jews killed Christ.

The Jews care only about money, money, money.

The Jews betrayed Muhammad.

The Jews are the sons of monkeys and pigs.

The Jews are a nation with no state.

The Jewish state is the cause of all the trouble.

The Jews care more about Israel than about America.

The Jews control Hollywood.

Every agent in New York is a Jew.

The Jews own the media.

The Jews agitate for war.

What you have here is a symbol, the way the man in the black hat is a symbol; only, this particular symbol has the misfortune of being an actual person.

In each era, the Jew is the villain. In the age of religion, he is the Pharisee and Christ killer. In the age of capitalism, he is the union organizer. In the age of communism, he is the profiteer. From this, you conclude either that the enemies of the Jews are correct, and the Jews are devious and eternal, or that the enemies of the Jews are psychotic, in which case you have to explain the persistence of the psychosis, which is as mysterious as the persistence of the Jews. In *The Second Coming*, by Walker Percy, the protagonist continually asks people if they think the survival of the Jews is a sign. But what seems more like a sign, the survival of the Jews or the survival of the hatred of the Jews?

According to Martin Buber, the Jew is hated for this very survival, which challenges the authenticity of new faiths and new nations. "Against all oppression stood the unfortunate Jewish people, bearing the book which was its own and at the same time part of the holy book of the nations," he writes.* "That is the real reason for their hatred. Their theologians argue that God rejected this people, who no longer have any heritage because that heritage has now passed to Christianity. But the Jewish people continued to exist, book in hand: and even though they were burned at the stake, the words of the book were still on their lips. That is the perennial source of anti-Semitism. In this sense, there is an essential truth in the verse of the medieval Hebrew poet, Yannai, 'Hated we are, for Thee we love, O Holy.'"

Some historians believe the hatred of the Jews can be traced back to a single Egyptian screed written in the heat of an ancient war, then translated and copied. That is, the Jews are hated because they've been around so long and so have been the object of the most propaganda and gossip.

Take the example of the blood libel. In the early years of the Church, when Christians were a Jewish sect, they were accused of ritual murder by the Romans: it was said that Christians killed pagan ba-

Israel and the World: Essays in a Time of Crisis, by Martin Buber.

bies for their blood, which was then used in the Sacrament. This was a gross parody of the Mass, in which Christians drink the blood and eat the body of Christ. Later, when the Romans became Christians, the slander survived, only its object changed. It was now the Jews who were said to kill babies for their blood, which, in this new telling, was used to make matzo. In other words, the Romans slandered the Christians when the Christians were Jews; then, when the Romans became Christians, they continued to slander the Jews, telling a lie that had started with a misunderstanding of their own Catholic Mass.

If you can make sense of this, you can understand everything.

As science replaced religion, many believed that hatred of the Jews would simply fade away. In the twentieth century, the wave of pogroms that swept Russia were dismissed as the last outbreak of a disease that had been defeated. We now know the truth: the old hatred did not disappear but was instead remade in the image of the modern era. A hatred based on the murder of God was replaced by a hatred based on "science," evolution, racial theory. What is the story of the world as told by Darwin if not a new religion, with its own myth of creation? And doesn't every religion need a devil? It was in these years, as Darwin's theory came to be accepted, that the Jews were first described as a race, an organism, likened to a parasite that sucks the blood of higher species. (Note the echo of the blood libel.) Books were written to explain the Jew's biological nature: skilled in manipulation, in imitation, in fakery, the Jew cannot create, so must live off the work of others. In this way, the age ushered in by Napoleon, which was to be a golden age for Jews, culminated in an even more toxic version of the ancient hatred.

The term *anti-Semitism* was first published in 1879 in a pamphlet written by Wilhelm Marr, a German journalist who said he had been fired from his newspaper job "at the behest of the Jews." Marr adapted the term from an article he was reading on languages, in which all tongues of the Near East, including Hebrew, were described as Semitic. By renaming his hatred of the Jews anti-Semitism, he was presenting himself as a student of science. He did not hate the Jews because the Jews had killed God. He opposed Semites, because that race was inferior. Hating the Jews was crude. Espousing anti-Semitism was respectable. A Jew hater was filled with anger, superstition. An anti-Semite was filled with theories, the big one being that the Semites are responsible for every societal ill.

In this way, the Jew was redefined. He had been a member of a religious community, characterized by its beliefs; if he changed his beliefs, he could (in theory) change his identity; now he was remade into a member of a race. Which meant there was no hope of redemption. He could never be a German or a Frenchman. The flaw was in his blood. A Jew is a Jew is a Jew. Kinky hair and beady eyes and clawlike hands and bowlegs and narrow shoulders. Even if he does not look like this on the outside, you will find it in his genes—the soul of the Jew is bacterial.

According to Walter Laqueur in *The History of Zionism*, the appearance of modern scientific anti-Semitism

> constituted a turning point, even though few realized it at the time. Carried to its logical conclusion, it meant the end of assimilation, the total rejection of the Jew. The magic circle was replaced by a new ghetto whose walls could no longer be scaled. For racial characteristics, according to the new doctrine, were unchangeable; a change of religion and the rejection of his own heritage did not make a Jew into a German, any more than a dog could transform into a cat.

In the Christian era, an ambitious Jew might be baptized to change his fate. In the modern era, there was no escape. This was an age characterized by Jews trying to think their way out of the trap. The most brilliant of them designed utopias in which a Jew could participate fully. I am not saying this was done consciously, but I do think a restless desire for freedom set the wheels of their inventions in motion. Marxism, Zionism—each, in its way, was an effort to create a world in which a Jew could be cured of his Jewishness.

Think of Karl Marx, a middle-class German Jew whose entire system can be read as an attempt to create a world in which Karl Marx would finally be free of the Mosaic curse. In his utopia, national and ethnic classifications would fall away and people would instead be identified by class. The word *Jew* would become a quaint thing of history. To Marx, who believed in every stereotype, the Jew was always a capitalist. A world without capitalists would therefore be a world without Jews, where even a Jew would be free of the Jews. Marx was Moses saying "Let my people go," only he was not freeing them from Pharaoh but from their tortured past. In *On the Jewish Question*, which he wrote when he was twenty-five, Marx called for a "society which would abolish the basis of huckstering, therefore the possibility of huckstering, rendering the Jew impossible."

In *The Jewish Century*, Yuri Slezkine says that Marx was, in fact, revolting against his own father, a merchant, a member of the petite bourgeoisie. With his shaggy beard and blue eyes, his musty books and far-fetched theories, Marx is a character out of Kafka, pacing in his room, going over and over the argument with his father, an impotent little man to everyone else, but an unmovable giant to his son. The old man is the past. The old man is tradition. The old man is the JEW. Marx has to kill the old man to be free. To accomplish this, he devises a way to destroy capitalism, which will end the reign of the JEW, which will free the boy from the father. Behind Khrushchev banging his shoe on the table at the United Nations is one man trying to get out from under his father. "What is the secular basis of Judaism?" writes Marx. "Practical need, self-interest. What is the secular cult of the Jew? Haggling. What is his secular God? Money. Well, then! Emancipation from haggling and money, i.e., from practical, real Judaism, would be the same as the self-emancipation of our age."

Marx sought to free the Jews by shaping the future; others sought to free them by rewriting the past. If you're defined by blood, if the racists have invented a science in which your identity is fixed in the ancient world, then the only real solution is to change the ancient world. If you change the past, you change the present and free the Jews.

Think of Sigmund Freud: in his final years, he wrote a book called *Moses and Monotheism*, in which he meditates on the origins of the Jewish people. This book is weird and astonishing, a work less of psychology than of fantasy, like a novel Borges might have written, in which

the epic of the Jews is seen in a convex mirror. Moses was not a Hebrew, says Freud. He was an Egyptian, a prince and priest in the court
of Pharaoh Akhenaton, who first championed monotheism: the worship of a single spirit that controls everything. It was called the Jahve
religion, a name corrupted to *Yahweh*. When Akhenaton died, the
Egyptians went back to the worship of goat demons and idols. Moses,
who continued in the way of Jahve, left the royal house. He went into
the streets and preached, eventually building a following among the
lowest of the low, the slaves who built the roads and pyramids, as Paul
built his following among the outcasts of Rome, and Trotsky built his
following among the outcasts of the Pale.

The slaves led the slaves in rebellion, then took them to the desert and
taught them the rituals of Jahve. (Circumcision was common among
royals in the Pharaoh's court.) Over time, the slaves became confused.
They thought that Moses was God. Because it was he who brought
them out of Egypt. When Moses spoke, they thought God was speaking. When Moses led, they thought God was leading. When Moses was
jealous or angry, they thought this, too, was God. When you describe
God's personality as depicted in Exodus, it's really Moses you're describing. For I am a jealous God, and I led you out of Egypt.*

The slaves grew restless. They chafed under the ruler's iron hand.
They rose up and killed Moses, which means they killed God—the
classic charge of deicide, discovered, by Freud, in the biography of
Moses—in the desert that remains the center of Jewish worship. The
murder of Moses was not just the murder of one prince; it was a repetition of a more ancient murder that stands behind every religion: the
brothers of an early tribe, ruled by a tyrannical father, who is Kafka's
father, who is Marx's father, banded together and killed their tormen-
tor, then cooked and ate his body. (This is the original sin, the secret
knowledge beneath every faith: I am a killer! My hands are covered in
blood!) "I have no qualms in saying that men have always known that
once upon a time they had a primeval father and killed him," writes
Freud.

---

*Freud: "It was one man, the man Moses, who created the Jews."

The sons made a pact: they were done with murder. This was the beginning of the law. Memory of this first murder was sublimated, but it reemerged, was recovered, slowly, over time, first in the animal cults, in which the crime was reenacted, the part of the father being played by the beast that was slaughtered, cooked, and eaten; then in the pagan cults, in which the gods were depicted with a human face; then in monotheism, in which the father has returned, one man with one face, the vengeful, murderous leader of the tribe. The history of the species is the history of an amnesiac remembering his crime.

The slaves reverted to paganism in the desert. Wandered, and drank, and fought, and killed. Forty years. Then Joshua brought them back to monotheism, with Moses as its prophet, the last man who had seen the Father face-to-face. All of which (says Freud) culminates with Christianity, in which the ancient sin is finally acknowledged: it's the dim memory around which the Church is constructed as the Temple was constructed around the holy of holies, the empty room, where, once a year, a priest whispered the secret name of God: "We killed You in the wilderness."

Jesus is murdered, his blood is poured into a glass, his body is torn to pieces and consumed by the faithful. "The murder of God was, of course, not mentioned, but a crime that had to be expiated by a sacrificial death could only have been murder," writes Freud. "Further, the connection between the delusion and the historical truth was established by the assurance that the sacrificial victim was the Son of God."

In other words, the murder of the father is paid for by the murder of the son.

The truth only suggested with the binding of Isaac is acknowledged with the crucifixion of Jesus.

Here's how Freud explains anti-Semitism: It's Christians talking to Jews on a classified frequency, saying, We hate you because you killed our father, and we, too, killed our father, but we have admitted it and paid for it, but you will not admit it, and will not pay for it, so the blood of it be on your head.

Freud wrote *Moses and Monotheism* in London in 1939, having been forced out of Austria by the Nazis. He was sick and old, in constant pain. The manuscript had to be smuggled to his followers on the Continent. There is no factual basis for his claims, though the book was presented as history. Its value is poetic. It's the blazing vision of a paranoid, persecuted, failing ghetto mind. (In another age, he would have been a prophet and books in the Bible would have carried his name: I Freud 8:12.) The book is driven by a persistent hidden impulse: he wanted to save his people from biology. To do this, he would rewrite their story. If he changed the Jewish past, he could change the Jewish present. ("To deny a people the man whom it praises as the greatest of its sons is not a deed to be undertaken lightheartedly," he writes.) If Moses was not a Hebrew, then the Jews are not Jews. They are Egyptians, which means the racial theories have to be reformulated, meaning Freud can return to Vienna.

Or think of Arthur Koestler, the Jewish novelist, early Communist, and early critic of communism, famous for his book *Darkness at Noon*, who, looking for a way out of the trap, turned to the Khazars. Koestler was thrilled by the legend of the lost kingdom, its Jewish warrior astride his war horse, with his sword and crimson beard, so different from the image of the ghetto Jew of Koestler's native Hungary. He was particularly interested in the fate of the Khazars. One year they were living in their fantastic cities; the next year they were gone.

What happened to them?

Koestler explored this question in *The Thirteenth Tribe*, a book in which he strings facts into a narrative in the manner of a private detective:

1247: The Khazars lose a tremendous land and sea battle.
1290: The towns of Khazaria stand empty.
1310: Travelers report red-bearded strangers on the trade routes.
1390: Any mention of Khazaria has ceased.
1410: Hundreds of thousands of Jews are living in the small towns of Poland.

Conventional history has these Jews migrating to Poland from western Europe at the invitation of King Casimir III, who promised to protect them as a "people of the King." According to Koestler, who builds his case on the work of other historians, then extrapolates wildly, there were simply not enough Jews in western Europe to account for the size of the influx. He therefore has the Jews coming not from the west but from the east. To Koestler, the Jews who migrated to Poland were none other than the Khazars, the remnant that fled the ruined kingdom. He knew that 70 percent of modern Jews had roots in Poland, so he also knew he was saying that the Jews, a majority of them, descended not from Abraham and Isaac and David, but from the khagan. We're not Judeans. We're Turks. The fact that Jews of eastern European descent are called Ashkenazi—Ashkenazi was the grandson of Japheth and brother to Togarma, the father of the Turks; in the Bible, the term is used to denote people living near Mount Ararat in Armenia—suggests, says Koestler, that Jews themselves once understood their identity clearly.

The shtetl of Sholem Alecheim was a Khazarian farm town. The Jewish peddler wore a long black coat because that is what his great-grandfather wore on the steppe. His hair was red and his beard was scraggly because he was a Russian. He was bowlegged because he descended from the rider who fought with Hulagu Khan, whose bowlegs made him impossible to unhorse.

Arthur Koestler:

> The evidence . . . adds up to a strong case in favor of those modern historians, who, independently of each other, have argued that the bulk of modern Jewry is not of Palestinian, but Caucasian origin. The mainstream Jewish migration did not flow from the Mediterranean across France and Germany to the East, then back again. The stream moved in a consistently Westerly direction, from the Caucuses through the Ukraine into Poland and thence into Western Europe. When that unprecedented mass settlement in Poland came into being, there were simply not enough Jews around in the West to account for it; while in the East a whole nation was on the move to new frontiers.

To make this case—it has been largely dismissed by historians—Koestler pursues a Melville-like examination of the "Jewish nose."

(This includes diagrams.) To Koestler, the nose of the Jew is like the whiteness of the whale, the surface detail that unlocks the secret history. Koestler says the type of nose considered most Jewish, hooked, is rarely seen on the faces of Sephardic Jews, who come from the Middle East and Spain, but is quite common among the tribes of Central Asia. In other words, the Jewish Nose is not even a Jewish nose. It's a Turkish nose. ("The North American Indians also very often have 'Jewish noses,'" he writes.) Koestler shows a picture of an Ottoman caliph who looks like Nosferatu: sloped shoulders, weak chin, hooked nose. (Koestler also includes an essay on nostrils, which, he says, are even more important than the bridge in determining the character of a nose.) Semites, he says, are straight-nosed or flat-nosed or broad-nosed. Never hook- or needle-nosed.* Which suggests to Koestler that hook-nosed Ashkenazim are not Semites. They do not hail from the Near East but from the Caucasus, and are therefore, by the racist definition, Aryans.† If this theory is true, writes Koestler, "the term *anti-Semitism* would become void of meaning, based on a misapprehension shared by both the killers and their victims."

I go to synagogue every Rosh Hashanah. I sit in the balcony or in the annex, or wherever they make room for Jews who aren't full-time members. I know how the service goes, what follows what, when you sit, when you stand, when the shofar is blown as it was blown in the ancient days, when Jews left the Temple stained in blood. But all this

---

*Koestler: "One of the most prominent features—both literally and metaphorically—which is said to characterize that particular type is the nose, variously described as Semitic, aquiline, hooked, or resembling the beak of an eagle. But, surprisingly among 2,836 Jews in New York City [a study] found that only 14 percent—i.e., one person in seven—has hooked noses; while 57 percent were straight nosed, 20 percent were snub nosed and 6.5 percent have flat or broad noses."

†Koestler's argument was picked up by anti-Semites who said it proved that Jews, in addition to everything else, were not even Jews: they were frauds, perpetrators of identity theft on a massive scale. This argument—when it was used, which was not often, because it's nuts—stripped Jews of the only thing many of them had: their story, their sense of self. To some it proved that Zionists had no historical claim on Palestine. If the Jews of Europe are not Hebrews, if they are Caucasians or Turks, then the Zionist project is a fraud. (This argument, like the Nazi argument, accepts blood as the key factor in faith.) Zionists are either liars or the most deluded colonists in history—the colonist who thinks he's a native.

ritual washes over and does not touch me, because it's dead and the men leading it do not believe in prophecy. At some point, after I have gone out for air and come back, I pick up the book on the back of the seat in front of me—not the abbreviated volume passed around before the service, but the Hebrew Bible. I flip to stories that have no immediate relevance: Esther and the milk, Daniel in the lion's den. I get caught up in the strangeness of these stories, and for the first time of the morning recognize myself in the epic of the Judeans.

It was in this way that I recently reread the story of Jonah, which I have known from the scriptures but also from *Pinocchio*, *Moby-Dick*, and *Jaws*. Though I have read it many times, it suddenly seemed urgent, as if it had been written for me. It spoke of the condition of the Jew, alone in his strangeness, on the same train as everyone else, but not making the same stops.

It starts with Jonah hearing God's call: "Arise, go to Nineveh, that great city, and cry against it; for their wickedness is come up before me."

So what does Jonah do?

Does he pack a bag and heed the call?

No. He flees. He runs from the voice, which is his fate. He does not want to prophesy. He is tired of looking and looking and being a pair of eyes. He does not want to be different. He wants to live his own life. The story of Jonah is the story of Marx, Freud, and Koestler. It's the story of the Reform Jew of Germany and the modern Jew of America, of all those people who want to get lost in the world of fishermen and ships, where the only voice in your head is the voice that says, "It is time to get up. It is time to lie down. It is time to eat."

Jonah rose to flee unto Tarshish from the presence of the LORD, and went down to Joppa; and he found a ship going to Tarshish: so he paid the fare thereof, and went down into it, to go with them unto Tarshish from the presence of the LORD.

When the ship was out at sea, a tremendous storm blew across the water. The hull pitched on the waves. The sailors stood in the spars, searching for a break in the clouds. They pulled in their sails, shouted and cried. Jonah went belowdecks, got into a bunk, and pulled a blanket over his head. He knew the storm was God looking for him, combing the waters.

> So the shipmaster came to him, and said unto him, What meanest thou, O sleeper? arise, call upon thy God, if so be that God will think upon us, that we perish not.

Jonah, though feigning sleep, had in fact been dozing from the moment he fled the call. He was sleepwalking through life, but God was shaking him awake. The captain ordered all passengers on deck. He cut up pieces of straw and said, "Come, and let us cast lots, that we may know for whose cause this evil is upon us."
Jonah drew short.

> [The sailors] said unto him, Tell us, we pray thee, for whose cause is this evil upon us; What is thine occupation? and whence comest thou? what is thy country? and of what people art thou?

Jonah confessed he was a Hebrew in flight. That he had run from the divine voice. The sailors lifted him up and "cast him into the sea," which is the fate of the Jew in exile: what the goyim do to the Hebrew when the storm is raging, and the markets fail.
He sank to the bottom, where he was swallowed by the whale, which carried him in its belly for five days. "And Jonah prayed unto the LORD out of the fish's belly," and the fish surfaced and "vomited him" onto the shore of his native land. He crossed the beach, stopping for a moment to gaze in wonder at the glass towers of Tel Aviv, then went on to Nineveh. He was a Zionist, broken by the storm, eaten by the whale, devoured, digested, and beached in the old country. He talked in the squares and markets of the city. He warned and prophesied, then climbed a hill, "made him a booth, and sat under it in shadow," and waited for Nineveh to be destroyed. Is this the mission of a Jew who stops running? To be a witness, to be an eyeball? To sit in

the shade as the world is devoured? Is this why people hate the Jew? Because they see their own tragedy reflected in his eyes?*

Now I will tell you what the story of Jonah means: the ship is Europe; the journey away from God is the journey into the Diaspora; Jonah on the ship is the Jew in the ghetto; Jonah in the whale is the Jew in the camps. Who has no choice. Who must feed himself to the beast to survive, who must return to history to be free.

*The people of Nineveh repented, and God spared the city.

SEVEN

House Hunting

Who was the first Zionist? It's like trying to determine the original teller of a joke, or trace a rumor to its point of origin. It's a question impossible to answer. Maybe there was no first; maybe the idea was in the wind. Maybe it grew naturally, as certain flowers grow when the conditions are right. The Jews had been promised a life free from the ghetto. The Jews had embraced this promise only to find, after they lost their old world, that the new world was still closed to them—in no European nation were they accepted as citizens. It was merely a question of time, then, until some of these outcasts decided that the solution was not to change the nature of the European states, nor to give up on the national dream, but to create their own nation in which a Jew could live a normal life. Such a state would end the neurosis of the Jew, which was the neurosis of exile. Maybe no one thought of it first. Maybe the idea appeared in many minds at the same instant. A dream dreamt by thousands.

If you study old books and pamphlets, you sense the presence of these dreamers, but can't make them out; or you hear them, but can't see their faces; or you see their faces, but only for a moment, through a window, and the bus is moving. The members of this generation were obscure to the point of abstraction—a smear of color, a storm of paint. But if you look long enough, a figure appears amid all those brushstrokes and lines. An old rabbi with a white beard and a head full of sparks. His name was Yehuda Solomon Alkalai. He was a mystic, a master of Kabbalah, hypnotized by numbers. He said that a smart man can understand the sentences, but a knowing man can read between them. He turned each letter in the Torah into a digit, then tallied them, the result being the year the messianic age would dawn.* He was born in Sarajevo in 1798. In 1825, he became the rabbi of Semlin, then the capital of Serbia. Over the years, his sense of the Jews as a community, and his fear for their future, grew, strengthened. He was deeply affected by the campaign for Serbian autonomy, which was itself influenced by the Greek War of Independence against the Ottoman Turks. If these ancient nations could be restored, why not Israel? In 1834, after years of preparation and prayer, Alkalai published a pamphlet called *Shema Yisrael* ("Hear O Israel"), which was the first known call for Jewish political independence.

He went on a sort of lecture tour, traveling, with his pamphlet, to the great Jewish capitals of Middle Europe. He said that Jewish life in Europe was coming to an end. He told the Jews to save themselves by forming a state in Palestine. He was perhaps the first Jewish leader who said that the Jews could return before the Messiah.† Which was blasphemy. Forcing the hand. He was a bridge to the modern era. He expressed a modern idea in the language of Kabbalah. He spoke of neither political parties nor soldiers, but of signs and symbols. He looked like an ancient, but his ideas were new. By telling the Jews to re-

*1840.

†Alkalai is seen by many as a curiosity whose writing had limited long-term impact, but he was in fact good friends with a man who had a son, who had a son, who was Theodor Herzl.

turn, he was telling them that return was possible. His words would not find an audience for another half century.

T he notion of Jews living in a modern Jewish state was not unprece-
dented. It had, in fact, been in the air for centuries. It had, in fact, been proposed again and again. You can start in the Age of Discovery. In 1652 the British, working through the Dutch West India Company, tried to establish a Jewish colony in Curaçao. In 1659 the French, also working through the Dutch West India Company, tried to establish a Jewish colony in Cayenne. In 1749 the Polish prince Maurice de Saxe proposed the establishment of a Jewish nation in South America, over which he would rule.* (Almost as soon as there was a New World, people wanted to ship the Jews there.) In 1819 the British entrepreneur W. D. Robinson tried to form a Jewish state on the Mississippi River in the Missouri Territory. But the idea really got under way with Napoleon, the man who opened the ghettos. (The founding of Israel can be seen at the end of a long chain that began with the storming of the Bastille.) After his victory in Egypt, Napoleon, standing beside the Pyramids, called on the Jews to restore their ancient kingdom.

You can start with Pavel Pestel, a leader of the Decembrists, the cabal of Russian military officers who, in the early 1800s, a century before the Bolsheviks, called for revolution against the czars. As part of his visionary plan, Pestel proposed the establishment of a Jewish state in Asia Minor, less because he loved the Jews than because he wanted to get rid of them. Pestel was executed with other plotters in December 1826.

You can start with Benjamin Disraeli, the British prime minister, and the son of a prominent family of Sephardic Jews.† He inspired by

*See the essay on Zionism by Hugh Chisholm in the *Encyclopædia Britannica.*

†Disraeli was baptized at his father's insistence when he was thirteen years old. This was the ticket you had to punch to enter the fair. But he spoke often of his Jewish heritage, and remained proud, though he attended the Anglican Church.

example: a proud man dressed like a parrot, in tall hat and candy stripes. "We are hated," he said, "because we are superior." In 1855 Disraeli, a novelist before he entered politics, published *The Wondrous Tale of Alroy*, a Zionist text written before Zionism. "You ask what I wish?" Alroy tells the caliph. "My answer is this: 'Jerusalem, all we have forfeited, all we have yearned after, all for which we have fought.'"

You can start with Mordecai Noah, an American journalist who called for the establishment of a Jewish state in Palestine in 1818. In 1812 Noah, who was the editor of the *City Gazette* in Charleston, South Carolina, published a series of articles under the pseudonym Muley Molack that brought challenges to duel, this being akin to a letter to the editor. (As a result, he killed an angry reader.) Noah later served as the American consul in Tunis, but was recalled, according to James Monroe, then secretary of state, because he was a Jew. A trip to Europe convinced Noah that the Jews needed a state of their own. He proposed this in a speech called "A Discourse on the Restoration of the Jews." It would eventually be located in Palestine, but he argued for an interim home outside of Buffalo, New York. He purchased 2,555 acres on Grand Island in the Niagara River and was given the deed in a ceremony led by the New York legislature on September 15, 1825. Noah called his state Ararat, after the peak on which the biblical Noah landed his Ark. No Jews ever lived in Ararat, but the cornerstone stood at its entrance, with somber Buffalo brooding beyond.*

Though each of these men was unique, they were all dreaming the same dream, a collective hallucination that culminated in 1862 in the frontal lobe of the pamphleteer Moses Hess. He was born in Bonn, Germany, in 1812, but his father came from Poland, which means he was like the rest of us, trying to fit in here, with antecedents back there. His father was a rabbi, but Hess cared only about current events. He

---

*Or you can start with the novelist George Eliot, whose book *Daniel Deronda*, published in 1876, was taken by many as an argument for Jewish restoration. In it, a Jewish character says, "The effect of our separateness will not be completed and have its highest transformation unless our race takes on again the character of a nationality."

was a newspaperman, an ink-stained wretch. He passed his afternoons in smoke-filled coffeehouses. He knew Marx and Engels and attended rallies, catching cold in the rain. He shouted until he was hoarse. All these pioneers were true believers: they gave themselves entirely to whatever they were championing, the cause often seeming secondary to the ecstasy of belief. Republicans, anarchists, Communists, Nationalists, more German than the Germans, more Russian than the Russians. They became Zionists only later, as a result of a scandal or a massacre that destroyed their faith in the first cause, that made them realize they were not more German than the Germans, not more Russian than the Russians.

For Hess, it was the Damascus Affair, in which several prominent Jews were accused of blood libel, that is, killing Christian babies for their blood, then used (said the accusers) to make matzo. To Hess, this affair, which was followed credulously by the German press, came as a shock. He was seeing the world not as he wanted it to be, but as it actually was—seeing himself as he was himself seen. It changed everything.

The book for which Hess is remembered was published in 1864. It's written in the form of twelve letters, or epistles, and reads like a sacred text minus God. In it, the author, while comforting a woman in mourning, ponders every aspect of the Jewish Question. The book was originally titled *The Revival of Israel*, which was to be accomplished through a return to Zion—the Jews will revive the land, the land will revive the Jews—but was changed to the more stirring *Rome and Jerusalem*, which suggests the never-ending battle between Gentile and Jew.

Hess said two ancient peoples had been crushed by tradition: "The Chinese, a body without a soul, and the Jews, a soul without a body, wandering like a ghost through the centuries." Notice how Hess sets the Jew in time instead of in place. Notice how he echoes the Christian depiction of the Jew as the wanderer. Notice how, from the beginning, the Zionists seemed to accept the stereotype of the Jew: as weak, as fallen, as bloodless, as lost, "a soul without a body." Jews who opposed Zionism in these years considered men such as Hess to be self-haters.

He talked about "The Jewish Condition," as if being a Jew were an illness in need of treatment.

Hess called on the leaders of France, which controlled vast stretches of land in the Near East, to open Syria to Jewish settlement. He said all other efforts to assimilate would fail. "Even an act of conversion cannot relieve the Jew of the enormous pressure of [Jew hatred]," he wrote. "Germans hate the religion of the Jews less than they hate their race; they hate the peculiar beliefs of the Jews less than they hate their peculiar noses. Reform, conversion, education, emancipation—none will open the gates of society to the Jew; hence his desire to deny his racial origin."* The only solution, said Hess, was the creation of a state in which everyone was Jewish so being Jewish would be normal. Only in a state filled with Jews can a Jew stop being Jewish.

The Jewish Encyclopedia, compiled before the creation of Israel, distills the teaching of Moses Hess down to three major points:

(1) The Jews will always remain strangers among the European peoples, who may emancipate them for reasons of humanity and justice, but will never respect them so long as the Jews place their own great national memories in the background.

(2) The Jewish type is indestructible, and Jewish national feeling can not be uprooted, although the German Jews, for the sake of a wider and more general emancipation, persuade themselves and others to the contrary.

(3) If the emancipation of the Jews is irreconcilable with Jewish nationality, the Jews must sacrifice emancipation to nationality. The only solution of the Jewish question lies in the colonization of Palestine.

In its first year of publication, *Rome and Jerusalem* sold 160 copies. It hit the water and vanished. When it touched bottom, a tiny bubble

*Moses Hess was a particular foe of the Reform movement, by which Judaism would be made less exotic and less foreign so therefore less an obstacle to assimilation. He said such reforms would merely cause the Jews to lose connection to their past, and in the end they still would not be accepted by the Germans.

came to the surface and went *pop*. A second edition was printed, but most of these copies vanished. The book was a failure. Hess stopped talking about it. Then died. His survivors gathered the remainders in a pile and burned them—because they feared scandal. Only in retrospect was the significance of *Rome and Jerusalem* evident. It was really the first book to make the case for the modern nation. Hess died a failure, but history has turned him into a legend.

EIGHT

The Flâneur

Theodor Herzl appeared on the scene relatively late, at the end of the nineteenth century, yet he is still considered the father of Zionism. Not because he was first, not because he was most eloquent, but because he was singing just the right song at just the right time. He was the messiah of that particular moment. What he wanted was really no different from what previous messiahs wanted—to save the Jews, to restore the kingdom—but he lived in a different era. Sabbatai Zevi, David Alroy, and Jacob Frank lived in a religious age, so expressed themselves in the language of the Bible. Herzl lived in a secular age, so expressed himself in the language of the Enlightenment.

Look at the pictures of Herzl at the beginning, then look at the pictures of Herzl at the end. Year by year, he turns into a prophet. *Is not the story of Herzl written in the Chronicle of the Book of Kings?* He is clean-shaven in early photos, or sporting a neat beard, what old-timers called a Van Dyke. He is a young man on the make, in a tailored suit, carrying a watch on a chain. His gaze is level and you can hear the coins jingle in his pocket. He does not look handsome to me, but was often described as such: tall and slender, with dark eyes and fine features. He takes his coffee in a swallow and bounds onto the trolley that rattles through the streets of town. He's going places. It's morning in Europa. In photos taken at the end, his eyes are fixed on the distance, on a storm gathering beyond the horizon. He is thin and his face is lost in a terrific beard. He's the prophet of a religion without a god. In a famous photo, he stands on a balcony, leaning over a balustrade, looking out at the land, at the future, which is hidden from us, but which he has been allowed to see.

> And Moses went up from the plains of Moab unto the mountain of Nebo, to the top of Pisgah, that is over against Jericho. And the Lord showed him all the land of Gilead, unto Dan, and all Naphtali, and the land of Ephraim, and Manasseh, and all the land of Judah, unto the utmost sea, and the south, and the plain of the valley of Jericho, the city of palm trees, unto Zoar. And the Lord said unto him, This is the land which I sware unto Abraham, unto Isaac, and unto Jacob, saying, I will give it unto thy seed: I have caused thee to see it with thine eyes, but thou shalt not go over thither.

Herzl was born in Budapest in 1860. His father worked in the rag trade, like Daryl Zanuck's old man. When he was twelve, he read a book on theology and was tormented by dreams. In one, which Herzl wrote about in his diary, "the King-Messiah came, a glorious and majestic old man, took me in his arms and swept off with me on the wings of the wind. On one of the iridescent clouds we encountered the figure of Moses. The features were those familiar to me out of my childhood from the statue by Michelangelo. The Messiah called to Moses: 'It is for this child I have prayed.' But to me he said: 'Go, declare to the Jews that I shall come soon and perform great wonders and great deeds for my people and for the whole world.'"

In other words, the Messiah prayed for Herzl.

In other words, the Messiah believed in Herzl, who did not believe in God.

For the most part, though, Herzl did not think about his faith or his people. He was a Reform Jew. He went to temple twice a year, on the High Holidays, but otherwise did not much trouble himself. He wanted to be a German, a modern man, known for his talents, not for his kinky hair. For this reason, Herzl can seem alien to modern Israelis. He is not one of their heroes. They do not identify with him: he was never part of a Jewish majority, he never saw a Jewish army, he never knew of Jewish power, or the corruption that comes with such power. He was less like an Israeli than like an American Jew. His fears were the fears of the exterminated Diaspora of Europe, part of which survives in America.

I feel I understand Herzl better than do my Israeli cousins, who use money with his picture on it and drive roads with his name on them, but who are baffled by his insecurity and desire. He wanted to conform, I tell them. He wanted to disappear so he could be seen.* His generation was promised everything, then discovered that the promise was a lie. In this gap, between expectation and reality, Zionism bloomed.

Herzl moved to Vienna, where he practiced law. He stopped going to synagogue in these years, and lost contact with his faith. ("But deep in my soul," he wrote, "I always felt myself to be Jewish.") One Christmas he was visited at home by the chief rabbi of Vienna (Rabbi Moritz Güdemann, who became a leading anti-Zionist), who was shocked to find Herzl decorating a Christmas tree. "I was lighting the tree for my children when Güdemann arrived," Herzl wrote. "He seemed upset by the 'Christian' custom. Well, I will not let myself be pressured."

Herzl wanted to be a novelist and playwright. He wanted to capture the essence of Germany in language. In this, he cut a path parallel to Hitler's, an artist from the provinces haunting the streets of Vienna's Ring. Herzl's plays were performed on small stages, then big stages. There was a flash of fame, then it was gone. "As an author, particularly as a playwright, I am held to be nothing, less than nothing," he wrote. "Yet I feel that I am by instinct a great writer, or was a great

---

*"Herzl's dream was the American dream," Yossi Beillin wrote. "Give the Jews the chance to live as human beings—to assimilate. In many respects, he was the prophet of Jewish life in America much more than he was the prophet of the Jewish state."

writer, who failed to yield his full harvest only because he became nau-
seated and discouraged." He later suggested he had given up his literary career to lead the movement—that is, if history had not called,
he might have been another Ibsen or Chekhov. In fact, Herzl took
up prophecy only when stagecraft failed—or perhaps prophecy was
a continuation of stagecraft, a bigger drama on a bigger stage with
higher stakes. The greatest character created by Herzl the dramaturge
was Herzl the prophet.

To support himself, Herzl worked as a journalist. This took him
everywhere. He was wildly successful. At twenty-six, he had a column
in the *Neue Freie Presse*, in Vienna, which was among the most respected
papers in the world. He mastered the popular form of the day: the
feuilleton, in which the reporter, or flâneur, functions as a giant eyeball, drifting through a city, observing and recording. Herzl, in other
words, was a professional dreamer, paid to work himself into the de-
tached state conducive to epiphanies. He published his first book before he was thirty, a collection of feuilletons, in which the word *Jew*
appeared just once, in a description of the Roman Ghetto:

> What a steaming in the air, what a street! Countless open doors and
> windows thronged with innumerable pallid and worn-out faces. The
> Ghetto! With what base and persistent hatred the unfortunates have
> been persecuted for the sole crime of faithfulness to their religion.
> We've traveled a long way since those times: nowadays the Jew is de-
> spised only for having a crooked nose, or for being a plutocrat even
> when he happens to be a pauper.

Herzl was made the Paris correspondent of the *Neue Freie Presse*. He
rented an apartment on the Right Bank of the Seine and explored the
city. He was a young man, in a new town. He went to the local synagogue. He spent time in the Marais, then the Jewish Ghetto. He was
comforted by the faces, so much like the faces of his childhood. It was
here, far from home, that he first came to see the Jews as a nation. He
covered everything for his newspaper: political campaigns, diplomatic
missions, bicycle races, fashion shows. In 1894 he found the biggest story

of his career, the trial of Alfred Dreyfus, the Jewish army captain who had been charged with treason by the French government. The Dreyfus Affair was not just the case, but also the spectacle surrounding it.

It started when a newspaper reporter discovered a breach in French national security. A spy, someone in the military, had been leaking secret information to the German High Command. A secretary in a staff office found a sheet of paper in the trash. It was covered with figures and maps. This document, later determined to be a fake, was said to show the position of various French fortifications. Experts went through the military files, seeking to match the handwriting on the paper. Dreyfus was arrested on October 15, 1894. He was a captain in the army, attached to the General Staff. He was also a Jew, which made him suspect. As a Jew, he was not considered a full citizen, so could not be trusted. Where did his loyalty lie? With France, or with his co-religionists in Germany? In the end, his faith was the only evidence against him.

For Herzl, this case—not just the charges, but the way Dreyfus was treated: dragged from the barracks, stripped of his rank, degraded before his men—came as a shock, the sort that makes you say, "Oh, so all of that was a lie."

Dreyfus was, after all, not the bearded Jew from the East, not the stooped rabbi from the ghetto. He was the flower of the age, handsome and strong. He did not even consider himself a Jew; he considered himself a Frenchman. He wanted to die fighting for France. In prison, he did not compare his trials to those of Job or Moses, but to those of St. Stephen and the Christian martyrs. He worshipped his tormentors. *Dreyfus, you didn't even know who your friends were!* Years later, when Dreyfus wrote his memoir, *Five Years of My Life* (1901), he did not once mention that he was a Jew, though his being a Jew was the entire story.

The men who championed his cause—freethinkers, liberals, Jews— were known as Dreyfusards. A famous Dreyfusard named Bernard Lazare tried to explain to Dreyfus why the case was significant. "Never shall I forget what I suffered in my Jewish skin the day of your degradation when you represented my martyred and insulted race."

When Dreyfus protested, saying he was not a Jew, Lazare said,

"You are more a Jew than you think, with your incoercible hope, your faith in the best, your almost fatalistic resignation. This indestructible fund comes to you from your people; it is your people who have sustained you."

When Herzl looked at Captain Dreyfus, he could not help but see himself, stripped of rank, pulled out of uniform.

He was a regular in the press gallery. He watched the generals come and go in their stiff uniforms, their heels ringing on the marble floor. He stood on the steps, where the mob chanted, "Death to the Jews!" He was shaken by the trial, shaken by the crowds, by the press. He followed every journalistic account, paying special attention to the stories in *La France Juive*, an anti-Semitic newspaper. This led him to a study of anti-Semitic literature and the science of race in general. He was stunned by Eugen Dühring's *The Jewish Problem as a Problem of Race, Morals and Culture*.* Words that appeared in this book—*usurper, defiler, inferior*—stung like a whip. "There is only one way out," Herzl wrote in his diary. "To return to the Promised Land."

This is the core of Zionism. Not the land, not the Book, not the gun, but the Jew realizing that anti-Semitism is an evil that lives even on the Right Bank of the Seine. "The Dreyfus case embodies more than a judicial error," Herzl wrote. "It embodies the desire of a vast majority of the French to condemn a Jew, and to condemn all Jews in this one Jew. Death to the Jews! howled the mob as the decorations were being ripped from the captain's coat. Where? In France. In republican, modern, civilized France, a hundred years after the Declaration of the Rights of Man. The French people, or at any rate, the great part of the French people, does not want to extend the Rights of Man to the Jews. The edicts of the great revolution have been revoked."†

Herzl worked up his plan slowly, in the course of months, but later, when his story was written, his idea for the state was said to have come

---

*He had actually first read this book a few years earlier.

†Dreyfus was found guilty, sent to prison on Ile Royal, then to another prison on Devil's Island. He was kept in solitary confinement. Not even the guards were allowed to talk to him. He grew frail, but survived. He was eventually cleared, but was not released until 1899. His rank was not restored until 1906.

in a flash, in the way of a mystical insight. Because he was a prophet and this was a vision. Here is how historian Alex Bein described Herzl in his fit of inspiration* (notice how the prophet receives the teaching whole, as if it comes from elsewhere, and needs only be written down):

> Then suddenly the storm breaks upon him. The clouds open. The thunder rolls. The lightning flashes. A thousand impressions beat upon him at the same time—a gigantic vision. He cannot think; he is unable to move; he can only write; breathless, unreflecting, unable to control himself or exercise his critical faculties lest he dam the eruption, he dashes down his thoughts on scraps of paper—walking, standing, lying down, on the street, at the table, in the night—as if under unceasing command. So furiously did the cataract of his thoughts rush through him that he thought he was going out of his mind. He was not working out the idea. The idea was working him out.

Why was Herzl open to such insight? Why did he see the trap when the most brilliant Jews of his time continued on their way to Auschwitz? I think it had to do with his turn of mind, his style. Herzl was a flâneur, a magazine writer, the author of whimsical essays. He trained himself to be open to the sudden insight, the detail that illuminates the whole. Isaiah Berlin said it was because he was an outsider—not a scholar, not a rabbi, not a professional Jew. (With Zionism, the amateurs took over from the pros.) He approached the oldest issue as if it were new, because it was new to him.

Isaiah Berlin, *The Power of Ideas*:

> The distinguishing characteristic of Herzl was that, despite his origin and milieu, he came to the problem, as it were, from the outside; and possessed a somewhat romantic conception of the Jews, scarcely recognizable to those who themselves grew up in the thick of a closely-knit traditional Jewish community. There is something about great radical solutions of political questions which seem to make it necessary for them to be born in the minds of those who in some sense

*This is from an early introduction to Herzl's book *The Jewish State*.

stand on the rim, and look in from the outside, and have an over-simple ideal, an over-simple purpose, a lucid, usually violent vision, based on indispensable ignorance of detail. Those who know too much—know too many detailed facts too closely—cannot, as a rule, produce radical solutions.

Herzl wanted to explain his idea for a state to bankers and money-men, who, he imagined, would then sit with world leaders and make it happen. He wrote a list of the wealthiest Jews in Europe: the Roth-schilds, the Montefiores, the Mendelssohns, the Warburgs. He was like the producer of an offbeat independent film in search of financing. He sent letters and made appointments, identifying himself as not the champion of a strange new ideology but a correspondent for the *Neue Freie Presse*. He did not say he was working on a story for the news-paper, not exactly, but neither did he dispel the impression. He let these men believe what they wanted. That is, Herzl initiated his move-ment with a slick act of salesmanship, a bait-and-switch, in which you want the journalist but get the prophet.

Imagine Herzl traveling to one of these meetings, boarding a train in Paris, the country rolling backward out the window, fields going by, the strange land of Pharaoh, the rush of arrival, crossing the platform, a handsome young man with a black beard taking a carriage to town, the steeple pointing to heaven, only it's not our steeple and it's not our heaven, rolling through a gate that reads ROTHSCHILD. He waits in the foyer—the small Jew come to the house of the big Jew, the intellectual come to the house of the moneyman. In his bag Herzl carries a plan that tells the story of the next hundred years. A servant brings him into the library, where the banker sits before a wall of books, dressed like a country gentleman.*

Herzl spoke in dramatic sentences that followed, one to another, like figures in an equation. Emancipation had been a success for the Rothschilds, but a failure for the millions of Jews who lost their ghettos and still had not found a home. For these people, calamity is just over

*Herzl met with Lord Nathan Meyer Rothschild, the head of the British wing of the banking fam-ily, on July 4, 1902.

the horizon. There is only one solution: a state in which Jews will find safe harbor and the Jewish character will be redeemed. Ideally, it will be located in the biblical homeland. Herzl made the case to several financiers, calling on each to bankroll the project* and lobby the imperial powers. If we succeed, he said, "a wondrous breed of Jews will spring up from the earth. The Maccabees will rise again. We shall live at last as free men on our own soil, and in our own homes peacefully die."

Notes survive from one of these meetings: Herzl talking to Baron de Hirsch, who had funded a Jewish colony in Argentina. Hirsch was skeptical. He asked Herzl how long he figured it would take to cure the Jews of their condition. "They are to be transformed into men of character in a reasonable period of time," Herzl said. "Say, ten or twenty years, even forty—the interval needed by Moses."

Why now? asked Hirsch. Why after two thousand years of struggling vainly to return, do you think the moment is finally right?

Herzl spoke with his hands, indicating new horizons, new visions. He spoke specifically of the wonders of the modern world, how technology at last made the old dream possible. He spoke of the miracle of train travel, which made far-off lands accessible. "Distance has ceased to be an obstacle," he said. He spoke of modern agriculture, pipes and pumping stations that could bring water to the wastes. He said the Jews would return to the East with the learning of the West, and heal the land that had lain fallow since being devastated by Rome. "The word 'impossible' has ceased to exist in the vocabulary of technical science," he said. "Were a man who lived in the last century to return to earth, he would find the life of today full of incomprehensible magic. Wherever the moderns appear with our inventions, we transform the desert into a garden."

*Many of these philanthropists had already given millions to set up colonies in Palestine—these were meant for poor Jews from the East, Russia mostly, displaced by pogroms. There was a degree of self-interest in such charity: the rich Jews wanted to settle their destitute cousins in Palestine so they would not migrate to Berlin and London, where, with their beards and bodies, they would be an embarrassment. In other words, these philanthropists funded settlements in Palestine to protect the image of the assimilated Western Jew, and to protect their own position. If you go to Israel today, you see, on a hill in West Jerusalem, overlooking the old city, the luxurious black carriage that Lord Montefiore brought by ship from London on visits to the pre-Herzl settlements. It's a monument to an early benefactor, but seems more like a shrine to a lost way of life, to the luxurious estates and titles of the super-rich who turned away from Herzl.

He spoke of the wealth that the Jews of Europe had accumulated since emancipation, which, for the first time, gave them the capital necessary to pursue the dream. He spoke of England and France, of Western soldiers in Eastern cities, Western ships in Arab seas. He spoke of the religious revival sweeping Great Britain, how the Books of Daniel and Revelation had come to be read literally. Thousands of Christians favored the creation of a Jewish state as a necessary step toward the Second Coming.* He spoke of the Ottoman Empire, which ruled Palestine, but was bankrupt and receding slowly, like a glacier. He said the Jews could buy land for their state from the cash-hungry sultan. "We will be like the boy who plucks the thorn from the lion's paw."

He spoke of the danger the Jews faced if they remained in Europe. The Damascus Affair. The Dreyfus Affair. The Russian pogroms. To most people, these seemed unconnected events. But Herzl saw the pattern, read the signs. Because he was paranoid. He framed the issue in the way of God in the Bible: it is either the Promise, a state in which the Jews recover their dignity, or the Curse, in which the Jews are massacred.

Herzl was received without enthusiasm in most of these meetings. For starters, there was the way he presented himself. He did not grovel, nor did he regard these men with special respect. He did not even consider them his equals. Herzl was a visionary. These men, most of whom had inherited their wealth, were cash. In a letter to Baron de Hirsch, he wrote, "You will be the money and I will be the spirit."

Then there was the ideology, which, to the wealthy Jews, came as a challenge to their way of life. To them, Judaism was not a nationality; it was a religion, like Catholicism; you could therefore be a German Jew in the same way you could be a German Catholic. If Judaism were a nationality, as Herzl said, then a Jew could never be anything but a stranger, even if, as was the case in Germany, he had been in the land

---

*It was in these years that John Darby, a British religious leader, pioneered the notion of the Rapture, in which, in the moment before the final moments, the righteous are carried away to heaven, from where they watch the people of earth perish in the last great conflagration. To Darby, Zionism, when it appeared, came as a fulfillment of prophecy. In other words, Israel was built, to some degree, with the help of other people's insanity.

longer than the "natives." To these men, Herzl could sound like an anti-Semite. Like an anti-Semite, he said the Jews were alien. Like an anti-Semite, he described the Jews as weak and grasping. Like an anti-Semite, he said the presence of Jews caused instability and war. Like an anti-Semite, he wanted the Jews out of Europe.

The men in these meetings lived on estates, dressed well, ate well, traveled, held offices and titles. Herzl told them these lives were an illusion; that they were not who they thought they were; that they were neither respected nor loved by their countrymen. In a meeting with Herzl, Nathan Rothschild shouted, "You are nothing but a simple-minded dreamer of dreams!"

"It takes a simple mind to lead men," said Herzl.

"And where will you lead them?" asked Rothschild.

"Away from the hate that engulfs them in Europe," said Herzl.

"There will never be anti-Semitism in Britain!" said Rothschild.

In 1895 Herzl spoke to the Maccabean Society, a group of powerful British Jews. He was then asked to turn his notes into an article. It was in the course of writing this article that the pieces fell together, and the ideas of many generations coalesced into a plan. It was later called Zionism, though the word did not appear in Herzl's speech or in the article.* The article ran in *The Jewish Chronicle* on January 17, 1896. Four months later, it was published as *Der Judenstaat* (*The Jewish State*), which many consider the founding document of Israel.

It's short, less a book than a pamphlet. It radiates the kind of imperial, can-do optimism that disappeared in the First World War. Its ideology is characterized by will. "The Jews who wish for a state will have it," writes Herzl. "The world will be freed by our liberty, enriched by our wealth, magnified by our greatness. And whatever we attempt there to accomplish for our own welfare, will react powerfully and beneficially for the good of humanity." Despite such language of universalism, Zionism is really the opposite. It's particular. It's peculiar. It's nationalism for the Jews. Nationalism in the age of nationalism:

---

*The term had, in fact, been coined on January 23, 1892, in an essay by the writer Nathan Birnbaum.

the Serbs, the Greeks, the Croats. There is a feeling of "me too"-ism about it. And of diminishment. It takes the landless faith that bloomed in the ruin of the Temple and returns it to fixed borders.

Yet Zionism was, in important ways, different from other nationalisms. Yuri Slezkine calls it "nationalism in reverse." German nationalism, for example, sought to turn a people into a nation, then sanctify it. Jewish nationalism sought to take a universal faith that was already sanctified and reduce it to the level of a state—that is, to make Jews "normal." In creating a German nation, the mundane things of German life were made sacred. The German language, which had been the language of the marketplace and the pub, was made sacred by German poets. The landscape of Germany, which had been the frontiers of Rome, was made sacred by German painters. Zionist poets and painters, however, took a language (Hebrew) and a landscape (Canaan) that was holy already, not just to Jews, and restored it to everyday life. This was the only way to free the Jews from history. "The idea was not to sanctify popular speech but to profane the language of God," writes Slezkine. "Not to convert your home into a Promised Land but to convert the Promised Land into a home. The effort to turn Jews into a normal nation looked like no other nationalism in the world."

W here *The Jewish State* was reviewed, it was reviewed poorly. Mostly it was ignored. It was not mentioned in *The New York Times* until 1905, ten years after its publication. By then, Herzl was famous. It was not mentioned in *Harper's* until 1925. It was reviewed only in small political magazines and the Yiddish press, where it was either dismissed or used as an occasion to attack Herzl for his presumption, for acting like Moses.

How did Herzl react?

Did he walk the streets? Did he let his long coat trail on the dirty ground? Did he look in the windows of Parisian cafés where families were sitting down to dinner and poets were penning verse:

Gentle, the sound of rain
Pattering roof and ground!
Ah, for the heart in pain,
*Sweet is the sound of rain!**

Or did he tell himself the struggle is long and hard and every prophet is ignored in his hometown?

He waits. He broods. Then the news came: Herzl's book was being devoured and debated in Warsaw, in Vilna, in Bielsk. Why did it flop in the West but become a hit in the East? Because Jewish suffering was greater in the East, so the Jews there were more open to the radical solution; because Herzl, the epitome of the modern Jew, was to them a fascinating exotic; because the Jews in the East knew nothing of Herzl so could project on him their fantasy of redemption. According to the historian Alex Bein, Herzl "dawned on the Jews of Eastern Europe as a mystic figure rising out of the past."

He made his first trip to Russia that year, arriving in a small town by train. The platform was overrun. People shouted, tugged his coat. It went to his head. This magazine writer, this transcriber of events, had himself become the event. He turned away from the Rothschilds and Warburgs. What does it say in Psalms? "Do not put thy trust in Princes." Zionism would not be a movement led by wealthy Jews in the West, but a revolution driven by poor Jews in the East. He traded the drawing room for the open road, traveling town to town, fields stretching before, fields stretching behind, prophesying in synagogues filled with sweaty faces. He could not read Hebrew, did not know Yiddish, or Russian, or Polish. His words were a half-understood torrent, stanzas as beautiful as Romantic poems. "Herzl, with his magnificent appearance and visionary gaze, came like a prophet from a distant land," writes Isaiah Berlin. "Many were dazzled by the strangeness and distance which divided them from this Messianic messenger from another world, who

---

*"Like city's rain, my heart . . ." *One Hundred and One Poems by Paul Verlaine* (translated by Norman R. Shapiro, University of Chicago Press, 2000).

could not speak to them in their own language—that remoteness made him and his message all the more magical and magnetic."

"The transformation of a dandy and a man of letters into a leader and man of action was miraculous," writes Walter Laqueur. "He sacrificed everything to his idea and movement—marriage, money, health. The narcissistic streak in his character played a great part in it. Herzl relished the role of Messiah-King."

He spoke to political leaders and rabbis. He spoke to crowds, every word a promise, every word a curse.

He said, "They do not suspect it, but [the Jews] have ghetto natures, quiet, decent, timid. That is what most of us are. Will we understand the call to freedom and manhood?"

He said, "In our native lands where we have lived for centuries we are still derided as aliens, often by men whose ancestors had not yet come when Jewish songs had long been heard in the country."

He said, "In the Promised Land, we can have hooked noses, black or red beards, and bowlegs, without being despised for it."

He established funds, wrote letters, published pamphlets. He was building the bureaucracy that would become the government of the Jewish state. He was a whirlwind, a dervish. He recruited the men who would lead the next generation. David Ben-Gurion, the first prime minister of Israel. Chaim Weizmann, the first president. He was sometimes disgusted by his ragged followers in just the way Moses was disgusted by the Hebrew slaves. "I have only an army of schnorrers," he wrote in his diary. "I am in command of youths, and beggars, and sensation mongers."

As the movement swelled, the Western press finally took notice. Herzl began appearing in the newspapers not as a flâneur, nor as the author of an obscure book, but as the leader of a revolution. It was only then that *The Jewish State* began to be discussed in Paris, London, New York. Herzl became a kind of king, in exile from a nation that did not yet exist. He paid official visits to heads of state as if he were himself a head of state. He met ministers and members of Parliament. At a rally in London in 1899, a priest introduced him as "a new Joshua come to fulfill the words of the Prophet Ezekiel."

Herzl's work of these years culminated in the First Zionist Congress, where his followers drew up the nation's founding documents. The congress was originally to take place in Munich, a city of broad avenues and Hitler, but the local Jews protested—they did not want their town overrun by this army of schnorrers. It was instead held in Basel, Switzerland, in August 1897. Men arrived by carriage and train, crowded the hotels and restaurants, argued, predicted. This was the pinnacle of Herzl's career. When he stood to give his speech, the crowd stood with him and cheered. "This was no longer the elegant Dr. Herzl of Vienna," wrote Alex Bein. "It was no longer the easy-going literary man, the critic, the feuilletonist. It was a scion of the House of David, risen from among the dead, clothed in legend and fantasy and beauty."

"If I had to sum up the First Zionist Congress in one word," Herzl said, "it would be this: at Basel I founded the Jewish state. If I were to say this today, I would be greeted by laughter. In five years, perhaps, and certainly in fifty, everyone will see it."

The men at the congress, most of them from towns in eastern Europe, had never been to Rome or Paris, let alone Palestine. To them, Palestine was a place in the Bible, a setting in a book, the background in a painting by Van Dyke. The term *Arab* hardly appears in early Zionist literature. If it does, it is in the way *cactus* or *oasis* appears in an Owen Wister novel, a bit of local color. Not because Zionists were evil, or filled with bad intent, but because they were unaware—lacked imagination, did not know. If a Zionist did visit Palestine, he was usually shocked. In his imagination, it had been barren and empty;* in reality it was full of life.

----

*The most famous expression of this sentiment is the phrase coined by Israel Zangwill: "A land without a people for a people without a land." In the early 1900s, Zangwill was the most popular playwright in Britain. In *The Jewish Encyclopedia* published in 1923, he gets a thousand more words than Herzl. He made his name with depictions of Jewish life in London's West End, particularly with the play *Children of the Ghetto*. He attended the meeting of the Maccabean Society where Herzl made his case—he thereafter converted to Zionism. (He died in 1926.) He first spoke his famous words in 1905, at a Zionist convention in New York. He had never been to Palestine, but that was not the point. The phrase was an advertising slogan meant to encourage Jews to go east. Ever since, it's been used to demonstrate the flaw of Zionism: for my dream to come true, it suggests, you cannot exist.

Herzl made his first trip to Palestine in the fall of 1898. It was a momentous journey—he had organized his entire life around a place he had never seen. He traveled with a delegation. They landed in Jaffa, the ancient town from which Jonah sailed for Tarshish. (Herzl is Jonah, vomited out of the belly of the fish.) Jaffa is built on a cliff. It's a maze of streets, arches, walls, vertiginous drops to the sea. Compared to a European town, it was primitive. Trash was piled in the streets. You could smell it from a long way off. Herzl sickened. He suffered culture shock, got the shakes, the sweats, could not eat. In other words, the old land, which he had long imagined, made him ill. He spent one week in the country, all of it in a fever. This was a side effect of Zionism, the nausea caused by going from the universal, which is a story in a book, to the particular, which is an alley in the Near East. "Jaffa makes a very unpleasant impression," he wrote. "Though nobly situated on the Mediterranean, the town is in a state of extreme decay. Landing is difficult in the forsaken harbor. The alleys are dirty, neglected, full of vile odors. Everywhere misery in bright oriental rags. Poor Turks, dirty Arabs, timid Jews—indolent, beggarly, hopeless. A peculiar, tomblike odor of mold caught one's breath."*

He traveled to Jerusalem by train, a narrow-gauge British railroad. He sat by the window looking at hills and towns. The train ran on a dry riverbed, its whistle echoing in the barren canyons. "The landscape is desolation," he wrote. "The lowlands are sand and swamp, the fields look burnt. The inhabitants of the blackish Arab villages look like brigands. Naked children play in dirty alleys. Over the distant horizon loom the deforested hills of Judea. The bare slopes and the bleak, rock valleys show few traces of present or former cultivation."

There were sixty thousand people living in Jerusalem, perhaps forty thousand of them Jews. Herzl entered on foot. He paused to look at the domes and towers gathered beneath the strange ethereal sky that is the city's best argument for God. He walked to the Western Wall. He touched the stones, said the prayers. The men with him burst

---

*Herzl's writings are quoted from his diaries and letters, as well as from his novel *Old New Land*, which borrows heavily from the diaries and letters.

into tears, but he was unmoved. No matter how hard he looked, he could not find the majestic capital in this dirty provincial town. "The once royal city could have sunk no lower," he wrote. "We walked down the noisome little lane that led to the Wailing Wall, and were revolted by the appearance of the praying beggars there."

He stayed in a small hotel. He could hear camels in the desert at night. He did not think Jerusalem should be the capital of the Jewish state. Jerusalem was the haunted past. Herzl wanted to a build a new nation populated by a new race of men.

I n May 1901 Herzl traveled to Constantinople to meet the sultan, Abdülhamīd II, who, with the stroke of a pen, could make the dream a reality. (In letters, Herzl referred to the sultan in code as "Mr. Cohn.") The sultan was a small man with a full dyed beard and a hooked nose. In my imagination I see him pass the hookah. Herzl breathes the smoke into his lungs. It pools behind his eyes. The walls fall away and he is above the city, looking down at streets and canals, at the palace, where, in a room filled with carpets, he recognizes himself sitting before the sultan, who does not give Herzl land for a state, but does give him a diamond scarf pin.*

H erzl was in a hurry. He said that refuge was needed before a disaster came. He hoped such refuge would be created by one of the colonial powers. He lobbied the political leaders, who, now and then, floated a vague proposal: settle the Jews in the Sinai, or in South Asia. On July 13, 1903, he submitted an official request to the British government. The response was written by Joseph Chamberlain, colonial secretary, who had just returned from a trip across the Empire. Chamberlain was the father of Neville Chamberlain and therefore the

*Abdülhamīd II later described Herzl as "regal, a prophet, a leader of his people."

grandfather of appeasement. "On my travels I saw a country for you," he told Herzl. "Uganda! On the coast it is hot, but in the interior the climate is excellent for Europeans. You can plant cotton and sugar. I thought to myself, that is the country for Dr. Herzl."

Uganda was a barren stretch of sub-Saharan Africa, as far away as you could get from Europe. It was jungle and beasts and painted men. It was a Union Jack planted on the moon. This proposal was apparently serious. Five thousand square miles on the Mau Plateau in what is now Kenya. Chamberlain said it would solve Herzl's problem and the problem of many Europeans, also called the "Jewish Problem." Herzl thought about it, said no, then went back and asked, Is Uganda still available? Pogroms had broken out in Russia. A safe harbor was needed before more people died. To Herzl, the location of the harbor was never paramount. This put him at odds with those who valued the land (because it was promised by God) more than anything else. To Herzl, the worship of the land was no different from the worship of the past. It was a kind of sacrilege. Palestine was out of reach for the immediate future, and to Herzl, the immediate future was what mattered.

He presented the Uganda Plan at the Sixth Zionist Congress in 1903. A temporary shelter, he explained. It would serve as forty years in the wilderness had served the ancient Hebrews. He suggested that the congress create a committee to visit Uganda and report. He called for a vote.* The room filled with jeers. When Herzl tried to talk, he was shouted down. For the rest of the week, whenever he appeared, he was booed. It aged him like Moses. His beard was flecked with gray, the luster went out of his eyes. He had seen his own corpse. After that, the masses never trusted him in the same way. The Uganda Plan, and speeches Herzl made to defend it, brought out something many had long suspected: that Herzl was not like them, did not understand them; that he was as much a German as he was a Jew.

---

*This vote, held later, was, in fact, carried by Herzl 295 to 178. A delegation was sent to Africa, and the land was inspected. It was on a plateau, and the climate was fine, but according to the delegation, it was filled with dangerous animals, mostly lions, as well as "not-very-welcoming Maasai warriors." The British proposal was rejected. A group of Zionists then formed the Jewish Territorialist Organization, which proposed to establish "a Jewish State where possible, not just Palestine."

Herzl tried to dismiss the episode as a misunderstanding, reiterating that he had never intended Uganda as a permanent home, only as a temporary shelter. But the more he talked, the clearer it became that the dispute was not superficial. There was a real split between the Jews of the East and the Jews of the West, and it runs through Israel to this day. To some, the land of Palestine is the point: because it is the only place a Jew can live an authentically Jewish life. To others, the land of Palestine might be the best place for a state—because of its historical resonance—but the point is not to live an authentically Jewish life, but to be free to live a normal life in which it does not matter that you are a Jew. In other words, some wanted a state so they could be Jews, some wanted a state so they could stop being Jews.

H erzl emerged from the Uganda episode disillusioned, melancholy. He wanted to win back the love of the people, yet resented the people he wanted to win back: how quickly they had turned! He decided to write a novel. He would show the masses what was in his mind. The book, which would occupy his final years, was visionary in the way of Thomas More on Utopia. It was called *Old New Land*.

If I worked in a bookstore, I would shelve it under Science Fiction/Fantasy, or Judaica, or Judaica/Science Fiction, or Political Theory, or Sports (much is said about the athletic trim of the future citizens of Israel). In it, Herzl follows several characters into the future, where they visit a thriving Jewish state. He does not describe the founding of this state, but instead skips directly from the present, the bleak reality of early twentieth-century Europe, to the fantastical future. Whatever you think of the book as fiction (not much), it's a fascinating document. I know of no other instance in which the founder of a nation depicted the life of that nation in the distant future; it's as if Thomas Jefferson had described a typical afternoon in America in 1973. Herzl's imagined state is nothing like modern Israel, of course. It's a vision, and visions were the point of his effort. He was a futurist. He believed that it was his role to imagine the world that others would build.

The novel follows Dr. Friedrich Lowenberg as he wanders through nighttime London, where Jews behave like whipped dogs. Lowenberg meets a poor boy named David, who dreams of Zion. Lowenberg shows the boy a kindness, then, disgusted by a civilization in which the Jew must be the Jew every time, he flees to the docks, where he meets a German misanthrope named Kingscourt, who plans to sail to the South Seas and pass his remaining years in peace. Lowenberg agrees to go on this trip, receiving, in return for his companionship, a life of leisure. En route the men stop in Haifa. Kingscourt suggests they tour the Holy Land, which he calls "the land of your forefathers."

"You are mistaken," says Lowenberg. "I have no connection with Palestine. It does not interest me. My ancestors left it eighteen hundred years ago. What should I seek there? I think that only anti-Semites can call Palestine our fatherland."

"I don't understand you Jews," says Kingscourt. "If I were a Jew, I should be mighty proud of that sort of thing. Yet you are ashamed of it. You needn't wonder why you are despised. Present company excluded, of course."

They visit the ancient towns of the Bible and the modern colonies that had been established for the poor Jews from the East. "Rishon-le-Zion, Rehobot, and other villages that lay like oases in the desolate countryside."

Lowenberg is moved by his first sight of Jerusalem: "He did not understand why this strange city affected him so powerfully. Was it a memory of words heard in early childhood? In passages of prayer murmured by his father? Memories of Seder-services long forgotten, or one of the few Hebrew phrases that still rang in his ears: 'Next year in Jerusalem!'"—but its reality dispirits him. "Shouting, odors, dirty colors, crowds of ragged people in narrow, musty lanes, beggars, sick people, hungry children, screeching women, shouting tradesman."

The travelers sail away to the Pacific Islands. Years go by. They grow bored. They sail back. When they reach the Suez Canal, they find it empty. A dockworker tells them that most ships now use the Red

Sea Canal, which the Jews have built on the southern border of their state. Their state? The men hurry on to Haifa, which they had last seen as a ruin. Lowenberg stands at the rail like Rip Van Winklestein. "How changed it all is!" he says. "There's been a miracle here."

> A magnificent city had been built beside the sapphire-blue Mediterranean. The magnificent stone dams showed the harbor for what it was: the safest and most convenient port in the Eastern Mediterranean. Craft of every shape and size, flying flags of all the nations, lay sheltered.*

Lowenberg and Kingscourt meet a Jewish man on shore. He is big, strong, healthy. This is the boy David, all grown up. He never forgot the kindness of Lowenberg, so has made that name great in the old new land. There is even a city named Friedrichsheim. (Herzl foreseeing Herzliya?) Lowenberg marvels at David's physique. "Yes," says David. "Jewish children used to be pale, weak, timid. Now look at them! The explanation of this miracle is the simplest in the world. We took our children out of damp cellars and hovels, and brought them into the sunlight. Plants cannot thrive without sun. No more can human beings. Plants can be saved by transplantation into congenial soil. Human beings as well. That is how it happened!"†

David takes the visitors on a tour of the country, in the course of which the reader sees the state as envisioned by Herzl. It is years beyond the obsolete nations of Europe, a fantasy of bullet trains and glass towers. "You are a damned shrewd nation," says Kingscourt. "Left us with the old scrap iron, while you travel about by the latest machines."

They visit Haifa, Tiberias, Jerusalem.

---

*This encapsulates the mission of Herzl, who was not out to invent something new but to uncover what he believed had always been there, but was long obscured by centuries of abuse, neglect, and decay.

†In the edition I have, published in 1959, this passage carries a footnote: "Israeli children are indeed, remarkably sturdy specimens with a great love of the out-of-doors and athletics."

"What's the wonderful structure of white and gold, whose roof rests on a forest of marble columns with gilt capitals?" asks Lowenberg.

"That's the Temple!"*

Jerusalem has been hosed off, deodorized. "The spell of the moon was over the city, freed from the filth, noise and vile odors that so often revolted pilgrims of all creeds when, after long and trying journeys, they reached their goal," writes Herzl. "In the old days, they had had to endure many disgusting sights before they could reach their shrines. All was different now."

At the end of the day, the men sit on a verandah over the Galilee talking about old Europe. "What a degraded era," says Lowenberg, "when Jews had been ashamed of everything Jewish, when they thought they made a better showing when they concealed their Jewishness, yet in that very concealment revealed the temper of the slave."

David introduces the travelers to an Arab named Rechid Bey and it's through this character that Herzl describes the life of Arabs in the Jewish state. (Herzl creates an Arab puppet, in other words, then uses this puppet to bless Zionism.) We are told that Bey grew up poor but now lives in splendor, in an Arab neighborhood "on Mount Carmel, where there are many elegant mansions surrounded by fragrant gardens."

Kingscourt asks if the creation of the state has harmed the Arab population.

"What a question!" says Bey. "It was a great blessing for us. Naturally, the land owners gained most because they were able to sell to the Jewish society at high prices, or to wait for high ones. Those who had nothing stood to lose nothing, and could only gain. And they did gain: opportunities to work, means of livelihood, prosperity. Nothing could have been more wretched than an Arab village at the end of the nineteenth century. The peasants' clay hovels were unfit for stables. The children lay naked and neglected in the streets and grew up like dumb beasts. Now everything is different. They benefited from the progressive measures of the New Society whether they wanted to or not. When the swamps were drained, the canals built, and the eucalyptus

---

*No mention is made of the Al Aqsa Mosque, or of what happened to the Dome of the Rock.

trees planted to drain and 'cure' the marshy soil, the natives (who, naturally, were all acclimatized) were the first to be employed, and were paid well for their work."

Herzl looked at the world as a modern European: that is, as a materialist, as if there were nothing but property, whereas the never-ending lure of Jerusalem, which, for many Jews, is at the center of Zionism, suggests there is indeed something beyond the material.

"Don't you consider the Jews intruders?" asks Kingscourt.

"You speak strangely, Christian," says Bey. "Would you call a man a robber who takes nothing from you, but brings you something instead? The Jews have enriched us. Why should we be angry with them? They dwell among us like brothers. Why should we not love them?"

Old New Land was published in April 1902.* Herzl envisioned it as a popular novel that would reach far more people than could ever be reached with a treatise like *The Jewish State*. He gave a copy to Nathan Rothschild with the inscription "Dear Baron, I send my latest, knowing well you will again accuse me of being a dreamer of dreams." For Herzl, the book's publication was traumatic: this was the last great event of his life. He had been attacked and denounced. He hoped *Old New Land* would bring back his followers. On the last page, he wrote a message to the book itself: "Now, dear Book, after three years of labor, we must part. And your sufferings will begin. You will have to make your way through enmity and misrepresentation as through a dark forest."

The book did not become the mainstream success Herzl had hoped. It was, however, a sensation among Zionists. It was reviewed in every variety of Jewish newspaper. Students carried it in their bags, dog-eared and underlined. They quoted from it, debated it, denounced it. Herzl thought people would read his book and see what he saw and love him; the book instead confirmed what people already believed: that Herzl was not like them. You think, well, if I can just explain myself, people will understand, and not be angry, but the more you explain, the angrier they get, not because they don't understand—but because they do.

---

*The cover of my copy (1941) shows Jaffa, with the sea breaking on its cliffs, side by side with the Bauhaus buildings of modern Tel Aviv.

To detractors, it seemed there was nothing particularly Jewish about Herzl's futuristic state. Its citizens happened to have Jewish mothers, that's all. In fact, Herzl seemed less concerned with the Jewish state than with what Europeans would think of such a state; less concerned with the Jews than with the Jew haters. He wanted to settle his people in Palestine less than he wanted to unsettle them from Europe—get them out of the bourgeois struggle for food and jobs and money that, according to Herzl, was the real cause of anti-Semitism. (He said Jews were hated because they were competition.) In his writing, there is little sense of the landscape of Israel, its beauty or geology, its historical importance or its mystical power. To him, it was just a means, the place where the Jew would shed his ghetto nature. Ahad Ha-am, a Zionist thinker from Russia,* called Herzl's state an abomination. It has no Jewish soul, he said. All that remains of the ancient covenant are a precious few cultural artifacts.

I ask you, friend, what is a corned beef on rye without Torah?

Old New Land was not a good book when it was published, and it is not good now, yet time has given it a patina that sadly hints at what might have been. It shows Israel as Herzl dreamed it, so you cannot help but compare the dream to the nation in the newspaper, where the jets fly fast and low and the Black Hawk helicopters go *whump, whump, whump* as they drift over the sea. I think of the book whenever I drive through the Jezreel Valley, which was a sleepy Bedouin nowhere before the last century found it.

Here's the valley as envisioned (in the future) by Herzl:

> There was less traffic here than in town, but numerous bicycles and motor cars speeded past, and horseback riders appeared and disappeared on the soft bridle path which ran parallel with the road. Some of the riders wore picturesque Arab costume and others conventional European clothing. Occasionally, too, camels filed past, singly and in cavalcades, picturesque and primitive relics of an obsolete era. The

---

*A Russian-born Zionist, his real name was Asher Ginsberg. He argued against a political state for the Jews, instead favoring a spiritual center in Palestine. He was one of Herzl's fiercest Jewish critics.

car rolled along comfortably on the smooth roadway, to the left and to the right they saw small houses with garden plots, and behind them well-cultivated fields that were freshly green.

Here's the Jezreel Valley today: on the left are Jewish towns, red-roofed houses backed by fields, not unlike those imagined by Herzl, but on the right is the fence that the Israelis built to keep out suicide bombers, or grab land, or both, or neither—I can't hear myself think over the constant bickering and the exploding of bombs. In places the wall is made of chain link; in places it's made of concrete slabs. It reminds me of the wall along the Long Island Expressway that shelters suburban towns from the dirt and noise of passing traffic. It reminds me of a blast wall, of a siege wall, of a ghetto fence. Behind it, Rechid Bey is smoldering in his forsaken town.

Ariel Sharon, the prime minister of Israel at the time of the fence's construction, explained it by quoting the Robert Frost poem "Mending Wall": "Good fences make good neighbors." None of the journalists covering the speech looked up the poem, which is a shame, because, read with the fence in mind, it's filled with revealing, unintended meanings. For example, the poem is not written in the voice of the man who says "Good fences make good neighbors," but in the voice of the stranger beyond the wall, who seems to mock the fence builder:

> *There where it is we do not need the wall:*
> *He is all pine and I am apple orchard.*
> *My apple trees will never get across*
> *And eat the cones under his pines, I tell him.*
> *He only says, "Good fences make good neighbors."*
> *Spring is the mischief in me, and I wonder*
> *If I could put a notion in his head:*
> *"Why do they make good neighbors? Isn't it*
> *Where there are cows?*
> *But here there are no cows.*
> *Before I built a wall I'd ask to know*
> *What I was walling in or walling out,*

And to whom I was like to give offence.
Something there is that doesn't love a wall,
That wants it down." I could say "Elves" to him,
But it's not elves exactly, and I'd rather
He said it for himself.

When the neighbor enters the frame—and this is Ariel Sharon, or the part in which Sharon has cast himself—he is a brute, unknowing, uninterested in knowing.

I see him there
Bringing a stone grasped firmly by the top
In each hand, like an old-stone savage armed.
He moves in darkness as it seems to me—
Not of woods only and the shade of trees.
He will not go behind his father's saying,
And he likes having thought of it so well
He says again, "Good fences make good neighbors."

Herzl fell out of favor in his final days. He had torn open his chest and shown the world his craven, accommodating heart. He was living in Austria, in the foothills of big mountains. The years of argument and travel had weakened him. He spoke too long, took everything too hard. He died on July 3, 1904. He was forty-four years old. Most prophets die young. The power of the message is too strong, the filament cannot hold the charge. They flash. You see the coil glow orange. Then: *pffft!* Gone. Though Herzl did not say anything especially new, nor say it especially well, he was the man whom all the others followed. His story exemplifies Eastern wisdom, which is the opposite of the romantic truth: "It's not the singer, it's the song." With Herzl, it was only the song. It did not matter who was singing it, only that it was sung.

His funeral was in a shul in Austria. Thousands of people stood in the street weeping. He was forgiven at the moment of his death. In his will, he asked "to be buried in the vault beside my father, and to lie there

till the Jewish people take my remains to Palestine." His coffin was dis-
interred in 1949, flown to Tel Aviv, and reburied on Mount Herzl.

Young Zionists traveled in schools, men sharking along in bad suits,
turning, all at once, in a pivot, swimming city to town to country.
They had green eyes, or yellow eyes, or brown eyes, or their eyes were
so blue they were black, and their noses were hooked, or broken, or
turned up, and their hair was brown, or red, or blond, that Yiddish
kind of blond, and was curly, or as fine as string. They were forever
planning to head to Palestine, but never going because there was still
so much to do. Before the First World War, they were all in their twenties and named Teitlebaum and Green. Later, they were in their thirties and had changed their names to Ben-Gurion and Shahak. This
was the generation that came after Herzl, when Zionism boomed.
These men did the hardest work, left behind the world of their fathers,
crossed over into a new life.

Most came from towns in Eastern Europe, were idealists and fan-
tasists. They wanted to build a new Jew, who would look a lot like the
stereotype of the Gentile: big, square-jawed, quiet; not so clever, so not
so talky. They would, in other words, rid the world of people like
themselves. At the Second Zionist Congress, Max Nordau spoke of
creating a "physical ideal." By the Fifth Congress, this notion had
been fleshed out and given a (ridiculous) name: "muscle Jewry." According to the critics, the real aim of men such as Max Nordau was to
cleanse the Jew of the very uniqueness that made him Jewish. The
same goal as the Nazis: a world without Jews. When the tenets of this
faith were explained to the philosopher Hermann Cohen, he said,
"Oho! So the gang wants to be happy, does it?"

These men were converted not by rational persuasion but by holy
epiphany. Most had been nationalists of, say, Russia who experienced
some trauma, witnessed some brutality, that made them realize there
was no place for Jews in the nations of their birth. Like Calvinists,

each had a story of conversion. (For Herzl, it was the Dreyfus Affair.) The story of that generation is maybe best told in the person of Vladimir "Zev" Jabotinsky, who grew up in Russia and went on to found the movement that would become the political right wing in Israel. Jabotinsky is the spiritual father of every Israeli hawk.

He was born in 1880, in Odessa, Russia, a summer resort on the Black Sea. I cannot think of it without thinking of Isaac Babel's descriptions of the city, its waterfront dives and Jewish gangsters. "The sun hung from the sky like the pink tongue of a thirsty dog, the gigantic sea rolled on to Peresyp, and the masts of far-off ships rocked on the emerald water of Odessa Bay." I mention Isaac Babel in part because I love him, in part because his life plays counterpoint to the life of Zev Jabotinsky.

Jabotinsky grew up in the same town as Babel, in the same kind of family, in the same class. He, too, dreamed of being a famous writer, a successor to Pushkin and Gogol. He sold his first story when he was sixteen, to a local newspaper. He was gifted; everyone said so. His eyes were dark, his hair swept back, his words quick and elegant. After high school, he was sent to Switzerland, then to Rome to continue his studies. He is just the sort of man Isaac Babel had in mind when he described the Jewish writer as one with "autumn in his heart and glasses on his nose."

Jabotinsky published novels in the late 1800s, some of which are still read. He established himself as a rising star on the Russian literary scene. He was twenty-three in 1903, the year of the pogroms. Riots broke out in Odessa that summer and again in the spring. Babel, who was nine years old, later wrote about them in his story "The Story of My Dovecot": "Somewhere far off rode disaster on a lame and lively horse, but the sound of its hooves grew faint, died, and silence, the bitter silence that sometimes afflicts children in misfortune, suddenly annihilated the boundary between my trembling body and the earth that was moving nowhere."

Babel became a Communist. He wanted to make a new world in which being a Jew ceased to have meaning. He rode with a Cossack regiment in the Civil War and filed dispatches for *Pravda*, an experience he later turned into his masterpiece *Red Cavalry Stories*. He fell afoul of Stalin, was arrested, tortured, executed. (The last photograph of him shows him without his glasses, bruised and defeated.) He set out to be the voice of a universal nation but ended up right back in 1903 Odessa. Jabotinsky went the other way, quitting literary life, giving up fiction. He decided he never could be a great Russian writer, because Russia did not want him; even the liberals said a Jew could not be the voice of the people, as a Jew could never be an authentic Russian. If he was going to be a Jew, he decided, he wanted to be a Jew in a nation where Jews controlled the guns. That's what experience taught him. He attended the Zionist Congress in Basel in 1906, soon after the pogroms. He turned all his energy and skill to the new cause.* He became an advocate, one of the school, sharking along with the rest.

Jabotinsky settled in Palestine early in the twentieth century. He edited a daily newspaper and went into politics. For a time, he served on councils and boards set up by Herzl, but quit because he found the members of these committees weak and accommodating. Too often they wanted to be liked, said Jabotinsky, whose own experience told him it was better to be feared. He formed a party to counterbalance mainstream Zionism, which was left wing and composed of socialists. He called his party the Revisionists. It would become Israel's right wing. Menachem Begin, Ariel Sharon, Benjamin Netanyahu, all come to us via Zev Jabotinsky.

He was the first successful politician to speak of establishing Jewish sovereignty on both sides of the Jordan River. (This makes Jabotinsky the great-grandfather of the settler movement.) He formed a Zionist version of the Boy Scouts, in which young Jews were trained as pioneers. He dressed them in brown shirts, which, he said, represented the land of Israel. On parade, the boys chanted the phrase "Conquer or die!" He pushed them toward a physical ideal, expressed by the word *hadar*, which means dignity, beauty, self-respect. He was, in short, the boy who has seen his father beaten by a mob.

Chaim Weizmann:

*Maxim Gorky called Jabotinsky's Zionism a great loss to Russian literature.

Jabotinsky, the passionate Zionist, was utterly un-Jewish in manner, approach and deportment. He came from Odessa, Ahad Ha-Am's home town, but the inner life of Jewry left no trace on him. When I became intimate with him in later years, I observed at closer hand what seemed to be a confirmation of this dual streak; he was immensely attractive, well spoken, warm-hearted, generous, always ready to help a comrade in distress; all of those qualities overlaid with a certain touch of the rather theatrically chivalresque, a certain queer irrelevant knightliness, which was not at all Jewish.

Jabotinsky said he understood the Arab grievance—being crowded out by foreigners—but believed that the Jewish claim on Palestine was simply more compelling.

He said, "The Arabs are safe everywhere, the Jews are safe nowhere."

He said, "The Arabs have many lands, the Jews have none."

He said, "A drowning man does not ask permission to survive."

"One fraction, one branch of [the Arab] race, and not a big one, will have to live in someone else's state," wrote Jabotinsky. "That's the case with the mightiest nations in the world. I could hardly mention one of the big nations, having their states, mighty and powerful, who had not had one branch in someone else's state . . . it's quite understandable that the Arabs of Palestine would also prefer Palestine to be Arab state No. 4, No. 5, or No. 6 . . . But when the Arab claim is confronted with our Jewish demand to be saved, it's like the claims of appetite versus the claim of starvation."

In 1920, in the wake of anti-Jewish riots that swept across Palestine, Jabotinsky wrote an essay called "On the Iron Wall (We and the Arabs)." In it, he says that the Arabs will never willingly accept a Jewish state. "Every indigenous people will resist alien settlers as long as they see any hope of ridding themselves of the danger of foreign settlement," he explains. "This is how the Arabs will behave so long as they possess a gleam of hope they can prevent 'Palestine' from becoming the Land of Israel."

If the Jews are to survive in Palestine, he writes, the Arabs must be made to believe the Jews will not leave, that the Arabs cannot win. To accomplish this, he said, the Jews must build "an iron wall," a phrase that has haunted Israeli politics ever since.* Only after the Arabs have banged up against this wall for a generation or more—this is what you see happening at checkpoints in the West Bank—will they accept Jewish sovereignty. (Which is the policy of Israel to this day: the air force is the iron wall; the nuclear bomb is the iron wall; the iron wall is the iron wall.)† "The sole way to agreement is through the iron wall, that is to say, the establishment in Palestine of a force that will in no way be influenced by Arab pressure," writes Jabotinsky. "In other words, the only way to achieve a settlement in the future is the total avoidance of all attempts to arrive at a settlement in the present."

H istory is an argument recounted as a story. (This is what people mean when they say it's written by the winners.) In textbooks you might hear a raised voice, but rarely the voice that voice is raised to. It's like watching just one of the boxers in a fight, or seeing a film in which the challenger has been Photoshopped out of existence. Of course, the remaining fighter looks insane. Why is he dancing, you wonder; why is he sweating and throwing haymakers? This explains the stridency of the early Zionists—when you hear Jabotinsky ranting about the iron wall you are hearing a man in the middle of a fight. What you are not hearing are the men he is fighting with, the anti-Zionists, who were not anti-Semites, or racists, or Arabs, or goyim, but Jews who saw in Jewish nationalism a disaster for their people. Middle-aged men, mostly, public officials, rabbis, the filthy rich—all those with

---

*In response to criticism of this article, Jabotinsky wrote "The Morality of the Iron Wall," in which he makes the case for the nation at war: "A sacred truth, whose realization requires the use of force, does not cease thereby to be a sacred truth."

†With construction of Israel's security fence, something amazing happened: the metaphor of a literary artist was made real. They actually built the thing.

a stake in the system. Who wore fur hats. Who owned horses and had country houses. Who avoided rooms where people gave their candid opinions. These men resented the Zionists because the Zionists wanted to trade the many identities of the modern European man who happened to be born Jewish for just the one: the Jew.

Together they were a chorus, a cacophony of naysayers united only by their opposition to Zionism:

There were the Orthodox rabbis who said only God can anoint the Messiah and only the Messiah can return the people to Palestine. They accused the Zionists of forcing the hand of God, thus subverting the divine plan.

There were the Reform Jews of, say, England, who said they were British before they were Jewish, and so looked on the creation of a Jewish state as a threat to their identity: they feared such a state would lead to charges of dual loyalty. In 1917 Claude Montefiore and David Alexander, the leaders of the Anglo-Jewish Association, co-wrote an article in *The Times* of London* in which they said Zionism, meant to make the Jews at home in the world, would instead mark them everywhere as "strangers and foreigners."†

There were the Jewish progressives who saw in Zionism a step backward, a retreat into clannish parochialism. Moritz Güdemann, the chief rabbi of Vienna, said Zionism would tie the Jews to the particular, making specific what had survived only because it was universal. He called it "a spiritual regression."

In 1910 the American Council for Judaism released the following statement:

> We oppose the effort to establish a national Jewish state in Palestine or anywhere else as a philosophy of defeatism . . . we dissent from all these related doctrines that stress the racialism, the national and the theoretical homelessness of the Jews. We oppose such doctrines as in-

---

*"Palestine and Zionism: Views of Anglo-Jewry."

†Here's what Chaim Weizmann wrote about the English journalist Lucien Wolf who was opposed to Zionism: "He found it impossible to understand that English non-Jews did not look upon his anti-Zionism as the hallmark of a superior loyalty."

imical to the welfare of Jews in Palestine, in America, wherever Jews
may dwell.

Why trade a universal vision for a piece of land? To many, the idea
seemed un-Jewish. Here's Albert Einstein in a letter written before the
Holocaust:

> My awareness of the essential nature of Judaism resists the idea of a
> Jewish state with borders, an army, and a measure of temporal power
> no matter how modest. I am afraid of the inner damage Judaism will
> sustain—especially from the development of a narrow isolationism
> within our own ranks, against which we have already had to fight
> strongly, even without a Jewish state. A return to a nation in a polecat
> sense would be equivalent to turning away from the spiritualization of
> our community which we owe to the genius of our prophets.

There were the Jewish bankers and industrialists, the Rothschilds,
the Warburgs, the Frankfurters, who heard in Zionism a call to overturn the existing order, so saw no play in it, as, for them, the existing
order worked.

There were the American Jews, many of whom resented this
wordy search for Zion, as they believed they had already found it—in
the United States. In 1904 the congregants of Sherith Israel, in San
Francisco, California, installed a stained-glass window that showed
Moses descending with the tablets from the snowy heights of El Ca-
pitan, the peak of the Sierra Madre. When you have a last shot like that,
right out of a John Ford movie, why keep asking for another ending?

There were the Arabs living in Palestine, who saw in the coming of
the Zionists a conspiracy and a nightmare, a development so improb-
able it was almost impossible to believe, even while it was happening.
Depending on your point of view, the Zionists were either like the
American settlers who pushed out the Plains Indians, or like a tribe of
Iroquois who suddenly started building settlements in Westchester,
driving families out of Scarsdale and Armonk in an effort to reclaim
their ancient nation. When the Arabs responded, it was almost always

via ambush and militia, in ways that hardened the Zionists, and strengthened those who argued the most extreme position: that there could be no compromise; it's us or them.

There was Judah Magnes, the founder and first president of The Hebrew University, who said military might corrupted even worse than money. The idea of a Jewish army sickened him. He urged Zionists to give up their "love of force" and become holy pacifists. Later, when the British promised to create a homeland for the Jews, Magnes said, "The British have no right to give anything to anyone." Magnes spoke against the state in front of the United Nations. (Ben-Gurion called him a naïve child.) Yes, a Jewish state is a lovely idea, Magnes said, but is it worth the price? The ways in which the people will be warped by power, and the Jewish soul, which is the soul of the holy wanderer, will give way to a stunted steely warrior soul.

There was Asher Ginsberg, who wrote under the pseudonym Ahad Ha-am—it means "one of the people"— who believed in returning to Palestine before Zionism and saw in the rise of Theodor Herzl a disaster for that cause. Ha-am opposed *The Jewish State* with an essay entitled "The Wrong Way," in which he called the very notion of worldly Jewish power an abomination. He was more interested in faith for the Jews than in a state for the Jews. He moved to Tel Aviv in 1922, and was surprised by what he found. "From abroad, we are accustomed to believe Eretz Israel is almost totally desolate, an uncultivated desert, that anyone wishing to buy land there can come and buy all he wants," he wrote, "but in truth, it's not so. In the entire country, it's hard to find tillable land that is not already tilled." He argued for a binational state in which Jews and Arabs would share power; a popular notion in some Jewish circles—more popular when the state seemed an impossible dream, less when it came within reach. (The idea was repeatedly rejected by the Arabs, making the argument moot.)

Ha-am agreed with the Zionists about one thing: the state would create a new kind of Jew, only to him this sounded less like a promise than a curse. He was disgusted by the young Jews he met in Palestine. "They were slaves in the land of exile," he wrote, "and they suddenly find themselves with unlimited freedom, the kind of wild freedom to be found only in a country like Turkey. This sudden change has engendered in them an impulse to despotism, as always happens when 'a slave becomes a king,' and behold, they talk with the Arabs in hostility and cruelty, unjustly encroaching on them, shamefully beating them for no reason, and even bragging about what they do."

There was Martin Buber, who considered the Zionists simple-minded men who had missed the point, who started with a faulty premise and went from there. The Exile cannot be ended by migration, he said. Because the Exile is not physical, it's spiritual. The Diaspora is merely a symbol of a metaphysical condition. If you return the Jews to Palestine, you destroy the symbol, but the condition remains. In their effort to end the Exile, the Zionists will therefore make the people forget that they are in exile—they will be lost forever. "Of all the kinds of assimilation in the course of our history, this is the most terrifying, the most dangerous, this national assimilation," Buber wrote in *On Zion*. "That which we lose on account of this state we shall perhaps never acquire again."

NINE

The Night Squads

The first Zionist settlement had been established in Palestine in 1882, more than a decade before Herzl's first trip there. It was the punk corpuscle that heralds the disease, the lonely pimple that portends the general outbreak, the tiny bud that suggests the sea of wildflowers. Pick your metaphor. It was called Rishon Le-Zion and was about sixty miles south of Haifa. It's since been subsumed in greater Tel Aviv, but you can pick out its buildings by their white walls and red roofs. Despite the name—Rishon Le-Zion means "first to Zion"—its occupants were not Zionists. They did not want to form a state, fight in an army, win a war. They were Russian Jews who wanted to get their fingers in the soil. They were like hippies. Their vision was entirely personal.

There had always been Jews in Palestine, of course, the community that survived the destruction of the Second Temple and the Expulsion by Rome. They were massacred when the Romans became Christian, and again when the Arabs became Muslim. They were killed by the Crusaders and by the armies that defeated the Crusaders. Their numbers were thinned by migration and conversion, but a remnant re-mained. They had a protected place under Muslim rule as a "People of the Book," an example of other, earlier creation, like the horseshoe crab. By the mid-nineteenth century, when the Ottoman Empire be-gan its slow decline, thirty thousand Jews were living in Palestine, mostly in the Jewish Quarter of Jerusalem. There were smaller com-munities in Haifa and Tiberias. Sfad, perched on its hill, its head full of visions, remained the capital of Jewish mysticism.

When European Jews first emigrated to Palestine, they found a hodgepodge: Sephardic Jews living alongside Arabs, Greeks, and Turks; pilgrims coming and going from every Christian nation; colonies of Russians, Germans, Brits, the most devout of them living in monasteries in the sandstone cliffs. For a strange, romantic moment, different cultures, different historical eras—the West was riding a wave of innovation, was awash in machinery; the East had faded, was rot-ting—seemed to exist side by side.

T. E. Lawrence, *Seven Pillars of Wisdom*:

> The sword had been the virtue of the children of Othman, and swords had passed out of fashion nowadays, in favour of deadlier, more scientific weapons. Life was growing too complicated for this childlike people, whose strength had lain in simplicity, and patience, and in their capacity for sacrifice. They were the slowest of the races of Western Asia, little fitted to adapt to new sciences of government and life, still less to invent any new arts for themselves.*

The first Zionist settlers called themselves "Lovers of Zion." They were ideologues, wild-eyed, touched in the head. You had to be. Think of it, traveling from the cold cities of Russia, with their brooding skies and rivers frozen mid-current, to this wide-open nowhere. They left behind families and towns, sweethearts and vistas. The first group comprised students from Kharkov. They traveled to Odessa in 1881,

---

*I like this quote because it tells more than it intends to—about what the British were like and what the Arabs were faced with.

crossed the Black Sea to Constantinople, then got a ship for Jaffa. Of three hundred who signed up for the trip, only fifteen made it all the way. The rest got distracted. Met a girl—gone. Were moved by a line of poetry—gone. As I said, they were less interested in a political state than in the state of their own lost souls. They longed, needed, chased, craved. They did not want to live as their parents had lived. They were Russian intellectuals. They worshipped Tolstoy and believed, like Tolstoy, that a man could find salvation in physical labor. For them, the peasant, in touch with the soil, was the only holy figure of the age. They wanted to be peasants, but because they were Jews, they could not be,* so decided to go to the place where Jews had been peasants once, long ago: Palestine, where they would get their hands in the dirt and be reborn. Their quest for an authentic life grew in response to industrialization. The more monstrous the cities became, the more these Jews craved a simple existence. They built their ideology around a few paragraphs from *Anna Karenina*.†

I n the late nineteenth century, hundreds of thousands of Jews left Russia. Most went to America; others went to Germany, France, England. A few—three or four thousand, no more—went to Palestine.

---

*Since the Middle Ages, Jews had not been allowed to own land anywhere in eastern Europe.

†"[Levin] thought of nothing, desired nothing, except not to lag behind and to do the best job he could. He heard only the clang of scythes and ahead of him saw Titus's erect figure moving on, the curved semicircle of the mowed space, grass and flower-heads bending down slowly and wavily about the blade of his scythe, and ahead of him the end of the swath, where rest would come.

"Not understanding what it was or where it came from, in the midst of his work he suddenly felt a pleasant sensation of coolness on his hot, sweaty shoulders. He glanced at the sky while his blade was being whetted. A low, heavy cloud had come over it, and big drops of rain were falling. Some muzhiks went for their caftans and put them on; others, just like Levin, merely shrugged their shoulders joyfully under the pleasant freshness.

"They finished another swath and another. They went through long swaths, short swaths, with bad grass, with good grass. Levin lost all awareness of time and had no idea whether it was late or early. A change now began to take place in his work which gave him enormous pleasure. In the midst of his work moments came to him when he forgot what he was doing and began to feel light, and in those moments his swath came out as even and good as Titus's. But as soon as he remembered what he was doing and started trying to do better, he at once felt how hard the work was and the swath came out badly." (Translated by Richard Pevear, Larissa Volokhonsky, Penguin Classics.)

Given the choice between New York or Jerusalem, money or ideology, only the crazies chose ideology. Grandpa Morris came to the Lower East Side because he had a family. Uncle Hymie went to Rehovot because he was out of his mind. That's the back story of Israel.

That early wave came to be known as the First Aliyah, a term taken from the Hebrew word for "going up," which in ancient times was used to describe the climb a pilgrim made to the Temple Mount. They built the first settlements, some of which grew into cities: Petach Tikva (1878), Rehovot (1890), Hadera (1891), Metulla (1896). Few members of the First Aliyah stayed in Palestine, however. They were stunned by how hard the life was. Palestine was primitive in a way that shocked even the most determined Tolstoyans. This was a world of tribe and blood and veil and no toilets or running water. Jews usually purchased land from absentee owners, rich men living in Cairo or Constantinople, who sold vast parcels with the happy glee of a sharpie unloading Florida swamp. The land was sandy, dry, next to impossible to cultivate. The first spring went by with no crop, followed by an autumn with no harvest.

This is from the diary of an early Jewish settler:

[The land is] infested with malaria and typhus, and is a quagmire of mud in the winter. It has to be drained by cutting canals, while the men working on the reclamation shake with fever.

Within a few years, the majority of the early settlers were gone. Some got malaria and died, some got dysentery and died, some recovered, then left, back to Europe, or on to the United States. Most of the settlements went broke. A few were bailed out by rich European Jews, including Edmond de Rothschild, who gave millions, then used the occasion to plant the family's first vineyard on Mount Carmel. A few survived, but only by hiring Arabs to work the fields, which, of course, defeated the whole point—to redeem the land, to become peasants. Had Jews traveled all this way just to be landlords? By 1900 most of the original settlements had been abandoned, overgrown by skunk grass and wild grape. Little evidence of the First Aliyah remained.

The few Russians who persisted did so by sheer will. The land needs me, that's what they told themselves. It has fallen like the people have fallen, because the people have fallen. But if I can redeem the land, and bring it to harvest, it will redeem all of us. No matter what else you might think of the greater project, you have to admit this is a sort of beautiful idea.

The Second Aliyah came more than a decade later, largely in response to the call made by Herzl. Its members were different from members of the First Aliyah: harder, cooler, less emotional, the little brother come to finish what the big brother had started. They were singleminded to the point of mania. They could see no side but their own. As Jabotinsky told the Arabs: You are right, but we are more right. Many carried dog-eared copies of *What Is to Be Done?* by Nikolai Chernyshevsky, which tells the story of a group of Russian noblemen who quit their position and property for a life on the land. "The pioneers of 1905 were the strangest workers the world had ever seen," Walter Laqueur wrote. "Manual labor for them was not a necessary evil but an absolute moral value, a remedy to cure the Jewish people of its social and national ills." David Ben-Gurion and Golda Meir were members of the Second Aliyah.

You don't need to know everything about them, just that they were radical and tough—and all had the same idea at the same time. They built the kibbutzim, invented the mechanics of settlement, houses thrown up at night, walls built, fields planted. Here's how it worked: a group of Zionists from a city such as Bielsk or Kiev purchase a piece of land from an Arab aristocrat living in, say, Baghdad. A Jewish scout travels to Palestine, surveys the fields, draws a map and a plan. The other Zionists meet in Rehovot or Metulla or wherever, select a crop, buy saplings or seeds, load the trucks. An advance team sets off at sundown, rolling onto the land at night, checking it against the map, dividing tasks, laying out stakes, setting up huts and fences, working fast, so that, in the morning, when the Bedouin shepherd crests the hill, the settlement will seem like an established fact, as if it's always been there.

The first kibbutz was called Deganiah. It was founded in 1909 by

Russian Jews, two men and a woman. (Imagine the life of that woman!) The land, purchased by the Jewish National Fund, hugged the shore of the Galilee. From a distance, it must have looked like a painting by Mark Rothko: a green field beside a shimmering sea. The first settlers grew wheat. They worked till their bodies ached, pounding out the sin of their fraudulent old lives. Nothing was simply done; it was thought about, then done. Deganiah was a hothouse of ideology. The inhabitants considered themselves people of substance yet were consumed with the image of the Jew—that is, with what people thought. They looked at their Arab neighbors with a kind of longing, envied their freedom, how easily they seemed to live in their bodies and dwell on their land. Some Zionists wore Arab headdresses in the fields and grew the sort of pencil-thin mustaches favored by the Arab noblemen. These Jews were wannabes, or wanna-not-bes. They did not want to be Jews as Jews had been viewed in Europe. The Arabs called them *Moskub*, "Russians."*

Deganiah was a breeding ground for great figures of the Zionist movement. A. D. Gordon moved there in 1919, close to fifty by then, but still working in the fields every day. At night, he sat in his cottage writing essays. In photos, he looks like the old Tolstoy: his piercing blue eyes have seen through every artifice. He was raised an Orthodox Jew in Russia, spoke of sin and redemption, but had long since lost his faith. He did not believe in God. He believed in action and human will. "The Jewish people have been cut off from nature and imprisoned within city walls for two thousand years," he wrote. "We have been accustomed to every form of life, except a life of labor—of labor done on our behalf and for its own sake. It will require the greatest effort of will for such a people to become normal again."

His essays were saturated with Jewish history. Everything was in them: the flood, the covenant, the promise, the curse. Each was a big picture made of many other pictures. In this one, Jerusalem is in flames. In that one, Sabbatai Zevi bows before the Sultan. In this one,

*Yuri Slezkine describing Zionists at work in Palestine: "Russian shirts, Russian boots, peasants' caps . . . the flowing Cossack forelock was one of [their] most recognizable features . . . they sang Russian folk songs and talked about Russian literature."

Theodor Herzl waves from a balcony. In that one, A. D. Gordon works in the wheat. To Gordon, the body and soul were connected by a tether. Only when the body was exhausted could the soul transcend. "We are engaged in a creative endeavor the like of which is not to be found in the whole history of mankind," he wrote. "The rebirth and rehabilitation of a people that has been uprooted and scattered to the winds."

D eganiah was the birthplace of Moshe Dayan, perhaps the greatest military figure in modern Israeli history. Dayan was, in fact, the second child born on the kibbutz. In other words, for one moment, in the fall of 1919, A. D. Gordon was the oldest person in Deganiah, Moshe Dayan was the youngest—this should give you a sense of the intensity of life in those settlements. Dayan's parents came directly from Russia. For young Russian Jews, moving to Palestine was often a way less to a new life than to escape the routine of a tired old one. On the kibbutz, even the familiar took on fresh meaning, became portentous, ecstatic. The trip to the store, the cigarette at sundown, the schnapps in the evening chill—these actions became notable, important snapshots of the revolution. In this way, the quotidian stayed quotidian yet also became heroic. The old man in the fields, scythe raised high, was still an old man in the fields but was also a symbol of the Jew reclaiming his land.

Dayan's mother had a long, complicated childbirth, in the middle of which a family friend named Moshe was sent out to find a doctor. This was late at night. Hours went by, the baby was born, and still the man did not return. At dawn, his horse wandered into the kibbutz alone, the riderless steed being everywhere an omen of a world without leaders. They found his body in the wheat. He had been killed by a militant gang of Arabs known as the Bearded Sheiks. Dayan was named after this man, the image of the bloodthirsty Arab having a place in his imagination from the beginning.

Dayan later described his childhood on the kibbutz as idyllic—

swimming the breadth of the Galilee, leaving his clothes on the distant shore, hiking into the hills. He wandered through Judea using the Bible as a guide and camped above the Dead Sea, dazzled by the nearness of the stars. He went everywhere in his life, and experienced every kind of victory and defeat, but the spirit of Deganiah never left him. It's what made him great. To Dayan, each setback was a challenge. It was good to be tested, he said, an honor to be hated, an opportunity to be attacked.

Here is a eulogy he gave in the 1950s for an Israeli soldier killed in battle:

> And so let us make our reckoning today. We are a generation of settlers, and without the steel helmet and the gun barrel, we shall not be able to plant a tree or build a house. Let us not be afraid to see the hatred that accompanies and consumes the lives of hundreds of thousands of Arabs who sit all around us and await the moment when their hand will be able to reach our blood. Let us not avert our gaze, for it will weaken our hand. This is the fate of our generation. The only choice we have is to be prepared and armed, strong and resolute, or else our sword will slip from our hand and the thread of our lives will be severed.

As soon as the Jewish settlers began to establish themselves on the land, and bring in crops—this was accomplished by tricks of modern agriculture, by draining swamps and piping water onto land Arabs had sold because they considered it waste—there was conflict with the Bedouins and tribal chiefs who had long controlled the valleys. To be sure, there were some, on both sides, who looked for accommodation, who searched for good news. Such leaders saw a counterpoint in the other: established together in the land, the communities would rhyme. King Abdullah bin al-Hussein (Abdullah I), the legendary figure who ruled Arabia in the last days of the Ottoman Empire as the sharif and emir of Mecca, and was later made king of Transjordan by the British, heralded the arrival of the Jews. These are not Moskub, he said, but long-lost cousins returning with a knowledge of science that will enrich the region. (The Jew will teach the Arab how to make the most of his land; the Arab will teach the Jew how to live in his own skin.) In 1910 Hussein's newspaper extended an official welcome to the members of the Second Aliyah, calling them, "The original sons of the country from which their Arab brethren would benefit materially as well as spiritually."*

For Jews, accommodation would mean a binational state, a popular notion among many Zionists up to the Second World War. That is, one state for two peoples—Arabs and Jews, equal citizens under a single law. This was proposed several times by Jewish leaders, but always rejected by Arabs, who, perhaps understandably, did not think they should give half of what, as far as they were concerned, was entirely theirs. Even now, when Israel is rich and the Territories are poor, the majority of Palestinians reject a binational state, as many reject two states. Many Arabs would rather be poor without a Jewish state than rich with one, which is why, in 1951, King Hussein, who supported accommodation, was killed by a Muslim extremist while visiting the Temple Mount.[†]

The early Jewish settlers were harassed, shot at, ambushed— attacks most often carried out by ragtag militias, dozens of men in keffiyehs, shouldering flintlock blunderbuss rifles. The fighters were fierce, with piercing eyes. These were mostly Muslim Arabs, farmers and merchants who lived in the towns and waste places of Palestine, many of whom could trace their family trees back hundreds of years. They were recruited in mosques and town squares, and pledged to take the land back from the Jews. They aimed to make life so difficult that the interlopers would simply go home. The militias left their forlorn, mud-caked villages at sundown, in groups of six or twelve, their shadows stretching behind them. They went in search of Moskub, lin-

---

*In 1918 Chaim Weizmann met King Hussein's son Faisal in Akaba in an official, kiss-on-each-cheek, drink-tea-and-work-it-out sort of way. This is the father-and-son team portrayed in the movie *Lawrence of Arabia*, in which they are seen in grand Bedouin tents, which, at night, fill like sails with the cool desert wind.

[†]Standing with King Hussein at the time of the assassination was his grandson, the future King Hussein, who would, in 1990, finally sign a peace treaty with Israel.

gered beyond the gates of the kibbutzim, hid in the ditches along the road. They threw stones, shot up convoys, killed horses, burned fields. Their guns went *ka-blam!* You heard a cheer, then saw a puff of smoke.* The casualties were few, but every loss was felt keenly, because everyone knew everyone, and every name was a story.

The first organized Arab militant group was formed in 1919. Called the Black Hand, it vowed to drive the Jews into the sea. The Black Hand would, in a sense, become Fatah, Hamas, et al. The first Zionist militia was created in response to the Black Hand. It was called the Watchmen. It would, in a sense, become the Israel Defense Forces. This was the beginning of the dance in which the Zionists act, the Arabs respond, the Zionists respond to the response, the Arabs respond to the response to the response, and on and on, forever.

The Ottoman Empire, long considered the sick man of Europe, finally died in the First World War. In history books, the death is a date on a time line, a picture of an old man in a Turkish uniform. In Palestine, it was British soldiers marching from El Arish to Beersheba, in the Negev Desert, high ground from which the wounded Turkish army could be seen spread out, bleeding. The British advanced as the Ottomans fell. By December 9, 1917, the former were camped outside Jerusalem. Two days later, the city surrendered. General Edmund Allenby entered that afternoon, as the sun went down. He approached on horseback. If you go there today, a guide will show you the path he took. He will describe Allenby's posture and bearing. Allenby was a graduate of Sandhurst, a veteran of the Boer War, a student of history, and a believer in Christ. He had been reading the Gospels. He knew what he was doing. When he reached Jaffa

---

*The Zionists responded by building walls and training men to guard those walls. But more walls meant more attacks, which meant still more walls. In this way, Jews were closing themselves off from the very land they meant to redeem. In 1911 Arthur Ruppin, a founder of Deganiah, called for the transfer of the Arabs of Palestine—he wanted to round them up and ship them off to land that the Jewish National Fund would purchase in Syria. (The modern term for this is "ethnic cleansing.")

Gate, he got off his horse and said, "A better man than I entered this city on foot."

That's how they tell it, and there is no reason to doubt them. Such events were stage-managed then as they are stage-managed now. The victory was sold as a high-water mark of the British Empire: the Christians, gone since the Crusades, had retaken the city of Christ.

A few days later, however, Allenby returned in a Rolls-Royce convertible with leather seats and flags on the hood. It went up Jaffa Road. You could see it across the valley, ascending like an angel climbing the ramps to heaven. Allenby was in back, smoking a pipe. His eyes were blue crystals, his face was porcelain. The car stopped at the gate. The driver got out. He talked to an Arab standing at the threshold.

What's the problem? asked Allenby.

Well, you see, sir. The car is too wide. Simply won't fit. These gates were made with camels in mind.

Then fix it.

Fix it, General?

Get a demolition crew up here and blow it open!

A few minutes later, a British soldier set a charge in the wall next to Jaffa Gate. The general went back downhill, waited for the blast, nodded to his driver, then rode into the city. The hole was cleaned up and a proper road was laid. This remains a primary way into the old city by car.

A week or so earlier, Lord Balfour, then serving as the First Lord of the Admiralty, issued the political statement that changed everything: the Balfour Declaration. It was presented as an open letter to Lord Rothschild, because if you want to say something to all Jews, why not say it to the Jew with the most money?

Foreign Office,
November 2nd, 1917.

Dear Lord Rothschild,

I have much pleasure in conveying to you, on behalf of His Majesty's Government, the following declaration of sympathy with

Jewish Zionist aspirations which has been submitted to, and approved by, the Cabinet.

"His Majesty's Government view with favour the establishment in Palestine of a national home for the Jewish people, and will use their best endeavours to facilitate the achievement of this object, it being clearly understood that nothing shall be done which may prejudice the civil and religious rights of existing non-Jewish communities in Palestine, or the rights and political status enjoyed by Jews in any other country."

I should be grateful if you would bring this declaration to the knowledge of the Zionist Federation.

Yours,

Arthur James Balfour

Why did the British issue this declaration?

To some, it proves the conspiracy that explains both the founding of Israel and its continued existence. How have the Zionists, who are just a fraction of the Jewish people—that is, a fraction of a fraction—been able to win the Great Powers, starting with Britain, continuing with France, then America, to their cause, a cause that cannot help but antagonize millions of Muslims? With their money, of course, their influence, their voodoo. That is, Jews, with the tricks of their race, seduced the British into acting against their own national interest.

To some, it was cunning propaganda. Note when the Balfour Declaration was issued: not at the beginning of the war, nor at the end, but in the middle, when it seemed Germany was winning. By promising the Jews a homeland, Lord Balfour, so goes the reasoning, would change the balance of power. If "world Jewry," whatever that means, came to favor the British, then the big-money Jews would use their economic and political influence to choke off and defeat Germany.

Then there was Balfour himself: this is where personality enters politics, where taste determines history. Lord Balfour, educated at Eton and Cambridge, a member of Parliament descended from members of Parliament, was a fantastic Judeophile. He said the Greeks and Jews were the most talented people the world had ever produced.

Taken together, they told the entire story of civilization, with reason coming from the Greeks, passion coming from the Jews. An obsessive reader of the Bible, he saw the Jew on Fleet Street as no different from the Jew in the Book of Kings. They must return. God was merely waiting for them to hear the trumpets, which were blowing, and always had been.

Lord Balfour had lunch with Chaim Weizmann most Thursdays. Weizmann, who would serve as the first president of Israel, was then working on Balfour's General Staff. He was a chemist and served as a scientific advisor, and would brief Balfour on breakthroughs and discoveries. Weizmann was in the process of developing a new kind of TNT, acetone, that would ignite even when wet. It was said to be a factor in victory on the Western Front, as it meant the Allies could attack even in the rain. But the relationship was more than professional: Balfour and Weizmann spent hours talking about the Bible and the future of the Jews in Palestine.

Some said the Declaration was an act of hubris: Balfour wanted to attach his name to the fulfillment of prophecy, the in-gathering of the exiles, so that future generations would not be able to discuss the Jews without mentioning Balfour, as I am doing here. Some said he wrote it because he thought it was right, believed in it. Some said he wrote it to pay a debt: the general debt Christendom owed the Jews for the slander of deicide, the particular debt that Britain owed Weizmann for acetone. In other words, the Declaration, though addressed to Rothschild, was actually a gift for Chaim Weizmann, who had long lobbied for such a document.

The news was, in fact, broken first to Weizmann, who was sitting in an anteroom on Whitehall Street while the Declaration was being debated. The diplomat Mark Sykes came out first. He gripped Weizmann by the shoulder, shook his hand, and said, "Dr. Weizmann, it's a boy!" British officials who disagreed with the policy later tried to downplay the Declaration, reinterpret it out of existence, but its meaning was clear at the time.

Here's how it was reported in the *Daily Express*, November 8, 1917:

A STATE FOR THE JEWS

Arab crowds gathered in Palestine. Imams gave sermons, and riots broke out. Scattered attacks grew into regular attacks, then into the first Arab revolt: it was the start of the war that never ends, that only mutates, grows more brutal. (Here's the progression: stone, stone, stone; stab, stab, stab; shoot, shoot, shoot; bomb, bomb, bomb.) Even today, when you watch a correspondent in a helmet, with the letters *T V* taped on her back, filing a report from Tel Aviv, where a suicide bomber has bloomed like a flower, you are seeing the front wall of a fire that burns clear back to London 1917, where Mark Sykes grips Chaim Weizmann by the shoulder, saying, "Dr. Weizmann, it's a boy!"

The spirit behind that first revolt was Haj Amin al-Husseini, the grand mufti of Jerusalem, the original Yasser Arafat. (As late as 2001, Arafat called the mufti the hero of Palestine.*) In those years, the grand mufti, more than anyone else, determined how the Arabs would respond to Zionism; he set the pattern that still dominates.

Husseini was appointed to office by the British high commissioner of Palestine, Herbert Samuel, who, curiously, considering Husseini's views, was Jewish. Well, not so curious if you believe in the conspiracy—in which case the choice was brilliant, in that Haj Amin al-Husseini's leadership led directly to the Arab disaster in Palestine. (As God tells the Jews in *Samuel*, "I will slay you, and I will slay those who slay you.")

Husseini was born in Jerusalem in 1893, and died in Beirut in 1974. Which meant he saw his world change in ways that are almost inconceivable. In his lifetime, Palestine went from sparse, agrarian, drowsy, peaceful Turkish hinterland to ultramodern Jewish Sparta. In these years, Husseini, who wore a fez and a high clerical collar, joined secret

---

*Here's Arafat, quoted, after the U.S. invasion of Afghanistan, in the London-based Arabic newspaper *Al Sharq al Awsat*. "We are not Afghanistan. We are the mighty people. Were they able to replace our hero Haj Amin al-Husseini? There were a number of attempts to get rid of Haj Amin, whom they considered an ally of the Nazis. But even so, he lived in Cairo, and participated in the 1948 war, and I was one of his troops."

societies and brotherhoods. His family was prominent and old, filled with landowners and politicians. He had terrible luck. In every battle, he chose the wrong side. (If history had broken another way, his face would be on T-shirts for sale in American shopping malls.) He supported the Ottomans in the First World War, the Germans in the Second. He made speeches against the Allies and threatened the Jews with extinction. In 1942, British police in Palestine issued a warrant for his arrest. He fled to Transjordan, then to Berlin, where he spent the rest of the war. He praised the Nazi Party, and sent its leaders long, flattering letters. He met with Ribbentrop and Goebbels. He drafted a document for the Germans to sign, his own chilling version of the Balfour Declaration. (They refused.) In it, the Arabs were promised "the right to solve the problem of the Jewish elements in Palestine and other Arab countries . . . by the same method in which that question is now being settled in the Axis countries."

From Husseini's memoir, written after the war:

> Our fundamental condition for cooperating with Germany was a free hand to eradicate every last Jew from Palestine and the Arab world. I asked Hitler for an explicit undertaking to allow us to solve the Jewish problem in a manner befitting our national and racial aspirations and according to the scientific methods innovated by Germany in the handling of its Jews. The answer I got was: "The Jews are yours."

Did Husseini know what he was saying? Did he know the details of the death camps? Adolf Eichmann, at his trial in Jerusalem, said that Husseini had not merely known, but had been one of the instigators of the Final Solution.* Historians note a speech given by Husseini during the war, when there were thought to be thirteen million Jews living in the world. In it, Husseini spoke of "the eight million Jews now living," which suggests that he not only knew the details of the Holocaust, but the minutiae.

---

*Not the most trustworthy witness, of course.

This is expressed as an algebraic equation:

$$13,000,000 - X = 8,000,000$$
$$\text{What is X?}$$
$$5,000,000$$

On November 28, 1941, Husseini met with Adolf Hitler. There is a picture of the men seated side by side in deep, comfortable chairs. Hitler is leaning forward, talking with his hands, like a Jew, hair pushed to the side, that terrible hyphen of facial hair, a dash between before and after, beneath his nose. The mufti sits upright, his fez placed neatly on his head. In another, the mufti inspects the ranks of the Waffen SS. In this way, Husseini associated the Palestinian cause with that of the Nazis. He fled to Switzerland after the war, was captured and brought back. He was tried for war crimes and sentenced to three years in prison, but escaped and was smuggled out to Egypt, where he carried on his struggle against the Jews.

The rioting that began after the Balfour Declaration continued sporadically, with days of battle separated by months or years of peace, until 1929, when the countryside exploded into the orgy of violence that is sometimes called the real first Intifada.

It started at the Wailing Wall in Jerusalem—the Bitching Wall, the Tear Your Hair Out and Curse Your Maker Wall, the last remnant of the Temple complex, which was the center of the ancient kingdom. Above it is the Dome of the Rock, planted like a flag on the grave of another people, staff driven right down into the corpse. For centuries, the Wall had been a curiosity to Muslims, a Jewish ruin. After Herzl, it became a threat. Imams who had never seen much importance in it now decided it belonged only to the Muslims. It was here, they said, that Muhammad tied his flying horse, al-Buraq, before he made his night journey to heaven. The Wall became a flashpoint. Arabs dumped trash in the alley and harassed Jews who prayed there. The

British, asked to settle the dispute, promised to protect all existing rights: neither side would be allowed to upset the status quo.

Then, in early August 1929, a devout Jew put a barrier up at the Wall to separate male worshippers from female worshippers. The Muslim Authority complained; the British removed the barrier. The Zionist Federation issued a statement: If Jews are not allowed to pray as they want at the Wall, it said, then Jews will never be free. The next day, a hundred Zionists gathered at the Wall, chanted and sang, and raised a blue-and-white flag. Arabs held a counterdemonstration on the Temple Mount. That crowd then went down into the alley beside the Wall. The Zionists had gone, so the Arabs attacked Orthodox Jews who had come to pray.

On August 8, 1929, full-scale rioting broke out across the country. Jews were beaten and stabbed, shuls sacked, stores looted. The British dispatched soldiers with orders to shoot to kill. By the fifteenth of September, 133 Jews had been killed, and nearly as many Arabs. In Jerusalem, the crowds chanted: Death! Death! Death! Behind the rioters were the Bearded Sheiks and the Black Hand and the Grand Mufti, whose face drifted, laughing across the Jerusalem sky.

H ebron is among the holiest places on earth to Jews. David made his first capital there, and ruled from the city for seven years. It was home to the Ark of the Covenant. It's also where the Hebrew patriarchs are buried, deep in a cave called Machpelah which, according to Genesis, Abraham bought from a local sheik to bury his wife (Sarah), himself, and his sons. This transaction, described in detail in the Bible, is used by Jewish settlers to prove their ownership of the city. The sheik wanted to give Abraham the cave as a gift, but the canny old Jew refused, insisting on paying full market value—four hundred shekels of silver—so there could be no argument about ownership. The bill of sale is right there in the Torah, say the modern settlers.

Whether or not the cave is actually the Tomb of the Patriarchs is in dispute, but it has been worshipped as such for at least two thousand years.

Josephus described it soon after the destruction of the Second Temple:

> If the inhabitants are to be believed, Hebron is more ancient than any town in the country—older even than Memphis in Egypt; its age is reckoned at 2,300 years. They affirm that it was the home of Abraham, the ancestor of the Jews, after his migration from Mesopotamia, and that his descendants went down into Egypt from there. Their tombs are pointed out to this day in the little town, of the finest marble and beautifully fashioned.

Here's how Benjamin Tudela described it in the 1200s:

> At a distance of six parsings is St. Abram de Bron, which is Hebron; the old city stood on the mountain, but is now in ruins; and in the valley by the field of Machpelah lies the present city. Here there is the great church called St. Abram, and this was a Jewish place of worship at the time of Mohammedan rule, but the Gentiles have erected there six tombs, respectively called those of Abraham and Sarah, Isaac and Rebekah, Jacob and Leah. The custodians tell the pilgrims that these are the tombs of the Patriarchs, for which information the pilgrims give them money. If a Jew comes, however, and gives a special reward, the custodian of the caves opens unto him a gate of iron, which was constructed by our forefathers, and then he is able to descend below by means of steps, holding a lighted candle in his hand. He then reaches a cave, in which nothing is to be found, and a cave beyond which is likewise empty, but when he reaches the third cave, behold there are six sepulchres. Those of Abraham, Isaac and Jacob, respectively facing those of Sarah, Rebekah and Leah.

Hebron is the Middle East in a drop of rain. It had perhaps twenty thousand residents in 1929, including a sizable Jewish population. It was home to probably the oldest Jewish community in the world, which had lived in the city since the early sixth century, more than a century before Muslim rule. The life of this community ended with the riots in which sixty Jews were killed and the rest fled. It's a Muslim city today, with a tiny minority of fanatical Jewish settlers living in a walled compound at its center. The presence of these settlers makes life miserable for Arabs. This is what the world sees. The Hebrew foot in the Muslim face. The most radical of the Jews there demand "transfer" of the Arab population from the city. As I said, the other word for this is "ethnic cleansing," removing a population as if it never existed. You cannot be a normal, fair-minded person and believe these settlers are anything but a problem. Monstrous. They should go; they should never have been allowed to move here in the first place.

But the story is complicated. Hebron was mixed for centuries. It became Muslim only after the riots of 1929. In other words, Hebron already has been ethnically cleansed—of Jews. When the settlers came in 1968, it was, supposedly, to reestablish the oldest Jewish community in the world. Of course, these Jews were not those Jews. Those Jews had been a poor, ancient, devout community. These Jews are ideological, steely, determined, extreme. Let me address this directly to the mufti: Look what you did! You pushed out the old peaceful Jews and in their place got these wild-eyed Zealots! Who have come to fulfill the word of God! Who have come to redeem the land! Who have come to be kings among the defeated Philistines! You, with your bloodlust and riots, created the Jews, who, with their bloodlust and planes, created the Arabs, who created the Jews, who created the Arabs. The mufti gives birth to Sharon, who gives birth to Nasarallah, etc., etc.

It's called a spiral.

B efore the riots, each Jewish settlement looked after its own defense. The amateurish guards were called Watchmen. Every kibbutz was laid out in the same way: common buildings, cottages, fields, fences, towers, wilderness. It's referred to as the fence-and-tower era of settlement. Did you ever see the John Ford movie *She Wore a Yellow Rib-bon*? Well, it was just like that. There was inside the fence (civilization), there was outside the fence (chaos). The ultimate goal was to bring everything inside the fence. As a rule, the Watchmen "stayed inside." It was their policy. Wait, hope, react. I can give you a picture of a Watchman: a middle-aged man named Schmuely, in peasant boots and flop-brim hat, a Russian rifle slung over his shoulder, walking the last planted field. Or a kid named Jacob sitting in a wooden tower studying the land through a pair of antique opera glasses. On the kib-butz where my cousins live—it's called Ein Hahoresh and it's near the sea north of Tel Aviv; I have spent many summers there—the guns are stored in a locked room to be opened only if the Arab armies break through. The key was kept, for a time, on a string around my cousin Gadi's neck. Gadi in the dining hall, eating cucumbers, the tiny weight felt even when he was swimming (when it swung to the side, you saw the tan mark left by each notch)—to me, this is the image of the Watchmen.

Moshe Dayan described them as ragtag bands of the "we few, we happy few, we band of schnorrers" variety. Reading now, you sense, oddly, considering the violence of their lives, that they were having fun. It was only after the 1929 riots that the leaders of the movement turned these scattered militias into the professional force, the Hagana, that would eventually become the Israeli military. They built it the way you might build a national soccer team: recruiters went from town to town, meeting members of each militia, watching them train, select-ing the standouts. A few weeks later, hundreds of them gathered in a field, where Zionists who had attended military academies in Russia, or Prussia, or Britain, or America, watched them run, climb, shoot, and bayonet. The British had banned all private armies in Palestine. (Merely being a member of the Hagana was a crime.) So this was all done in secret, the soldiers inducted in a ceremony known, with vari-ation, to underground soldiers everywhere. A man on his knees in a cellar, the face of the leader flickering in the candlelight, a husky whis-per. He asks three questions, then has the recruit swear an oath, right hand on a Bible, left hand on a gun.

In the beginning, the Hagana fought as the Watchmen had fought: behind the fence. But the Jewish community in Palestine, known as the Yishuv, was simply too small, its territory too meager, to stay on the defensive. If Zionism was to succeed, the Hagana needed a new strategy. Interestingly, it came not from a Jew but from an Englishman, an officer in the British army, a Judeophile filled to the brim with the Bible. His name was Orde Wingate and he was, in a sense, a perfect expression of the Empire. Wingate was born in Naini Tal, India, in 1903; his father was an army officer, his mother a missionary. And insane. Did she believe the end was near? Did she believe a Jew could be normal? Did she believe the Jews would be either saved or smote? Yes, no, yes.

Mrs. Wingate taught her son to believe in the chosen-ness of the Jews, and to regard every word of scripture as a promise. He was sent to England for school. He studied at the Royal Military Academy at Sandhurst and dreamed of service in the Near East, the land of the Bible. He learned Arabic, Hebrew, Farsi. He used his connections, specifically his cousin Sir Reginald Wingate, the governor general of Sudan, to get posted overseas. In 1928, he commanded a battalion in the no-man's-land between Sudan and Abyssinia. He was ordered to arrest poachers and slavers and smugglers but quickly realized his uniformed soldiers, at their checkpoints, with their trucks and fixed guns, were useless against these pirates. In considering the problem, he read books on the Roman wars and studied stories in the Bible in which Hebrew bands defeated much larger armies. He paid special attention to Gideon, who, with three hundred men, vanquished the Midianites. In this story, which appears in the Book of Judges, you find all of Wingate's tactics: the ambush, the feint, the trick. He trained a band of elite soldiers. To beat pirates, he told them, they would have to become pirates. Ditch their uniforms and posts, vanish into the bush. This was the birth of modern counterinsurgency.

In 1936 Wingate sailed for Palestine, where the Arabs were rioting in response to increased Jewish immigration, which came with the rise of Hitler. This was called the "Arab Revolt." It took three years to suppress. In the end, to mollify the rioters, the British issued a white paper that severely limited Jewish emigration to Palestine. At the moment the Jews of Europe most needed a way out, the last door had closed.*

Wingate was posted to the General Staff and told to learn native culture with a mind toward intelligence. He was a captain. He could be seen walking in the city at sundown, broad-nosed and solid with gray eyes, one of those reserved men who proves surprisingly strong. He impressed everyone: the way he listened, the nature of his focus. He was troubled by the violence of the rioters and asked permission to teach the Jews how best to defend themselves. To Wingate, Jewish military prowess was a precondition of a Jewish state, and a Jewish state was a precondition of the Second Coming. (He was Lawrence of Arabia for the Jews.)

If the Jews can defend themselves properly, he told his commander, Lord Archibald Wavell, then British soldiers will not have to risk their lives defending Jewish settlements.

"We heard Wingate was someone with unconventional ideas about how to deal with Arab terrorism and sabotage, and, unlike his military colleagues, thought well of Jews," Moshe Dayan wrote. "In fact, he had become an ardent supporter of the Zionist idea."

In the spring of 1938, Wingate met the leaders of the Hagana. If the Jews want to prevail, he told them, they have to learn to fight as the British learned to fight in Sudan. "You do not have the people, or the size, to wait for the next attack," he explained. "Given the choice, you must fight in their towns, in their fields, not in yours."

"Wingate taught us everything we know," Dayan said.

The Jews took to him, in part, because his ideas meshed perfectly with the ideals of Zionism. In urging them to come out from behind the fence, he was urging them to fulfill their ideology: take possession of the land, redeem it, be redeemed. He led them through the countryside, instructed them in night fighting and weed crawling, surprise attack, psychological warfare, in timing each mission to the cycle of the moon. He taught them the art of ambush, how to read the land.

---

*By rioting, the Arabs actually made the outcome they feared more likely. In the 1930s, no one would have the Jews, and millions died. Ironically, the quota enacted in response to the riots demonstrated the need for a Jewish state.

Memorize the terrain until it becomes your own body and you will never be lost—this became the ethos of the new Jewish soldier.

Wingate led the Hagana on several missions. They would set out at sundown, walking single file through the darkening fields. He called them night squads. They raided villages, ambushed militias, counter-attacked. If a Jew was killed, they might go into the nearest town and burn down Arab houses. "We could not guard every water pipeline from being blown up and every tree from being uprooted," Moshe Dayan explained. "We could not prevent every murder of a worker in an orchard or family in their beds. But it was in our power to set a high price on our blood, a price too high for the Arab community, the Arab army, or the Arab governments to think it worth paying."

The night squads returned at dawn, gathered in a house on a kibbutz and talked over the mission—what could be learned from each mistake. As the men sat around, drinking coffee, Wingate read from the Bible. He was a bit of an eccentric. He wore a bathing cap in the shower and issued orders in the nude. He had an onion on a string around his neck and now and then bit it like an apple. He built missions on stories in scripture, which he read aloud before the men set off. In his diary, Lord Moran, who would serve as Winston Churchill's private physician, described Wingate as "Hardly sane—in medical jargon, a borderline case."*

Moshe Dayan:

> [Wingate] had an unbreakable belief in the Bible. Before going on an action, he would read the passage in the Bible relating to the places where we would be operating and find testimony to our victory—the victory of God and the Jews. At dawn, we would return to Shimron and prepare breakfast. We would enter the wooden structure which served as the communal kitchen and watch the scores of cockroaches scurry away at our approach. There we would fry omelets and potatoes on a primus stove and prepare tomato salad. While this was going on, Wingate would sit in a corner, stark naked, reading the Bible and munching raw onions as though they were the most luscious

---

*Jerusalem Syndrome.

pears. Judged by ordinary standards, he would not be regarded as normal. But his own standards were far from ordinary. He was a military genius and a wonderful man.

On leave in England in 1939, Wingate spoke publicly in favor of the creation of a Jewish state, and as a result was recalled from Palestine. He had been in the country for just three years, but in that time had basically invented the modern Israeli fighting style. In the Hagana, his code name was The Friend.

He went back to Sudan to organize a guerrilla campaign against the Italians, who had invaded Ethiopia. His army of irregulars included Jewish veterans of the night squads as well as British and Sudanese. He called it the Gideon Force. He contracted malaria in the course of the campaign, which he self-treated with high doses of Atabrine, a medicine he purchased from a witch doctor. This resulted in temporary dementia. He had visions: saw faces, streets filled with blood. He tried to kill himself and was sent home. He recovered. By then, the newspapers had made him a legend. Orde Wingate, the swashbuckling guerrilla. Franklin Roosevelt was fascinated by Wingate's theories on counterinsurgency. In 1942, the British command sent him to Burma to harass the Japanese. For this, he developed the "long-range penetration unit," a squad of elite soldiers that would operate hundreds of miles behind the lines. He called them Chindits, Burmese for *lions*. He was dropped, with his men, into the jungle. On March 6, 1944, returning to India, his plane, an American B-25, was shot down. He was buried in the Naga Hills, in Burma, at the site of the wreck, inside Japanese territory.

TEN

Killing Adolf Again

I have a cousin named Ruzka. Had, actually. I wrote a book about her, and what happened to her and her friends during the Second World War. They fought as partisans in the woods outside Vilna. The book was called *The Avengers*. I did not like that title. I chose it, but changed my mind. I thought it sounded denigrating. Possibly because there is a cartoon called *The Avengers* that features a character who shoots poison darts out of an umbrella. I wanted to call it *Night March*, which is the title of a poem written by Abba Kovner, who led the partisans. This poem seemed to encapsulate the mood of the story and the message of Zionism.

It goes like this:

> *And someone stood up in the field,*
> *And his voice was like this night:*
> *"Will we get there—and how?"*
> *Who will know? This night*

—as on all other nights—
It's the one who will stand up and go.

My editor preferred *The Avengers*. She said a book called *Night March* might be confused with the Elie Wiesel book *Night*. But to my mind, this overlap (*Night*) is interesting, even instructive. In these titles, *Night* and *Night March*, you have opposing styles in Jewish history. *Night* is a Jew in the evening time of the Holocaust. *Night March* is the same night, only this Jew is moving.

I struggled with the name Ruzka, too, which sounded so foreign. I wondered if an American reader could identify with a woman named Ruzka. I don't care about things like that anymore. (I was a craven, beholden ghetto Jew, but now I am free.) Besides, the story of *The Avengers* *is* foreign. It's the story of young people who lost everything, then formed an irregular army and started blowing things up. I mean, it's not our story, not the story of Jews in America. It's important to remember that. Nor did Ruzka look familiar or act familiar. She was tiny and strange. Too short to go on the roller coaster. Melancholy smile. Cigarette after cigarette. Quoting Herzen, discussing the dialectic. Suspicious, cynical, but very warm. She was my grandmother's niece, known only from an occasional postcard. Her entire family was killed in the first weeks of the Second World War. These were the people who did not make it to the camps, who were just stood against a wall and shot.

Ruzka survived by running away. Her father ordered her to. It's a panel in a graphic novel: a man in an overcoat, eyes dark and moist, because this is the great thing he can still do, one hand on his daughter, who is young and small, the other pointing up the road, which is a charcoal line bending in the undergrowth. Until now, I have been viewing Jewish history through a wide-angle lens, showing the mega moments—Temple, ghetto, etc.—but, in a way, this small girl going down the road is Jewish history in its purest form. It's like one of those paintings by Chuck Close: when you stand back, you see a big picture, but when you move in you realize the big picture is made of hundreds of little pictures, each a tiny epic.

Ruzka went to Vilna. In this panel, you see her walking through the dives, a pack on her shoulder, the city reeling around her. She met Abba Kovner, already a famous Zionist leader, lived in a house for refugees, then, with the rest of the Jews of Vilna, was forced into the medieval ghetto. She spent her time in the basements of the city, training to fight. This is how Jewish life ends in Europe: a girl in a cellar with a gun. When the ghetto was destroyed, she went through the sewers to the forest, lived in a hole in the ground, fought until the country was taken over by the Russians. She then traveled to Romania to make contact with a Zionist agent, who had come looking for survivors. She went by train and foot, and in these panels you see her in burned-out towns, on the back of slow-moving trains. When she told her story in Bucharest, the Zionist agent said she had to return with him to tell the story in Palestine. In these panels, you see her on the deck of a ship, the foghorn blowing. She was arrested in Haifa by British military police—she had been traveling on forged papers—and locked in an internment camp in Atilt.

She was in prison for three months. In this panel, you see her with fingers hooked through the barbed wire. She was visited by Chaim Weizmann's wife, Vera. With each telling, Ruzka's story became less like something that happened than like something she'd read in a book. Vera Weizmann was beautiful, with dark eyes and long lashes. Ruzka was a peasant, plain, with short hair and clothes more suitable for a boy. (I know this from Ruzka, who told me about it later.) The meeting stayed in Ruzka's memory, as it was here, while talking to Vera Weizmann, that she first heard the number that would become holy to the Jews. It was at the end of the conversation. Weizmann had turned to leave, stopped, and said, "Is it true what they say? Did six million Jews die in Europe?"

"Do you know what I did," Ruzka told me. "I ran. I left that lady standing there. It was the first time I heard this number: six million."

For Ruzka, it was the moment a number became *the* number. More than a tally of the dead, a symbol and a sign, a number tattooed on the body of the people as a number was tattooed on the forearm of the prisoner in Auschwitz. It whispers. It tells you what it means to be a Jew, what happened and what will happen.

Of course, no one knows exactly how many Jews died in the Holocaust. No one even knows how many Jews were alive before the war, or how many are alive today. It's a guess. Six million is six million because someone decided to round up or round down, or decided a whole number looked better in the paper. I have tried to determine the precise moment that six million was first used as we use it today. As I have tried to determine the moment the word *holocaust* was first used as we use it today. Because this is when the tragedy turned into a religion.

I searched the archive of *Time* magazine for "Six Million." I also searched "Six Million Dead," "Six Million Corpses," "Six Million Souls," "Six Million Lives," "Six Million Stories," "Six Million Tragedies," "Six Million Jews." The results show how a number can evolve, with time, from something general and valueless, neither good nor bad, into something specific and terrible. It's like watching a man being made out of clay, malleable at first, taking on and throwing off features, then hardening into a familiar and recognizable shape.

Time's debut issue was dated March 3, 1923. On its cover was Joseph Cannon, the Speaker of the House of Representatives. From then until the end of the Second World War, the term *six million* appeared in the magazine sixty-one times, first on September 22, 1924, in which story the chairman of the Steuben Society promises Robert La Follett, the senator from Wisconsin, the support of "six-million U.S. citizens of German blood." Interesting that the first mention of six million is from a German American who speaks not of culture but of blood, a worldview that will have consequences.

In the thirties and early forties, *six million* turns up again and again, like a premonition. If you read *Time* as the Evangelicals read Isaiah, then it's prophecy. In the issue dated October 1, 1934, Pope Leo XIII reminded the world that "today no less than six-million people still live in slavery." In the issue dated January 12, 1942 (the story is called "On to Six Million"), a reporter tries to determine the exact number of Americans under arms, and how long until the army has "the six-million most military wizards figure it must have before the U.S. can defeat Hirohito, Hitler and hangers-on." The May 18, 1942, issue includes this sentence: "Six-million U.S. people move every year. In big cities they usually move only a few blocks, in small towns, across the street. Their reasons: to be near the Joneses, to get more sun in the living room, an extra bedroom for Junior, a bigger garden, lower rent—or restlessness." The February 5, 1945, issue includes a story about "Maharaja of Patiala, 31, the leader of India's six-million warrior Sikhs": "Walking in his socks while his mustachios curled magnificently skyward, the Maharaja carried a takri (basket) of earth from the site of the shrine. While thousands of his subjects chanted: 'Sat Sri Akal!' ('Truth is eternal!'), the Prince bore his burden on his turbaned head in token of his total humility."

Other stories reference it: "six-million prisoners captured on European and African battlefields"; "six-million francs a day" made by French citizens working in German factories; "six-million farms" that constitute America's most fertile land; "six-million words" written by the Hollywood screenwriter Adam Berg; "six-million surplus pairs of dungarees" the navy is trying to unload.

After 1945 the term was used almost exclusively to describe the tragedies of war. (The world had entered the era of millions, billions, trillions.) Six million Germans displaced by the new borders of Poland. Six million bushels of wheat to feed the starving people of Hungary. It was first used in relation to the Jews in the issue dated January 21, 1946, in a story about a feud among the Allies. British general Sir Frederick Morgan had spoken of an "organized Jewish 'plot' to smuggle Jews out of Europe."* American Jews, including the comedian Eddie Cantor, were outraged by the term "Jewish plot." It sounded like Nazi propaganda. *The New York Times* editorialized, calling the comments "an insult to six million tortured dead." *Time* summarized the back and forth. This was probably the first widely circulated mention of the number sacred in modern Jewish life.

The issue of *Time* dated March 11, 1946, has a story about Jewish

---

*There was such a plot. It was called the Bricha and it was led by Zionists, including Abba Kovner.

life in Europe since the war. In it, *six million* has assumed its familiar resonance: "six million tortured dead" has become "the six million," as if the victims have turned into a single holy body.

> Everywhere, the Jews were strangers and everywhere they were haunted by the past. Europe was a burial ground that held six million Jewish corpses; the survivors found life among the dead unbearable. They knew that the massacre had not been the work of a handful of Nazis alone, and they had acquired a bitter, all-inclusive suspicion.

You can likewise follow the evolution of *holocaust* from a hyperbolic term used in newspapers and magazines for seasoning to a righteous word that stands for the suffering of all Jews. Little by little, it was sanctified, removed from the dictionary, printed in a black book. It's not yours. It's ours. It's what happened to us. It has one meaning. It cannot be used like that. At some point, it appeared in all caps. It looms over us like a monument: HOLOCAUST. Which means it can be sacked, burned down. Which means it can be used to torment us, played with, goofed on, denied. He is a Holocaust denier! He denies the Holocaust! To demonstrate the progression, I will use just three stories, like the magician who uses just three rings to show you that nothing is as it seems.

The first is from *Time*, November 17, 1947. It tells of a fire in Bar Harbor, Maine, that killed thousands of lab mice—brown mice, white mice, black mice:

> After the blackened buildings cooled, Director Clarence Cook Little walked sadly among the cages of roasted or suffocated mice. A few "little fellows" looked up with frightened eyes, among them two elderly, fat yellow mice. But survivors were few. Out of the 90,000, only 55 were alive. The mouse holocaust was a major disaster to researchers in medicine and biology . . .*

---

*With Art Spiegelman's *Maus* in mind, it's not hard to read this as an allegory on the fate of the European Jews.

Of course, what's interesting is the word *holocaust* used to describe the death of lab mice—a last fleeting glimpse of the word used the old way. The second story is called "Hornet's Nest" (*Time*, October 8, 1945):

> The Palestine cauldron was aboil again. Jews, now driven by the need to save survivors from the European holocaust, were demanding the immediate reopening of large-scale immigration into the Holy Land.

This is the first use (I know) in an American periodical of *holocaust* as "the holocaust." Specifically, "the European holocaust," though the qualifier will soon be dropped. It will fall away as the fuel tanks fall away as the capsule glides into the blue orbit of outer space.

Third is a letter written to the editors of *Time* (November 15, 1949) by a rabbi angered at a police photo the magazine ran of Jacob Wasserman, who had been killed in a robbery in New York.

> Sir:
>
> Not just another "Manhattan Street Scene"—and far more than mere dramatic photography: Jacob Wasserman died of the wounds he received.
>
> Wasserman had survived the Nazi holocaust in Europe, but had lost his entire family. He came to the U.S. in 1946, and for four years he and his wife struggled to retain some form of economic security. Six weeks ago they had opened that little jewelry shop.
>
> What six years under Hitler could not do was so neatly accomplished on that Saturday in Manhattan.
>
> Rabbi Asher Dov Kahn
> Tulsa, Okla.

Rabbi Kahn uses *holocaust* as it is still used today (it belongs to the rabbis now, who wave it over our heads like a divining rod): it's the name given to a historical event, but it also describes a mood or disposition. It's the gloom that came out of the camps, the tragic sense that what happened will happen again. It might seem that Wasserman died in a holdup, because it was late and he was in a room filled with gems, but Jacob Wasserman was killed because he was a Jew.

The first Holocaust museum was built five years after the war, in Negba, a kibbutz south of Tel Aviv. It was designed by Abba Kovner, and its exhibits, which are run-down and dated, seem meant less to tell the story than to motivate Israelis in their struggle with the Arabs. The museum reads like a novel, with a point of view and characters and a story to tell. Less is said by the photos and statistics than by the layout of the museum, how, without quite noticing it, you leave behind pictures of Europe, where the Jews are stacked in piles, for pictures of Palestine, where the Jews are in full battle dress.

I went to the museum with Kovner's son, Michael, who is a friend of mine. He served in Sayeret Matkal, an elite unit of the Israeli army. He's an artist, a painter of great complicated landscapes. Some show Arab houses in Gaza. Some show the Jericho Road climbing to Jerusalem. Some show the Temple Mount from a distance, an object in a sea of objects, with no special claim on our sentiments. Now and then, Michael would stop before a display and say, "You see, to describe the flight from Europe to Palestine, Abba used the word that is used in the Bible for *ladder*, which means to go up—the ladder that brings my parents to Palestine is the same ladder on which Jacob sees the angels coming and going from Heaven." Or, "You see, in this museum, Abba had a big idea: that the story of the Jews in the Holocaust and the story of the Jews in Palestine is the same story."

Abba Kovner was typical of a certain kind of Israeli. He was an ideologue. Everything had an idea behind it. Everything was intentional. He was a fine poet, but in his work you find no poem about a meadow, or the joy of riding the bus. It's only barbed wire and desert and ships and live-or-die fighting. He went on to design the Jewish Diaspora Museum in Tel Aviv, where he invented a brilliant way to show the fate of the Jews (as he saw it) in Exile. As you go along, you follow the story of particular Jews living in Europe in the middle of the twentieth century. As you walk from room to room, and the fate of each person unfolds, the message becomes plain. Though each Jew had a different beginning—some wore side curls; some wore lab coats; some wore gowns; some wore uniforms; some studied Sun Tzu; some wore suits; some prayed in a synagogue that looked like a church; some did not consider themselves Jews at all;

some drank absinthe; some smoked opium; some were nervous; some were calm—they all had the same end. You might live the life of a Gentile, but you will die like a Jew.

The little museum in Negba has since grown into a network of museums. These are said to tell the story of the Holocaust, but their unstated purpose is to justify the state of Israel. This does not mean that I am against Israel. (I am for Israel.) I simply do not believe the Holocaust justifies the state, nor do I think it needs to. Israel does not need to be justified. It is. Or, as it said on the T-shirt my best friend was wearing when he returned from a trip to Tel Aviv in 1977:

Israel

Is

Real

Did the Holocaust change Zionism?

Of course it did.

First of all, it ended the argument.

For decades, Jewish intellectual life had been characterized by the debate between Zionists and anti-Zionists, nationalists and assimilationists. It went back and forth. The assimilationists dismissed Zionism as parochialism, as particularism, a spiritual retreat—a fever that chilled the people when the people were afraid. The good life is to be had by those who abandon their tribal identity and give themselves to the life of their nation. In trying to normalize the Jews, they said, Zionism will make them objects of suspicion everywhere. The Zionists called such reasoning backward. It's not our dream that causes Jews to be suspect, they said. It's because Jews have always been suspect that we have our dream. To them, the assimilationists were worse than fools. They were dangerous. They put the people to sleep when they most needed to be awake. There is no such thing as assimilation, said Abba Kovner. In the end, all roads converge at the grave.

If you want to know who was winning the argument, look at the statistics: for every Jew who went to Palestine, ten went to America. By 1930, when there were fewer than a half million Jews in Palestine, over one million were living in New York alone. (You've seen them in the old photo taken at the meeting of the cousins' club, gray men with sad eyes. The one in the middle is Grandpa N, who is Abraham, having come across from Poland. His sons and nephews flock around him— he who chose this world (Brooklyn) over the next (Jerusalem). My father is in front, on the ground in short pants, surrounded by girl cousins. He tells me his life has been nothing but a progression through the rows, from the floor to the chairs, then to the seats in back, looking like his own father now, with the great black maw reeling behind.*) The assimilationists had it, and it wasn't even close. When given a choice between the Promised Land and the shopping mall, most chose the latter. It seemed there was little future for a Jewish Palestine. But the Holocaust changed that.

The Nuremberg Laws, the ghettos, the cattle cars, the camps, the ovens, the smokestacks, the warehouses filled with shoes and human hair, the survivors on the road—these images remade Jews even in America, even in Russia, where tribal identity was called a thing of the past. After 1945 it became impossible to dismiss the Zionists as paranoid, small-minded, parochial. The Shoah had demonstrated the truth of their main insight: that Europe is the graveyard of the Jews. Assimilation, which promised a golden age of tolerance, had shown itself a lie. If Germany, the land of Mendelssohn and Heine, the land of universities, was not safe, there was no safe place. The ground could give way anywhere, anytime. In short, the Holocaust reminded the Jews what it meant to be Jewish.

Here's a poem written by the Russian poet Margaret Aliger in 1946. It's called "Your Victory."

> *Our freedom's firstborn generation,*
> *Raised in blissful ignorance of Hell,*
> *We forgot about our ancient nation,*
> *But the Nazis—they remembered well.*

---

*When my aunt Renee, who, in the photo, is the girl in pigtails next to my father, showed this picture to me and my brother, she said, "Almost everyone in this picture is dead." "Oh my God," said my brother. "Did they just prop them up like that?"

This is from an article written during the war by Ilya Ehrenburg:

I grew up in a Russian city. My native language is Russian. I am a Russian writer. Now, like all Russians, I am defending my homeland. But the Nazis have reminded me of something else: my mother's name was Hannah. I am a Jew. I say this with pride. Hitler hates us more than anyone else. And that does us credit.

Zionists considered the Holocaust their failure—they had not convinced the masses in time, had lost the debate, so there was no refuge when refuge was needed. In the 1930s the Nazis had been willing to let Jews emigrate, but no nation would have them, so they died. If there had been a Jewish state, millions would have lived. So appears the phrase that falls on me like a shadow: *Never again*. Never again will Jews be without resource or refuge. Never again will Jews be led like sheep to the slaughter. Next time there will be a safe haven. We will rush to it by boat and plane, pull up the ladders and bridges, huddle behind the walls and peer through the turrets at the legions below.

These arguments were not all academic. There were a million Jews trapped in Europe after the war, most in DP camps, built for displaced persons on the grounds of liberated Nazi concentration camps—old hotel, new management. Some Jews remained in these camps three, four, five years. (The last closed in 1951.) Those who tried to return to their homes in, say, Kielce, were met by squatters who chased them off, beat them, whistled rifle shots over their heads. There were several pogroms in Poland in 1946, most set off by Jews returning from the camps. These accomplished what they were probably meant to: they cleansed the country of its remaining Jews.

Even then, few survivors were offered refuge in Britain, France, or America. Most were simply left in the DP camps, behind the wire. Thousands slipped away to the forests, where they met Zionist agents, who smuggled them to Palestine. This was Sir Frederick Morgan's "organized Jewish 'plot.'" It was called the Bricha, "the Flight." The refugees were led down trails, from city to city, then out to the sea, where they were packed into rickety old ships, which carried them to

Tel Aviv and Haifa. The British navy blockaded the coast of Palestine. Many refugee ships were stopped, boarded, turned back. Most famous was the *Exodus*, an antique steamship boarded three miles off Haifa. (Passengers could see the stone buildings of the city rising in terraces above the sea.) The ship was escorted back across the Mediterranean, shown the door. Everywhere it landed—Turkey, Italy, France—it was turned away. It sailed from port to port, finally returning to Germany, where the passengers were sent back to the DP camp. This battered ship, in its desperate wandering search for a harbor, became a symbol of the Jews after the war.

When the Western nations voted to partition Palestine, it was not, as history books tell you, an act of altruism, nor was it about guilt. It was the best solution to the Jewish Problem. With the creation of Israel, the Europeans could finally ship off the refugees and close the DP camps. Israel is not a nation—it's a landfill, a garbage dump, where Europeans heaped the ashes after the war.

The Holocaust changed the nature of Zionism, scrambled its DNA. It had been utopian: Jews as an example, a light unto the nations. It would now be about survival. The mission, which had been to create a new man, became prickly and small. It would not be a city on a hill; it would be the last refuge. Herzl's *Old New Land* came to mirror the ghetto: the Jewish condition experienced at the national level, life behind the wall, the horizon seen through a turret. The ideal is still there, only sublimated. The combination of these two visions—utopia plus the struggle to survive—was a new creed that proved wildly powerful. It justifies every action, every violence. In it, the Jews found a way to be both strong and righteous.

Avraham Stern was typical of the new sort of Zionist who came of age in the twenties. He made Aliyah from Poland in 1925, went up to the Temple, where God sits on a velvet throne, surrounded by cherubim, each armed to the teeth, their fat little bodies crossed by strings of ammunition. He studied humanities at Hebrew University, a young man in a suit and tie, crossing campus with the earnest, hawk-nosed look of all those who went in the front gate and came out the chimney. He studied in Florence, then returned to Palestine, where in 1929 he was recruited by the Hagana. He grew disillusioned, accused his commanders of excess moderation. He said the Hagana was too concerned with the approval of the British.

In 1931 he and a few others split to form their own militia. They called it the Irgun.* This was the military wing of Vladimir Jabotinsky's Revisionist Party. Its members, who defined themselves in opposition to the more moderate members of the Hagana, preached a kind of holy fanaticism.† They wore matching shirts and marched in ranks. They demanded a violent response to violent attacks. It was not just a question of survival. It was a matter of ideology. Action will cure the Jew of the weakness bred by exile. They were young, zealous, hyperarticulate, driven by a big idea. In 1947 *The New York Times*‡ described the typical member of the Irgun as "a lower middle-class man about 31 years old, probably of Polish origin, who previously worked at a skilled occupation. But for his political convictions and activities, he would probably be an ordinary man working at an ordinary job and living on an ordinary street in the all-Jewish city of Tel Aviv."

The *Times* reporter quotes a British document in which Menachem Begin, a leader of the Irgun, is described as you might describe someone in an online Jewish dating service:

> A thin-faced sallow young man with large brown eyes and enormous horned rim glasses. Age 38, Height 5 foot 10. Build: thin. Nose: hooked. Flat footed, bad teeth. Occupation: clerk

When people speak of Jewish terrorists in Palestine during this period, it's almost always the Irgun they have in mind. Most of the Irgun's missions were against the British, who had severely curtailed Jewish emigration. They blew up bridges and raided arms depots. After sev-

---

*Irgun means simply "Hebrew organization."

†On occasion, the Hagana worked with the British to thwart the Irgun. The leaders of Israel eventually brought the rogues under control by force. During the 1948 War, the Israeli navy sank a ship carrying weapons to the Irgun, whose fighters were then absorbed into the Israel Defense Forces. This incident—the Altalena Affair—is often cited as an example for Palestinians: it shows what Fatah should have done with Hamas when they had the chance. As Shimon Peres says, "You can have many political parties, but only have one gun."

‡"PALESTINE HUNTS TERROR CHIEFS."

eral underground leaders were executed, the Irgun kidnapped British soldiers, who were then found hanging from trees in the north.* Most famously, in 1946 the Irgun, led by Begin, blew up a wing of the King David Hotel in Jerusalem, where the British had their military headquarters.†

Avraham Stern considered himself a throwback to the Jews of the kingdom, the last of whom died on Masada, or, I should say, the Israelis of the kingdom, as the Jew was the creation of the ghetto and the rabbis. (The citizens of his state would be Israelis.) His code name was Yair, taken from Eliezer Ben Yair, the leader of the Zealots. He wanted to dwell in the land as David dwelt in the land in 2 Samuel, smiting and procreating. He was a writer of Hebrew poetry, and left behind fifty-seven psalms, many of them erotic. He identified less with the Jews of his generation than with the ancient Israelites. He was the Zealots all over again. Or it was the Zealots, then Stern.

In 1939, when Britain declared war on Germany, the Irgun halted all attacks. Menachem Begin said the defeat of the Nazis was more important than the end of the British occupation. (Thousands of Palestinian Jews joined the British army.) But Stern refused to accept the cease-fire. He said Britain posed the greater threat, as it was the British who could smother the nascent Jewish state, the only hope for the warrior Jew. He advocated making an alliance with the Nazis, who, he explained, wanted to rid Europe of the very Jews the Zionists needed in order to build their state. The Nazis had the product, Stern had the market. A handful of men followed him out of the Irgun. They formed the Stern Gang, known by the acronym Lehi: Fighters For Israel's Freedom.

In the early 1940s, the gang went on a spree that turned Stern into a folk hero. He was like Dillinger or Pretty Boy Floyd, a righteous outlaw, unsound in his methods, pure in his heart.

---

*In his autobiography, *In My Own Words*, Mickey Cohen, the Mafia's man in Los Angeles, who had been running guns to the Irgun, claimed he ordered these killings: no dead British, no more guns. Cohen said he was first introduced to members of the Irgun by the writer Ben Hecht.

†Though members of the Irgun issued several warnings, the last fifteen minutes before the explosion, the hotel was not evacuated, and ninety-one people were killed.

Here's how it looked in the newspapers:

STERN GROUP THREATENED SLAYING
It Boasts a Record of Terrorism

POLITICAL TERRORIST GROUPS KEEP PALESTINE
IN TURMOIL
Violent Action Is Condoned by the Younger Element
and Condemned by Others

SCHOLARLY JEWISH IDEALISTS KILL TO DRIVE
BRITISH FROM PALESTINE
"Stern Gang," Copies Tactics of the Irish Republican Army

SIX POLICEMEN SLAIN IN PALESTINE
Curfew and Death Penalty Invoked
JERUSALEM, March 25—Jewish political terrorists belonging to a minority group struck Thursday night in a series of coordinated land-mine and shooting outrages that killed six British police officers and injured at least a dozen in Jerusalem, Tel Aviv and Haifa.

PALESTINE DISSIDENTS WAGE WAR ON POLICE
Abortive Land-Mine Outrages Laid to "Stern Gang" Survivors
JERUSALEM, May 3—Three recent abortive land-mine outrages have drawn attention again to the activities of the irreconcilable political terrorist group known here as the "Stern Gang."

Stern lived underground. He grew thin, wispy, strange. To many, he was an expression of Jewish misery and pain. He was the Jew who would emerge from the Holocaust, the Jew in love with the gun. The most symbolic thing he could do was die. This happened in March 1942, in a room crammed with books, sunlight coming through the windows. Gunshots, car engines, voices. *Ye gads, they've got us surrounded!* The British stormed the house, the secret headquarters of the gang, which means someone had turned rat. Your last questions are questions of betrayal: Who is Judas? Stern was twenty-eight. The British said they captured him alive, but he died trying to escape. Others said he was shot the moment he was identified. (He was, in fact, pushed down a flight of stairs and then shot.)

You Stern?

Yes.

Bang!

After Stern, the leadership of Lehi passed to Yitzhak Shamir, who would later serve as prime minister of Israel.*

The Holocaust turned Jews into a haunted remnant. History had confirmed their worst fear: it's not our homeland they won't accept, but our right to exist. Which is why every threat is existential—note the root of that word. (When France misbehaves, no one questions its right to exist.) The result is a syndrome, like the Vietnam Syndrome, only worse. It's characterized by the belief that every battle is the final battle, that every enemy is the Nazi, that every solution is the Final Solution.

David Grossman, *Death as a Way of Life*:

> How can we free ourselves from the tragic deformation that the Holo-
> caust still dictates in so much of our life and consciousness? This is ev-
> ident in our absolute, eerie insecurity about whether our children and
> we have a future, and in our feeling that death still shadows us, so that
> we are doomed to experience life as a living death.

---

*Shamir was prime minister from 1983 to 1984 and again from 1986 to 1992. The spirit of the gang under him was perfectly captured in an article that ran in *The New York Times* on June 28, 1944: "SINGS AT DEATH SENTENCE: Palestine Terrorist Renders Anthem in Court Room. Jerusalem, June 27—Unusual scenes were witnessed in the courtroom this afternoon when Shmayahu Smulevitz, alias Raphael Birnbaum, 24 years of age, belonging to the so-called Israel's Freedom Fighters terrorist group founded by the late Abraham Stern, was sentenced to death after his conviction on a charge of illegally carrying firearms and explosives and firing on the British police when accosted in Tel Aviv last April. After a British army major who presided over the military court pronounced the death sentence Smulevitz rose up in the dock and sang the Zionist anthem Hatikva. The prisoner had previously told the court that he did not expect mercy and knew that he was going to the gallows."

Each year, Israel sends thousands of its high school students to Poland, to wander around Treblinka and Auschwitz, barracks and crematoriums, as teachers hammer them with a chilling message: This is where you come from! This is who you are!*

I f you want to observe the Holocaust Syndrome in action, you could do no better than study Menachem Begin—when his pulse was elevated, Shoah came out his pores—who served as prime minister from 1977 to 1983. Begin was a disciple of Zev Jabotinsky and the leader of the Irgun, a little man with thick glasses and a jones for powerful bombs. (If you wrote a calypso about Begin, it would stretch to rhyme Menachem with explosion.) He was born in western Russia, where his family traveled a common route: his grandparents were rabbis (they believed in God), his parents were Zionists (they believed in progress).

They were killed in the Second World War, neither fighting nor fleeing, but in a factory whose product was dead Jews. The boy escaped by running east, one of thousands of refugees shaken loose by the German invasion. In September 1940, he was arrested by the Soviet Secret Police and charged with being "an agent of British Imperialism." He was sentenced to eight years of hard labor in Pechora, Siberia. It saved his life. When the Einsatzgruppen—the shock troops of Hitler's SS—shot the Jews of his town, when his parents were drawing like smoke, he was breaking rocks in the frozen north, night coming down like a storm shutter. *Ka-chunk!* But in 1941, as the Red Army seemed on the verge of collapse, the prisoners were released. Begin joined the Polish army in exile. When this army passed through Palestine, he deserted, slipping away to join the Hagana.

Begin would later found the Likud Party (with Ariel Sharon) and become the first right-wing prime minister in Israeli history. It was

*David Grossman, *Death as a Way of Life*: "Tens of thousands of high school students, on the verge of enlistment in this army, make pilgrimages to Auschwitz to discover their 'roots.' For nonreligious young Jews, the Holocaust often becomes the central element in their national identity, taking up a bit of the space filled in others by religious identity."

an odd image for the nation to project: the dark, slumpy, Yiddish-inflected Jew, not the new Jew, but the old Jew, backed by a modern army. He looked like my grandma Esther's second husband, Izzy Greenspun, of Skokie, Illinois, who stuttered and repeated and got flustered and died while wiping a dish—"I thought Izzy had dropped the dish," said Esther, "but it turns out what Izzy had dropped was dead." One of the thousands of Polish Jews scattered by history, an army of tiny men, surrounded by tchotchkes and photo albums, Holocaust-haunted, all in for Israel, ready to drop the big one, each a summation of the Eastern Jew, the last of a breed, a tchotchke like the tchotchkes in their curiosity cabinets.

Philip Roth, *The Counterlife*:

> My father died and so he missed Menachem Begin. That's too bad, for not even Ben-Gurion's fortitude, Golda's pride, and Dayan's valor taken all together could have provided him with that profound sense of personal vindication that so many of his generation have found in an Israeli Prime Minister who could pass, from his appearance, for the owner of a downtown clothing store. Even Begin's English is right, sounding more like the speech of their own impoverished immigrant parents than what emanates, say, from Abba Eban . . . After all, who better than the Jew caricatured by generation upon generation of pitiless enemies, the Jew ridiculed and despised for his funny accent and ugly looks and his alien ways, to make it perfectly clear to everyone that what matters now isn't what goyim think but what Jews do.

Begin could take bold action—he signed a peace treaty with Anwar Sadat, of Egypt—but in times of stress he was right back in Europe 1943. This characterizes the syndrome: the belief that every war is the last war.* Here's how he announced Israel's invasion of Lebanon:

---

*"He has no 'complex'—only an inescapable memory of the Holocaust," Alexander Haig wrote in his memoirs. "His letters, his conversations, his speeches—and unquestionably, his thoughts—were dominated by the sense that the lives of his people and the survival of Israel had been personally entrusted to him."

The hour of decision has arrived. You know what I have done to prevent war and bereavement. But our fate is that in the Land of Israel
there is no escape from fighting in the spirit of self-sacrifice. Believe
me, the alternative to fighting is Treblinka, and we have resolved that
there will be no more Treblinkas.

Later, when Ronald Reagan demanded the siege of Beirut be
lifted, here's how Begin responded (in a letter):

Now may I tell you, dear Mr. President, how I feel these days when I
turn to the creator of my soul in deep gratitude. I feel as a Prime Minister empowered to instruct a valiant army facing "Berlin" where
amongst innocent civilians Hitler and his henchmen hide in a bunker
deep beneath the surface. My generation, dear Ron, swore on the altar of God that whoever proclaims his intent to destroy the Jewish
state or the Jewish people, or both, seals his fate so that which happened once on instructions from Berlin . . . will never happen again.

When this letter was published in *The Jerusalem Post*, it shocked Israelis. It was like coming around a corner and catching your reflection
in a store window and wondering, "Who is that nut?" Chyka Grossman, a Knesset member who fought in Warsaw, addressed Begin in
the newspaper: "Return to reality! We are not in the Warsaw ghetto!
We are in the state of Israel!"

"This urge to revive Hitler only to kill him again and again is the
result of pain that poets can permit themselves but not statesman,"
wrote Amos Oz. "You [Menachem Begin] must remind yourself and
the public that Hitler is dead and burned to ashes."

Zionism is an ideology. The Holocaust was an event. Zionism plus
the Holocaust is a religion. (Marc Ellis calls it Holocaust theology.*)

*Marc Ellis: "Holocaust theology, emerging out of reflection on the death camps, represents the Jew-
ish people as we were, helpless and suffering; it does not and cannot speak of the people we are today
and who we are becoming—powerful and often oppressive. Holocaust theology argues correctly for

As with many other religions, it's historical—built around a narrative.
The way that Pilate and Calvary is a narrative. The way that Mecca
and Medina is a narrative. The Holocaust is the Flood and the return.
(When Chaim Potok, in his book *Wanderings*, marvels, "From Auschwitz
to Entebbe is a single generation," his sentiment is religious. He's writing about death and rebirth.) As with other religions, worship is performed with holy books and shrines. *Night*, by Elie Wiesel. *Survival in
Auschwitz*, by Primo Levi. The museums at Majdanek and Auschwitz.
As with other religions, observance requires a pilgrimage. The Israeli
students wandering through the crematoria are on pilgrimage. As with
other religions, there are prayers, sacred dates, magic numbers. Never
again. April 19, 1943.[†] Six million. As with other religions, there is belief in Apocalypse, with lessons on how to behave in the end-time. (Better to die as free men fighting!) As with other religions, believers are
constantly reliving the events in scripture. It seems like you are camped
outside Beirut, but when you look through the scope it's Berlin you see.
The power of this new religion comes from a unique combination of
fear (of another holocaust) and power (of the IDF): mix two stable
chemicals, and the resulting compound starts to smoke. "The realization of the scale and nature of the Nazi genocide merged with the
Zionist pioneer tradition to produce a warrior culture of remarkable
intensity," writes Yuri Slezkine.

The following parable appears in David Grossman's *Death as a Way
of Life*:

> I participated in an encounter between Israeli army officers and
> Holocaust survivors. Two brothers, now in their sixties, sat on the
> stage. As children, they had lived in Vilna, at the time of the Nazi in-
> vasion. One day, while they were playing soccer with their Christian

---

Jews to be empowered; it lacks the framework and skills of analysis to investigate the cost of that em-
powerment. Holocaust theology speaks eloquently about the struggle for human dignity in the death
camps and radically about the question of God and Jewish survival, but has virtually nothing to say
about the ethics of a Jewish state possessing nuclear weapons, supplying military arms and assistance
to authoritarian regimes, and expropriating land and torturing resisters to Israeli occupation." (*Toward
a Jewish Theology of Liberation: The Challenge of the 21st Century*, Baylor University Press, 2004.)
[†]The day the Warsaw Ghetto uprising began.

friends, the Nazis began rounding up Jews. The brothers were kidnapped from the playing field and put on a train that took them to a death camp. Through the cracks in the side of the train, they could see their friends continuing the game. The two brothers told their story in quiet voices, and the officers began crying. Some ran out of the room. I especially remember one of them, little more than a boy, with a wiry body and curly hair. I cannot forget the way he kept banging his forehead, over and over again, on the barrel of his M-16.

Fanatics dream of blowing up the Dome of the Rock and in its place building the Third Temple. To them I say: The Third Temple was built in 1953. It's called Yad Vashem,* the Holocaust Martyrs' and Heroes' Remembrance Authority. Like the Temple, it's in Jerusalem. Like the Temple, it sits on a hill—the Mount of Remembrance, near the Knesset. (To reach it, you make Aliyah.) Like the Temple, it can be seen from a long way off. It sulks. It broods. It's the center of the modern nation as the Temple was the center of the ancient nation. It's where Jews go to weep and pray. The road climbs until the trees are beneath you, their tops tossing in the wind, because not only did God make everything, he makes everything move, bloom, wither, and die. There is a line of taxis out front, waiting to return the pilgrims to their hotels. The drivers listen to the news on the radio, which is always bad, or smoke hand-rolled cigarettes, spitting out the leaves that stick to their tongues. Most are Arabs, dark-eyed, unshaven, unsmiling, idling before this shrine to the martyred European Jew.

What will happen to Yad Vashem if Israel is overrun? Will we see a mob looting its exhibits? Will we see singed scrolls that survived the burning of a Polish synagogue unrolled and mocked? Will we see photos of the death camps torn and scattered? Will we see Anderson

---

*The name comes from Isaiah: "To them will I give in my house and within my walls a memorial and a name (Yad Vashem) that shall not be cut off."

Cooper in an infantry helmet interviewing a man as he walks off with the antique pistol used by the leader of the Jewish resistance? Will the buildings be set ablaze, like the Temple, glowing like a torch, the eternal flame of the Jews? Will the hilltop sit desolate for a generation, until an Arab leader clears it with big machines and in its place builds a shrine to the sufferings of Palestine?

Yad Vashem is a campus, with its buildings offset by gardens and trees, like the buildings on the Temple Mount. As you walk from building to building, you feel as if you are in a painting by de Chirico, in a desolate, surreal landscape where pennants flag but no wind blows. Inside are halls where your head is forever bowed before the misery of the past. (Each generation builds its own temple without realizing what it has done.) Most visitors start in the Hall of Remembrance, a room filled with candles, each representing a town where Jewish life was blotted out. It's the holy of holies, a void where you speak the secret name of God. When a dignitary visits Israel, he or she is brought first to Yad Vashem, usually to this room. (The museum is the gate you pass through to reach Canaan.) Nixon, Kissinger, Chirac, Sadat—you must have seen the pictures. He says a prayer and lights a candle as if he were at Mass. What is he doing? He is confessing. He is asking forgiveness. He is acknowledging his sins. He is saying he is sorry for being a part of the world that martyred the six million.

In 2005 a wing was added to Yad Vashem; it's a beautiful bit of ideological architecture. You enter through a dark tunnel, which is the dark tunnel of Jewish history. You wander through strange rooms. You become disoriented, the way the Jews became disoriented in Europe. It's a labyrinth. At its center, a minotaur demands human sacrifice. It's always the same beast, but it goes under different names: Nebuchadnezzar, Titus, Hitler. You are wrong-footed, confused. Your heart starts to race. At every turn, you come upon another pile of dead bodies. You wander into a room about Abba Kovner. He's on a TV screen, skinny as a matchstick, reading his famous manifesto at the trial of Adolf Eichmann, Jerusalem, 1961. Eichmann, with cloudy myopic eyes, looks on from his bulletproof bubble.

Do not believe those who are deceiving you. All roads lead to Ponary,* and Ponary means death. Oh, despairing people,—tear this deception from your eyes. Your children, your husbands, your wives—are no longer alive. Everyone is shot. Let us not go like sheep to the slaughter. It is true that we are weak, lacking protection, but the only reply to a murderer is resistance. Brothers, it is better to die as free fighters than to live at the mercy of killers.

This clip plays on a loop, a circle, so it is endless, replicating the infinity of the story, how, no matter how far you go, you keep coming upon the same clearing.

In the last room you see pictures of ships crowded with Jewish refugees, the port of Haifa from a mile out to sea, then there's an escalator. It's long but climbs fast, carrying you out of the maze to a platform above, which is the Temple Mount. You step into the desert light. You walk under the blue sky. In every direction, you see hills. Israel is the last exhibit, its creation being the only way to redeem the past. This is what the architect is saying: that all that suffering is not meaningless if it leads back here, to the stony waste, the Old New Land.

Israel is the Holocaust with a happy ending.

*This is the name of the forest where the Jews of Vilnius were dumped in pits.

ELEVEN

First Good War in a Long, Long Time

When Samuel Zemurray died in 1961, *The New York Times* called him "Sam the Banana Man," "the fish who swallowed the whale." Unmentioned was the work he did for the Jews in Palestine. If you want to understand Israel, you should study David Ben-Gurion and Chaim Weizmann, but also Sam the Banana Man, who, along with a few dozen others, was an unknown agent of its creation.

More on that later: first a gray town in Bessarabia, Russia, where Zemurray was born and raised until he was ten; then the ship, steam pouring out of its funnel, people waving from the docks; then the ocean; then Galveston Bay, Texas, sheds and outbuildings, the plain shimmering away in the heat; then the quiet, porch-lined streets of Selma, Alabama, where—who knows why—the Zemurrays settled. A colony of Jews lived in mean shacks across the river, stitchers and sewers and salesmen and laborers who hauled and stacked, families stranded by the eccentric sweep of Jewish history.

Sam was like a kid in a Walker Evans photo, slouched against a fence in a snap-brim hat. Behind him, in the doorway—you see only the shadow, but know he's there—stands the old man in the skullcap. The family came with nothing, saved only their Hebrew skins. Sam went to work when he was a boy. He had one of those faces—as an old man, I mean, because I've only seen pictures of him from when he was old—that tells you he was cynical even as a child. His eyes were hooded, his mouth intelligent. Not handsome—familiar, everyone and everything the Jews brought from the little towns of Poland and Russia, all the mannerisms and wisdom that would be bleached out in the hot American sun.

He worked in machine shops and groceries, wherever there was money to be made. He sold tinware to pig farmers, earning a dollar a week. When he was fifteen, he got hold of an old pushcart and began hawking bananas in the markets of Selma and Mobile. Because he was a kid, he took what he could get: bananas that were a little too yellow, starting to freckle and stink. In the business, these are called ripes. His cart was piled high with them, the junk of the trade. If you don't move them in an hour, you never move them. Out of necessity, he became a great salesman, a boy with a clock over his head, making deals, unloading product—yes, at a discount, a tremendous discount. (It's a metaphor for the human condition. Entropy. The salesman on the edge of the abyss, closing before the innards turn to paste.) Green bananas, yellow bananas, fresh bananas, piles and stacks and heaps of rotten bananas—his head was filled with the business. His problems were logistical: getting the product to the consumer before the sun did its work. He decided to skip the markets altogether, pushing his cart directly to the train depots, so he could meet the grocers as soon as they reached town. It was in these years that Sam, behind his cart overloaded with reeking produce, came to be known as the Banana Man.

He saved every dime, then borrowed more. He bought a ship, a relic from the glory days of the river trade, when the Mississippi was crowded from Cairo to New Orleans. I would like to focus on this ship, as it will be important later: a two-deck steamer with a side wheel and a pilot's house, the paint splintered, the name faded beyond recognition. It's dilapidated to the point of being picturesque. Zemurray could now skip both the market and the railroad siding and go directly to the store owner, saving still more time. His work continued on a grander scale, the decks and cabins filled with bushels of ripes. He cruised the river. In each town, he was met by grocers and market bosses. Business boomed. He repaid his creditors and accumulated enough money to move into the more legitimate sectors of the trade—yellow bananas, even green bananas. A man who buys green bananas is said to have faith in the continued existence of the world.

On his twenty-first birthday, Zemurray had a hundred thousand dollars in the bank. Today we would call him a baby millionaire. He rented an office in New Orleans, the financial center of the trade. He lived in the French Quarter, in a house with tall windows.* He lingered on pier landings, reading the names of the ships, or haggled with sellers in the French Market. He sat in the coffee shops on Jackson Square, drinking café au lait and reading *The Picayune*. He spoke with a thick Yiddish accent and said things like *a bi gezunt*, or *bei mir bist du shayn*. He said smart people had a *Yiddische kupp*. He called old men *alter cockers*. It meant trouble if he called you a *momzer*.

He studied shipping charts, sales figures, farm yields. He learned Spanish. He read the Latin American newspapers. He was obsessed with supply, and dreamed of cornering the trade. He traveled to Honduras in 1910. He stayed in a small hotel. The courtyard was filled with palm trees and parrots. The town backed up to the jungle. He toured the country. After the rain, fog pooled in the valleys. He visited the delta where the Cuyamel River flowed into the sea. This was America as Columbus found it. He bought five thousand acres on the coast, then hired Indians to hack a plantation out of the jungle, then planted banana trees. He renamed his company Cuyamel Fruit. He bought a second steamer and soon had ships, heavy with bananas, running back and forth across the Gulf of Mexico.

In 1911, when the policies of the Honduran government imperiled

---

*He later bought and rebuilt the mansion on St. Charles Avenue that serves as the official residence of the president of Tulane University—one of many gifts Zemurray made to the school. This is how I first heard the story. As a student at Tulane, I had a professor named Joseph Cohen, who was himself fascinated by the role Zemurray played in the founding of the Jewish state, a fascination he passed on to me.

Zemurray's plantations, he began meeting with government officials and foreign agents. He talked in back rooms, in whispers, his face shrouded in cigar smoke, cursing a blue streak: *Those sons of bitches! Those momzers! When I buy a country, I expect it to stay bought!* He traveled to Miami, then a sleepy town on a hibiscus swamp, where he found General Manuel Bonilla, the deposed president of Honduras, drinking in a seaside bar. Zemurray told Bonilla he could return him to power. Then, back in New Orleans, he hired two mercenaries, Lee Christmas, an unemployed railroad brakeman from Livingston Parish, Louisiana, later famous for his adventures in half a dozen Latin American countries, and George "Machine Gun" Kelly, later famous for bank robbery.

That December, these men—Samuel Zemurray, General Bonilla, Machine Gun Kelly, Lee Christmas, and a handful of other mercenaries—left New Orleans in a skiff, from which they boarded one of Zemurray's steamships. In some accounts, he stays back, but in most he leads from the front. The men went down the Mississippi, through the bayous and around barrier islands, then across the Gulf of Mexico. They anchored in harbors where the water was so clear they could see every rock on the bottom. Spanish towns hung from the cliffs. They sailed into the Cuyamel River, tied up at a pier head, went into the jungle with rifles, pistols, grenades, and a Thompson machine gun, bribed peasants and rebels, crossed into Guatemala, where they were promised the support of the government, then went to Tegucigalpa, the capital of Honduras, a colonial town in the hills. They walked down the main street with guns on their hips, dragging the Thompson behind. (I am imagining.) Men watched them from windows, Miskito Indians drinking rum from leather sacks.

Do you think these men will get what they're after?

No, these men will be lucky to live through the day.

The government building was set on a green. As the sentries looked on, the mercenaries put together the machine gun. Zemurray went in to see the president. (Still imagining.) A clerk asked the nature of his business. Zemurray presented an order written on official-looking paper. It said that the sitting president was to step down and call for new elections. Zemurray came out of the building, waved his arm. George Kelly opened up with the machine gun. Bullets pocked the building's stone facade. There was an exchange of fire. The officials came out with their hands up. The president abdicated. A vote was held. Manuel Bonilla was returned to power. A few days after he took the oath of office in an elaborate ceremony, Bonilla signed a paper that exempted Zemurray from paying taxes in Honduras for twenty years.*

Over the course of the next decade Zemurray bought plantations across Central America, insuring himself against future overthrows, spreading his risk. He owned property in every nation between the Panama Canal and Mexico. In 1930, having spent every moment of the two previous decades working, he sold his business to his largest competitor, United Fruit, the staid old-money Boston concern that had long dominated the trade. The deal was structured as a swap, with most of the payout coming in stock—three hundred thousand shares of United Fruit. This made Zemurray, the immigrant from shtetl-land, the largest owner of the blueblood behemoth. As part of the arrangement, the board of directors in Boston would continue to run the company.

Zemurray retired, slept late, took up causes. He became a fierce opponent of Huey Long, the governor of Louisiana. In the 1930s, however, as the effects of the Depression spread through the economy, the share price of United Fruit stock began to fall, which meant that Zemurray, by reading the financial trades, could watch his fortune diminish.

A bi gezunt, what are these momzers doing to me?

He made an appointment with the board of directors in Boston. He had ideas, notions, ways to revive the business. He stood in a frumpy suit, with his dark eyes and big hands, talking of his own experience. He had a thick accent, as I said, and spoke the way my grandparents spoke, with a lot of spit, heavy vowels, rolling *R*s, and *W*s that

---

*Here's how the episode was reported, years later, in *The New York Times*: "In the course of his career, Zemurray dabbled occasionally in Latin revolutions. Once he outfitted an exiled Honduran president and two soldiers of fortune with rifles, ammunition and a yacht. Within six weeks, they overthrew a regime. And, incidentally, protected Mr. Zemurray's interests."

sounded like *Vs*: *Vat is da problem chere, gentleman?* When he finished speaking, a member of the board, Daniel G. Wing, chairman of the First National Bank of Boston, smiled and said, "Unfortunately, Mr. Zemurray, I can't understand a word of what you say." The men at the table laughed. Zemurray stormed out. He owned the most stock, but not a majority, so he spent weeks meeting with other shareholders, talking about the business, how it was being ruined: *And this you can see in your share price.* He put together about a dozen men, who, among them, controlled more than 60 percent of the stock. He then called a meeting. It was loud and contentious. The old board was voted out. A new board was voted in, with Zemurray as its managing director. Here is what he said: "You gentlemen have been fucking up this business long enough. I intend to straighten it out." This is how Samuel Zemurray became the head of United Fruit. This is how the fish swallowed the whale.

He revived the company. By tightening his hold on supply, and forcing out his competitors, he came close to the old dream of monopoly. By the mid-1940s, he was perhaps the most powerful man in Central America, controlling, with his ships, not just the fruit trade, but entire economies. When a firebrand said, "Yankee, go home," he was talking about Samuel Zemurray.*

This man lived the entire dream, crossed in steerage, went from nothing to everything, and, like many such men, came to see his success as hinging, to no small degree, on luck—that his parents carried him out of Russia, that the family settled in Selma, that he found his way to ripes—so he saw in the fate of the Jews of Europe something that was happening not far away, to someone else, but to him. It was not just, "Well, that could have been me," but, in some way, "That *is* me." Which is why he read the newspaper with such intensity—why all old Jews read the paper that way, folding it back, scanning, underlining.

*Zemurray is considered a factor in the CIA coup that, in 1954, overthrew the government of Guatemala. He persistently lobbied Congress, arguing that Guatemala's president, Jacobo Árbenz Guzmán, whom Zemurray saw as a threat to his plantations, was a Communist and thus represented a dangerous Russian foothold in the Western Hemisphere. (In 1961, United Fruit provided two ships for the Bay of Pigs invasion.)

He was searching, seeing what horror had befallen his people. He was the sort of man who responds to every development by asking, "Is it good or bad for the Jews?"

He closely followed the story of Jewish survivors in Europe after the war. He studied the photographs, criticized the headlines. He had a special interest in the *Exodus*, the refugee ship turned back from Palestine by the British. Here's the headline and lead of a story he would have read in *The New York Times* in August 1947:

BRITAIN ASSAILED ON REFUGEE THREAT
Plan to Return 4,400 on Ship to Germany Called
"Brutal" and "Ill-Advised" Act

The reported decision of British authorities to send back the 4,400 Jewish refugees of the ship Exodus 1947 to Germany brought vigorous protests from American Jewish organizations here yesterday. Several groups asserted that the proposal to ship the refugees now in the French port of Port-de-Bouc to Hamburg inevitably would lead to retaliation and more bloodshed.

Now I am going to focus on the *Exodus*: a two-deck steamer with a side wheel and a pilot's house, the paint splintered, the name faded beyond recognition. It was the very same ship Zemurray had used to haul his ripes up and down the Mississippi. He had stripped it, outfitted it, and donated it.* (This perfectly captures the relationship of American Jews to Israelis.)

In 1947 Zemurray began to curtail his hours at United Fruit, then, in 1948, without explanation, he resigned as president altogether. Two years later, he resumed his post. What was he doing? It's one of the mysteries of his career. Though it's impossible to answer this question with perfect certainty, the sequence of events offers a clue:

September 1947: Zemurray curtails his hours.

---

*This detail is so stunning that I've spent hours in the archives trying to nail it, figuratively, to the mast. Though the lore does indeed have the refugees crowded into the Banana Man's first boat, some skeptics say it was more likely another, less storied ship from the Zemurray fleet.

November 1947: The United Nations votes to partition Palestine into two states, one Arab, one Jewish.

May 11, 1948: Zemurray resigns from United Fruit, citing "personal reasons."

May 14, 1948: Britain withdraws its soldiers from Palestine, Israel declares its statehood, and war begins.

June 1949: The armistice is signed; Zemurray returns to work.

Is it unreasonable to suggest that Zemurray left United Fruit to campaign for partition, then help Israel fight its war of independence?

Especially telling is the tally of the partition vote: thirty-three in favor, thirteen against, ten abstentions. This is closer than it looks, as the motion required a two-thirds majority. The European nations voted in favor (as a bloc), the Muslim nations voted against (as a bloc), which left the tie to be broken by the nonaligned states with no obvious interest in the outcome. In the end, it was carried by the republics of Latin America: Costa Rica, Dominican Republic, Ecuador, Guatemala, Haiti, Nicaragua, Panama, Paraguay, Peru, Uruguay, and Venezuela. These votes, which might otherwise strike you as inexplicable and strange, suddenly make sense: behind them, and thus behind the realization of the ancient dream, is none other than Samuel Zemurray, with his accent and his pushcart piled high with stinking ripes.*

O f course, it was not just the nations of Latin America that made Israel real. It was those eleven added to twenty-two others scattered around the globe, each voting in favor for its own reasons, few having anything to do with a love for Jews. America because President Truman once owned a haberdashery with Eddie Jacobson, a Jewish friend from the army; Russia because Stalin wanted to embarrass the

---

*For information on the life of Zemurray see the *New York Times* obituary; the United Fruit Historical Society website; *Banana: The Fate of the Fruit That Changed the World*, by Dan Koeppel; *Empire's Workshop: Latin America, the United States, and the Rise of the New Imperialism*, by Greg Grandin; and *1948: A History of the First Arab-Israeli War*, by Benny Morris, which specifically references Zemurray's work on behalf of partition.

British; France because de Gaulle wanted to close the DP camps; the Czechs because the Czechs did whatever Stalin told them; the West Germans because, you know, they felt just crummy about what had happened. It was the kind of perfect alignment that might occur once in a millennium: because the Ottoman Empire had collapsed, because the Arab world was in decay, because the Allies had won the war, because the British had gone broke, because the cold war was on, because six million had died.

The resolution was greeted as a triumph in the Jewish world. This, and not the V-days celebrated in Times Square, may have been the real end of the war. It seemed biblical, not in the way of the Old Testament, which is the Jewish Bible reordered by Christians, but in the way of the Torah, which culminates in Chronicles, with the Hebrews streaming back from the Babylonian exile and King Cyrus calling them "to go up to Jerusalem," to make Aliyah. I have known old Brooklyn ladies, fund-raisers for Hadassah, who, on the night of that vote, got down on the linoleum floors of Brownsville and Flatbush and thanked God.

In Palestine, people followed the tally on the radio. It's like a scene in a folk painting: tense faces in blue light, shotguns and floorboards and dirty hands. Jewish peasants—meaning intellectuals drunk on Tolstoy—singing in the village squares. The night was wild with stars, each surrounded by worlds, on each world a hounded Jew waiting for his moment of joy. People danced in great circles. I've seen photographs. It's called the hora. It's noisy and inelegant, but, in a way, this was the point of the project—to root the hora, and all it represents, in a particular place, thus making it authentic, thus making it elegant. Later,* when the British were leaving Palestine, David Ben-Gurion went on the radio to declare statehood. He sat beneath a picture of Herzl. He spoke in a stilted Hebrew, a language that, a hundred years before, had lived only in sacred books.

Here is what he said:

*May 14, 1948.

By virtue of the national and historical right of the Jewish people and by resolution of the General Assembly of the United Nations we hereby proclaim the establishment of the Jewish state in Palestine to be called "Israel."

Then, "Two thousand years of wandering have come to an end." Then, "The ancient dream has been fulfilled."

The founders of the state had argued over its name. Some wanted to call it Judea, some wanted to call it Zion, some wanted to call it Eretz Yisrael, the "land of Israel." They finally agreed on Medinat Yisrael, the "state of Israel," grounded not in the mystical history of kingdoms (the land) but in the modern life of nations (the state). The name *Israel* is as old as time—it has been found on an Egyptian tablet carved in the thirteenth century BC, where it refers not to a nation but to a tribe of wanderers. In the Torah, it's the name Jacob wins from the angel, whom he wrestled to a standstill in the course of a long night before battle.

And [the angel] said, Let me go, for the day breaketh. And [Jacob] said, I will not let thee go, except thou bless me. And [the angel] said unto him, What is thy name? And he said, Jacob. And [the angel] said, Thy name shall be called no more Jacob, but Israel.

Thus the Hebrew sheds his old name, which meant heel-clutcher—Jacob, a twin, came through the birth canal grasping his older brother, Esau, by the foot. In naming their new state Israel, the Zionists were therefore laying claim to the transformative moment in Jewish history, when the grasper became Israel, "he who wrestles with God."

The war began soon after Ben-Gurion declared independence, first as declarations and threats to drive the Jews into the sea, then as soldiers crossing the frontier from each of the surrounding Arab states.

To Jews, it's the Israeli War of Independence. To Palestinians, it's Nebka, or the Disaster.

It's remembered as headlines and news clips, as battle reports and images, as pins moving across a map.

As the Egyptian army, singing and marching, kicking up dust, shooting and looting, fighting in the Negev, being stopped, digging in.

As Jews running the embargo, smuggling in weapons, outfitting the army, which was short on everything.

As pilots from around the world, some Jewish, some who just wanted to fly, shoot, and kill, meeting in Quonset huts to build the Israeli air force, which, for a time, consisted of a single German plane.

As battles and charges and the sky filled with smoke.

As snow falling on the high plains.

As the green peaks of the Golan, with Damascus glowing in the distance.

As the Syrian army in the north, the Iraqis in the west.

As explosions and showers of debris.

As Robert Capa taking pictures for *Life* magazine, which are frozen in the Jewish mind: soldiers marching up a stony hill, the landscape an essay on geology and time, their capes turned in the cold mineral wind.

As the Jordanians blockading the road to Jewish Jerusalem, the sky lit by tracers. The trucks and half-tracks destroyed trying to break the blockade have been left as a memorial in the ditches and overlooks, where you see them today, rotting and beautiful, on your way to Jerusalem.

As Ariel Sharon, a skinny officer, leading his men in a raid up the cliffs, smoke and gunfire, a bullet going in his shoulder and coming out his leg,* waking in the hospital to learn half his men had been killed.

As the smell of burning rubber and burning towns and burning bodies.

As fields filled with corpses, some pristine, some desecrated.

Ariel Sharon, *Warrior.*

---

*He was shot from directly above.

By mid-July I was well enough to return to my battalion, which was now holding the Kuleh hills northeast of Lod. Just a few days earlier, the Jordanians had launched a counterattack, overrunning a unit, then massacring the wounded. Twenty-eight bodies had been found, many with ears missing, some with their genitals cut off and stuffed into their mouths. For days we scoured the area looking for missing pieces, and scattered around the hills we found them: fingers, ears, penises caked into the dusty earth.

As the siege of the Jewish Quarter of Old Jerusalem, a sandstone warren where the ancient kingdom came to an end.

As the Jordanians pushing out the last of its defenders, looting the synagogues, ripping up gravestones and graves.

As the flowers that came in the spring, the heat that came in the summer, the cool evenings that came in the autumn, and the chill that came in the winter.

In the end, Israel suffered three thousand dead, one percent of its population. Many were immigrants, having gone from their homes in Europe, to the ghettos, to the camps, to the ships, to Palestine, where a gun was thrust in their hands and a kid yelled at them in a strange language and they were killed.

In the spring of 1946, a Bedouin chased a sheep across the desert. This was on the western shore of the Dead Sea, a few miles from Masada. He followed a trail over a hill into a kind of natural amphitheater, its walls riddled with caves. He tossed a rock into one of the caves and heard something shatter. He went inside. The cave was filled with clay pots. Did the sheep lead the man to the caves, or had the Almighty used the sheep as a pointer? *Here, shepherd, over here!* Or is it just the way of things: if you live in a graveyard, you are bound to stumble on a body. Each pot was filled with scrolls; the cave turned out to be part of a vast library. The Bedouin carried a scroll back to his tribe. Several Bedouins then returned to the caves, which have since been identified as Qumran, an ancient site, which, depending on the historian, was the library of an aristocrat, a pottery workshop, a hiding place, a fort, or the home of the Essenes, a monastic order that thrived early in the first millennium.

The Bedouin brought one of the scrolls to a dealer in Bethlehem, who gave it a quick look, then declared it junk. But the Bedouin kept trying, eventually finding his way to Father Roland de Vaux, a French priest who managed a religious library in Jerusalem. Father de Vaux had the scroll carbon-dated. It was two thousand years old. Several scrolls were then put on sale in an antiquities market, which is where E. L. Sukenik, the head of the Archeology Department at Hebrew University, came across them. Sukenik was the first person to properly identify the Dead Sea Scrolls. Some are books familiar from the Torah, he said, some are different versions of those books, and some are completely unknown.

Sukenik was a Russian-born Zionist. He wanted to rebuild the nation. His weapon was neither gun nor pen, but a shovel—biblical archeology, wherein you dig with scripture in your hand, seeking to prove the legend. By unearthing the ruins, you not only fix the Jews in the land, but suggest that the Diaspora was just a moment, a dream. When the new state is made, the ruins will rise as the dead will rise at the end of time: there were the Essenes, then the modern Zionists, and everything between was unreal. To Sukenik, the scrolls were a deed, a title of ownership, proof of prior occupancy. They were the project of his life. He shared every aspect of his work with his son Yigael Yadin, an archeologist* and a soldier. When Sukenik died, Yadin finished his father's work on the scrolls.

Yadin was the chief of operations of the Israel Defense Forces. He commanded the army in the north. Veterans tell stories of him reading the Bible before battle, not for inspiration, but for intelligence. He predicted the Syrians would invade along the route the Assyrians took 2,800 years before (he was right) and positioned his soldiers accordingly.

In 1948, during the darkest days of the battle, Yadin presented the

---

*Yadin excavated Masada in the 1950s. (See his book *Masada: Herod's Fortress and the Zealots' Last Stand.*)

War Scroll to a room of reporters. He believed it would inspire the nation. The press conference was held in Jerusalem while the city was being bombarded.* Plaster fell from the roof, the lights flickered, a reporter fainted, but the general went on. He was reading from his father's translation. The scroll tells the story of the last battle, in which the sons of light will clash with the sons of darkness. Its language is eschatological and symbolic and weird. It's said to be a comment on an older text, the Book of Habakkuk—Habakkuk was a Hebrew prophet from an earlier age—but as with all books was actually a comment on what was happening at the time it was written, in the last days of the ancient kingdom.

The discovery at Qumran is the kind of miracle modern science has taught us not to recognize. The fact that these scrolls, hidden in a cave circa AD 70, when Rome was crushing the last of the Zealots, were not found for two thousand years, until a Jewish army was again fighting for a Jewish nation—well, it's uncanny. When archeologists searched the caves, they found, in addition to the scrolls, coins minted with the face of Emperor Hadrian and letters Bar-Kokba had written to his generals. "It's as if these manuscripts had been waiting from the destruction of Israel's independence until the Jewish people returned to their home and regained their freedom," Yadin wrote. "The symbolism is heightened by the fact that the first three scrolls were bought by my father on 29 November 1947, the very day the United Nations voted for the re-creation of a Jewish state in Israel after two thousand years."†

The truth of the 1948 War was not in the tally of the dead, or in the names of the battles, or in the names of the generals, or in the miracle of the scrolls, but in the nature of the fighting, the atrocities

---

*Edmund Wilson was at this conference, doing research for his *New Yorker* stories on the Dead Sea Scrolls.

†A facsimile of the Isaiah Scroll is on display at the Israel Museum in Jerusalem in the Shrine of the Book, a building made to look like one of the pots in which the scrolls were found. The originals, so delicate, would disintegrate in even indirect light.

perpetrated by both sides as the struggle turned desperate. These would set the tone for decades to come. (There are some lessons you can't unlearn, some stories you don't forget.)

Deir Yassin was in the hills that control the western approaches to Jerusalem. In the weeks before the war, an Arab militia made the town its base, using its cliffs to attack cars crossing the valley below. There had been a series of skirmishes between Jewish irregulars and members of the militia. Then, on April 8, 1947, soldiers from LEHI entered the town, ostensibly to drive out the militia, but instead, either by accident or by design—I leave it to the polemicists to argue the motivation—massacred dozens of Arab civilians, including women and children. Two hundred and fifty killed. The rest of the population fled, taking what they could carry. This was the start of the crisis that turned two hundred thousand Arabs into refugees. Some historians say that the Deir Yassin Massacre gave rise to this crisis: Palestinians did not have to be driven out of their homes; fearing another Deir Yassin, they went without having to be told. In other words, Deir Yassin worked. (This is something we don't talk about.) It happened, the Arabs fled, Israel was built (in part) in the void left by these fleeing Arabs. It's what the peace activists mean by original sin—the massacre that portends all others. The Zionists wanted to change the Jewish character—well, they did. They successfully weakened the moral certainty of the ghetto, what the old men meant when they said, "Jews don't do that."*

Martin Buber:

It happened one day, that outside of all regular conduct of war, a band of armed Jews fell on an Arab village and destroyed it. Often in earlier times Arab hordes had committed outrages of this kind, and my soul bled with the sacrifice; but here it was a matter of our own, my own crime, of the crime of Jews against the spirit. Even today I cannot think about this without feeling guilty. Our fighting faith in the spirit was too weak to prevent the outbreak and spread of false demonic teaching.

*Immanuel Kant: "The wielding of power inevitably destroys the free judgment of reason, it is not to be expected that kings should philosophize or philosophers be kings."

By the summer of 1949, the war had settled into a stalemate, with armies dug in and lines drawn. Jerusalem was divided. Israel controlled the modern city in the west, Jordan controlled the old city in east. The ancient Jewish Quarter had been destroyed. Syria controlled the Golan Heights and the eastern shore of the Galilee. (This would become the 1949 border, or Green Line, to which Israel is so often asked to return.) David Ben-Gurion said Israel needed to make a final thrust—a drive into the Negev to open a way to the Red Sea, which was crucial to the nation's economic survival. There was only one road south, however. It ran through Gaza, along the Mediterranean, and was controlled by the Egyptian army. A direct attack would mean heavy casualties without promise of success. This problem (out of time, no way south) was presented to commanders of the army as a puzzle: see if you can solve this.

Yigael Yadin first noticed the odd marks on a satellite photo of the Arabian Peninsula: dashes scattered across the Negev, in the scrub waste. He ran his pen along the dashes, as if to connect the dots. They seemed to form a single line that ran from the Sinai to the fields east of Ashkelon. He went over to his bookshelf and took down an ancient text. He read a passage about the Romans, how they moved their soldiers from garrisons in Egypt to the towns of Judea. Yadin read the passage again, then looked at the photo, tapping the dotted line with his finger. The Romans must have built a road, he told himself. And it must have run through the middle of the desert.

He sent a scout, who found the road, here and there buried, here and there exposed. The Bedouins had always known about it, but did not know that the little stretches of brick made a single highway. (This is what people mean by missing the big picture.) Hundreds of Israeli workers went south. Moving quickly and quietly, they excavated the road, then covered it with wire, so tires and treads would not rip out the decayed stones. Then, one night, when the moon was down, a battalion of Israeli soldiers followed the road past Gaza, turned west, then, with the sun rising behind them, attacked the Egyptian flank. It's a kind of Zionist fairy tale—though much of it's true—for it connects the ancient and the modern, showing how the Jews reclaimed the past, or were reclaimed by it. The Egyptian army collapsed. Israel took control of the Negev, with its port on the Red Sea, and won the war.

The creation of Israel changed what it feels like to be Jewish. For American Jews, it meant a kind of normalization. A Jew in New York suddenly had an old country and a homeland, just like the French, the Greeks, the Italians. (We have a team to root for in the World Cup!) A Jew voting for Israel is not evidence of a conspiracy—it's the American way, no different from the Irishman rooting for Sinn Fein or the Pole supporting Solidarity. (My love for Israel is a dual loyalty only in the way most Americans with foreign relatives feel the pull of various connections.) Which is what people mean when they call the United States "the melting pot," a phrase coined, not incidentally, by Israel Zangwill, the Jewish playwright who also coined the phrase (about the Jews and Palestine) "a land without a people for a people without a land." The fact that the same man coined both phrases tells you something about the nature of the Jewish identity that has emerged over the last century: the Jew is now tied to both America and Israel, two Promised Lands. It's an identity that depends on radical freedom, the sort that comes from ignorance of the past.

What's more, Israel gave Jews in the Diaspora, the vast majority of them living in America, a place to escape to if the political winds turned sour. This is Israel as a safe haven: a place to go in a bad time, when all other doors have closed. This explains, in part, anyway, the Right of Return, the Israeli law that lets any Jew in the world become a citizen without delay. It's symbolic—it says these people are ours, they belong to us—but it's also seen as necessary, a way to keep the gates visibly open. It was under this law that Jews were brought to Israel, en masse, from North Africa, Iraq, Russia, Ethiopia. Ben-Gurion, as his first order of state, revoked the British white paper that limited immigration to a thousand Jews a year. If Israel had existed in the 1930s, he said, millions could have been saved.

Israel gave American Jews a new sense of freedom, which, in turn, made their lives in the United States more meaningful. Not making Aliyah became choosing America. "The fate of individuals—whether to stay or to move—is now morally in their own hands, and each can settle it freely, as he wishes, as best he can, with as much wisdom and good fortune as may fall to his lot," Isaiah Berlin writes in *The Power of Ideas*. "In this sense, the creation of the State of Israel has liberated all Jews, whatever their relation to it."

Most profoundly, the creation of Israel changed the very character of the Jewish people. This happened subtly, over time, probably as a natural consequence of statehood. With the birth of Israel, Jews went from the universal—because the values of exile were transcendent, stateless values—to the particular: a particular territory with particular enemies at a particular time. The Jews were "normalized" as a result, and so were beset by the normal cravings: land lust, power lust, blood lust. This was the fulfillment of ideology: Zionism is, after all, the desire to vanish into the quotidian, to get the yellow star off your arm, to get the invisible deity off your back—to live like everyone else. (As Chaim Weizmann said, "You will know Zionism is a success when you see a Jewish cop chasing a Jewish criminal.")

According to Robert Alter, the first critique of such "normalization" was spoken in the Book of Samuel, when the Hebrews, who had lived in a theocracy, demanded a king so they could live like everyone else:

> And [Samuel] said, This will be the manner of the king that shall reign over you: He will take your sons, and appoint them for himself, for his chariots, and to be his horsemen; and some shall run before his chariots. And he will appoint him captains over thousands, and captains over fifties; and will set them to ear his ground, and to reap his harvest, and to make his instruments of war, and instruments of his chariots. And he will take your daughters to be confectionaries, and to be cooks, and to be bakers. And he will take your fields, and your vineyards, and your olive yards, even the best of them, and give them to his servants. And he will take the tenth of your seed, and of your vineyards, and give to his officers, and to his servants. And he will take

your menservants, and your maidservants, and your goodliest young men, and your asses, and put them to his work. He will take the tenth of your sheep: and ye shall be his servants. And ye shall cry out in that day because of your king which ye shall have chosen you; and the LORD will not hear you in that day. Nevertheless the people refused to obey the voice of Samuel; and they said, Nay; but we will have a king over us; That we also may be like all the nations; and that our king may judge us, and go out before us, and fight our battles. And Samuel heard all the words of the people, and he rehearsed them in the ears of the LORD. And the LORD said to Samuel, Hearken unto their voice, and make them a king.

In other words, to become a nation, the Jews had to give up their ancient Jewish souls. It was the price of admission. "By being faithful to the covenant that advocated a return to Zion," Jean Daniel writes in *The Jewish Prison*, "they became unfaithful to the injunction to be nothing but priests and witnesses."

Here's how Nathan Zuckerman, on a bit of a goof, assesses the trade in Philip Roth's *Operation Shylock*:

Better to be marginal neurotics, anxious Assimilationists, and everything else the Zionists despise, better to lose the state than to lose your moral being by unleashing a nuclear war. Better Irving Berlin than Ariel Sharon. Better Irving Berlin than the Wailing Wall. Better Irving Berlin than Holy Jerusalem! What does owning Jerusalem, of all places, have to do with being Jews in 1988?

TWELVE

The New Jew

Let me show you a few pictures. Imagine them spread out across a table in the design department of *Life* magazine, circa 1950, with the art director, in a black turtleneck, studying them through an eyepiece as Robert Capa leans against a wall smoking a cigarette.

"Were these shot in Jerusalem?"

"Ashdod."

"These men here, are these Jews?"

"Sure, why not?"

"Marvelous, just marvelous."

The photos were taken soon after the 1948 War and were published in a book with an essay by Irwin Shaw. They were said to depict the "New Jew" who had come of age in the new Israel. Some showed men smiling in the sun. Some showed men patrolling beneath walls, packs on their backs. Some showed scouts in the bush, as free as Red Indians. Some showed men resting between missions—"most were very large, with bold, tanned faces and clear eyes, and gave the impression of a group of good-humored athletes whose faces had been stamped by profound experiences," writes Shaw; some showed men hiking up a road; some showed airplanes; some showed tanks; some showed infantrymen, who, according to Shaw, "had the tough confident look of victorious troops."

In the forties and fifties, a golden age for Israel—because the country was still humble, and truculent, and small—the spirit of the nation, personified by this normalized new Jew, was being forged in the army, which was seen as a kind of lab, where officers were not merely training soldiers for war, but curing Jewish recruits of being Jewish, or inventing a new way of being Jewish altogether.

The ethos of the army was the ethos of the state.

First there was the physical appearance of the soldiers, many of whom grew bushy mustaches and went everywhere without a hat, tanned to a deep olive. They were reclaiming the land and the land was reclaiming them, turning them into desert rats, the wandering tribe of Joshua. They changed their names—shed the *steins* and *bergs* of Europe, which were exile names, slave names, and took Hebrew names that suggested power, nature, or the land itself. The most popular included Peled (steel), Tzur (rock), Avni (another kind of rock), and Allon (oak), as in, *This New Jew is as solid as an oak!* When Shmuel Goldfein—it means something like Sam the Moneygrubber (in Europe, Jews were given surnames by their Christian neighbors)—made Aliyah from Plotsk, he changed his last name to Barak (lightning), and named his son Ehud, which means something like "popular." Sam the Moneygrubber begat Popular Lightning.

Then there was the fighting style of the Israelis, how Jewish soldiers were taught to comport themselves in battle. If fired on, for example, they were told to return fire immediately, before taking cover. If ambushed, a common tactic in the region, they were told to charge into the source of fire. Israeli commanders were reeducating the Jews, who had been taught, by history, to cower and hide. The New Jew would behave less like his grandfather the ghetto Jew, than like his ancestor the Zealot, who went out at sundown, when the sentries blew their horns and the archers darkened the sky with arrows.

The Israelis believed they were creating a soldier different from any other kind of soldier in history. Because these were Jews, they would be smart as well as strong, creative, humane, decent, compassionate. Officers spoke of "the purity of arms." It meant disobeying an order if it was immoral. It meant wars without war crimes. The army was egalitarian—no service academy, no ruling class; everyone went in as a grunt. To make the point, commanders led not from a tent or a hut in the rear, but from the front, first into the ambush, first to die. "After me" was their slogan. As in, "Come on, come on!" As in, "Here I go, here I go!" Some spoke of retiring the word *Jew* altogether. A Jew is in the Diaspora. A Jew is cowering and weak. "We are not Jews," said Shimon Peres. "We are Israelis."

Recruits trained in the desert, ran, shot, jumped from planes. The standouts were tapped to serve as officers. Those who accepted were taken into the wilderness blindfolded, turned around, and left to find their way home. They picked a service: paratroopers, infantry, scouts, commandos. You saw them in the city squares on leave, with insignia on their chests and berets pinned to their shoulders. Or at intersections on the main road, hitching a ride back to their base, the fiery sun dropping into the sea, the stars coming out.

The paratroopers were inducted on Masada. This was Yigael Yadin's idea. He wanted to connect modern Israeli soldiers with the ancient warriors who had made the peak their last redoubt. As in, "What died here is born again!" Soldiers followed the Snake Path in the dark, the desert yawning below. When the sun came up, it pressed on their backs like a warm hand. Cloud shadows crossed the valley. The sea shone in the distance like an amethyst, the flat eye of a lusterless God. The paratroopers were encouraged to think of themselves as the first Jews to retake the mountain from Rome. Everything that had happened was happening again. As the men stood in rank—the sun high now, the wastes bleak and going away—there was the *thwump*, *thwump* of a helicopter descending through the dust. Then a man climbed out: General Yadin. He stood on a platform, speaking of antiquity, return. One at a time, the soldiers came forward to have a pin stuck on their chests.

A fter the '48 War, Israel demobilized its army and returned its soldiers to civilian life. The barracks were empty, the borders sparsely defended. In these months, the Arab militias resumed the guerrilla war by which they tried to erode the Jewish state, erode and erode until the last Yehud stood with his wife on a pier in Haifa, waiting for a ship to take them to some merchant house in Antwerp or New York. These militias, known as fedayeen—Arabic for "freedom fighters"—ambushed Israeli convoys, shot up Israeli markets, planted bombs in Israeli hotels, stabbed and killed Israeli civilians.* Casualties mounted: 137 killed in terrorist attacks in 1951; 163 killed in terrorist attacks in 1952. There were more than 1,000 attacks in 1953, in which 162 died. The Israeli soldiers who responded were ill equipped, not properly trained. They were tricked, ambushed, and routed. Fearing such losses would demoralize citizens, Ben-Gurion decided to form an elite unit trained specifically to hunt the fedayeen. He asked Ariel Sharon to devise a strategy, recruit and train the men.

To many, Sharon is the fat old kosher butcher, with blood on his apron and a sly grin on his face—and his fingers are missiles and his teeth are bullets—but in the 1950s he was the fit young Sabra[†] who had been wounded in battle and was beloved by his men and superiors, especially David Ben-Gurion, who saw in Sharon a personification of the strong, inarticulate new Jew. Israel was still small that way: the leader of the nation could spot a recruit going up the rope and over the wall and say, "Bring him to me." Ben-Gurion would sit Sharon beside him at dinner, give him advice, tell him what books to read. The *Iliad* and the *Odyssey. The Peloponnesian War.* According to Moshe Dayan, Ben-Gurion loved Sharon because Sharon was "a daring fighter with

---

*It was said the fedayeen took inspiration from Algeria, where, beginning in the early 1950s, Muslim irregulars waged an insurgency that finally, in 1962, drove the French out of the country, which they had occupied for more than a hundred years.

[†]A term used to describe native-born Jewish Israelis. It's Hebrew for *cactus*, and so said to describe the sons and daughters of the new nation: prickly on the outside, tender within.

confidence in himself, who was unapologetic about his Jewishness, at home in the terrain, knew the Arabs and knew his profession."

In 2001 David Grossman called Sharon "one of the last living Sabra heroes, the native-born Israeli who is daring, rooted in the land, and prepared to fight for it to the death, in both his appearance and character he reminds many of a Biblical figure*—a man of great physical prowess and primal urges, cunning, shrewd, and brave."

Sharon called the unit 101. Composed of only the best of the best, it would be a kind of distillation of the national ethos. He began searching for members in 1952. He recruited in the manner of the Samurai in the Japanese film: this one because he can shoot, that one because he knows the enemy, this one because he can vanish in the tall grass, that one because he can stick the blade. He invited twenty men to a base in the Negev. These men were short, tall, handsome, homely, as Jewy as can be, or Aryan in a way Goebbels might have admired.[†] Sharon trained them not only for marksmanship, obedience, and discipline, but also for endurance and creativity. How will a man perform when he is alone and hungry, has had no sleep, and feels the world has forgotten him? He wanted men who could fight without support, for weeks. He drilled them inside Egypt and Jordan so that they became accustomed to going back and forth across the border. Israel is too small to play defense, he explained. We must attack. His strategy echoed that of Orde Wingate: if you have to fight among civilians, make it *their* civilians.

He led the first operations. The unit set off at dusk, a truck drop-

---

*Which figure from the Bible? Is Sharon David, as many of his supporters believed? Wherever he went, crowds chanted, "Arik Melech Yisrael!" "Ariel, King of Israel!" Or is he Jeroboam, David's strongman, his Luca Brazzi—the story of Michael Corleone is the story of King David. ("I'll try, but even Sonny can't call off Luca Brazzi.") Jeroboam fights the battles and secures the throne but kills with a little more zeal than is necessary, so, in the end, must himself be killed on the altar of God.

†Several years ago, I met a dozen or so men who served in Unit 101 and its successor, Sayeret Matkal ("General Staff Reconnaissance Unit"), the counterterrorism force responsible for, among other things, the rescue at Entebbe. They showed me a video that members of Sayeret Matkal had made for their commander, Uzi Yairi, who was leaving to head the paratroopers. It was a parody of a James Bond film, handsome young men in razor-sharp suits, smoking and laughing; in fatigues, at the stick of a helicopter, ascending, jumping from planes, smiling as their parachutes bloomed open behind them; in drag, scuba gear, space suits, having fun, being silly in the way of young men with no sense of consequences or cost.

ping the soldiers near the frontier, the men cutting the border fence, scrambling on their bellies under the wire, vanishing into the shadowy hills across the Dead Sea. There were several missions. Some were reconnaissance, some led to firefights, some were manhunts, but most were retaliation—Israelis attacking because Israel had been attacked.

Here's what Sharon told his men: It's simple economics. Because of the Holocaust, the number of Jews, the supply, has been greatly diminished; we are short on inventory. As a result, the price has gone up. If they want to kill Jews, okay, but it's going to cost them. "I came to view the objective not simply as retaliation or even deterrence in the usual sense," he wrote. "It was to create in the Arabs a psychology of defeat, to beat them every time and beat them so decisively they would develop the conviction they could never win."

Unit 101 existed for just five months—here, then gone. As a strategy, it turned out that hitting back twice as hard had perils. In short, all that training led to a disaster. In the winter of 1953, Arab militiamen infiltrated Yehud, a dusty Israeli town near Tel Aviv. Some of these men threw a grenade into a house, killing a family in their sleep: mother, daughter, baby. Within days, Israeli intelligence had determined the whereabouts of the militia: they were living in Jordan, in a town called Kibbya.

In February 1953, Israeli paratroopers attacked the town, driving its people from their houses, then searching for members of the militia. At the same time, Unit 101 attacked a Jordanian army base a few miles away. This was a diversion, meant to draw away soldiers who might otherwise come to the aid of the militia in Kibbya. Sharon wanted to inflict heavy casualties on the Jordanians, making them pay for sheltering the fedayeen.

At first light, the commander of the paratroopers radioed Sharon.
The mission is a success, he said. *We're withdrawing.*
Sharon asked about Kibbya.
Where are its people? What's it like on the street?
Deserted, said the paratrooper. *The people ran away.*
Members of 101 then entered Kibbya. They set bombs in the foundations of forty-five houses. The wires came out in a tangle and led to

the detonator a soldier carried on his belt. He counted to three—*aleph, bet, gimmel*—then pressed the button. Debris went into the air and came down in a shower. Smoke lingered over the town.

Ariel Sharon, *Warrior*:

> Kibbya was to be a lesson. I was to inflict as many casualties as I could on the Arab Home Guard and on whatever Jordanian army reinforcements showed up. I was also to blow up every major building in town. A political decision had been made at the highest level. The Jordanians were to understand that Jewish blood could no longer be shed with impunity. From this point on, there would be a heavy price to pay.

The members of 101 celebrated on their base: successful missions often ended with a party. The phone rang. Sharon took it in the back. When he came out, his expression was grim. There were people in those houses, he explained. Women and children, in the basements, hiding, probably waiting for us to leave. Sixty-three of them died.

Sharon said the fault lay not with his men, or his plan, but with the previous Israeli policy of limited response, from which, according to him, the Arabs took the wrong lesson: that the Israelis were not serious, that if you hid and waited they would just go away. The Arabs, in other words, were not victims of Israeli strength or aggression; they were victims of Israeli weakness, which had been provocative.

Kibbya made headlines around the world. This is what the incident seemed to suggest: the Jews are as bad as everyone else. Sharon's policy actually seemed to echo the Nazi policy of collective punishment, in which the masses suffer for the crimes of the few. There was an investigation. The Israeli government promised to be more careful in the future. Unit 101 was disbanded. Its members became paratroopers, but its legend lived on.

Here is the real lesson Israelis took from Kibbya: it was a terrible accident, but it worked. "While the civilian deaths were a tragedy, the Kibbya raid was also a turning point," Sharon wrote. "After so many defeats and demoralizing failures it was now clear that Israeli forces were capable of finding and hitting targets far behind enemy lines.

What this meant to army morale can hardly be exaggerated. The past years had been a time of impotence and frustration, again and again IDF units had been chased off by Arab militia. But with Kibbya a new sense of confidence began to take root."

Sharon met Ben-Gurion in Tel Aviv. "It doesn't make any difference what will be said about Kibbya around the world," Ben-Gurion told him. "The important thing is how it will be looked at in this region. This is going to give us the possibility of living here."

I n a sense, all this—training, fighting, raids—was not just a means to an end (secure borders, safe towns) but an end in itself. Through this struggle a new Jew would be born. "We are not Yeshiva students debating the finer points," Ben-Gurion wrote in 1922. "We are conquerors of the land facing an iron wall." It seemed thus to people everywhere: Israel was bringing a new type into the world, a ruddy, sandy-haired Jew, in the jet, on the tank, at the post, a kind of peasant, everything the Galut Jew was not: strong, simple, decisive, brave. He turned up again and again in the literature of the fifties, sixties, and seventies:

Saul Bellow, *To Jerusalem and Back*: "The young men wear skullcaps but their frames are big and their forearms thick with muscle."

Irwin Shaw, *The New Yorker*: "The housewives of Tel Aviv get up practically at dawn and seem to go, almost as one woman, immediately to the radio, which, with peasantlike delight in mechanical noise, they turn on full blast."

Edmund Wilson, *The Dead Sea Scrolls*: "The visitors at the King David Hotel present an unattractive contrast . . . to Israelis, who are active, industrious people, with skins that have been darkened by the Eastern sun."

In a letter to Lyndon Johnson, Henry McPherson, the president's special counsel, wrote: "Israel at war destroys the prototype of the pale scrawny Jew. The soldiers I saw were tough, muscular and sunburned."

The new Jew would look unlike any Jew the world had ever seen. Yes, it all seems superficial. Achingly so. What nation has ever been so concerned with the appearance of its citizens? (Well, Nazi Germany.) But there is a reason. In Europe, the appearance of the Jew—as caricatured—was said to mirror his inner nature: his foreignness, his forsakenness. The Jew is pale and narrow because he killed Christ. As if, in his anger, God smudged the Jew as you might smudge a wet painting. In the modern age, when people stopped attributing everything to God, the old caricature was kept, with its reasons rewritten. The Jew was still bent and pale, only now it was because of his inferior genes. Christ killers in the age of Christ; parasites in the age of Darwin. The modern Israeli was stronger and straighter because he had been redeemed.

What strikes me about the idea of the new Jew, which is at the core of the national project, is how Zionists seemed to accept the old stereotypes, seemed to believe, in their hearts, that the racists were at least partly right. Dreams of creating a new Jewish character were premised on the belief that the old Jewish character was diseased. In wanting to build a state to cure the Jew of his condition, early Zionists were in fact displaying a ghetto mentality. They were the slaves who had internalized the prejudice of their masters. For all his talk of autonomy, Theodor Herzl was mostly interested in creating a Jew the world could love—a Jew who wasn't Jewish.

No one hates a Jew like a Zionist.

THIRTEEN

God Made the World in Six Days

In May 1967, Egypt blockaded the Straits of Tiran, closing the Red Sea to Israeli shipping, then moved its armies into the Sinai Desert. These moves, which came as the result of a false intelligence report—a Soviet agent said Israel was amassing its soldiers on its northern border—were followed by weeks of threats issued from Arab capitals: "If Israel tries to set the region on fire, then Israel itself will be completely destroyed in this fire" (President Gamal Nasser, Egypt); "Our goal is clear—to wipe Israel off the map. We shall meet in Tel Aviv and Haifa" (President Ardur Aref, Iraq); "The war of liberation will not end except by Israel's abolition" (King Hussein, Jordan).

Abba Eban, Israel's ambassador to the United Nations, traveled the world seeking assurance or support, but everywhere was turned away. The UN, led by Secretary General U Thant, withdrew its peacekeeping force from the Sinai as the Egyptians moved in—the very development that the peacekeepers had been there to prevent. The UN force had been stationed in the Sinai since 1956, as part of the settlement that ended the Suez Crisis, during which Israel, France, and Britain invaded Egypt and seized the Suez Canal, which had been nationalized by Nasser. To Israelis, the removal of the peacekeepers, meant to guarantee the nation's security, felt like a betrayal, like being left to fate.* (U Thant later called it the great mistake of his career.) But when Abba Eban went to the White House for help, he was met only with riddles. "You will be alone," Lyndon Johnson told him, "only if you go alone."

This is how Hugh Smythe, of the State Department, analyzed the crisis for the president: "On the scale we have Israel, an unviable client state whose value to the U.S. is primarily emotional, balanced with the full range of vital strategic, political, commercial/economic interests represented by the Arabs."

It was the old Jewish nightmare of abandonment. Take, for example, that statement from Cairo. It echoed a statement made by Hitler before the Second World War—a fact not lost on Israelis. "If the Jews think they can bring about an international world war to annihilate the European races," Hitler had said, "then the result will not be the annihilation of the European races, but the annihilation of the Jews."

There is a rhetorical term for this: it's called a false premise.

(If . . . then.)

The noose tightened. Commerce stopped. Israelis were on the verge of hysteria. In Tel Aviv, the streets were ghostly, the buildings stark against the sea. The city squares had that strange feeling you get in old horror movies, when the crowd walks stiffly, with frozen faces, as a disc-shaped UFO hovers above—then, suddenly, a woman screams and swoons, which sends the crowd racing, boiling over, because *we're all going to die!*

Yitzhak Rabin was the chief of the Israel Defense Forces (IDF). He was forty-five years old, a kind of Sabra aristocrat. He had been recruited to the Hagana—irregulars trained to defend the early Jewish

---

*The United States currently has 960 soldiers in the Sinai. These men serve the same function the UN force was to serve before 1967.

settlements in Palestine*—by Moshe Dayan himself, and was then asked to join the Hagana's elite unit, the Palmach ("Strike Force"). Rabin was famous for daring exploits, especially his raid on the internment camp at Atilt, where he spirited dozens of Jewish refugees through the wire. (Paul Newman based his character in *Exodus* on Rabin.) He was, in short, the Israeli as imagined by the Jewesses of Long Island: the blond, bare-chested new Jew, with a gun in his hand and wire cutters between his teeth.

Rabin learned of the Egyptian move into Sinai while watching a military parade in Jerusalem. He was sitting in the bleachers, saluting and smiling, when a lieutenant whispered in his ear. He listened, nodded, then slipped away to headquarters, where he could study the photos and question the generals. Enemy soldiers were massing on every border. Israel's only southern port had been blockaded. The nation itself was being choked. The situation was so dire, in fact, that the only sensible course seemed to be a preemptive strike: kill him before he kills you. Rabin was told that with each passing day the chances of success dwindled—because the Egyptians were bringing in more troops, because their lines of supply were becoming fixed. If Israel struck first, Israel would be blamed for the war, and called the aggressor, and so be without allies. This is what President Johnson meant by "You will be alone only if you go alone." But if Israel waited, it might be destroyed, and so never need allies again. The dilemma was expressed most succinctly (this is Israel in a nutshell) by General Yigal Allon: "If we preempt the world will condemn us, and we will survive."

For a time, Rabin did nothing. This indecision was taken by many as a sign of weakness, even fear. In fact, he seemed nervous, shaky. According to his wife, he was getting no sleep, was hardly eating, was staring at maps, estimating the dead, comparing scenarios, living on coffee and cigarettes. He felt responsible not just for the here and now of Israel, but for the fate of the Jews—ten years from now, a hundred years from now.

---

*The Hagana became the Israel Defense Forces, that is, the regular army, in 1948.

On May 22, 1967, three weeks after Egypt closed the Straits, Rabin was summoned by David Ben-Gurion. Ben-Gurion called on Rabin instead of the prime minister, Levi Eshkol, because Ben-Gurion had built the state, so he knew how it worked—the politician is the public face, gives the speeches, comforts the children, the hysterical, over-wrought, and weak; but the military and its leaders, the elite first anointed in the age of Wingate, are ultimately responsible.*

Ben-Gurion had retired to a farm in the desert a few years before. He was eighty. His hair was falling out; he was haunted and pes-simistic. He did not go to synagogue, did not say the prayers or wear tfillin, but he was as Jewish as can be. He knew the world had ended several times, and would end again and again. He sat in his office, the blinds drawn, desert light streaming through the slats. He served Ra-bin tea, asked questions, then cut him short. (The human voice can be a cold, hard thing.)

He said, Where are our allies?

He said, What are our options?

He said, It is you, Yitzhak! This is your fault!

He said, You did this!

He said, The end of the Jewish people, this is what you have taken on yourself.

I'm imagining these words. The men were alone, the old Jew and the Sabra, who was handsome and strong but starting to buckle. Too much pressure, too much responsibility. "You have led the state into a grave situation," said Ben-Gurion. (These are the exact words accord-ing to Rabin's memoirs.) "We must not go to war. We are isolated. You bear the responsibility."

Rabin stepped out of the house, waved for his driver, lit a cigarette, exhaled. To a general on the eve of war, all smoke is smoke from can-nons. He slumped in the backseat, looking at the hills going by. He was in a daze.

---

*Politicians come and go, but a strong general can go on for decades. (See Sharon.)

Finally, the driver asked, "What did the old man say?"

"The old man . . ." said Rabin. "The old man is not happy."

Later, speaking to no one, Rabin muttered, "The higher you climb, the higher the wall."

This was probably a statement of general anxiety: what a bridge thinks as it starts to collapse. He said it the way you say, "The bastards got me by the throat!" Or: "When will it be enough?" That is, as an expression of personal frustration. But I think Rabin was saying more, even if this was not his intention. That's the power of language. Rabin was like Jesus: a saint who will never get old, who was killed in public in Jerusalem. He was speaking in parables. "The higher you climb, the higher the wall." It's the paradox of Jewish history: the farther you travel, the farther you are from your destination. With every passing year, Zionists, who have accomplished so much in the last century, who created a state, who won the wars, who built an economy, who raised generations of new Jews, seem more distant from their dream of normalcy. "The higher you climb, the higher the wall."

Rabin went to the Pit, the bunker beneath Tel Aviv where the military had its headquarters. He spoke with Moshe Dayan, who was then serving as defense minister. According to Dayan, who wrote about the meeting in his autobiography, Rabin was in a bad way—"unsure of himself, perplexed, nervously chain-smoking."

"So what did the old man say?" asked Dayan.

Rabin mumbled, excused himself, went home, collapsed. His wife found him on the floor. She called Eliyahu Gilon, the army's chief doctor. He examined Rabin, listened to his heart, looked in his eyes—murky green—checked his blood pressure, then diagnosed "acute anxiety disorder." In other words, on the eve of battle, Israel's commanding general had had a nervous breakdown. He was given a tranquilizer and sent to bed. Leah Rabin made the necessary phone calls. Rabin's condition was kept as quiet as possible; news of it might panic the public. Newspaper reporters were told that he had suffered a bout of "nicotine poisoning."

"I sank into a profound crisis brought on by guilt that I had led the country into war under the most difficult circumstances," Rabin said later. "Everything was on my shoulders, rightly or wrong. I had eaten almost nothing for nine days, hadn't slept, was smoking non-stop, and was exhausted."

Ezer Weizman, the commander of the air force, went to visit Rabin, sat by his bed, talked in a soft voice. Rabin was depressed, said he would resign. Weizman took Rabin's hand and said, "Please, Yitzhak, just get better."*

There is a storied tradition of such breakdowns in Israel. (Levi Eshkol, who was then prime minister, broke down a few weeks before Rabin.†) Such swoons are explained either by the nature of the Jews (a sensitive people), or by the nature of the threat, which is existential. It's not just the fortunes of the state that are in jeopardy, but the state's very existence, thus the existence of the people.

Rabin stayed in bed for thirty hours. When he returned to the Pit, he was weak, unsteady. One of the first people to greet him was General Haim Bar-Lev. "Yitzhak was not—how shall I say it?—in full form," Bar-Lev wrote. "Of course, he was briefed on all the developments, but he lacked his usual strength."

Rabin met the prime minister in the Knesset. He offered his resignation, which was refused, went back to the Pit, and gave the order for the preemptive strike. It had been planned down to the most minute detail. It was called Operation Nahshonim after the chief of Judah, the first tribe to walk between the parted waters during the Exodus. Nahshonim led from the front ("After me!"), setting the example for the other tribes to follow. With this name, all middle distance was obliterated: there was just then and just now, with the modern warriors burning a trail back across the Red Sea.

---

*Ezer Weizman was Chaim Weizmann's nephew. He was a historian as well as a fighter pilot, having flown in the Second World War in the RAF. These details come from his memoirs.

†At the start of the crisis, Eshkol, while trying to calm the public, instead seemed to crack up during a live speech. "The speech was awaited with expectancy," wrote Moshe Dayan. "In every house, in every tent and tank in the field, ears were glued to the radio. At last there would be a clear analysis of the crisis, a lucid presentation of government thinking. But the Prime Minister faltered and bumbled through his address, stumbling over words. What the public heard was the halting phrases of a man unsure of himself. The effect was catastrophic. Public doubt gave way to deep concern."

Pilots crossing runways, climbing into cockpits, pulling on helmets, fighter planes, Mirages and Mysteres, with their short wings and blunt cannons,* huddled together as if for warmth. 7:40 a.m. The mission commander, Motti Hod, is on the radio: "The spirit of Israel's heroes accompany us to battle," he says. "From Joshua Bin-Nun, King David, the Maccabees, we shall draw strength and courage to strike the Egyptians who threaten our safety, our independence, our future. Fly at the enemy, destroy him and scatter him through the desert so Israel may live." Again, the middle distance—which is yesterday, and the day before, and the day before that—is gone, and all we have is two thousand years ago and right now: time is a moving picture of eternity.

The planes go up, one after another, the contrails twisting away. The pilots shut off their transmitters. It's radio silence from here. If a pilot needs to communicate, he does so with hand signals. If his engine fails and he needs to ditch, he does it coolly and quietly, almost politely. Bobs in the sea till someone can come pluck him out. The planes traveled in waves. Group B headed south, over the Negev and the Red Sea, into Egypt. Imagine what those pilots saw, closed in their helmets, closed in their heads, their radios off, the ancient towns of the West Bank speeding beneath them, then the sea, with shafts of light penetrating to the bottom, lighting up the reef, which is a wall holier than the Western Wall, because the Western Wall is dead but the reef is ribboned with life. "It is just an extraordinary experience," an Israeli pilot explained, "flying above Bethlehem, Hebron, Jericho, feeling this time we're fighting on our historic homeland."†

Group A went over the Mediterranean. If you were in a boat off Gaza at 7:45 a.m., on June 6, 1967, you would have been amazed by the sight, plane after plane, flying so low you could see the eyes of the

---

*The United States did not really supply Israel with aircraft until after the Six-Day War.

†This pilot died a few days later; he was shot down above Syria.

pilots, under their helmets, all looking in the same direction. They flew a hundred miles out to sea, turned in a pivot, like a school of fish pivoting in the shallows, then rushed back toward Cairo. A mile from their targets, the runways and towers used by the Egyptian air force, they climbed to nine thousand feet. Radar screen blank one moment, then a blizzard of dots, each an enemy jet, not on the edge of the screen, but in the middle, here. Then, two by two, the dots vanished; the planes were diving.

The plan was designed around intelligence gathered years before by Wolfgang Lotz, a German Jew who had presented himself to the Egyptians as a Nazi SS officer wanting to exchange military know-how for protection. Lotz was found out in 1964 and executed, but not before he had given the Israelis the location and the configuration of every runway in Egypt, the name and rank of every pilot, war plans, flight schedules, rotations. The Israelis knew Egypt expected an attack from the east, at first light, jets flying out of the rising sun. (Egypt sent its pilots up each morning to patrol the eastern skies; by 8:00 a.m. they were back on their bases.) So the Israelis attacked from the west, the sea, arriving after 8:00 a.m., when the Egyptian pilots were in their mess halls. The first wave knocked out most of Egypt's runways, grounding its planes and leaving its skies undefended. The next wave strafed Egyptian pilots running to their planes. The third wave took its time, methodically destroying the Egyptian air force on the ground—bombers, then MiG fighters. In the first thirty minutes, Egypt lost more than two hundred planes—half its fleet. "A fighter jet is the deadliest weapon in existence—in the sky," Motti Hod said. "On the ground, it's defenseless."

Israeli tanks crossed into the Sinai. Wherever it was engaged, the Egyptian army, beset by rumors and confusion—What happened to the air force? Who is in charge?—came apart like wet paper: some units fought, some units retreated, some units fled. The sky above the desert was buzzing with Israeli jets. They strafed, bombed, strafed again. Egyptians were captured, wounded, scattered, and killed. These scenes—a generation after the Holocaust, following weeks in which Israelis felt abandoned by the world—inspired awe: Jews in Jeeps, Jews in tanks, crossing the desert, routing their enemies, missiles whistling, planes circling, like something awesome prophesied in Joel. "The Egyptian Sixth Division entered a terrible killing field," wrote Ariel Sharon. "It was a valley of death. For miles the desert was covered by ruined tanks and burned armored personnel carriers. Bodies littered the ground, and here and there you came across groups of Egyptians with their hands behind their heads."

Saul Bellow, *To Jerusalem and Back*:

> I had never seen a battlefield before 1967 and at first didn't understand what I was looking at. Riding through the Sinai Desert, I thought it odd that so many canvas or burlap sacks should have fallen from passing trucks. I soon realized that these bursting brown sacks were corpses. Then I smelled them. Then I saw vultures feeding, and dogs or jackals. Then suddenly there was an Egyptian trench with many corpses leaning on parapets and putrefying, bare limbs baking in the sun like meat and a stink like rotting cardboard. The corpses first swelled, ballooned, then burst their uniform seams. They trickled away; eyes liquefied, ran from the sockets; and the skull quickly came through the face.

The Hebrews followed a column of smoke through the desert, and now the Israelis were doing the same—only it was not the smoke of the Lord, but the smoke of guns. (You are what you follow.) Tanks rumbled by. Men marched in rank, weapons gleaming. Israel took more prisoners than it could feed, so began to free enlisted men, take their weapons, send them back across the canal. The Egyptian officers stripped off their insignia and claimed to be grunts. But the Israelis identified the officers by their underwear: enlisted men wore army-issue cotton briefs; the officers wore silk. *Oh, the trouble made for the men in cotton by the men in silk!* "Those with silk drawers we shipped off to the POW camps," wrote Sharon. "Those in cotton were sent back to the Canal."

Jordan made a determined effort to stay out of the war. King Hussein was, after all, a kind of moderate, more willing to make peace with Israel than any other Arab leader. In the first hours after the preemptive strike, when everything was smoky confusion, he seemed to ponder: If I go in, I open my people to ruin and myself to revolt; if I stay out, I forfeit the spoils and ostracize my nation. Nasser sent Hussein a cable (he must have known the war was already lost) in which he said Israel had been defeated and Jordan must enter the fight if she wanted to share in the victory. The Jordanians began shelling West Jerusalem, rounds coming out of long metal tubes, the kind worked by two men, a loader and a shooter, one dropping in the ordnance, the other hitting the switch: *VOOOOOM!*

Six thousand shells landed in West Jerusalem. One hit Hadassah Hospital, shattering a section of stained glass designed by Marc Chagall. Every American Jew who has been frog-marched through Jerusalem, from landmark to landmark—this happened here, that happened there; bow before this, weep before that—has seen these windows, which depict the twelve tribes of Israel. They filter the sunlight to a beautiful blue, so you feel you are on the bottom of a Jewish Sea. You meditate on the windows, or on the meaning of the windows, or try to meditate but feel nothing, so feel guilty, so meditate on that.

Israel did not immediately respond to the shelling. The strategists argued against opening another front while war was still being waged in the south. Some worried about the long-term effects of such a campaign, fought not in the Sinai, which is nowhere, a hall you pass through on your way someplace else, but in the West Bank, Judea, and Samaria, the heartland of the ancient kingdom. Thirty-five miles wide at its widest point, this was part of the territory the UN originally set aside for a Palestinian state, but it had been occupied by Jordan since the '48 War.* Its population was Palestinian, either people who had always lived there, or refugees from what became Israel. By defeating Jordan, Israel would take possession of the ancient hills, but also of a hostile population.

By June 5, however, the shelling had become intolerable. Buildings were hit all over the city. Israeli pilots took off from bases across the country. They met Jordanian pilots in the sky above the West Bank. In Nablus, people stood on their balconies to watch the dogfights. Dozens

---

*Jews lived in the West Bank until the mid-twentieth century, when they were driven out first by mobs, then by armies.

of Jordanian planes were shot down in the first hour: the whine of a dying engine, a trail of black smoke, the impact lighting up the distant hills. Israeli planes ghosted over Hebron, Bethlehem. They flew over herds, sheep thrown into the sudden dusk of jet shadows. They dropped bombs on the Jordanian army, hit fixed guns and barracks. The sound of the blasts was immense and swept across the valley like a wave, breaking on the cliffs of Moab. When the infantry moved in, the Jordanians fell away, away, away. By morning, the Jordanians had retreated across the Jordan River. It was in this way, without quite meaning to, that Israel took possession of the West Bank.

East Jerusalem remained in Jordanian hands. The city had been divided in the '48 War. East was separated from West by a no-man's-land of pillboxes and checkpoints and trenches and wire. The Jewish Quarter of the Old City had been razed, the holy places closed to Jews. The Wailing Wall, which could be seen from tall buildings in the modern city, was as far away as it had been at any time since the Roman Expulsion. To go there from the West, you had to pass through the Mandelbaum gate, where travelers were required to show a certificate of baptism proving they were not Jews.* This only made the ancient city more alluring.

Jewish soldiers were positioned on every side of the ancient city. It was like the Remington print in which the Indians creep up on the fort through the tall grass. Meanwhile, a grand argument was raging among Israelis. It pitted officers in the field, who were gung-ho to take the Old City, against commanders in the Pit, who were not so sure: Do we really want ancient Jerusalem with its mosques and its churches and its cargo of history? Is it our destiny, or is it a tangent from the primary mission, which is to escape history? They worried about the international response: Would the Christian nations boycott Israel? Would the Muslim nations attack? To Ben-Gurion, Jerusalem was a dangerous mirage; you follow it like you follow the Sirens' song onto the rocks. Tel Aviv is modern Israel, he said. Jerusalem is a grave. But

---

*Or you could travel to Europe, catch a plane to Amman, then drive back to Jerusalem from the east. The longest ten yards you will ever cross—this is what A. J. Liebling, a Jew, so not in possession of a certificate of baptism, did when reporting a story about the city for *The New Yorker*.

Menachem Begin (and others on the right) said that Israel was obligated to take the Old City. Only then would the dream be fulfilled. We must go all the way, even if it drives us insane.

Moshe Dayan opposed the invasion of East Jerusalem. At first, anyway. For the same reasons as Ben-Gurion. I mean, who wants it? Nothing but ghosts and dust. He warned his generals to "keep out of all that Vatican!"* But events have a logic of their own—there is a direction to the tide. Something wants you to behave in a certain way. No one knows where this comes from. Maybe it's the collective will of the people. (That's what Tolstoy believed.) Or maybe it's your own subconscious. No Jew who grew up with the Bible, who in his sleep was haunted by visions of the man astride the white horse and the proud towers burning, could be so close to the still point without taking that last step.

On June 7, 1967, Moshe Dayan gave the order, qualified with the following: "No heavy weapons in the Old City." A stray shell hits the Dome and it's World War III. The attack was led by a thirty-seven-year-old colonel named Mordechai "Motta" Gur. He was slender and dark with eyes that shade of Jewish green that suddenly seemed less like the green of money than the green of uniforms and tanks. He led the paratroopers through the hills above the Old City. You can follow their route as you follow the stations of the cross: first to the Intercontinental Hotel on the Mount of Olives, which is barnacled with graves and glows white in the sun. From the entrance of the hotel, you can see the shrines across the valley. Through Gur's binoculars, the Jordanian soldiers were close in their pillboxes and trucks. Then to Abu Dis, an Arab town that commands the hills east of the city. Then to the valley of Gethsemane, where Jesus prayed on his last night. Gur spoke to his men on the radio: "We occupy the heights overlooking Jerusalem, which, for generations, we have dreamt of and striven for," he said. "We will be the first to enter. Israel awaits this historic hour. Be proud. Good luck."

At 9:45 a.m., a Sherman tank crossed the valley, its cannon clicked into place, took aim at the Lion's Gate: *Ka-bam!* Paratroopers poured through the breach. History is a film in reverse: Jewish soldiers rushing

*Gershom Gorenberg, *The Accidental Empire*.

back into Jerusalem, fighting on the ramparts, beneath the standards. (As the Arabs say, "What has been taken by force can only be restored by force.") Other soldiers breached other gates, and soon the city was filled with Israelis. Bullets whistled past. Gunmen hid in windows. Israelis walked behind half-tracks, armored trucks with treads in back and wheels in front, like a mythological beast, head of a lion, body of a snake. Now and then, a sniper fell from a window like a sack of coins, coming apart on the stones. There was every kind of noise: gunfire, grenades, screams, prayers, curses, the throb of diesel engines, the whine of jet planes. There was every kind of color: green of Jeeps, brown of stone, black of guns, red of blood, blue of sky. There was every kind of smell and taste: spice from the market, incense and sweat, meat twitching on the lines, bodies in the dumps, copper in your mouth.

The battle was intense but short. The Israelis outnumbered the Jordanians, had better guns, were better trained and more motivated. They were fighting for history, whereas the Jordanians knew they had been abandoned, that their officers and army had gone across the river. These were grunts, having been left in the city in the manner of a bookmark, to save a place. If they fought, they fought only for fear of capture. Hundreds surrendered. The windows of the Jewish Quarter, which after 1948 had been destroyed by Muslims, were filled with white flags. Men came out with their hands up, fell to their knees.

Israeli soldiers converged on the street beneath the Dome of the Rock, ran up the stone ramp, then burst through the Mugrabi Gate and onto the Temple Mount. Where God fashioned Adam. Where Abraham bound Isaac. Where the Temple stood. Where the Zealots made their stand. There was a visual shock: going from a dark alley, where there is no sun, into a plaza filled with light, the roofs of the city suddenly below. (This is why mountaintops are holy.) There was a brief exchange of fire; then it was over. Clerics came out of Al Aqsa Mosque and stood before Captain Gur, heads bowed. They surrendered, then led the Israelis into the mosque, where a cache of weapons was hidden. Gur then radioed Uzi Narkis, his commander, and spoke the sentence that became iconic in Israel: "The Temple Mount is in our hands."

Israeli soldiers wandered in and out of the mosques, stunned. They had gone through the looking glass, into a landscape many had seen only from a great distance, in a book, through binoculars.

Arik Akhmon (one of the first soldiers to reach the Dome):

> There you are, on a half track after two days of fighting, with shots still filling the air, suddenly you enter this wide open space that everyone has seen before in pictures, and though I'm not religious, I don't think there was a man up there who wasn't overwhelmed. Something special had happened.

There are photographs: soldiers on their knees, weeping; soldiers looking on with dumbstruck eyes; a crowd of soldiers posed before the Dome, like fishermen showing off a catch; soldiers assembled in rows, as you assemble for the end-of-the-year photo. (In these, the Temple Mount is the fanciful backdrop painted on the studio photographer's screen.) Israelis pulled down the Jordanian flag and ran up their own. It was not just victory that excited them. It was victory coming after the weeks of anticipation and fear, itself coming in the context of the Holocaust. It was a release, pure glee. It finally seemed that the Jews had a future, a place in the world. There was a sense of the miraculous; even the atheists felt it. All that has happened since—war, occupation, settlement, terror—is just a hangover from that perfect moment.

Motta Gur asked a Muslim cleric if he knew the way to the Western Wall. The man took the captain by the wrist and led him to the stone stairs that went down to the holy place.* Gur and his men came out in front of the wall as another group of Israelis arrived from the opposite direction. The soldiers brushed the stones with their fingertips as you might brush the fur of a sleeping animal, thrilled and afraid. The Wall formed one side of a narrow alley. To see the whole thing, you had to look up, which meant these soldiers were looking at a narrow band of sky, and so were in the position of small men imploring. I have a post-

---

*This bookends a moment, following the capture of Jerusalem by Omar in AD 638, when an old Jew came out of the shadows to lead a Muslim general to the Temple Mount.

card that shows an Israeli with a gun slung across his back—he carries it
the way Bruce Springsteen carries his guitar while playing harmonica—
bowed to the Wall in prayer. It expresses the mood of modern Zionism:
vulnerability plus power, sorrow in a moment of great joy.

Among the first soldiers on the Mount that day was a compact man
with a wild gray beard and piercing eyes. He wore fatigues, but did not
look like an officer. He had traveled to St. Stephen's Gate by Jeep, and
from there, went on foot. He did not notice the gunfire or the shells exploding around him. He was carrying a Torah scroll and a shofar.
When he spotted the ramp that led to the Temple Mount, he broke
into a sprint. This was Shlomo Goren, an Israeli general, a veteran of
the paratroopers who, in 1967, served as the military's chief rabbi.

Goren grew up in a town outside Haifa and was educated at a
yeshiva, where he learned, among other things, to read the Book as if it
were a country, and to live in the country as if it were a book—in which
every object is placed, a thing in itself but also a symbol. Take for example that shofar, which, even now, he is raising to his lips and blowing, the
strangled blast added to the cacophony of shouts and cries and shots and
engines. To Goren, it's a ram's horn, but also a symbol that tells the Jews
on the Mount: *"Break! You are nearing the end!"* According to Hasidic legend, the Messiah, on the day of Judgment, will blow a shofar made from
the ram that Abraham sacrificed on this mountain in place of Isaac.

Goren went into the Dome of the Rock and touched the old stone,
said to be the foundation stone of the world. He opened the Torah scroll
and read, swaying and chanting. According to a newspaper account,
he then made the following statement: "I, General Shlomo Goren,
chief rabbi of the Israel Defense Forces, have come to this place never
to leave it." Goren was among the first of a new kind of New Jew,
driven mad by the victory of 1967. Religious men who once believed
that by creating a state, Zionists were forcing the hand of God came to
believe, because of the scope of the victory, that the creation of modern Israel was evidently the will of God. As such, the state must popu-
late the entire land promised in the Torah. It was the start of an era.

In the way that all Russian literature is said to have come out from under Gogol's overcoat, the entire settler movement was blown out of Shlomo Goren's shofar.

Rabbi Goren found Uzi Narkis, the commanding officer on the Mount. Goren took him by the sleeve, pulled him aside, spoke in a whisper. These men appear as members of a comic duo that has performed often in our history: the crazy Jew with his mind fixed on the next world and the rational Jew with his mind fixed on the here and now. First they're playing a basement room in Vilna, then they're playing the big Zionist convention in New York, then they're playing for the troops during a war, one in fatigues, the other in fatigues and a prayer shawl.

GOREN: General! General! Now is the time! Do it!

NARKIS: Do what, Rabbi!

GOREN: One hundred explosives. In the Mosque of Omar. That's all we need. That's enough. The whole thing will come down, and once and for all we'll be done with it.

NARKIS: Rabbi, stop.

GOREN: Listen to me, Uzi! If you do this, you will go down in the history of your people!

NARKIS: I've already put my name in Jerusalem's history.

GOREN: Uzi, you don't grasp the meaning of this. This is an opportunity that can be exploited. Now we can do it. Tomorrow it will be impossible.

NARKIS: Rabbi, if you don't stop now, I'm taking you to jail.*

Moshe Dayan arrived in the Old City after the fighting had ended. In his autobiography, he writes of approaching Jerusalem from the west, driving through the Lion's Gate, walking to the Temple Mount. He shuddered when he saw the Israeli flag over the Dome. "Down!" he said. "Take it down."

*Narkis told this story on his deathbed to a reporter named Nadav Shragai. It has since appeared in several books, including *Six Days of War*, by Michael Oren, and *The Accidental Empire*, by Gershom Gorenberg.

"If there is one thing we should refrain from doing," he explained, "it is putting flags on top of the mosque and the Church of the Holy Sepulcher."

Dayan was slender, small. His distinct accessory was the patch that covered his left eye, which he'd lost while scouting in Lebanon for the British during World War II. (He was looking through binoculars, saw a flash, a bullet came through the lens.) The patch gave him a fierce bearing, but he was a humorous man. He took the long view. He came onto the scene at the Mount like a cool drink of water. Just the opposite of Rabbi Goren, he behaved not as if the world were ending but as if it would go on and on. He shook hands, smiled, went down the ancient steps. He stood before the Western Wall. "The narrow plaza was crowded with soldiers who had taken part in the grim battle for Jerusalem," he wrote. "All were moved, some wept, many prayed, all stretched out their hands to touch the stones."

Dayan met with Muslim clerics the following day. When he reached the entrance of Al Aqsa, he told his staff to wait outside, unstrapped his sidearm, took off his shoes. The mosque is cavernous, with a pitched ceiling that mimics the vault of heaven. He sat cross-legged on a carpet, surrounded by imams. Here's the first thing he said: *What can I do for you?* He was like a Chicago politician meeting with a ward boss. You get to the center and here's what you find: men cross-legged on the floor trading chits.

We need water, said the imam. *We need electricity.*

Dayan signaled a member of his staff.

Water and electricity, he said. *Get them going.*

He turned back to the imam.

What else?

There are too many people here, said the imam. *Too many soldiers. The people can't attend to their prayers.*

Let's talk abut that, said Dayan.

He and the imam then worked out the arrangements that, for the most part, are still followed in the holy places: Israelis would keep off the Mount, which would remain under Muslim control. This decision was given additional weight by the chief rabbi of Israel, who, over the objection of Shlomo Goren, advised Jews to stay off the platform. In this era, he explained, when all Jews are presumed to have come in contact with the dead, there is no one pure enough to tread near the holy of holies, the precise location of which has been lost.* Zerah Warhaftig, Israel's minister of religious affairs, later told Amos Elon that even though the Temple Mount had been Jewish property since King David "paid the full price for it (fifty shekels) to Araunah the Jebusite," the rabbis were willing to wait: "We won't take possession until the Messiah comes," he said. Jews were instead directed to the Western Wall, which would be under Israeli control. In this way, each community would have its own religious space.

Israeli officials flooded the city. It was a pilgrimage. Even the most worldly spoke of it in religious terms—how they stood before the Wall, which was covered in flowers, which was breathing, soft like skin, which was bleeding, wet with tears. A mad moment at the end of a mad age. Yitzhak Rabin wrote a prayer on a piece of paper and shoved it between the stones. Whoever does this is talking to history, worshipping the past. "It was the peak of my life," he said. "For years I secretly harbored the dream that I might play a role in restoring the Western Wall to the Jewish people. Now that dream had come true, and I wondered why I, of all men, should be so privileged."

He gave a speech:

> The sacrifices of our comrades have not been in vain. The countless generations of Jews murdered, martyred and massacred for the sake of Jerusalem say to you, Comfort yet, our people, console the mothers and the fathers whose sacrifices have brought about redemption.

In less than a week, Israel had destroyed the Egyptian air force and defeated its army, opened the Straits of Tiran and taken possession of the Sinai Peninsula—Jewish soldiers were now stationed on the Suez Canal—defeated Jordan and conquered the West Bank, including its

---

*This ruling was promptly violated by Shmuel Gonen, who, in August 1967, on Tish B'Av, the Ninth of Av, which marks the anniversary of the destruction of the Second Temple, went up to the Mount with a Torah scroll, an ark, and a pulpit, to pray. He was quickly taken away.

capital in East Jerusalem, and defeated Syria, taking possession of the Golan Heights in the north.

The phrase "Six-Day War" first appeared in *The New York Times* about two months later. The name, which is not properly descriptive—by most measures, the war lasted more than a week—stuck because it echoed the holiest numbers in the Jewish lexicon: six days of creation, six million dead. The war was named like a TV show, with a demographic in mind: the Holocaust-haunted Jews of the world. It's a slogan: Six-Day War. It tells you that the story of modern Israel is the story of creation: something from nothing, desert in bloom—it's a miracle beyond normal history, so beyond question, so beyond doubt. It's a matter of faith. The United States, the most Christian nation on earth, really began supplying Israel with weapons only after the war—in part, I'm convinced, because, by winning, Israel proved it had won back the blessing of God.

Israel agreed to a cease-fire with Egypt on June 8; with Syria, on June 10. That night, bulldozers rumbled into the Old City through the Dung Gate, then idled at the edge of Mugrabi, an Arab neighborhood of ramshackle stone houses beneath the Temple Mount. (These stone houses remind me of center-hall colonials across the street from the Bahai Temple in Wilmette, Illinois, which is towering and awesome; the mundane in the shadow of the divine.) Israeli soldiers then went from house to house, banging on doors, ordering people out. Most of the inhabitants had fled at the start of the war, but there were stragglers: women and children, the same sort who stayed behind when Unit 101 brought down Kibbya. These people were marched through the streets, their numbers growing as dust grows before the broom, swept onto buses and taken away.

The bulldozers flicked on their headlights, shifted into gear, lowered their plows. By morning, the entire neighborhood had been knocked down. The stone was pushed into piles, then carried by trucks to dumps east of the city. In this way, the plaza where Jews gather before the Western Wall—it's familiar to any tourist—was carved from the destruction of an Arab neighborhood. It's like Piazza San Pietro in Rome, or Piazza San Marco in Venice: a transitional space where you leave behind the noise and commotion of the market and prepare to confront the sacred. The fact that it was built from the ruin of old homes is typical: Because our peace always comes on the back of someone else's disaster. Because epoch leads to epoch. Because the Jews built on the Muslims, who built on the Christians, who built on the Romans, who built on the Jews.

The Israelis knew they were doing something the international community would prevent if they could, condemn if they couldn't. (By the rules in the United Nations Charter, it was an illegal population transfer.) Which is why they did it so fast, the moment the war was over, in the middle of the night. "Do it now!" Teddy Kollek, the mayor of Jerusalem, told Moshe Dayan. "It may be impossible later, and it must be done!" It was in this same moment that Rabbi Goren asked Uzi Narkis to blow up the Dome of the Rock. Dayan did not blow up the Dome of the Rock; he tore down Mugrabi instead. He wanted to make a place in Jerusalem for the Jews. He called it either/or: either make room beneath the Wall, or the Jewish crowds will wander to the nearest open area, which was the Temple Mount. Dayan cleared Mugrabi to protect the mosques, he said, and to prevent another confrontation, this time not between armies but between religious communities, that could turn into a religious war. Dayan was channeling Jewish euphoria away from the flashpoint.

He was also working against time, not merely because the eyes of the world were on him, but because, in 1967, Shavuot, an ancient festival in which Jews, if able, travel to Jerusalem, fell on June 15, a week after the cease-fire. With the city in Jewish hands for the first time in millennia, the crowds would be enormous. In fact, two hundred thousand made the trip that year—8 percent of Israel's population. They filled the streets wall to wall, tower to tower. Imagine it! The city restored, the pilgrims returned, each in his own dream, in his own Bible, which had been a book and was again a place.

Jerusalem is composed of rings—as was the Temple—that get holier as you approach the center: first the desert, crossed by highways, dotted by towns; then the outskirts; then the new city, with its traffic and its mirrored buildings; then the Old City, with its markets and its monasteries; then, at the center of the Old City, at the center of the center, in place but also in time, is this Western Wall, which, in the hours after the victory, was fronted by a sea of hysterical Jews.

Look at this scene. Fix it. Underline it. Because this is the moment the Jews went batty. This is the moment the ripes turned brown. This is the moment people were touched in the head, contracted the Syndrome, went howling down the alleys of the haunted city. This is the moment the old man in the deli realized he was a hero in a book. Jewish soldiers fighting in Jerusalem, the shofar blown on the Temple Mount, the Israeli flag hanging over the Golden Dome—the images were simply too intense. No one could live with them and keep a clear mind. People went mad, came to sense the coming end. For what are these but the sort of things you expect to witness at the start of act 3, at the close of which everything will burn and the secret author will finally be revealed.

Gershom Gorenberg, *The End of Days*:

> The creation of Israel in 1948 and its conquest of Jerusalem in 1967 are not ordinary history. For those inclined to hear them, they are divine proclamations that the hour is near. For literalists, the venue for the final events is Jerusalem—and at its center, the Temple Mount.

This is when the Rabbi Gorens took a leading role in Jewish history, when the secular and pragmatic began to give way to the apocalyptic and eschatological. In the process, some Israelis forgot reality and began to think of themselves as a strong nation with a powerful army. Some came to love the gun, to see in violence a form of self-expression, a rebuke to the weak way of the ghetto Jew. In this way, some lost sight of the original mission, which had been about saving and redeeming people and instead became about holding and redeeming land. Some grew obsessed with the land. Settling it, dying for it. Historians sometimes say that after 1967, Israel went from being David to being Goliath; but that's not true. Israel is still David, only it's David in his middle years, after he has won, tasted power, summoned Bathsheba. The story of David ends with the toothless king standing in the gates of a town, weeping for his lost son, *Absalom, O Absalom*. The story of Israel, much of it, remains to be written.

FOURTEEN

The Jerusalem Syndrome

Moshe Dayan, while driving through the West Bank a few days before the cease-fire, came across some ruins.

"What's this?" he asked.

"It's the old Etzion Bloc," his aide told him. "What's left of it."

Dayan was going north on Highway 60, which runs through the Jordan Valley, climbing toward Jerusalem. He exited, then followed a potholed road to the Etzion Bloc, which before 1947 had been a cluster of Jewish towns. These towns, each with its own history, each approaching the dream from its own direction—one was communist, one was socialist—had a storied place in Zionist folklore. They were spartan farm colonies. Sometimes they grew oranges, sometimes they grew avocados, but their real product was always Jews—new Jews. The first was established in 1927, on land purchased from local Arabs. Most of its inhabitants were Orthodox Jews from Yemen. Other towns followed. They gathered together east of Jerusalem, animals leaning together on the plains. Four walled compounds, each with its guard tower and barracks, dirt roads and groves.

The towns waxed and waned with political conditions. Residents fled during the Arab riots in 1929, returned, fled again in 1939. They came under attack in 1948, as soon as the British withdrew from Palestine. The road was blockaded. Ben-Gurion asked the inhabitants to stay and vowed to defend the towns, which, in many ways, were indefensible. (Because every dead body is a statement of our intent to remain.) In other words, the Etzion Bloc entered the books not for how it lived, but for how it died. The caravans of Israeli buses coming to resupply the towns in the dead of night; the men in the guard towers, watching the fields; the ambushes and raids and counterraids; the sun getting bloody as it slumps toward the horizon. The 1948 siege culminated in a terrible final battle, at the end of which the defenders threw down their guns and surrendered, were stood against a wall and shot. One hundred and sixty-five of them died. According to Jewish survivors, the Arabs, many of them soldiers in the Jordanian army, were shouting, "Deir Yassin!"

The Jordanians built an army base on the ruins of the Etzion Bloc and a camp for Arab refugees who had fled Israel in 1948—that is, the survivors of the Deir Yassin Massacre settled in Etzion, which itself had been cleared by a massacre. Some of the survivors of Etzion were then settled in ruined Arab villages across the Green Line. It's called war.

Dayan parked and walked through the town. The houses were built in the boxy style of the old kibbutzim, which, for Dayan, who grew up in just such a place, would have brought nostalgia—mixed with horror. In Etzion, he was seeing what might have happened to his own town, what might happen still. If you want to locate the exact moment when the modern settler movement began, in the course of which the ancient hills of Judea and Samaria (and, really, what hills are not ancient, the world being the same age everywhere) would be riddled with bypass roads, fences, and towers, then this—Dayan, with his nostalgia and fear, walking in the ruins of Etzion—is probably it. "As I looked around," he wrote, "reflecting on what had happened to

the original pioneers of the Etzion, I felt quite certain that new kibbutzim would soon spring up on this site."

Of course, the birth of the settlements was not merely a matter of
Moshe Dayan, or anyone else, making a decision; the movement had
grass roots, came from below, from the imagination of people who
had been formed by ancient poetry. The romance of the West Bank
emerged naturally from psalms and stories and from the Hebrew language itself, which could be truly understood only in relation to the
land of Judea. *Peled* was not merely a rock, nor all rocks, but these particular rocks, which once groaned under the live weight of the sinful
king. Thousands of Jews felt the urge to go, to plant, to settle. To flour-
ish, the movement needed only leaders who could direct the mad
energy of the people. Here I'm thinking of the founder of the settler
movement, the teacher of the teachers, the perfectly named Rabbi
Abraham Kook, and his son, Zvi.

Every time you see a picture of a man on a hill in Judea with a
prayer shawl and a .38, barking orders, insulting and praising, in
search of the fiery wheel, the heavenly dynamo, the chariot of angels,
in which each wheel is a head and each head has seven faces, you are
seeing a replica of Abraham Kook, the rabbi from Latvia.

He was educated in a yeshiva in Europe, but unlike his own teachers he came to believe that the creation of modern Israel was not an
abomination, but a sign. He likened the modern Zionist who does not
keep the commandments to the dumb beast that pulls the cart knowing neither where he is going or the true purpose of his labor. To create a secular state where Jews can be normal and live normal lives?
No, of course not. To create the kingdom and gather together the exiles and fulfill the prophecies. Kook called the Zionists "good sinners."

Rabbi Kook studied Zionism with the mind of a believer. He was
less interested in what men such as Ben-Gurion had to say than in
what their actions truly meant, how, in their various proclamations
and declarations and wars, you could see the hidden hand of provi-
dence. His was a kind of hybrid faith: yeshiva plus kibbutz. It came to
be known as Religious Zionism, which remains the dominant belief
system of many of the Jews who settled the West Bank after the Six-

Day War. They believe that the final age is at hand, God is in the headlines. To them, a true Hasid does not stay in a room reading the Book, but lives in the world as if the world were the Book. He has a holy disregard for any characters who fall outside his story. If you come across a person who does not appear in the Book, ignore him, because he is not real, or make him into a character in the Book—which is why, to many settlers, the Arabs either do not exit, or exist as Amalek, the Canaanites that God commanded King Saul to exterminate. Saul fell because he failed to carry out this order. Extreme settlers likewise attribute modern Israel's troubles to its failure to drive out Amalek.

Rabbi Kook moved to Jaffa in 1904. He started a school to preach the good news: The age is at hand! Much suffering will result, he said, but God works through "creative destruction." Every people has a purpose on earth, he said, as every character has a purpose in a book, even a bit character. The purpose of the Jew is to bring the divine idea into the world. To bring this idea to yield, to bring the Lord back into the lives of man, he said, the Jews must return to Zion. In this way, the founding of the state became a step on the way to redemption. In this way, Zionism became holy, a matter of faith. In this way, any retreat or compromise—trading land for peace, say—became not merely a political decision but a religious failing, a sin. In this way, the Zealots got back into the Temple.

When Rabbi Kook died, his son, Zvi Yehuda Kook—Kook ben Kook, Kook son of Kook—carried these ideas, which had grown up in the dank rooms of Europe, where everything is soaked in Baltic gloom, into the hard air of the Middle East.* The son was the father shorn of politeness and niceties. There was no time for that. There was, in fact, something mean in his teaching. He said everything, even the most grisly crimes, were part of the plan. Events that would shatter other men only strengthened his belief in the holy wisdom. The Holocaust, he said, was "the cruel divine operation needed to lift [the Jews] up to the land of Israel against their wills" ("Creative Destruction").

Zvi Yehuda Kook had a thousand followers in early 1967. In the

---

*People say Zvi Kook is the father of the settler movement; Abraham Kook, its grandfather.

months after the war, that number doubled, then doubled again. The victory had convinced many of the truth and beauty of his teaching. By following Kook, they could toss away their ordinary lives and instead live like heroes in the Bible. Go into the land, he said, settle, redeem, because the land is the body of God. He said it's not enough to wait for the coming. You must hasten it, clear the way for the Messiah. "There are people who talk about the beginning of redemption in our time," he told a crowd. "We must see with open eyes that we are already in the middle of redemption. We are in the main hall, not the entryway."

Among Kook's followers was Moshe Levinger, who epitomized the movement. It was Levinger who took the teaching of the rabbi and turned it into facts on the ground. He was thirty-two years old when the war ended. He, too, was a rabbi, but the kind who wore a gun on his hip and considered himself a commando in the army of God. He was raised in Jerusalem, dipped in the Book as a wick is dipped in wax, then finished by the Kooks. He believed that Jews must govern all the territory promised in the Bible, river to sea. Only then would the land sing. Only then would its trees flower and its vines yield and sweet water fill its springs. Over the years, he amassed a criminal record: arrested for trespassing, assault, even for manslaughter, crimes always resulting from his run-ins with the Arabs of Hebron, the friction caused when a crazy rabbi wanders the Arab market armed to the teeth.

He was an interesting-looking man in those days, tall and dark-eyed, with a stringy beard. He wore baggy clothes and tennis shoes and was gaunt. He looked like he did not care what he looked like. He represents a familiar Jewish type: the organizer, the *shtarker*,* the revolutionary; his life has been an episode from start to finish.

He talked of settling the West Bank as soon as the cease-fire was signed. On September 27, 1967, he led a few dozen Jews to the Etzion Bloc, presenting their arrival as a return. Levinger would restore what the Arabs had destroyed. Several of the Jews who made this trip were,

---

*This is Yiddish for strongman, or tough guy.

in fact, survivors from the old Etzion Bloc, men and women who had been chased out when they were young. They returned in middle age, on buses made to look like those used in 1948, as if the last bus out was finally completing its circuit. The driver of the lead bus was indeed the same man who drove that route—Levinger was a savvy promoter. The buses themselves were covered in wood and painted silver to look like the armor that covered Israeli buses during the siege. A sign on each read, ONCE WE TRAVELED LIKE THIS. (In other words, the settler movement began in nostalgia.) The settlers slept in the Jordanian army barracks. One of the buildings was turned into a shul. A Torah scroll was brought from Jerusalem. It was dropped into the desert the way the core of depleted uranium is dropped into the reactor. Everything started to hum and spin, and soon the Jews were bowed together, chanting, *Hear O Israel, the Lord our God, the Lord is One.*

For Levinger, Etzion was just the start, a kind of test run. He wanted to see what was possible, how the government would react, though he always said he would move with or without government approval, there being laws higher than the laws of man. Of course, the real prize was Hebron, the ancient capital, the resting place of the patriarchs, purchased by Abraham for four hundred shekels. The minutes of Abraham's negotiation are right there in Genesis, pointed to by settlers as you might point to a receipt or proof of purchase. I'm not sure this tomb really is the Tomb of the Patriarchs—Dayan called it the tomb of some desert sheik—but people believe it's the tomb, which is all that really matters. It's holy because it's holy, or it's holy because people think it's holy, or it's holy because it's always been holy.

Is there a difference?

Levinger went to Etzion with permission. (Israel got around international law by identifying the settlement as a military base.) The government was far more wary of letting Jews move to Hebron, an Arab population center. For one thing, the Israelis—for the time being, anyway—were mindful of their obligations as occupiers. In September 1967, Levi Eshkol charged his attorney general, Theodor Meron, himself a Holocaust survivor, with researching the legality of West Bank settlement. "My conclusion," wrote Meron, "is that civilian settlement in the administered territories contravenes the explicit provisions of the Fourth Geneva convention: 'The Occupying Power shall not deport or transfer part of its own civilian population into the territories it occupies.'" Meron struck down Israeli arguments for the justice of settlement—that it was not settlement but return, as the Jews had been driven out of Hebron forty years before—noting that the relevant clause of the international treaty is "categorical and not conditioned on motives or purposes of the transfer, and is aimed at preventing colonization of conquered territory by citizens of the conquering state."*

What's more, many Israelis hoped to trade the newly conquered territory for recognition and peace with the Arab states. If Jews were living on that land, such a trade would be much harder to accomplish—which was the precise intention of many of the settlers. But Levinger had a few things working to his advantage: the passion of his followers, for one; their hysteria and persistence; the mood of the moment, which was millennial and triumphant; and, most important, the temper of the Arab world, which was wounded, uncompromising. Soon after the cease-fire, at a summit in Khartoum, the Arab leaders passed a resolution with their famous three nos: no negotiation, no recognition, no peace (with Israel). Which of course made the case of the settlers: if there will be no negotiation, then the occupation will never end; if the occupation never ends, it's not occupation, it's possession; if it's possession, let's possess.

Levinger was waiting only for a propitious moment. It came in 1968, the year after Israel conquered the West Bank. First, Levi Eshkol, who had been strongly opposed to the settlers, weakened and, as he weakened, became less effective. (He would die of a heart attack in 1969.) Then Moshe Dayan, a lucid voice against the settlement of Hebron, was wounded in a way that kept him off the scene for months.

The story of Dayan's injury is worth reporting: it's a parable as stories in the Bible are parables, a record of one life, but also a universal

*See Gershom Gorenberg, *The Accidental Empire*.

story in which Dayan is Dayan but also every Jew who has been touched in the head by the Syndrome.

Like a lot of Israelis of that era, Dayan was obsessed with archeology. By digging into the earth, he felt he was searching his own past and, in some way, communicating with history. It was an aggressive kind of archeology—it was the archeologist going through the sediment as the lawyer goes through the files, looking for the proof that will close the case. His fascination began years earlier, when he was in the fields with his nine-year-old son, teaching the boy to shoot. He was following a pheasant through his rifle scope when he noticed a row of clay jars poking out of the soil. "On inspection," he wrote, "I found that each one was whole, and all looked as though they had just come off the potter's wheel. It was evident that the heavy rains which had flooded the wadi had washed away whatever had hidden the jars."

He brought them home, set them on a table, looked and looked. He called on a friend, an amateur archeologist. The man examined the jars, said, yes, the find is genuine, the jars date from the ninth century BC, the time of the Hebrew Kings. "A new world suddenly opened to me," Dayan wrote, "giving me a glimpse of the life that had existed here three thousand years ago. Hidden beneath the roads, houses, fields and trees of the twentieth century were the remains of cities, villages, and artifacts created by the people who had lived in this land, the ancient Land of Israel. These ordinary articles that provide the bond, intimate, personal, with the wonderful world of antiquity, a world that had fallen silent but not vanished."

Whenever Dayan had time, he went in search of artifacts, which he brought to his house in Zahal, where he built a workshop. He researched and restored. It was a hobby, but also a way for the general to tell himself, *I belong.* His trove could be seen in the background whenever he gave an interview on TV, pots and plates gathered like children, the face he turns to the world, which says, "This is the best of me." (Experts called it "Moshe Dayan's illegal antiquities collection"—he pulled treasures from the ground and spirited them off without waiting for permission.)

One afternoon in the spring of 1968, Dayan, in the middle of dealing with a crisis—one of the first attacks by the PLO—excused himself from a meeting,* got in his car, and drove south. He had been awake for thirty-six hours, reading, arguing, planning. He stopped in Azur, a town near Tel Aviv, where a construction crew had been clearing ground for new roads. In the process, the workers had inadvertently uncovered a ruin. (Azur had been the site of an ancient Hebrew town mentioned in an Assyrian text from the eighth century BC; the Crusaders built a fort there called the Château des Plaines.) There was no official interest in this site—not yet—but word had gone out through the network of collectors. On his way across the sand, Dayan saw a boy playing in the dunes. (I mention this only because the boy saved Dayan's life.) He walked to the edge of a field, where the earth was as soft and rich as freshly ground coffee, got on his knees, and started to dig. Here was the general, during a break in battle, his mind filled with arguments and counterarguments, looking into the soil as another man in the same situation might look into the pages of a book.

He found a shard, a piece of stone, something that resembled something. He dug it out, kept on. He uncovered an opening. It led to a cavity or cave. He dug away the entrance, peered inside, squeezed through. He fell onto a smooth tile floor. He looked around, waiting for his eyes to adjust—his eye. *Where am I?* It was shapes, then the shapes took focus: a table? a jar? a room where people once lived? He had gone through a wormhole into ancient Israel. He would see Roman soldiers when he emerged, aqueducts and chariots. The father sits at the table, drinks from the goblet, un-scrolls the map. *Here is where we throw off Hadrian. Here, and here!*

He heard a sound like running water, then the ceiling fell in, first a shower of dirt, then a great heap of earth. He was knocked out by the blow. When he woke, he was buried to the shoulders. He shouted, cried out, heard the water again, and then was completely buried, interred in his glorious Jewish past. He later said that he could remem-

---

*Dayan was planning a strike on a PLO camp in Jordan. This was the battle of Karameh, in which twenty-nine Israeli soldiers were killed; to Palestinians, it was the founding battle of the resistance.

ber his exact thought. It was not about the Hasmonean kings or the fate of the Jews. It was: *I can't breathe!*

The boy in the dunes heard the collapse and ran for help. Two men working nearby in a metal shop came with tools and dug Dayan out. He woke in a hospital, where he spent the next month. He had damaged his vertebrae, severed his vocal cords, and broken his ribs.

This is a story with a message: dig your way into the past and root around for hints and evidence, and sooner or later the ground will shift and the roof will cave in and you will be buried in the sand, screaming to hear your own voice.

It was in these weeks, with Eshkol fading and Dayan recuperating, that Moshe Levinger made his move. He tried to buy houses in Hebron, but no one would sell to him. He then went to the Park Hotel in the center of the city, where he identified himself as a tourist from Switzerland. He asked to rent a block of rooms for the Passover holiday. He would need them for ten days, perhaps longer. He checked in with seventy others, including his wife.* It was the vanguard of the new movement: Religious Zionism. These were American and European Jews, yeshiva boys and lost Israelis, burning to give their lives to something grand. They had the zeal of the old kibbutzniks shot through with a thirst for the end-time. They were, in fact, a flip image of the early pioneers: whereas members of the Second Aliyah sought the ordinary, a way to stop being Jews, the Religious Zionists sought a life that was spectacular and strange.

Levinger planned a large Seder, at the end of which the Jews would dance in the streets of Hebron. He asked the Israeli army to stand guard over this feast. It was a dilemma for the generals: if Israeli soldiers protect the settlers, then Israel is complicit, the settlement is acknowledged, Levinger is encouraged; but if the army refuses and the settlers are attacked, Israel has failed in its primary mission, which is to

*With him was a Jewish native of Hebron, a survivor of 1929. This was Levinger telling reporters: this is not a conquest, it's a return.

protect Jews, even the wild men. In the end, Israel did guard the
Seder, then, soon after, ordered the settlers to leave Hebron. When
they refused, the army urged, asked, then finally pleaded.* The government worked out a compromise: the settlers agreed to move
from the hotel in the center of the city to a military base in Hebron,
then to apartment buildings on hills above the city. Over time, this
grew into Kiryat Arba. It's where Moshe Levinger still lives. You can
see him striding over the hills with his skullcap and his beard and
his gun.

On April 23, 1969, an article ran in *The New York Times* under the
headline "After 42 years, Jews Are Part of Hebron."

> In defiance of Israeli government policy—to say nothing of interna-
> tional law and world opinion—a hardy band of 73 ultra-Orthodox
> Jews arrived here on April 10, 1968, ostensibly to celebrate Passover in
> their faith's second holiest city, after Jerusalem. In reality, their plan
> was to implant Jewish life in a hostile Arab city and to defy their gov-
> ernment's power to negotiate it away.

Moshe Levinger's wife, Miriam, drawn in a few quick strokes,
seems to typify the settlers: a Jewish girl from the Bronx, the product of
the New York City public school system, swaying beneath the city
on the Number 9 train. "People tell me it isn't safe in Hebron," she
told the reporter, "but I would rather be killed by an Arab in Hebron
than by some nut in New York City—at least the Arab is killing me for
what he thinks is a good cause."

If, as this article suggests, the Israeli government opposed the settlers, why then did the settlements grow until they occupied every important hilltop and crossroad in the West Bank? Because the leaders of
Israel, most of them secular, and unmoved by prophecy, came to see
practical value in Kiryat Arba, Gush Etzion, Gush Katif, et al. In
short, the settlers were tolerated because the settlements were thought

---

*With this, we enter the age of special-interest politics, where settlements grow and grow and are
almost impossible to shrink—for the same reason, I suppose, that it's easy to gain and so difficult to
lose weight.

to protect Israel.* As this was really a kind of marriage of conven-
ience—it grew, and bloomed, and soured, and dissolved—it's probably best understood through the eyes of the groom, Ariel Sharon,
often called the father of the settlements.

For years foreign leaders who visited Israel were taken directly
from Yad Vashem to Ariel Sharon, who brought them up in a helicopter. (If Yad Vashem showed the horror of the Jewish past, the view
from the helicopter showed the horror of the Jewish future.) Sharon
sat beside the pilot, a map in his lap. The man on the runway, in the
jumpsuit, with the big orange earphones, gave the up-and-away,
which is the right index finger turning a corkscrew, the same as the sig-
nal used to indicate a man gone batty. The chopper ascended, the
landing pad falling away, turning into a postage stamp, the fields coming into view, big roads and small roads, the sea in the distance.
Sharon, speaking in that clipped way of Israelis, shouted over the roar:
*We go above Tel Aviv, Mr. President, but are not seeing it because we are going all
the time.*

They flew north, over the patchwork of farms and towns—millions
of people live here; it's where Israel has most of its industry—that runs
from the sea to the Green Line, a distance, in some places, of just nine
miles. Natives call it the slender waist of Israel. It's less landscape than
corridor. It runs from the suburbs of Tel Aviv to Haifa, where the
country balloons out again. (Israel, in its original borders, resembles
an old-fashioned barbell—thick on each end, skinny in the middle.)
The helicopter banked left. *You see,* said Sharon, pointing, *that is where
we start.* The helicopter banked right. *And that, Mr. President, is where
we end.*

In this way, Sharon demonstrated that the old frontier was unten-
able. A column of tanks could cross from border to sea in an afternoon, cutting the country in half. Not only did this make Israelis feel

*It's wrong to say the existence of these settlements prevented a peace deal—in fact, the settle-
ments came into existence in the absence of such a deal, even in place of such a deal. As in: If we
cannot have a piece of paper, then we will fill the land with walls. And the only people crazy
enough to live beneath those walls, in the forlorn desert nowhere, were the followers of Kook and
Levinger.

unsafe, it also caused conflict. Any would-be Saladin looking at the map would say, *It's easy. Let's go.* The settlements, built just east of the Green Line, were meant to thicken the country's waist, and thereby end the provocation. With the old border, we had a war every decade, Sharon would say. Now, with the settlements, we have not had a major war in thirty years.

Sharon was mapping the territory before the war ended, taking special interest in the hilltops that dominated the country. Even before Levinger came on the scene, he established outposts and moved his commando school to the West Bank. "It did not require personal experience or military genius to recognize the strategic significance of these territories," he wrote.

> The coastal strip they bordered was where two thirds of Israel's population lived. It was here that most of Israel's industrial infrastructure was located, where the three main power stations were, where the only international airport was. All that—the heart of the country— was open and vulnerable to terrorists who could cross the border, carry out their attacks, and return, all in the same night. It was within easy artillery range of the Samarian high ground. The entire depth of Israel's strategic center was less than what the American army considers tactical depth for a brigade of soldiers.*

Sharon was everywhere after the war, a map open on the hood of his car, the engine warm, because he had been tooling around the hills, determining where settlements should be built. As every invasion of the country—by the Babylonians, by the Assyrians, by the Greeks, by the Turks, by the Egyptians—had come along the same few roads, he decided to place settlements at the key intersections of these roads. In the event of an attack, the invaders would run first into a settlement filled with Religious Zionists, Zealots, who might not stop the attack, but who would slow it enough for Israel to mobilize. By putting ci-

---

*When making camp, in other words, American field commanders are required to leave a buffer between their brigades and the enemy that is greater than the (old) width of Israel.

vilians on the invasion routes, Sharon believed he was obligating the government to defend the land, even if its instinct was to retreat or appease. "Then, in our moment of weakness, we would not be tempted to give up," he wrote. "We would not be able to say to ourselves: Look, nothing is there. The easiest thing is to walk away."

"[Sharon's] endeavor was absurd from the start," Ari Shavit wrote in *The New Yorker*. "Fifteen years after the decolonization of Algeria, he attempted a colonial project that had an idiosyncratic rationale behind it: to force Jews to defend certain parts of the land whether they liked it or not."

Within a decade of the cease-fire, Jerusalem was ringed by settlements. This was done to secure Jerusalem, to surround it with Jews, protecting it from reliving the nightmare of 1948, when the Jewish half of the city was under siege. (Sharon was, after all, wounded trying to break that siege—the bullet went in his shoulder and came out his thigh.) It was also done to tighten Israel's hold on the city, to mix the populations and confuse the borders so that it could never again be divided, even if a future Israeli government wanted it divided. Sharon called these settlements "facts on the ground"—as in, let the journalists talk, let the negotiators negotiate, let the condemners condemn, but there they are, in their houses, with their God and their guns.

This phrase, "facts on the ground," is spoken with revulsion even by many Israelis. It suggests the worst of the nationalist impulse: taking without asking; taking without thinking. Stealing. Of course, the entire region, the frontiers and names on every one of the old maps, is the result of just this process. What is the Dome of the Rock—built on the pedestal of the Jewish Temple, supported by a faith and a narrative that make its removal unthinkable—but the most successful fact on the ground ever built?

The issue of the West Bank settlements remained the big debate. Just what should Israel do with the land? Some people believed it should be annexed: because the Arabs lost the war, and losing a war should have consequences; because the old border was itself the outcome of the 1948 War, thus no more legitimate than the new border; because the land would be needed to settle the millions of Jews who would flood in from America in the aftermath of Israel's victory. Other people, such as Ben-Gurion, who was old and lived in the desert, warned of the demographic danger: along with the land, he said, we will swallow a monstrous dose of Arabs.

Soon after the cease-fire, the United Nations passed Resolution 242, which called on Israel to exchange conquered land for peace. This resolution is often used as a stick to beat Israel, but it was, it seems, carefully crafted to acknowledge that the borders would probably change—Israel would not be asked to return to the old frontier, with its nine-mile waist, which some Israelis took to calling the Auschwitz Border.

The relevant passage calls for "the withdrawal of Israeli armed forces from territories occupied in the recent conflict."

"Territories" was a negotiated phrase, finessed so that it was non-inclusive. Note it's not "*the* Territories" but "territories," meaning some, not necessarily all. What's more, the resolution calls for territories to be exchanged as part of a larger process leading to recognition and peace: no recognition, no peace, no territories.

In Israel, many criticize the premise of the resolution, which calls for the state to exchange something tangible (territories) for something abstract (peace).*

Meanwhile, as the debaters were debating, the Levingers were building, and in this way settlement led to settlement, until we reached the current impasse. It's depicted on the map that runs with every newspaper story that tells why the shooting will never end. It shows the outline of Palestine, which, to a person like me, is as familiar as a successful corporate logo—it's shaped like a wedge, or a shard of broken glass—with the West Bank shaded and covered in lines and dots, each representing another bypass road (on which Palestinians are not allowed to drive) or settlement, another tiny point of friction, where the flint rubs and the sparks fly.

More than two hundred Jewish settlements have been built in the Territories since 1967. (This number does not include the plethora

---

*Ariel Sharon would have preferred the following trade: War for War, Peace for Peace.

of illegal outposts, which usually consist of a few dozen would-be re-
deemers in trailers on a windy hilltop.) There are two hundred thousand Jews living on the West Bank—half of them in East Jerusalem, in
neighborhoods Israel insists it will keep in any peace deal.* To protect
these settlements, Israel has built dozens of military bases. Each Arab
attack results in more Israeli soldiers, more infrastructure. In this way,
the settlement leads to the shooting, which leads to the checkpoint,
which leads to the roadside bomb, which leads to the bypass road,
which scoots past the town, which burns in the wadi, on and on, until
the landscape is a tangle, with Jews on the high ground and Arabs in
the lowland and soldiers at the crossings and walls through the fields.

How, even if you wanted to, could you unknot this spool?

And it's not just the infrastructure; it's the settlers themselves, a
generation of Jews who grew up out there, convinced they are living in
Judea and Samaria, in the time of King David, dancing and singing
before the Ark. These are the real facts on the ground, though not
the sort Ariel Sharon had in mind: a sea of believers, who, if there
ever is a peace, will have to be brought in as Crazy Horse had to be
brought in.

What are these people like?

Well, first you have to subtract those who moved beyond the Green
Line in search of cheap real estate (there were many); and those who
went in search of a kind of hippie adventure (there were many of
them, too). Then you're left with the hardcore summoned by Rabbi
Goren's shofar. To them, the will of the Israeli government is just as irrelevant as the command of all weak, worldly authority. In a sense, the
state of Israel is not even real to them. It is, as Zvi Kook said, just the
hall on the way to salvation.

Amos Elon, *The New York Review of Books*:

Some Jews abroad have never grasped that for Orthodox Jews in Israel, and in America, the "Land of Israel" was not a territorial but a
theological concept, one linked to salvation.

---

*See *The Other Israel: Voices of Refusal and Dissent*, edited by Roane Carey and Jonathan Shainin.

Among the settlers is a disproportionately large contingent from New York and its suburbs. (Fifteen percent of all religious settlers—there are nearly 140,000—are American born.*) Many made Aliyah in the seventies and eighties. These people can seem a perfect expression of Martin Scorsese's depictions of New York City. They search. They crave. They want to die, but want their death to have meaning. ("I would rather be killed by an Arab in Hebron than by some nut in New York City.") Each one is Travis Bickle, pointing a bloody finger at his temple, going *bang, bang, bang*. Each one is purely American in the way Mickey Mouse and trailer parks are purely American. These people can seem less like believers in Zionist ideology than like pursuers of the American dream. Which is about freedom. Fantasy. Living in the past.† Scores lit out from Borough Park and Flatbush. First they were listening to the Beatles and hallucinating on LSD, then they were poring over stories about the Six-Day War, then they were learning Hebrew, growing beards, boarding El Al jets piloted by stoical veterans of the Israeli air force, then they were wandering the Old City of Jerusalem. They turned up with nothing but a prayer shawl and a book but soon found their way to the settlements. Because they were lost. Because they wanted something. *Because I used to be Malcolm Little but now I'm Malcolm X.*

Meir Kahane was born in Brooklyn in 1932. His parents were Orthodox, but his religion was the street corner, its comedy and folklore. He was torn between being and becoming: Jew or American. Jew was the old man praying and weeping and telling the same story again and again. American was a bat hitting a ball, jazz, kids in the schoolyard. Kahane's story resembles that of a prophet—maybe all life stories

---

*A current leader of the radical West Bank settler movement is a twenty-four-year-old from Monsey, New York, named Akiva Ha-Cohen. He is called the architect of the "price tag" doctrine, whereby settlers, in an attempt to drive up the price of removing them—note the echo of the Hagana policy of raising the cost of Jewish blood—attack anyone who interferes with their settlements, even Israeli soldiers. Members of this movement, which includes many young runaways from New York and Tel Aviv, call themselves "the hilltop youth," as they are young and live in trailers scattered across the forsaken hilltops of the West Bank, where life is divided among three rooms: gun room, weight room, shul. (See "Radical Settlers Take on Israel," *The New York Times*, September 25, 2008.)

† *The Great Gatsby*: " 'Can't repeat the past?' he cried incredulously. 'Why of course you can!' "

do—in which the blissful childhood is interrupted by the divine call, from which he runs, trying to lose himself in the everyday; he finally submits, returns, is vomited out of the belly of the fish, preaches, then vanishes in a puff of smoke.

Kahane went to NYU and New York Law School. He was ordained as a rabbi but wanted to be a writer. His prose was American, untouched by ethnic inflection. He wanted to speak in a universal voice. He fled the particular and the peculiar. He changed his name to Michael King. (No different from Kirk Douglas or Tony Curtis, he tried to get away in another man's clothes.) He published articles and essays. He had an affair with a woman named Gloria Jean D'Argenio. Then, in 1967, when he was thirty-five years old, he had an epiphany: the voice had always been there, but he suddenly understood what it was saying: *Prepare the people for the feast.* He let his hair grow, his beard grow, his mind run. He was the man you see on the bench outside the Church of the Holy Sepulcher, head in his hands, wondering, "Am I? Could I be?" He changed his name back to Meir Kahane but now, in a sense, he was Meir Kahane for the first time. When he told Gloria Jean D'Argenio he could never marry her, she jumped off the Queensboro Bridge.

In a parable, everything is factual—Michael King really did become Meir Kahane and Gloria Jean D'Argenio really did die—but everything is a symbol for something else, too.

Meir Kahane formed the Jewish Defense League in 1968. Young Jews were recruited and trained to patrol neighborhoods in Brooklyn, to walk old Jews to and from shul, but this was never the main mission. Kahane was less concerned with the old Jews who needed protection than with the young Jews who needed to protect. He wanted to raise an army of militants. His symbol was a fist inside a Jewish star. He opened Camp Jedel in the Catskills, where American Jews were trained in guerrilla warfare by members of Israel's elite Golani Brigade. Feeling weak, particular, and peculiar, changing your name to King—all that was over. He later said he patterned the JDL on the Black Panthers. In this way, the history of Israel got tangled up with American identity politics.

In 1971, Kahane moved to Kiryat Arba. He was a whirlwind in these years. He founded a political party (Kach!*), opened a school (Yeshiva of the Jewish Idea), and wrote a political platform that called on the Jews to settle "the whole land of Israel," which he spoke of as Greater Israel the way people speak of Greater Detroit. It was Israel as it had been at its zenith, when King David united the upper and lower kingdoms and census takers canvassed from the Nile to the foothills of Moab. To properly settle Greater Israel, Kahane said, the West Bank must be cleared of Arabs. This was the policy of Kach and it remains the policy of politicians on the Israeli far-right fringe, who call it "Transfer."

Here's what their posters say: NO ARABS, NO TERROR.

Kahane was a prolific writer, with titles including *Never Again!*, and *Listen World, Listen Jew*. His argument was most famously made in his perfectly titled *They Must Go*. But most revealing is his memoir, *Forty Years*, which is like an episode from Marvel comics, in which an ordinary Brooklyn Clark Kent realizes he is in fact a hero in a book.

David Mamet, in *The Wicked Son*, wrote a passage that perfectly captures the spirit of Meir Kahane:

> Children, and especially unhappy children, fantasize that the adults with whom they live are not their real parents, that their real parents are noble kings and queens, who will one day come for them. This fantasy does not cease with childhood, it strengthens. We defend ourselves against the longing this fantasy represents, and turn against that which would, or might, weaken our defense.
>
> The depth of the wicked son's rancor is the depth of his longing. And, curiously, the childhood fantasy which we as adults so vehemently disclaim, is true.
>
> We are the children of kings and queens, and the children of a mystery which has not abandoned us, and which has come for us, and it is both described and contained in the Torah.

*It means: Thus!

Kahane was a true monotheist in that he followed just one God: power. To him, weakness was more than an embarrassment, it was a sin. If Jews are the Chosen of God, Jewish weakness suggests that God himself is weak. Which means Jewish power is more than a military circumstance; it's a moral value. It demonstrates the strength of the divine idea and the health of the world. Israel was not created by the UN to shelter Jews or to alleviate Holocaust guilt, nor by secular Europeans wanting to live decent lives. It was created by God to demonstrate the strength of God. In Exodus, Yahweh tells Moses that He will both deliver the plagues that devastate Egypt and harden Pharaoh's heart so that Pharaoh will not free the slaves, thus bringing more devastation. He does this to show his own power. (This is God playing solitaire.) The defeat of Israel would therefore mean the defeat not only of the Jews, but also of God. The destruction of Israel would mean the death of God.

This is also what the Zealots believed.

After several failed attempts, in 1984 Kahane won a seat in the Israeli Knesset. In Israel, political parties are represented by the proportion of their vote, which, for Kach, meant one seat for 1 percent. Kahane served two years, then his party was banned as racist. (This had to do with the language it used about Arabs in its platform.) He was fifty-four years old when he was turned out, and looked the way he probably always wanted to look: a twisted sage, who had seen and been changed by seeing, with white hair and a knotty beard and big hands marbled by veins. He went everywhere, preaching the gospel of Jewish Power. He was shaking hands after a speech in the ballroom of the Marriott Hotel in Manhattan when a man came out of the crowd and shot him in the face. Police arrested El Sayyid Nosair, an Egyptian associated with the Muslim Brotherhood. Nosair was acquitted of murder, but convicted on gun charges. A few years later, he was arrested again, this time as a conspirator in the case against Omar Abdel Rahman, the Blind Sheik, the cleric behind the first World Trade Center bombing. Money for Nosair's defense was put up by Osama Bin Laden.

Kahane's followers settled on Kfar Tapuach in the West Bank. They founded a new party: Kahane Chai! (Kahane Lives!). Some-

times you see members of Kahane Chai! on New York public access
TV late at night, sitting before a banner with the fist in the star, saying
something like "Die, Nasrallah, you scum-sucking pig," or "Here's a
fuck-you to Abraham Foxman of the Anti-Defamation League, you
weak, collaborationist, Nazi-loving kike!" Kahane Chai draws its members from a range of professions. One of them was a doctor from
Flatbush, Brooklyn, named Baruch Goldstein, who, in the fall of 1993,
was thirty-eight years old and living in Kiryat Arba. Goldstein often
treated the victims of Palestinian terrorist attacks. In December 1993,
he treated Mordechai Lapid and his son, who had been shot in a roadside ambush. Both later died. Goldstein spoke at the funeral.

Here (in essence) is what he said:

> Some will tell you that terrorists are responsible for this crime, but I
> say it's not true. You do not blame the wolf when the wolf mauls the
> baby. You hunt down and kill the wolf, but the wolf is not to blame.
> The wolf is a wolf. You blame the man who did not latch the gate.
> Jews are responsible for this tragedy, politicians in Jerusalem who were
> not strong enough to deter the Arabs. In such a case, we must protect
> our own. Responding with violence is not a matter of bloodlust or re-
> venge. It's a sacrament, a demand from the Almighty.

On February 25, 1994, which was Purim, Dr. Goldstein woke early,
wrote a letter in which he explained what he would do and why,
loaded a rifle, filled a bag with extra clips, then walked down the hill to
the Tomb of the Patriarchs. Before 1967, Jews were not allowed in the
tomb; they could get no closer than the bottom step. After the war, the
tomb was opened. Goldstein went into the Muslim chamber, where
hundreds of men were on their knees in prayer. He raised his gun—
the gun is the shofar, its call ringing through the hills—and fired. In
the half-light you would see blue flames and the terrified faces in the
muzzle flash. He shot until he emptied the clip, then reloaded. More
than a hundred spent shell casings were found. Twenty-nine Arabs
were killed, many more wounded. The crowd overcame Goldstein,
then beat him to death with their belts and shoes. People in Israel were

stunned. "Even in my worst dream," Yitzhak Rabin told a crowd, "I never imagined a Jew capable of such a crime."

Goldstein's grave, which is way out there in the wilderness, has become a shrine for fringe lunatics, a place of pilgrimage, covered with stones and flowers, men weeping and praying before it as men weep and pray before the grave of Joan of Arc. It's a temple, really, a holy place in the new faith, in which Jewish violence is the glory of God.

FIFTEEN

The Surprise

From Manhattan, the drive to JFK feels like forever, especially if you think the world is ending. Michael Kovner caught a taxi on Sixty-fourth Street and Third Avenue. He was in work clothes, a bag thrown over his shoulder. In the bag were two shirts, a pair of pants, and a book on the fate of empires. It was October 3, 1973, the first day of Yom Kippur. The cab took him down Second Avenue, through a maze of traffic, the river on his left, then turned around the cloverleaf and into the Midtown Tunnel. Michael listened to news the entire way. That morning, the Egyptian army had crossed the 1967 cease-fire line and attacked Israel in the Sinai Desert. A Syrian army simultaneously invaded the Golan Heights. These were the first hours of the Yom Kippur War, in which Israel, taken by surprise on two fronts, was almost destroyed. "We decided to let them have the first punch," Moshe Dayan said later, "and that first punch almost killed us."

The Yom Kippur War was a turning point for Israel. It took decades for many people to understand what it meant, but the astute knew instinctively: the struggle with the Arabs, which Israelis thought they had won in 1967, had not, in fact, been won, and would not be won, maybe for a generation, maybe forever. The long-term Zionist strategy, in which Israel beats the Arabs until, as Ariel Sharon put it, they "develop a psychology of defeat," and so come to believe they could never win, so come to accept the Jewish state, had failed. The fact that you could win and win and still not win came as a shock to most Israelis. One day it's victory and blue skies, and the next day it's war stretching in every direction to the horizon.

A few years ago I traveled around the country to meet some of the men who commanded the Israeli army in 1967 and 1973.* They were old and stooped but still had that jaunty physicality you expect from soldiers. They reached, grabbed, shoved, laughed. We spoke in coffee shops and apartments, the desert lark on the windowsill, the palm fronds beating out applause. Some spread maps between us, pointing out scenes of battle, or a pass they slipped through when the fog was heavy. Some showed photos of friends who had died, who were young, and so would stay young. Some showed photos of themselves with white teeth and dark hair. Some spoke English perfectly, some not at all, some as if they had a mouthful of gravel, each phrase broken by a shrug or a sigh.

I was with Jessica, my wife, and Michael Kovner, my friend, who directed us and sat with us and talked about what the officers were "really trying to say." This was in 2000, during the Second Palestinian Intifada—every day brought news of another terrorist attack—and the old soldiers were gloomy. They talked about the situation of Israel in the way their grandfathers once talked about the Jewish Question. It was hopeless, they said; each victory leads us back to this same grinding war. Most blamed not the setbacks but the triumphs, especially the Six-Day War, from which, they said, Israel had taken the wrong lessons. "It was the sin of hubris," a general told us. "This idea that we were big and strong, and winning, and would keep on winning,

---

*It's amazing how accessible the leaders of Israel are. At one meeting, someone gave me the home phone number of Ehud Barak. I called several times, talked to his wife again and again, until, finally, exasperated, she said, "You know, he is the prime minister."

and could have everything, as if we had solved the riddle of Jewish history."

There have really been three Israels: the scrappy little nation that existed from 1948 to 1967; the world strider that existed from 1967 to 1973; and the walled-in defensive nation that exists today—a country surprised by history.

Michael moved to New York in 1972, after his military service, to study painting at the New School with Philip Guston. He worked as a security guard in the Israeli consulate at night, and listened to the radio each morning. It was in this way, still heavy with sleep, that he learned of the attack. The first reports were sketchy. The next were more detailed. The Egyptians had crossed into the Sinai not with a few soldiers, but with an entire army. Eighty thousand men. They were advancing under a cover of Russian surface-to-air missiles. The frontier had been guarded by fortified outposts: the Bar-Lev Line. Many of these had already been destroyed—because it was Yom Kippur, most of the defenders were on leave when the first shots were fired—and the few forts that survived were trapped behind Egyptian lines. The Syrians had driven the Israelis off Mount Hermon in the Golan, and Syrian tanks were a few miles from Israeli towns in the Galilee. If they broke through, the war could end quickly.

Michael tried to call his parents, his sister, the commander of his military unit—he was a member of Sayeret Matkal, the commando force that, among other things, freed the hostages at Entebbe—but the circuits were busy; nothing was getting through. He packed, went to the street. He stared out the window of the taxi. He stood at the counter of El Al. He had no ticket, no reservation. It did not matter. The airline was bringing all the soldiers home. He went through the terminal to the gate. The seats and floor were crowded with Israelis, hundreds of young men, who, like Michael, had rushed to the airport as soon as they heard the news. It was a terrible moment but also sublime, all these young men gathered together at the gate, then on the plane, the world flashing below. This is what it means to be a nation, Michael thought. Going home to fight, maybe to die. The feeling welled up inside him: how they had come from every part of New

York and America as you come to the hospital when the phone rings and the voice says, "Hurry! The old man is in trouble."

W hy did the attack come as such a surprise?

Well, for starters, the Israelis (as I said) thought they had already won, that the victory of 1967 was a decisive end to the conflict. In 1971 Moshe Dayan, then the minister of defense, gave an interview to *Time* magazine in which he promised there would be no war for at least ten years. "We are at the threshold of the crowning period of the return to Zion," he explained. Each piece of intelligence, no matter how troubling, was made to fit this belief. In the months before the attack, the Mossad, the Israeli intelligence service, issued eleven general warnings. There were, in fact, dozens of clues. The Egyptians mobilizing their troops, moving their troops to the Suez Canal, purchasing weapons en masse, painting the headlights of their trucks black. Russian transport planes flew Soviet diplomats and their families out of the country. Then, a week before the invasion, which came during Ramadan, Muslim soldiers were told to break their fast. The next night, an Israeli patrol found footprints in the raked sand along the canal.

Golda Meir was born in 1898, in Kiev, Ukraine, where the Nazis stacked Jews like firewood. Her family moved to Milwaukee, Wisconsin, when she was eight. She took the bus, read paperbacks, ate custard, but remembered Zion. She married at twenty-one, made Aliyah. She picked almonds on a farm in the Jezreel Valley, but was outspoken and ambitious and made her way into positions of authority, first on her kibbutz, then in her political party. By the time of the UN partition, she had reached the top circles of the Zionist leadership. (Ben-Gurion famously called her "the best man in government.") In 1948 she was tapped for an important mission. Disguised as an Arab, she traveled across the Jordan River to meet Abdullah bin al-Hussein, then king of Jordan, whom she tried to persuade to stay out of the war. Nothing came of the meeting, but it made Golda famous. She went on to serve in various posts, including as ambassador to the Soviet Union and as foreign minister. She became prime minister in 1969, by which time she was a homely gray-haired grandmother with the weight of the world on her shoulders.

A few days before the attack, Golda was contacted by Hussein bin Talal, who had succeeded his father and his grandfather as the king of Jordan. "We have to meet," he said. He came across in secret, by helicopter, in a dark suit and a headdress, his eyes warm and larky. He took Golda by the arm. He said, "Something terrible is on its way." He said, "War is coming." He said, "The Syrians are already in their jump positions." Hussein did not want war; and he feared Syria more than he feared Israel. But the warning, because it did not fit the preexisting belief—that the war had already been won—was dismissed.*

The day before the attack, the head of the Mossad, Zvi Zamir, met with an Egyptian double agent in London who had long been sending information to Israel.† He told Zamir the Egyptians would cross at dawn. But he had been wrong before, so this, too, was dismissed.

In short, the Israelis had become overconfident and had stopped thinking with the edgy paranoia of Jews. They believed their own propaganda: that the new Jews were supermen, a handful of whom could defeat any Arab army. (They did not have nearly enough soldiers on the frontier.) They underestimated their enemy. After looking at satellite photos a few days before the war, Moshe Dayan told his commanders, "You can get a stroke just from the numbers. They have 1,100 artillery pieces compared to our 802. They have fifty thousand men compared to our five thousand. You people don't take the Arabs seriously enough."

Israel did not mobilize its reserves until it was too late. The Egyptians had feinted so many times the Israelis came to think every threat

---

*Here's what the analysts told the prime minister: The Syrians will not attack without the Egyptians; the Egyptians will not attack without missiles that can hit Tel Aviv. As they have no such missiles, there will be no war.

†The identity of this man remains a mystery—some Israelis think he was a ranking Egyptian official, a relative of Nasser's who had grown disgruntled in the age of Sadat.

was a bluff. Anwar Sadat had called 1971 the year of decision, for example, but 1971 came and went without incident. If Israel met every threat with mobilization, the country would go broke. Some believed this was Egypt's plan. So Israel's commanders decided to gamble, betting there would be no attack, or that if there were, the army would quickly repel the invaders. Shortly before the invasion, an Israeli general told a ranking Mossad agent: "It's Intelligence's job to safeguard the nation's nerves, not drive the public crazy, not undermine the economy. I don't permit you to think of mobilizing even a fraction of a reservist."

All of which was the fruit of Egypt's disinformation campaign, whereby the Israelis were kept guessing. Each day, Egyptian soldiers were sent to the canal with fishing rods, to sit slack-jawed on the bank, as behind them the real army was preparing its invasion.

Here is how Moshe Dayan described the first morning of the war in his autobiography:

> In the east the sky was red and gold. A light sea breeze came in from the west. A silent, tranquil dawn. Even the birds were quiet. It was Yom Kippur, the most sacred day in the Jewish calendar. There was not a soul on the streets.

That's how the day began. By the time it ended, there were hundreds of dead Israelis in the Sinai Desert. The frontier had been overrun and Israeli soldiers trapped in forts behind the enemy line. These were actually fortified bunkers—there were two dozen of them strung like beads along the canal*—where a handful of men held out for weeks; they became a metaphor for the nation at war, a tiny redoubt stranded in a great Arab sea.

A few miles east, a quickly assembled collection of Israeli soldiers, the first of those mobilized, tried to push back the Egyptians but were

---

*The construction of the line had been controversial: General Haim Bar-Lev considered it an impregnable defense that would require minimal manpower, while others saw it as a death trap.

decisively routed. It was the first shock: the Egyptians did not run, as they had in 1967. They fought.

Ariel Sharon, *Warrior*:

> I stood on the dunes as tanks and APCs withdrew past the observation post. I stopped some of the men to talk and saw something strange on their faces—not fear but bewilderment. Suddenly something was happening to them that had never happened before. These were soldiers who had been brought up on victories—not easy victories maybe, but nevertheless victories. It was a generation that had never lost. Now they were in a state of shock. How could it be that these Egyptians were crossing the canal right in our faces? How was it that they were moving forward and we were defeated?

By sundown, fifty thousand Egyptians had crossed the Suez—a development that, the day before, would have been dismissed as impossible. In a week, there would be a hundred thousand. They came over in dozens of places along the canal, on pontoon bridges that snaked across the oily water. Much of Egypt's early success resulted from equipment they had imported from the Soviet Union. Russian surface-to-air missiles (SAMs), deployed along the canal, drove the Israeli air force, which had long been Israel's great tactical advantage, from the sky above the battlefield. Russian-made rocket-propelled grenades drove back Israeli soldiers. Russian-made wire-guided suitcase rockets devastated columns of Israeli tanks.

In Israel, the mobilization orders came over the radio in code—*the sons of Boaz are to report to the shade of the terebinth tree; the daughters of Elijah are to rendezvous at the well of Midian*—or by messenger. (As it was Yom Kippur, many Israelis had turned off their radios.) These messengers sped along deserted roads, bringing news of both attack and mobilization. The fact that mobilization came on Yom Kippur, in many ways a disaster, also meant the roads were free of traffic and the Reservists were easy to find: they were either at home, or in shul wrapped in tfillin.

Within an hour of the call, a parade of vehicles was moving along the coast, trucks and tanks, Peugeots and Citroëns. It was exhilarating. Israelis had suddenly been freed from the obligations and worries of their everyday lives. That's why people love war. One moment, you are in your living room, wondering if the baby needs a nap; the next moment you are on the hot road, with your thumb out and a gun on your back.

Ariel Sharon was on his farm in the Negev when the news came. It's an hour south of Jerusalem, in the wilderness where the desert flower blooms and the lizard sits lazily in the sun, dreaming of mice. He was with Zev Amit, an old friend. Sharon had retired from active military service the year before but was still a general in the Reserves. He had since entered politics, where, with Menachem Begin, he founded the Likud Party. To many fellow officers, most of whom were members of the Labor Party, Sharon's politics made him suspect. They thought he took foolish risks in pursuit of professional glory.

Sharon spoke to his wife quietly, then started packing: Maps. Field glasses. Clips for his gun. He put on a uniform that had spent months in the back of his closet. Zev Amit decided to go along. He had been with Sharon through everything, and would stay with him now—well, for several more days, anyway, because Zev Amit would die in little more than a week, a mile from the canal, an artillery shell screaming out of the blue sky and erasing him. He had only the shoes on his feet, soft walking shoes, so Sharon tossed him a pair of his old infantry boots, saying, "Take these, Zev, they will get you through."

Sharon packed some food, including a basket of oranges he had picked that morning. The men set off in Sharon's truck. They drove south on empty roads, the skies clear but for the occasional plane. In Gaza, the roads were crowded with machines. They had turned a corner into the war. They went beyond the last outpost into the Sinai. Soldiers were scattered along the road, camped in fields, wandering away from the front. Sharon looked for signs of order but found none. Even the officers seemed confused. These soldiers were cheered by the sight of Ariel Sharon, who had always been associated with victories. He represented the old Sabra confidence. He stood in his Jeep waving, handing out oranges. When he got out, the men crowded around and shook his hand.

According to Robert Alter, the first line spoken by a figure in the Torah defines that figure's character. For example, when Saul wanders into strange territory, he says, "Come, let us turn back." When David, who succeeds Saul as king, sees Goliath in a field taunting the Hebrews, he says, "What will be done for the man who strikes down yonder Philistine and takes away insult from Israel?"* When Sharon arrived at his post, a bunker near Al Arish in Sinai, where he would command three battalions, he said, "When do we counterattack?"

Abraham Rabinovich, *The Yom Kippur War.*

> Even Sharon's bitterest opponents acknowledged that he was a superb field commander, the best Israel had, in the view of many. A daring and imaginative officer who could read a battle as it unfolded and inspire his troops. He remained a field officer even in high command, capable of studying a photo-stat of unfamiliar territory for a quarter hour, as a staff officer would testify, and then leading his unit through the terrain for an entire night without further reference.

Sharon sat in his post, surrounded by officers, with a map opened before him. "What happened to the forts along the Bar-Lev Line?" he asked.

"Most were destroyed," an officer told him. "Some were overrun."

"The defenders were killed, fled, what?" asked Sharon.

"Some were killed," said the officer, "some fled, but most are still there."

"Still where?"

"In the forts."

Sharon paused, then said, "You mean they're alive, trapped in those Goddamn bunkers?"

---

*This is from the Alter translation as it appears in (the excellent) *The David Story: A Translation with Commentary of 1 and 2 Samuel.*

"Yes."

"What's the plan?" said Sharon. "How do we save them?"

"There is no plan," said the officer. "General Gonen says we can't risk a division to rescue a few dozen men."

"No," said Sharon. "That's not right."

Sharon had been abandoned on the battlefield in 1948. The army retreated, leaving behind him and his men, most of whom were killed. He knew such seemingly small matters, the rescue of a few soldiers, could determine the outcome of a war. It told your men how much you valued their lives. "I don't care what Gonen told you," said Sharon. "We've got to get them."

He then said, "The men at the forts, is there any way to talk to them?"

"We can get them on the radio," said the officer.

"Good," said Sharon. "Get them."

The following exchange was recorded. In it, you hear Major Meir Weisel, the commander of Fort Haakon, talking to Ariel Sharon, who identifies himself by the codename "Forty."

Sharon asks about the battle. "Do the Egyptians seem tired or do they have momentum?" "How many tanks do you see?" "Are they moving toward Tasa?"

"It reminded me of six years ago," Weisel tells him.

"Were you in that war?" asks Sharon.

"I've been in four . . . well, three," says Weisel. "You're talking to an old man of almost forty-one."

"I just got here," Sharon says, "but I'm going to try to get you out. What vehicles do you have?"

"Two half-tracks and a truck," says Weisel.

Just then, the radio operator at the fort—his name was Max Maimon; he was a clerk in a bank in Jerusalem and he did not survive the war—breaks in, having recognized Sharon's voice. "Forty, Forty" he shouts. "We know you! We know who you are! We know you will get us out of here. Please, please, please, oh God, come to us!"

Sharon called Shmuel Gonen, the head of Israel's Southern Command. Gonen had been promoted to his job when Sharon retired. In other words, Sharon had previously been his commander. In 1967 Gonen led a tank division from Gaza clear to the Suez Canal. There were pictures of him everywhere after the war, stubble-faced, with a cigar in his mouth, giving a thumbs-up. He was rarely seen without sunglasses, mirrored aviators; you look at him but see only yourself looking at him. He had been called the Jewish Patton, which means he was bold and colorful and did what had to be done. (The Francis Ford Coppola–scripted movie, in which the American general says, among other things, "We will grease the treads of our tanks with their blood," had come out the year before.) After the '67 War, Gonen gave a speech* in which he said, "We looked death in the eyes, and it averted its gaze."

Sharon and Gonen argued throughout the war. Most of their calls ended in shouting. Gonen said Sharon was vainglorious and reckless. Sharon said Gonen was timid and defensive. Sharon wanted to counterattack immediately. Hit the Egyptian bridges. Pound them. Bloody them. Send a battalion across the canal, turn up behind their lines, remind them who we are. But Gonen never seemed to recover from that first blow. The losses were heavy, and he did not want to lose any more. He ordered his generals to fall back, dig in, wait. According to Sharon, all Gonen's errors derived from a single mistake: he did not lead from the front, but from a post dozens of miles from the fighting, so could never know the true nature of the war, its ebbs and flows.

When Sharon asked permission to rescue the men in the forts, Gonen said, "Negative. We do not have the resources."

Sharon then called Moshe Dayan, the minister of defense.

He said, "Moshe, we have to save them. It's our responsibility."

Dayan said, "Arik, don't do this—don't break the chain of command."

On October 8, Israel launched a counterattack in Sinai. It was supposed to be the decisive battle in the south, the moment Israel retook the momentum and, as Sharon said, reminded the Arabs who we were. But it was a disaster. The Egyptians did not break, but instead drove back the Israelis, who took heavy casualties. This panicked the

---

*The speech was called "My Glorious Brothers, Deserving of Fame."

Israeli commanders. It meant they had to question their basic assumptions about the Egyptian army and their own. What's more, Israel lost so much materiel in this counterattack that some worried they would not have enough tanks and planes to win even if they could turn the tide. People later referred to it as "the black day," "the darkest day."

Things were even worse in the Golan. In the first hours of the war, Syria had crossed the border in three hundred American-made Sherman tanks. Israel had only thirty tanks in the north, and many of those were out of commission or being serviced. (As Moshe Dayan told Golda Meir, "They caught us with our pants down.") The Israelis were quickly driven off the Heights. By the end of that first terrible day—well, terrible if you were an Israeli, or cared about Israel—the Syrians were less than a dozen miles from the Green Line. If they pushed through the last line of defense, the tanks would roll down the slopes of the Golan and into the Jordan Valley, the farm country of Israel, its towns and factories undefended.

Moshe Dayan grew up in one of those towns: Deganiah, on the shore of the Galilee. The morning of the second day, he drove north. Here is what he told David Ben-Eliezer, the chief of the army: "I am going to see if we will lose the Golan." He toured the front, looked at the reconnaissance photos, studied the numbers. The intelligence spooked him. He grew morose, ashen, dour. It was like the trick in the old movie that makes the dashing hero age before your eyes. The Syrians will break through, he said. They will devastate the country. It was in these hours that Dayan began to speak of Israel as the Third Temple. He said it quietly at first, to himself, then to friends, then to fellow officers. We did build the Third Temple, he explained. It's modern Israel. It's about to burn.

Dayan was perhaps the first Israeli leader to understand the true nature of the project: its grandiosity and presumption; that the Zionists had turned the Book back into a temple, which is small and holy and ringed by walls. The change was so revolutionary and had happened so fast that most people missed it. They're too close; it's still too soon. Perhaps if the sky clears, or they're filled with mania, or despair, they might glimpse it. Which is what happened to Dayan on the Golan Heights, as he watched Syrian tanks through his binoculars, their treads grinding up the ramparts.

On October 9, an Israeli general named Ehud Peled was driving into the Golan. He saw a man sitting alone on the side of the road, looking at the Hula Valley. Peled parked, walked through the scrub. When he was thirty feet away, he realized it was Dayan watching a tank battle. Now and then, there was a flash in the valley, a report, a puff of smoke. That is, this scene, in addition to being arranged horizontally, was arranged vertically. There was the ground, where bodies lay in their blood; there were the tanks, with men closed up in the dark, staring at dials and switches; there was the sky through which the bullets and artillery shells flew; there were the Heights, where, hidden in a crag, the one-eyed general had the same vantage point as the Archangel Gabriel watching the last battle. Peled put a hand on Dayan's shoulder. Dayan looked up with tears in his eyes. "Don't you see what's happening," he said. "We're losing our Third Temple."

Later that day, Dayan took a helicopter tour of the Sinai. He saw Israeli soldiers in retreat. He got out, walked among the men. The entire front was being bombarded. He refused to take cover. By then, he was talking constantly about the Third Temple. "I drank a good deal of black coffee in the South with General Gonen and his officers, but it did nothing to salve my unease," he later wrote. "As I flew back to Tel Aviv, I could recall no moment in the past when I had felt such anxiety. If I had been in physical straits, involved in personal danger, it would have been simpler. I knew this from experience. But now I had a different feeling. Israel was in danger, and the results could be fatal."

He briefed newspaper reporters in Tel Aviv, told them his fears: the nation is the Temple and the Romans have breached the outer wall. He said he would go on TV that evening to deliver this message to the public. After the meeting, several reporters went to Golda Meir. Here is what they told her: Do not let Moshe Dayan go on TV. He will cause a panic.*

Dayan met with Golda Meir and Ben-Eliezer and other Israeli leaders in the Pit. Many were less terrified by Dayan's report than by his demeanor. He seemed rattled. He suggested that the government draft old men and children into the army, as the Germans had done at the end of World War II. He suggested that sidearms and grenade launchers be handed out to all citizens in the north. He said, "Golda, oh Golda, our Third Temple is in danger." Ehud Peled, who was not as pessimistic, began to call the Pit "the Holocaust basement."

Moshe Dayan, *Story of My Life*:

> The prime minister and the other ministers were shocked, largely I think because I said I did not believe we could at this moment throw the Egyptians back to the other side of the Canal. It was clear from their critical cross-questioning after my realistic remarks that they thought the weakness lay not in our current military situation but in my personal character, that I had lost my confidence.

Dayan suggested the army form a defensive line in the middle of the Sinai, retreat, and save what could be saved.

Sharon, hearing this, exploded. *Have you lost your mind, Moshe? Now is not the time to give in. Now is the time to attack. Hit them! Hit them! Remind them who we are!* This might have been the most important role Sharon played in the war: by demanding and persisting and refusing to act defeated, he dragged his superiors along behind him. "Twenty-five years ago, when we were staring at our own extinction in the war of Independence, we never once lost our self-confidence," he later wrote. "How then had we been brought so low, when we were fighting almost two hundred miles from home? As bad as this war had been, I never

---

*Israel's chief of military intelligence appeared in Dayan's place and did not once mention the Third Temple.

felt we were on the verge of destruction. I knew how precarious our position had been on the Golan, and the Sinai too. But it was nothing like those first six months of the Independence War."

When Golda Meir heard Dayan's report—"No stone will stand on stone. All will be torn down and ruined"—the blood ran out of her face. She excused herself, went into the hall for a cigarette. Her heart was pounding, her mind reeled. She stood with her assistant, a young officer who later described the scene. Her eyes were weepy and wild and she spoke of suicide. She could see her body in the grave and the dead stacked in piles and the fire in the clouds and the spokes in the sun and the eye in the heavens. She was on the road to Babylon, the Hebrews gathered around her in chains. She finished her cigarette, started another, put it out. Her mind cleared. She said, "Let's go back to work."

Abraham Rabinovich, *The Yom Kippur War.*

> She was pale and her eyes were downcast as she walked slowly to her chair. Her hair, normally neatly combed and pulled back, was disheveled and she looked as if she had not shut her eyes all night. For the first time her ministers saw an old woman sitting in the prime minister's chair, slightly bent. She lit a cigarette, leafed briefly though a pile of papers in front of her, and declared the meeting to be open.

The Yom Kippur War was probably Israel's greatest military triumph. Because there had been surprise. Because there had been despair. I once spoke to a military historian at a party, and the conversation, for whatever reason, turned to Israel. "Well, you know, seventy-three, that was amazing," he told me, "because it was like this guy comes through your window in the middle of the night and, when you are still half asleep, he hits you as hard as he can, and you fall back, stagger, and think for a moment it is over, you're going to die, then you shake it off, load the gun, and blow his fuckin' head apart." (That's really what he said.) To me, Israel shaking it off is Golda Meir stubbing out her cigarette, saying, "Let's go back to work."

Henry Kissinger briefed President Nixon on developments throughout the war. On the fifth day, he came in with a list of equipment the
Israelis said they needed. Nixon said, "Israel cannot be allowed to
lose." He might also have said, "American guns cannot be allowed
to lose to Soviet guns." Nixon went through the list with a pencil. F-14
Tomcats (check), P-23 tanks (check), Jeeps (check), trucks (check), half-
tracks (check), Weasels (check), rifles (check), pistols (check), shells
(check), clips (check), bullets (check), night-vision goggles (check),
sniper scopes (check), grenades (check), cluster bombs (check). Everything but laser-guided missiles, the newest item in the American arse-
nal. The weapons were to be shipped secretly, at night, via a third
country, but since the Soviets had already rearmed the Arabs, and the
struggle had become a proxy, Nixon decided the delivery should be
made as publicly and as loudly as possible, so everyone knew exactly
what was happening and why.

The European nations did not let America use their air bases to
supply Israel. The Arabs said they would embargo any nation that
took part. (America had its oil imports cut by OPEC after the war, resulting in the first energy crisis.) The planes flew directly from bases
in the United States, the pilots, hopped up on amphetamines for the
twenty-hour round-trip haul, flying a convoy of C-5 Galaxies. They
landed at Lod on October 14, 1973. Ramps were brought out, and
American crews and Israeli crews stood side by side in flight suits as
materiel was rolled into the hangars: twenty-two thousand tons of ar-
maments. Most came too late to be used in the war; the fighting was
over by the time the guns reached the front, but the airlift had a
tremendous psychological impact.* It was a warm hand on a cold day.
It told the Israelis they were not alone. I met an American colonel who
had been on one of those planes. He described flying over the empty

---

*Also, knowing it was coming allowed the Israelis to be more liberal in their use of their existing
weapons, shoot more rounds, fly more sorties.

streets of Tel Aviv, the Israelis running out to meet him on the tarmac, drinking whiskey in the hangar. It was noisy, he said, with the engines kicking up dust and dirt. When the plane was empty, the colonel unstrapped his own sidearm and handed it to an Israeli, "because those were my orders," he told me, "give them everything you got, even the gun on your waist."

The turning point came in the north. On the evening of October 6, hundreds of Syrian tanks were racing across the Hula Valley toward Nafakh, the last outpost before the Green Line. It seemed only a miracle could stop them.

Zvika Greengold, a twenty-one-year-old tank commander, was in the fields near his family home. Greengold is the Israeli Sergeant York. There should be a movie about him. It would star a young William Holden. On the set, other actors would call him Bill and, between shots, toss cans of beer up to the tank, where he sits in the turret smoking a cigarette in the green-gold sun. Greengold's childhood would be seen in flashback. Eucalyptus and cypress trees, barns, and cows standing two-deep at the milking machine. He grew up on Lohamey HaGeta'ot, a kibbutz founded by veterans of the Warsaw Ghetto Uprising, including Zvika's parents. Even if your parents don't talk about it, such a history presents certain questions: What would I have done? How would I have acted?*

I've seen a picture of Greengold taken later, when he was in his twenties. The cap on his shoulder means he is a member of an elite brigade. The T-shirt under his uniform means he is no stickler for protocol. He can read off the sheet, but can play jazz, too.

By the time Greengold reported to his base, Israel's forward positions had been destroyed in the Golan. He was told to assemble as many tanks as he could and lead them to the Hula Valley, where they were to engage the enemy, slowing the Syrian advance until reinforce-

---

*I know this from Michael Kovner, who, like Zvika Greengold, had parents who fought as partisans, lived through the Holocaust, and survived, but were not really survivors.

ments could arrive. There were, however, only two tanks ready for battle. The rest had been knocked out in the first hours of the fighting. Some were being repaired, others were being brought from across the country. In the meantime, it was just Greengold and this other man. They set off at dusk, the sun behind them. Then, a few miles from base, the second tank sputtered and broke down.

A war comes down to a single battle, a single battle comes down to a single man, a single night, a single series of events. It's an old-fashioned idea, made nonsensical by modern weapons, but it seems to fit here, on the eighth night of battle, during which Zvika Greengold, fighting alone, turned back the Syrian advance.

The mission was simple: destroy everything you see. He pursued it for twenty-two hours, shut in his tank, which was hot as an oven, damaged, moving at half speed in and out of enemy ranks, destroying dozens of Syrian tanks; no one knows how many, but in the morning their shells were scattered across the valley. Greengold did have one advantage: Syria and Israel were both using Sherman tanks, meaning he could wander unnoticed among the enemy. He could, in the parlance of the ghetto, "pass." He crept into a row of Syrian tanks, gathered with their lights out, like trucks at a rest stop, lowered his cannon: *BLAM! BLAM!* What's more, as he was alone, there could be no mistakes: every tank was an enemy tank. He could shoot and shoot. Not wanting to give away this secret, he referred to himself on the radio as Force Zvika. When asked to describe his situation, he said, "Not good. Force Zvika needs a general."

He said he persevered by thinking of his parents and the Warsaw Ghetto: he could finally answer the questions, quiet the voices in his head. Here was another Jew driven mad by history, because every enemy is the Nazis. "This is what I kept telling myself," Greengold said. "It's just me between the Syrians and the annihilation of the Jews."

He slowed the Syrians long enough for reinforcements to arrive, a column of tanks groaning up into the Golan. Only then did the commanders understand Greengold's situation:

A battered tank crawls across a field; the hatch opens; a man sticks his head out; he is young and disheveled, with burns on his face and neck.

"Where are the others?" an officer asks.

"There are no others."

"What about Force Zvika?"

"I am Force Zvika."

He weaved downhill, as if the tank had been drinking, the sound of the battle fading behind him. When he reached base, he crawled out of his tank and collapsed. He spent the rest of the war in the hospital. Abraham Rabinovich, *The Yom Kippur War*.

Some officers involved in the battle would later maintain that Green-gold had single handedly prevented the capture of Nafakh by block-ing the Syrian drive up the Tapline Saturday night and that in saving Nafakh he had saved the Golan Heights.

Israel gathered enough tanks in the Hula Valley to stage the coun-terattack that would drive the Syrians off the Heights. It was led by Ori Orr, a commander with a shock of black hair. He did not know most of the men he was leading. The division had been patched together from spare parts, in the middle of the fight. (*Gonzo* means "learn to fly by falling out of a plane.") He sat on his tank, surrounded by other tanks, each man in his open hatch. He reached into his pocket, took out a chocolate bar, broke it into pieces, which he passed around. The wind blew through his hair—well, I don't really know what the wind was doing, but on the Golan the wind blows almost all the time; it comes over the hills and plays with every leaf and stick. "I know it's difficult for you," Orr told the men. "It's difficult for me, too. I've fought in a tough war, but this is something else. But we're going to survive. We've got no choice. Whoever hangs on longer wins."

The Egyptian advance had been stopped in the Sinai. The Israelis formed a defensive line. The crisis passed, but Israel needed a break-through to change the course of the war and force an acceptable cease-fire. In other words, they needed a plan, but it was unlikely to come from the leaders in the Pit, who had never really recovered from the first shock. They had grown sullen, defensive, did not want to muddy their tanks, deplete their munitions, risk, chance, lose. This left it to the officers in the field, in the muck and blood of it, and here I am thinking of Sharon, who had been criticizing his superiors from the start. "We should attack," he told them. "Attack, attack, and attack!"

One morning, some of Sharon's men, scouting in the desert, made a discovery that sent them into a frenzy. They called the general, who was a big man and wandered through camp in boots and flak jacket with Zev Amit at his side. Their voices were quick and excited. *We found it, General! We found the way through!*

The Egyptians had crossed the Suez Canal with two armies (the Second and Third), each of which had its own commanders, machines, and soldiers. These armies were supposed to be deployed side by side, flush along the front, but the scouts had discovered a gap. Fifteen miles wide, clear to the canal. The Egyptians did not know about this gap, of course. It was an error, the kind that loses wars. Instead of searching for a way to flank the Egyptians, the Israelis could simply slip between the Second and Third armies without firing a shot. In hockey, they call it the five hole: the most devastating way to score, a puck put between the goalie's legs.

Sharon knew he had to act fast. As soon as the Egyptians realized their error, they would close the seam, and the opportunity would be lost. He told his officers to prepare, then called Gonen and told him about the seam. Sharon said he wanted to take his men through at once, before it closed. Gonen said no. The army had already been driven back in one counterattack and could not afford another hasty maneuver that would result in more loss of life and equipment. Sharon pleaded. He talked of how rare and precious such a discovery was: a seam through enemy ranks! But where Sharon saw an opportunity, Gonen saw a disaster. What happens if you do get through, he said, and the Egyptians close it behind you? Have you thought of that?

It's an example of two sorts of brains grinding against each other in a crisis: given the same facts, Gonen sees only danger, whereas Sharon sees only glory, a ride through a conquered city in a cascade of flowers.

Sharon and his men were soon on the move, drifting toward the seam, which dazzled before them like a mirage, a threshold into another war. Later, when reprimanded by Gonen, Sharon said he must have misunderstood the order, heard it and forgotten, or never heard it. The next morning, Sharon and several hundred of his men were within sight of the canal. The eastern shore was desolate and gray; the western shore was vibrant, fecund, moist, aromatic, green. The canal was not merely a throughway, but a frontier, a transition between continents, climates. It's a line you can pick out on any map, no matter how small; it's where Asia ends. Israeli soldiers did not call the western shore Egypt. They called it Africa.

Ariel Sharon, *Warrior*:

> We stared across at the trees and lush green foliage. On our side everything was barren and dust. On their side the palm trees and orchards grew in profusion along the Sweet Water Canal. It looked like paradise.

Sharon talked to Dayan on the field phone. "Arik did not ring off before describing the wondrous sight he was beholding," Dayan later wrote. "Moving tanks silhouetted against the brilliant flashes of shells exploding in fireworks across the surface of the Great Bitter Lake."

Israelis had been stationed on the canal two weeks before; why then did it suddenly seem so exotic? Because it had been lost, that's why. Because Israelis had died trying to defend it. The canal was strange in the way that all common places are strange to a man following a near-death experience, a man who has been restored and so sees with new eyes, as if for the first time.

Sharon called Gonen. He was wild with excitement.*

> SHARON: Shmuely, Shmuely, we're near the canal! We can touch the water! The canal bank is in our hand! Request permission to cross.
> GONEN: What! No! No! [Then, away from the receiver, as if talking to someone else in the room, Gonen yells: Get him out of there!]
> SHARON: If we can get a bridge here, we can cross.

*This exchange was recorded and played for investigators after the war.

GONEN: Get out of there!

SHARON: I'm already here, Shmuely. The moment we cross, the
whole situation will change.

GONEN: No, no, no, no, no!

When Sharon hung up the phone, he turned to his officers and said
(in essence), "Find a way to cross."

After all else failed, Israeli soldiers hauled fifteen dilapidated, old
amphibious landing craft—called Gilowas—to the canal, where they
were pushed down a ramp to the water, then used to ferry vehicles to
the western bank of the Suez. I have seen no pictures of this sorry ar-
mada but have read descriptions. The rafts were beaters, shoddy and
tan, bobbing like ancient punts, heavy with men and equipment.
"There was still no bridge but there was now a way to get tanks across
the canal," writes Abraham Rabinovich. "Israel's major strategic move
in the war . . . was literally being floated by recycled junk."

Sharon tucked in his shirt and combed his hair. He was dirty, with
grease on his forehead and half-moons under his eyes. He was tired
but having fun. It was obvious. It was something that separated him
from the other generals. While the others were fretting and proclaim-
ing, he was grinning. He gave his comb to Zev Amit, saying, "Clean
up. We're going to Africa." Sharon issued the order: a convoy across
the canal on the rafts. These swayed, water sloshed over the tank
treads, but the maneuver worked. The soldiers made camp on the west
bank, a short drive through the fields from Cairo. Sharon ducked into
an armored truck and called his wife: "Lily, Lily! We made it! We're
the first ones across!"

Few people knew where Sharon was. Gonen assumed he had followed orders and was on his way back to the Israeli line. The Egyptians considered such a crossing impossible, so did not notice it when
it happened. Sharon figured the Egyptians would discover him eventually, so he wanted to take advantage of the situation while it lasted.
He left a group of soldiers at the crossing, which, for the time, was the
only way in or out, and led a second group north along the canal.
These men blew up Egyptian bridges and batteries and attacked out-

posts. When an outpost fell, the soldiers ran up an Israeli flag. "When the Egyptians across the canal see our colors behind them, they will panic," Sharon explained.

The Israelis operated behind the lines for thirty hours before the Egyptians accepted their presence as something more than a stunt. (That's how it was described to Anwar Sadat.) When Golda Meir went on TV and said, "Right now, as we convene the Knesset, an IDF task force is operating on the west bank of the Suez Canal," Sadat told reporters, "What you have heard from Israel is propaganda. There has been no crossing." Sadat's officers then had to tell him that Golda Meir had been right: the Israelis had come across, not with ten men, but with hundreds.

On October 17, Egyptian planes attacked Sharon's position, destroying a landing craft and ramp the Israelis had used to enter the canal. When the planes came in sight, the Israelis scrambled. Some jumped into foxholes, some ran for tanks. Sharon climbed into an armored truck. There was a gun on the roof. He got off several rounds, the tracers arcing up to the Egyptian MiGs. Everyone who had not found cover was hit, including Zev Amit, who died in Sharon's boots. Sharon himself was peppered with shrapnel. Blood ran around his eyes. For a moment, he looked at the battlefield through a red filter. His wounds were not serious. Pieces of metal were picked out of his face, the bleeders closed. A surgeon wrapped a bandage around his head. He looked like a wounded hero in a purple poem: the general on his tank, covered in gauze, blood showing through.

What did Gonen think when he got the news?

Was there a moment when he wished Sharon had been killed?

He summoned Sharon to a meeting in the Sinai. Sharon, who was back on the east side of the canal, drove to the rendezvous, from where a helicopter took him to a field. Other generals were waiting. In history books, this is called "the meeting of generals." There are photos. They show four middle-aged men crouched in the desert. Sharon draws a diagram in the sand: *Here's what happened, here's how we can win.* There was shouting and cursing. The generals were furious with Sharon: he did not listen to orders, or exceeded what he had been allowed; if an order he did not like was on its way, he suddenly became hard to reach; he was selfish, in search of glory. He was accused of forming a cult of personality. *What's this with tossing oranges out to your men? That's the gesture of a demagogue!* For a moment, it seemed Sharon and the generals would come to blows. They wanted to remove him but could not. His men loved him too much. Losing Sharon would mean losing the enthusiasm of a division; it's where demagogues protect themselves, in the warm embrace of the people.

When the final plan was approved, it was close to what Sharon diagrammed, only his battalion was mostly kept out of it. Another general would cross the canal, while Sharon gave support from its eastern bank. Sharon later said this was about politics. The men in charge of the army were also in charge of the Labor Party. They wanted to steal away the acclaim Sharon might use to advance the fortunes of Likud. Of course, it did not work out that way. No matter what the reporters wrote, no matter what the generals said, the enduring image of the war was Sharon with his bloodied, bandaged *Yiddische kupp.*

Ariel Sharon was conjured from the dreams of the Jewish people, from the centuries of fear and humiliation. He's the Golem, the automaton that the mystics animated with magic spells. He's the man prophesied in the Zohar, come to finish the unfinished work of Saul and wipe out Amalek. (As John Milius said of Arnold Schwarzenegger, "If we did not have Arnold, we would have to build Arnold.") People see in him what they want to see: either Arik, King of the Jews, or the kosher butcher, apron covered in blood. After the war, an Israeli newspaper editor described him as "this Aryan general with his shock of blond hair." Of course, Sharon is not an Aryan, but he was to this editor, with his memories of German demagogues. Sharon is the Jewish Aryan, the Jewish Rommel. It's the ultimate expression of emancipation: we are free to worship our own strongmen.

On October 20, 1973, the Israeli infantry crossed the Suez Canal. The battle lasted forty-eight hours. When it was over, the Egyptians, who had been on the march, were trapped, with Israelis on either side of them. Israel controlled the Egyptian supply lines. Three hundred thousand men: if Israel did not give them water, they would die. Anwar Sadat asked for terms. What had looked like an Egyptian triumph—bringing a huge army across the canal—suddenly seemed like a brilliant Israeli strategy. Military experts wondered if the generals had planned it this way: let the Egyptians advance, get behind them, and close the trap.

A total of 2,656 Israelis were killed in the war, and more than 7,000 wounded. The Arabs had 15,000 dead, and 35,000 wounded. Gershom Gorenberg describes these as World War I–size losses, making the point by computing equivalencies. By factoring in the size of Israel's population and rescoring on a curve, Israel's 2,656 dead equals 165,000 dead Americans. But such equivalencies probably say less about the realities of war—a life is a life is a life—than about the state of mind of Israelis after the shooting stopped. In the books, it looked like Israel won handily. The fighting lasted just three weeks, and at the end Israel had not only recovered what it had lost, but also increased its holdings, with its soldiers stationed on both sides of the Suez Canal.

But that's not how it felt. It was not the number of dead that devastated Israel. It was the nature of the struggle, the surprise and what had caused them to be so surprised. Many of them had thought the age of big wars was over, that the Arabs had been defeated, that Zionism had triumphed—this had suddenly been exposed as a fantasy, a dream. The Arabs had not been beaten in 1967, and would not be beaten. The struggle would go on. And yes, we're safe now, because we're stronger, but what about in ten years, or a hundred?

A few months after the cease-fire, Abba Kovner made a film about the history of his kibbutz, Ein Hahoresh. It showed pictures of Jews in cities and towns in Europe: old men in prayer shawls, gathered in wooden synagogues, not knowing how easily those synagogues would burn; steamships crowded with red-haired Hannahs leaving ports on the Black Sea, the stone towns rising in terraces above; crossing, islands slipping by in the fog, Palestine appearing on the horizon, Eretz Yisrael, the same earth God used to fashion the first man; the pioneers, in broad straw hats, hacking fields out of the weeds, piping in water, throwing up walls; the first harvest and the first harvest festivals, memorial candles glowing on a hillside, battles in the high places; survivors arriving from the camps, guns put in their hands, being told to fight; victories and pride in this new kind of Jew, winning and winning, but still more wars because the Arabs do not know they have lost. The film ends with ships gathered on the shore, the same ships crowded with the same Jews, only this time they are going away, to sea, the coast of Palestine fading behind them.

After the war, the Israeli government formed a commission to study what had gone wrong. It was headed by the chief of Israel's Supreme Court, Shimon Agranat.* The commissioners interviewed witnesses, experts, soldiers, officials. The preliminary report, released on April 2, 1974, was unusual in that it actually named names. The chief of staff (David Elazar), the chief of military intelligence (Eli Zeira), the deputy chief of military intelligence (Aryeh Shalev), the head of the Mossad's Egypt desk (Lt. Col. Yona Bandman)—all were called to resign or be dismissed. Though the report did not name Golda Meir, she came under intense pressure. It was her government and her ministers who had failed.

To see Golda Meir go through this, in public, was torture to Jews of my parents' generation. It was like watching their own mothers wilt. Golda Meir was one of the people who seemed to represent more than herself. Ben-Gurion was the old man, the grandfather of the project, but Golda was its Yiddish mama. (Which is why she is portrayed onstage and on-screen again and again: by Anne Bancroft on Broadway in *Golda*; by Ingrid Bergman in *A Woman Called Golda*; by To-

*Other members included Moshe Landau, a justice on the court, and Yigael Yadin.

vah Feldshuh and Valerie Harper in *Golda's Balcony*; by Lynn Cohen in *Munich*.) When I was a boy, it seemed her face, pictured on the cover of her autobiography, *My Life*, looked up from every coffee table in Chicago. It was gray and delicate and as wrinkled as an ancient document. She had a big nose and ears and seemed, in pictures, to be both here, in frame, and somewhere else, in a room beyond history, pondering. The old lady with the recipes and the tray of cookies, but whose eyes tell a different story: a hard life, things she knows but does not talk about. Because it was her life, does that mean it has to be yours?

(That's Golda's Zionism in a phrase.)

She epitomized what I've always suspected about the old ladies in the back row of the family portrait—old Sarah, old Rebecca, old Esther, in a dark dress and clunky shoes—that the half smile was hiding another self, that when it came to protecting her own, she could be steely, even ruthless, brutal, and mean. Such ladies, as they get older, lose the filter that separates what they think from what they say and so, on occasion, say remarkable things.

> GOLDA: This country is our own. Nobody has to get up in the morning and worry what his neighbors think of him.
>
> GOLDA: We've won all our wars, but we've paid for them. We don't want any more victories.
>
> GOLDA: The Arabs will stop fighting us when they love their children more than they hate Jews.

In Israel, the office of prime minister devastates everyone who touches it. Because the pressure is too intense. Because there is no margin for error. Because, as Golda said, "The Arabs can fight and lose, but we can only lose once." Because you're responsible not just for your own nation, but for the Jews. (The road winds through the mountains, with sheer drops on either side.) Eshkol wearied unto death; Begin went mad; Rabin was driven out by scandal, then killed by an assassin; Sharon's head imploded, and blood ran into his brain.

Golda Meir resigned on April 10, 1974, a week after the Agranat Commission filed its report. Here's what she said: "I cannot bear this

yoke any longer. I have reached the end of the road." She died of can-
cer in December 1978. She was eighty years old. She lived in Russia
and in Milwaukee but was buried on Mount Herzl. You can see her
tomb. It's a black slab, a modern sculpture on an ancient mountain,
where the desert stretches away on every side.

The commissioners saved their most biting words for Shmuel Gonen. He had been General Patton in mirrored shades, but became
Captain Queeg with his hysteria and tension balls. They called him
timid and nervous and faulted him for leading from behind. He had
been discussing when he should have been attacking. "[Gonen] failed
to fulfill his duties adequately," read the report, "and bears much of
the responsibility for the dangerous situation in which our troops were
caught."

He was cashiered in 1975, offered no posting, no job, no soft landing.
He went out the door in his stiff new civilian clothes. He looked for work
but mostly brooded, replaying each battle in his mind. He blamed his
disgrace on Moshe Dayan and often imagined walking into Dayan's office and shooting him dead.* He quit Israel, went away from there. He
was Lord Jim, wandering from country to country, seeking to outrun the
story of his shame. He lived in Africa for thirteen years, in cheap hotels
on the outskirts of cities, or in port towns where boats floated above
their restless shadows. He hiked through the jungle, in search of precious gems and gold. He said he would make enough money to return
to Israel and clear his name. He won and lost two fortunes—that was
the legend, what the locals would tell you about Mr. Kurtz.

An Israeli reporter tracked him down in Zaire in 1982. He seemed
calm, at peace. He quoted the Talmud. "Who is a hero? He who con-
quers his urges." He was a symbol of the Jewish nation reeling from
too much reality, going here and there trying to clear its name. He was
a premonition of the third exile as seen in a vision by Abba Kovner.
He died in 1991, on a business trip in Europe. His possessions were
sent to his family in Tel Aviv. These included a watch, a book on Kabbalah, and a map of the Sinai Desert.

---

*Gonen told this to a journalist years later.

SIXTEEN

Israel Is Too Real

I first went to Israel in 1975, when I was seven years old. For American Jews, such a trip is a kind of pilgrimage. It's what you might do instead of going to synagogue. It can turn you off, of course, going all that way and finding nothing but dank hotels and old cars and Israelis, who can be arrogant and rude. You might be done with Israel after that. But some of us are smitten, entranced, and so are condemned to a life of scanning the newspaper and worrying about what will happen next there. I remember every detail of that trip: the drive to the airport, the December sting of Chicago, the NON FUMER sign in the seat pocket, the city turning into a grid as we climbed, the stewardess bringing juice, the plane descending, the drops of cloud water racing across the window, the sun on the tarmac, the soldiers in the terminal. There was a line at Passport Control. We were surrounded by American Jews, who were all named Renee and Ralph. The agent went through our documents quickly. Without looking up, he asked, "Where are you staying?" "What are your plans?" Handing the stamped passports to my father, he smiled and said, "Welcome home."

For my father, being in Israel (I realized this only later) was a way to think about his own father, who had died a few years before.

We took a taxi to Jerusalem. My father and mother spoke to the driver. The drone of adult voices. My window open, a breeze on my face. It smelled of cut grass. The road ascended. Each turn opened on a vista of wildflower and cactus. The city waited in cooler air ahead. We drove by hills made entirely of graves. Jerusalem is a city where the dead greatly outnumber the living, where so much more has happened than is happening. I am trying to express how strange the city seems when you approach it for the first time, or after a long absence. Speeding on old stone roads, with rocks towering above, cresting a final rise and rolling into this place so talked about and obsessed over it seems unreal. I saw shops, parks, corners, cars, crowds, police, soldiers. Jews, Jews, Jews, I told myself, all of them Jews! Israel should feel narrow, suffocating—it's small and dominated by one faith—but to me it seemed the opposite. The world was bigger here, more various. Being a Jew where being a Jew is no big deal, you are free to think of yourself in ways other than as being a Jew.

Trips to Israel are organized to indoctrinate; the country is exhibited like a museum. There are things you must see, places you must go, which, together, form a narrative, an argument for the Jewish state. You enter through Yad Vashem as pilgrims once entered the holy city through the Golden Gate. Everything after is seen through the filter of six million dead. You visit Zionist sites, each with its message. Masada, which is Jewish Resistance and Never Again. The Wall, which is antiquity and return. Tel Aviv, which is the Sabra, the New Jew, who is on the beach late into evening like the heroes in books by Camus. The Dead Sea, which is wilderness and the buoyancy of Yahweh. But nothing is more stirring than Jerusalem itself, wandering in the Arab market where the merchandise hangs over arched doorways and the meat twitches fresh on the butcher's line. The light is ethereal, like light in a dream. This is where everything happened, where everything will happen. This is the gate and this is the light streaming through the gate. There is something terrible about the city. It's been the center of too many stories, too many fantasies; it's been tainted, stained. I felt all this on that first trip; it was a current, and it went through me, and I was shocked. Which is why I kept going back. I had come away with the Jerusalem Syndrome.

I have returned again and again, and each time I find a different Israel. Normally when you visit a place, you change, but it stays the same. In this way, you use it to gauge your own development. With Israel, you change, but it changes too. Because it's so new, because it's based on an idea, because it lacks stability. It's like one of those highstrung lapdogs, so small it's immediately affected by whatever it ingests. It's interesting, looking at a country this way, in visit after visit. It's like watching a country develop through a series of time-lapse photos.

I was there in 1977, when Menachem Begin and Anwar Sadat of Egypt began to negotiate their historic peace settlement—it would be the first such deal Israel reached with any of its neighbors. The treaty was made possible by the Yom Kippur War—not by Israel's victory, but by its reversals, which seemed to give the Egyptians self-respect. Anwar Sadat felt he could deal because he was dealing from a position of strength. The particulars could be negotiated, said Sadat. The real obstacle was the suspicion and fear inside the people, which could be dealt with only by bold, imaginative gestures, which is why Sadat flew from Cairo to Tel Aviv. (Before that, the only way to make this trip was through the desert, at the head of an army.*) He was met in Israel by rapturous crowds. He waved and smiled. He stood before the

---

*The reverse trip had, in fact, been attempted years earlier by Israeli peace activist Abie Nathan. Here's how it was described in Nathan's obituary in *The New York Times* of August 28, 2008: "A Royal Air Force–trained pilot, [Nathan] crashed into the national consciousness and the quagmire of the Middle East conflict with a dramatic solo flight from Israel to Egypt in an old rented biplane in 1966. A self-appointed ambassador, he wanted to talk to President Gamal Abdel Nasser of Egypt about making peace. After a forced landing in the enemy territory of Port Said, he was allowed to stay overnight in Egypt before being sent back to Israel. He never got to see Nasser."

Knesset and said, "No more war." It was a catharsis, like being told you can live.

Here's what Sadat said on the tarmac: "What about Sharon? Is he here?" Funny that he asked not for Shimon Peres or Golda Meir, but for the bloodstained warrior, Ariel Sharon. Say what you want, but this was a war and these men were generals. In the footage, you see them standing together on the runway, Sadat taking Sharon by the hand, whispering. "I tried to capture you," Sadat said. "If you attempt to cross to the West Bank again, I will have you arrested."*

The treaty was signed on September 17, 1978. I remember walking on the kibbutz in the evening, past the white cottages, which glowed with light, behind my father and Ruzka Marle. She was wearing a peasant dress, and was very small, with large, distinct features. They talked in that quiet way of adults when it is evening and there is serious business at hand.

"I don't trust them," said Ruzka.

"You have to," said my father.

"Peace is a state of mind," said Ruzka. "Who trades land for a state of mind?"

I was there in 1979, with my Grandma Esther, in an air-conditioned coach that climbed above Nazareth as the guide said, "Now we see the Galilee, where Jesus, a typical Jewish rabbi, led his congregation." There was an attack that summer. Members of the PLO ambushed and killed Israeli soldiers in Hebron. On the bus, hours of discussion followed. It was like we were members of the Mossad. An intelligence agent had dropped a file into our lap and said, "His name is Yasser Arafat. Learn everything you can."

Arafat was an engineer born in Cairo to Palestinian parents. In the mid 1960s, before the occupation, he formed Fatah, a group pledged to destroy the Jewish state. (*Fatah*, which is Arabic for "opening," is a

*This is according to Sharon, in his autobiography.

reverse acronym for "Palestinian National Liberation Movement.") The group was bundled together with various other groups to form the PLO (Palestinian Liberation Organization). Arafat had staged a series of attacks, the first coming in the mid-sixties, their frequency and audacity increasing greatly after 1973, when the Arab states basically quit the fight against Israel. My grandmother listed the atrocities: the raid at the Olympic Village in Munich (1972), where terrorists kidnapped and killed Israeli athletes; the attack in Ma'alot (1974), where terrorists blew up a school filled with Israeli children; the hijacking of Air France Flight 139 (1976), which was then diverted to Uganda. On the ground in Entebbe, the Jewish passengers were separated from the Gentiles, who were freed, which, to Jews of my grandmother's generation, seemed terrifyingly reminiscent of the Nazi selections. (The hijacking ended with Israel's miracle raid on the Entebbe airport.)

And others, so many others, skyjackings and bus bombings and kidnappings, planes exploding, buildings collapsing, images that, shuffled fast before your eyes, told you (if you were named Esther Cohen and lived in North Miami Beach) what it meant to be a Hebrew in this world: to be blamed, to be hated, to be attacked. Arafat was straight from the nightmare of the Galut Jew. In a sense, he gave us what we secretly wanted: a reminder, history made manifest. The fatigues and the keffiyeh, the stubbly beard and the pistol. Words my Grandma Esther used to describe him include *monster*, *killer*, *bully*, *murderer*, *terrorist*, *meshugenner*, *mental patient*, *Jew killer*, *Cossack*, *Nazi*.

I was there in 1982, when the IDF, in pursuit of Yasser Arafat and his ragtag army, which had made camp across the northern border, invaded Lebanon, advancing to the suburbs of Beirut. The Israelis besieged the city, demanding the surrender of the PLO.* During the invasion, Christian militias allied with Israel went into the Palestinian

---

*As part of the eventual cease-fire, Arafat and his lieutenants went into exile in Tunis, where they remained until they were brought back as part of the Oslo peace process.

refugee camps of Sabra and Shatila and massacred hundreds of people. News of these massacres provoked worldwide condemnation and sent the citizens of Israel, many of them, into a rage. Sabra and Shatila seemed to epitomize all that had gone wrong with Zionism. Is this really why we came all that way, to be the power, the Cossack, the gun? Has history so punished us that we can understand no suffering but our own? Apologists pointed to the region, saying, in essence, "We have done nothing that the other nations around here have not done routinely." It's what Israeli generals mean when they say, "We live in a tough neighborhood."

In other words, Israel has become what it has become in order to survive.

What happened in Lebanon, however, particularly in those camps, was simply too brutal for most Israelis to accept. Protesters filled the streets of Jerusalem and Tel Aviv. They waved signs, chanted. They demanded the end of the war and the resignation of the government. Most of their anger was directed at Ariel Sharon, in part because he was the minister of defense, and so the architect of the war, in part because the mission and the resulting massacre had all the markings of an Ariel Sharon production. (It was the culmination of all the other raids, in Kibbya, in Gaza, in the West Bank.) It was extreme and seemingly without purpose, unless, of course, the purpose was to send a message: this is who we are, this is what we'll do.

Sharon denied any responsibility. It was not Israeli but Lebanese soldiers who went into those camps, he explained, not Jews but Christians, fighting their own battle, settling their own scores, speaking in their own language. As soon as he learned of the killings, they were stopped. Of course, Sharon knew the terrain, knew the history and the players, so he should also have known what would happen if Christian militias went into the Palestinian camps. Perhaps he thought some bloodshed—just a little—would be proper punishment for people who had supported and given haven to terrorists who killed Jews. (Jewish blood is a commodity, and the price has gone up.)

But events have a way of following their own logic, of riding from emotion to emotion, of spinning out of control. Once inside the camps, the Christian militias were overcome by bloodlust. They went wild. The resulting massacre must have shocked even Sharon. It was a turning point: in how the world saw Israel and, more important, in how many Israelis saw their own leaders and nation. After Lebanon, there was no more pretending that Israel, because of its faith and its history, was immune, different, better. Like every other nation, it's capable of both the best and the worst.

The massacres were investigated by an Israeli commission, the Kahane Commission. Sharon was the villain of its report. He was charged with "indirect responsibility" for the killings and forced to resign his office. He did not regain a position of leadership for a generation.

I was there in 1987, when the Palestinians rose up in the First Intifada. It started with scattered riots but soon grew into a full-scale revolt. It took even the beat reporters a while to determine the exact incident or trigger that set off the conflagration:

On December 9 an Israeli lost control of his car in the Jabaliya Refugee Camp in Gaza. He skidded through an intersection, killing four pedestrians. A crowd gathered. Some people erroneously said the Israeli had steered into the crosswalk intentionally to avenge the death of his brother, killed by an Arab a few days earlier. Thousands of Palestinians were soon on the streets of the camp, first cursing the driver, then cursing Israel in general. The protest spread to camps and towns across Gaza and the West Bank. That it began as a misunderstanding does not mean it was bad luck and could have been avoided. It was a fire that was going to burn, had to burn, kindling in need of a spark. The accident was merely the occasion seized upon to make the point about life under occupation, without rights, in refugee camps and squalid towns. Since Arafat and his soldiers had been exiled to Tunis, the explosion came from below; it was a genuinely popular uprising, which made it almost impossible to put down. It was in the course of the First Intifada, in fact, that many Israelis learned the limits of their military power. "An army can beat an army," the Israeli political scientist Shlomo Avineri said at the time, "but an army cannot beat a people."

In the first months, the Intifada took the form of stone-throwing crowds, young men showering Israeli cars and soldiers with rocks. (This is when checkpoints first appeared in Gaza and the West Bank.) The army, which had never been properly trained to respond to a popular uprising, reacted rashly, dumbly, with machines and soldiers, bulldozers, water cannons, rubber bullets and real bullets.

Here's what you would see: Arabs throwing stones; Israelis sheltering behind riot shields; two or three quick bursts, a trail of smoke as canisters of teargas drop into a crowd; a yellow wind; the crowd running; men covering their mouths with scarves; Israelis shooting over the crowd; Arab prisoners chained to a truck. All of this—Jews, Arabs, smoke, weapons—played before the TV cameras, a long-running show in which Israel was the heavy. Yitzhak Rabin, then the minister of defense, reportedly told his soldiers—he later denied it—"Break their bones."

With every action, Israel seemed to undermine its own cause. In an effort to break the Intifada, they arrested thousands of Palestinians, who were then transformed, in Israeli jails, from a collection of protesters into a tightly organized movement. (Israeli prisons were said to be the finishing schools of the Intifada.) Then, in an effort to undermine the growing resistance, which was secular and nationalist, Israel tried to foster a Palestinian opposition, giving money to Muslim clerics, specifically to Sheik Ahmed Yassin, later assassinated by Israel, who went on to build Hamas.

Worse was the way the Intifada changed Israel's image in the West. Israel had once been championed by the Left in Europe and the United States. Here was David, the shepherd boy, slaying the monster with a sling. (In the 1940s, Luther Adler directed *A Flag Is Born* on Broadway, a heroic retelling of Zionist pioneer days starring Marlon Brando.) That ended with the uprising. Because who is the underdog now, who has the sling and the stone? That the rioters called themselves the "children of stones" was no accident. The Palestinians had become David. If the Arab is David, then who is the Jew? He is Goliath, of course. Something strange happened in those years, at least in the mind of the Left. The Palestinians became the Jews and the Jews became the Romans, or the British, or even the Nazis.

Edward Said, *The Question of Palestine*:

> There is an unmistakable coincidence between the experience of Arab Palestinians at the hands of Zionism and the experience of those black, yellow and brown people who were described as inferior and subhuman by 19th century Imperialists.

Worse still was the way the Intifada changed how Jews saw themselves. For the first time in two thousand years, Jews wielded the power of a state, which, to the Jewish community, had always been seen as an oppressive and corrupting power. The holiness of the Jew, the holiness of Jesus, had come from his very statelessness. Neither temporal power nor worldly dominion, free of involvement, free of guilt. With a Jewish army crushing what looked like an Arab peasant rebellion on TV, Jews everywhere had to reset their compasses. There is no way to exercise power without diminishing yourself. To be is to do, and to do is to be damned. It's the price of sovereignty, the hidden cost of Zionism.

The Intifada came as a shock to Israelis. It made them see themselves as they had long been seen. Which is why, in the early 1980s, there was an explosion of activity on Israel's political left, with the appearance of groups such as Peace Now, which questioned the very assumptions of Israeli life: maybe we don't need the wars and maybe we don't need the occupation. This was accompanied by the rise of a generation of revisionist historians: Benny Morris, Tom Segev, Avi Shlaim. They vowed to rethink every story and explanation. Who are we really, they seemed to wonder, and what lies have we been told? Though radical, these men were part of a tradition. They were, in a sense, behaving as prophets. They did not question King David as a metaphor for modern Israel so much as follow the metaphor through to its narrative conclusion: David as an old man, beset by violence and court intrigue, a witness to the world that will come after him. The state of Israel is, in other words, the story of David after David has won. After he has moved from slingshots to siege engines. After he has moved from wilderness to capital. After he has consolidated power and become satisfied and entitled. After he takes and takes, and so betrays the holy secret of the Jew, which is his knowledge of God. First he is a boy bringing water to his brothers, then he is in the valley with his slingshot and his stone, then he is dancing before the Ark of the Lord, then he is an old man weeping for his dead.

Absalom, O Absalom.

When Nathan the prophet spoke to King David in the palace, he did so as the revisionist historian spoke to the Israeli public during the Intifada. He showed him a picture of a brutal stranger and said, "Look at this man, because it is you!" David had seen Uriah the Hittite's wife, Bathsheba, in her bath ("And it happened at eventide that David arose from his bed and walked about on the roof of the King's house, and he saw from the roof a woman bathing, and the woman was very beautiful"), took her, then sent her husband to be killed in battle.

Here's what Nathan told his king:

> There were two men in one city; the one rich, and the other poor. The rich man had exceeding many flocks and herds: But the poor man had nothing, save one little ewe lamb, which he had bought and nourished up: and it grew up together with him, and with his children; it did eat of his own meat, and drank of his own cup, and lay in his bosom, and was unto him as a daughter. And there came a traveler unto the rich man, and he spared to take of his own flock and of his own herd, to dress for the wayfaring man that was come unto him; but took the poor man's lamb, and dressed it for the man that was come to him. And David's anger was greatly kindled against the man; and he said to Nathan, As the LORD liveth, the man that hath done this thing shall surely die: And he shall restore the lamb fourfold, because he did this thing, and because he had no pity. And Nathan said to David, Thou art the man.

I was not in Israel in 1990, when Saddam Hussein, who had threat-ened to incinerate half the country, ordered his armies into Kuwait and George Bush went before the American public and said, "This will not stand." I was right here, in New York, but I was watching on TV. The war played behind the bartender as my friend Todd said, "You know, this is just what we need, a bloodletting to test our sad, image-saturated generation." What I remember from that war, and why I bring it up here, in a book about Zionism, was a night soon af-ter the bombs began to fall on Baghdad. I was at a Rangers game at Madison Square Garden. When I went out for a beer, all the TVs were showing Tel Aviv, where Israelis were gathered in safe rooms, wait-ing for the chemical-tipped Scuds promised by Saddam. Network cor-respondents filed reports from shelters where Israeli families were gathered nervously—mother, father, daughter, son, all strapped into monstrous gas masks, a vision of the First World War. This image—which was terrifying and consoling in a way, because here were these families, in it together—was everywhere in Madison Square Garden, playing on a hundred screens, but no one seemed to notice. Which made it stranger still, as if it were being broadcast on a frequency only I, a Jew, could receive. It made me feel just the way I feel when a Hasid from the Mitzvah tank spots me in a crowd, and says, "You! Are you a Jew?" Singled out, as if history has business with me.

I was in Israel in 1993, when Yasser Arafat and Yitzhak Rabin shook hands on the White House lawn. This was the result of a long process that began in secret in Oslo, Norway (hence: the Oslo Ac-cords), before emerging into the afternoon light of the Rose Garden. I watched the broadcast of the signing and handshake in a hotel room in Tiberias:

"Come on," a friend was saying. "Let's go."

"No, wait," I told him. "I want to see this."

Here was Rabin, an iconic figure, the first Israeli prime minister born in Israel, the boy soldier grown into the gray-haired eminence.* He was among the few Israelis with the credibility to make such a deal. He had struggled and fought and bled and been defeated and gone on. His life was as various as that of King David. He was King David. His story would be impossible in any era but David's, or our own. He served with the Hagana in the Galilee, he scouted for the British in Lebanon, he freed the refugees from Atilt, he collapsed on the eve of the Six-Day War, then recovered to conquer Jerusalem. He had been through the Intifada, and believed that the struggle could not be won on the battlefield, no matter how many bones you broke.

Here was Arafat, the terrorist, the exile, the statesman. In fatigues and headdress. Having picked the wrong side. Having backed Saddam Hussein, which left him ostracized, and destitute. He was finally ready to recognize the Jewish state, finally ready, or so he said, to make peace.

I was fascinated by the handshake itself. The entire conflict was captured in this pleasantry. I mean, here were these two men, each a stand-in for his people and his cause, leaning together, leaning apart, and here was Bill Clinton, big, white-haired, bluff, smiling, happy-natured America, friendly as a golden retriever, bringing together these enemies. According to Rabin, who saw in Arafat a man marinated to his eyes in blood, there was not supposed to be a handshake. But Clinton, demonstrating the role of personality in history, forced them together—because what is a party without a dance? You could see Rabin grimace, hesitate, as if, for a moment, he felt the weight of the past. *What I am about to do, in front of all these cameras?* Recoil, pull it together, take the hand, and smile. The fact that Arafat demonstrated

---

*David Grossman: "Even his physical appearance could teach us something we didn't know. This youthful Sabra with the handsome face and uncombed wavy hair turned into an adult, then into an old man. Rabin's very real face allowed us to sense how our ideals and hopes slowly became flesh, became real life. We walked with him, watching him as if walking alongside ourselves, each according to his age, and we saw our own image in him." This was, in fact, Rabin's second stint as prime minister. The first, which followed the resignation of Golda Meir, ended in scandal. When Leah Rabin was discovered to be holding a U.S. bank account filled with American dollars, the prime minister was forced to resign.

no such hesitation—smiled, waved, went on—does not tell me he was more willing. Just the opposite. It tells me he took the day in stride, not as the end of the conflict, but as the beginning of a new phase.

The handshake and signing of the treaty were followed by euphoria. In Israel, people crowded the beaches and bars. My friend Michael Kovner hugged me and said, "I always knew if we went this way, took this step, took the hand, the whole thing could be over; then we could live and be just like other people." (There were tears in his eyes.) Soon after, King Hussein of Jordan signed a peace treaty with Israel. It seemed that Israel had entered a new era in which it would finally dream the humdrum dream of nations in repose. It's hard to overestimate the giddiness of that moment: the war was over, resolved not on the battlefield but at the negotiating table. In a gesture of friendship, King Hussein, who was a pilot, flew over Jerusalem, banking low above the ancient streets—I was in those streets, and saw the metallic shine in the flawless blue sky—signaling the end of Israel's life behind walls.

Rabin made peace with a kind of sad wisdom, in a minor key, like an old man who has seen the limits of his will.

Here's what he said:

> We, the soldiers who have returned from battle stained with blood, we who have seen our relatives and friends killed . . . we who come from a land where parents bury their children, we who have fought against you, the Palestinians—we say today in a loud and clear voice: Enough blood and tears. Enough.

I was in Israel on November 4, 1995, when Yitzhak Rabin was assassinated. It happened in public, with a hundred thousand people looking on. Everything about it seemed symbolic, ironic, as if staged by a dramatist. Rabin was killed at the end of a rally for peace, in the center of Tel Aviv. A moment before, he had been singing a song about peace. (A nurse found the bloodstained lyrics in his pocket.) A moment before that he had been saying (in a speech), "I believe that there is now a chance for peace, a great chance, which must be seized." He was shot three times by a slim little man. He was laid in state in the Knesset, where his coffin was visited by more than a million people. His funeral was attended by the leaders of the Arab world, including King Hussein, Hosni Mubarak of Egypt, and Yasser Arafat. He was buried on Mount Herzl.

The assassin was named Yigal Amir. He was twenty-five. Here is how he first appeared in *The New York Times:* "A short, dark-haired man dressed in a blue shirt and light colored pants, [who] was pinned to a wall by police officers and rushed to a waiting police car." After that, you saw him on TV, going to and from court, a sallow, trampy figure with dark pools for eyes—the chaos of history, which, in books, looks orderly, but in truth reels from disaster to disaster. He was pleasant and plain. His head was filled with stories and commandments. His parents emigrated from Yemen. He fell under the sway of charismatic rabbis who believed, as the followers of Jesus had believed, that "some of you will pass to the next world without tasting death."

He was educated in a yeshiva where students were trained in the martial arts. His teachers described him as sensitive, an intellectual who could lose himself in the library. His mother taught nursery school. After his military service, he went to Russia, where he taught Hebrew and encouraged Jews to emigrate. At the time of the assassination, he was in his third year of law school at Bar-Ilan University, near Tel Aviv, a center of Religious Zionism. He spent time in the settlements, on the hilltops. He registered as a resident of Kiryat Arba, which he was not, because this allowed him to carry a gun. He attended sermons where rabbis charged Rabin with treason. By trading land for peace, they said, Rabin was delaying the end-time, holding up the Messiah, betraying the mission. A few weeks before the assassination, some of these rabbis gathered in front of the prime minister's house in Jerusalem, where they prayed for the "angels of destruction" to swoop down and kill Rabin. In fliers passed out at the rally, the

prime minister was shown dressed as a Nazi.* Amir quoted the Halaka, a code of Orthodox Jewish law, during his trial: "A man who
gives his people and his land to the enemy must be killed"; "Any Jew
who helps the enemy endangers the life of Jews and must be killed."

"My whole life has been given to studying the Halaka," he told a
jury. "I have all the data. When I shot Rabin I felt as if I was shooting
a terrorist."[†]

I was in Israel in 2000, when Ehud Barak and Yasser Arafat, meeting
at Camp David in Maryland, tried and failed to work out the final
terms of a peace.[‡] (This was an attempt to close the deal that Rabin
and Arafat had opened in Oslo.) The particulars of the meeting—
what happened, who offered what, who refused, who is to blame—
have been so analyzed and debated that the details fade, leaving a
single scene, played and replayed in a loop: Ehud Barak, a short,
stocky man gone slightly to seed, walking beside Yasser Arafat. Behind
them is Bill Clinton in big-and-tall-man-type clothes. They come to a
door. Arafat steps aside to let Barak through. As in, "ladies first." This
is how Barak seems to take it, anyway. He drops an arm on Arafat's
shoulder, as if to say, "No, please, after you." Arafat smiles, puts his
arm on Barak. "No, be my guest." And on it goes, until, within a few
moments, the men are actually jostling, trying to shove each other
through the door. Clinton stands there, looking pained, like, you know,
what now? In other words, these two men, each the head of a nation,
cannot even agree who goes first through a door in Maryland. Even
this, it seems, will require a summit and an exchange of prisoners,

---

*Benjamin Netanyahu spoke at a rally: "You, Yitzhak Rabin. I accuse you of direct responsibility
for stirring up Arab terror and for the horror of this massacre in Tel Aviv. You are guilty. The blood
is on your head."

[†]See "Israel's Demons," by Amos Elon, *The New York Review of Books*, December 21, 1995.

[‡]The process had been moving in fits and starts for years, through the administrations of Shimon
Peres, Benjamin Netanyahu, and Ehud Barak. After the death of Rabin, the love, if there had ever
been any, went out of the peace process: Israelis continued to settle the West Bank, and Palestinians continued to incite and engage in terrorist attacks.

which is the conflict in a nutshell: *We will stop building when you stop attacking, and we will stop attacking when you stop building.*

There were more talks and concessions after that, glimmers of hope, but when you think back, the story jumps directly from the struggle to see who goes through that door first to Ariel Sharon striding onto the Temple Mount. Sharon was making a point. His famous walk was an act of theater.* As part of the Camp David deal, Ehud Barak had agreed to cede control of much of East Jerusalem, and Ariel Sharon was letting people know his position on that. It belongs only to us. It will never again be divided. He was, in other words, declaring Jewish sovereignty, which infuriated Palestinians. Not just the visit to the Temple Mount, but the way it was done, with a swarm of cameras and a thousand Israeli policeman. The Second Intifada began a few days later. It was not like the first. This time, the struggle was led not from below but from above, by the leaders of various militant groups. This time, Palestinians fought not with rocks but with guns, then bombs, then suicide bombs. It went on for two years, moving from atrocity to atrocity.

I was back in Israel in the spring of 2001, at the height of the conflict. Everything had changed. The hotels were empty, the streets deserted. When you saw a bus gliding to a stop, you imagined it bursting into flames. For a moment in the summer of that year, when the wave of suicide bombing reached its height, with several dozen each week, in malls, in clubs, at beaches, each with its aftermath of panic and blood and glass, and that weird tribe of limb-gathering orthodox Jews who came after the explosion as certain kinds of microbes come after an oil spill, it seemed that life would become impossible in Israel, that the Zionist dream would die. It was less the death toll than what the suicide bomber—talking of his own death on a video, wound up like a toy, sent into a market, smiling as he explodes—seemed to be saying. He spoke of annihilation. He spoke in the voice of Haman[†] and

---

*This walk broke the unwritten rule, established by Moshe Dayan in 1967, by which Israeli politicians stay off the Temple Mount. Sharon had asked Ehud Barak's permission, and Barak had given it, perhaps hoping Sharon's appearance on the Mount would be taken as a warning, spurring Arafat to deal.

[†]The nobleman who plotted to kill the Jews of Persia. (See the Book of Esther.)

Hitler. He said, "Here is how much I hate you." He said, "Here is how far I will go." He said, "You will never know a normal life in this land."

Then came the Israeli response: which was fear; which was war; which was invasion; which was checkpoints; which was assassination; which was death from above; which was F-16s; which was Ariel Sharon; which was the fence.

SEVENTEEN

Ninth of Av

In the summer of 2005, I went to Israel to cover the withdrawal from Gaza. To me, this seemed like the first truly significant thing to happen in the conflict in years. In deciding to pull its soldiers and settlers from the Strip, the Israeli government was finally accepting what should have been clear the morning after the Yom Kippur War. That Israel could not govern the Territories and remain Israel as it had first been envisioned: a sane, secular, Jewish republic. If the situation is allowed to follow its present trajectory, in fact, the Jews will eventually find themselves in the minority, ruling over a restive, disenfranchised, angry Arab population. At that point, Israel will stop being a democracy. The withdrawal, led by Ariel Sharon, the architect of the settlements, was a stunning moment of recognition. It was the old man realizing the dream had to be reimagined, Israel had to get smaller to survive. If you stood on a hill as the buses filled with religious zealots rolled out of the Strip, you might even feel like you were watching an ebb tide.

Ariel Sharon was elected prime minister in 2001. He was the villain of the Palestinians, but in many ways it was the Palestinians who put him back in office. It was the terror, the suicide bomber, the fanaticism and fear that sent Israelis into the arms of the general. They clung to him the way, in a storm, you cling to your father, even if he's a son of a bitch. He was the last of the generation that made the state and won its wars. He had been a hero in '48, he had been a hero in '67, he had been a hero in '73, and a villain in '82 (so what?). When a suicide bomber is wandering through the market wired up like a Christmas tree, you summon the toughest cop you can find.

Sharon was pugnacious, direct, an athlete grown fat with age, who ambles, who shakes a fist. He said he wanted to reestablish the nation's deterrence: if you hit us, you get hit back ten times as hard. It was only such deterrence that enabled the Jews to live as a nation, he said, but it had been dangerously eroded by years of negotiating and compromising: by not punishing Saddam Hussein following the Scud attacks, by not hitting back in the first days of the Second Intifada. Under Ehud Barak, the air force bombed empty buildings in the Gaza Strip. Barak wanted to pressure Arafat but avoid casualties. He would warn the Palestinians to evacuate in advance. According to Sharon, this further eroded Israel's deterrence; it made the terrorists believe they could get away with it, there would be no price. "From now on," said Sharon, "every time we hit, we draw blood."

His main achievement was simply persisting, carrying on. When Sharon came on the scene, people were in despair, convinced this new kind of terrorism could not be fought, because, as the leader of Hezbollah, Hassan Nasrallah, said, "They love life and we love death." Sharon wanted to show that the terrorism could be fought, that there was hope, a seam through the armies, a way to cross the canal.

He did, in fact, defeat the Second Intifada, which was less an uprising than a war. By various strategies, each of which has since been condemned: by invasion, by assassination, by checkpoint, by building a wall. The number of suicide attacks decreased dramatically. As a result, ordinary life returned. Sharon said the nation was still not secure.

It was as if he had woken from a dream, suddenly understood the danger posed by demographics, the drift of populations. Here's how the politicians on the Left explained it: if the occupation continues, then within a generation Israel will be either a Jewish state or a Democracy, but it cannot be both.*

In short, the Arabs were out-procreating the Jews. This is why some Palestinians don't want to end the occupation. Because, if they wait long enough, then demand "one man, one vote," there will be just one state and it will be Palestine. Arafat called it the "human bomb."

In the summer of 2004, for the first time in his life, Sharon began talking about ceding territory. He wanted to get Israel behind the blast wall before the Palestinians detonated the human bomb. How do you do this without destroying the deterrent? Israel is like a man who has had a fight that ended with him sitting astride his enemy. The trick is getting off without getting killed. He therefore has to make a deal before he gets off. But the man on the bottom says, "How can I make a deal while you're sitting on me?" So who gives? Who goes through the door first?

After you?

No, please, you first.

No, my friend, first you.

---

*In time, this position was accepted even by members of the old Likud aristocracy, such as Ehud Olmert, who, in the fall of 2008, in his last days as prime minister—he had been driven out by an ethics probe; this consisted most damagingly of a businessman from Long Island telling a judge of the cash-filled envelopes he once handed the politician—gave an interview to *Yediot Aharonot*, the largest newspaper in Israel, in which he recanted some of his oldest beliefs, including his belief in Greater Israel. "What I am saying now has not been said by any Israeli leader before me," he told the reporter. "The time has come to say these things. Who thinks seriously if we sit on another hilltop, on another hundred meters, that this is what will make the difference for the State of Israel's basic security? A decision has to be made. This decision is difficult, terrible, a decision that contradicts our natural instincts, our innermost desires, our collective memories, the prayers of the Jewish people for 2,000 years. We have to reach an agreement with the Palestinians, the meaning of which is that in practice we will withdraw from almost all the territories, if not all the territories. We will leave a percentage of these territories in our hands, but will have to give the Palestinians a similar percentage, because without that there will be no peace. I am not trying to justify retroactively what I did for 35 years," he explained. "For a large portion of these years, I was unwilling to look at reality in all its depth" ("Olmert Says Israel Should Pull Out of West Bank," *The New York Times*, September 30, 2008).

Sharon decided to act quickly, unilaterally, withdrawing troops and settlers from Gaza in the summer of 2005. If all went well, Israel could then leave parts of the West Bank. He was like an engineer preparing for a flood—of extremism, of populations. He was, in a sense, throwing up sandbags while watching the horizon. He reeked of sadness. You hear it in his last speeches. It was a melancholy, end-of-the-day sadness. It was the sadness of the father who watches the sky turn purple and shivers as the wind falls still. He fought the wars when he was young, built the settlements when he was in his middle years, and now, as an old man, he had come to see his mistake and was desperately trying to fix it before he died.

I stayed in the American Colony Hotel in East Jerusalem. At night, I sat in the bar listening to the reporters. The American Colony is a mecca for foreign correspondents. Their talk was complicated, knowing, involved, and inane. Israel is the only place I know where a reporter can cover a war in the afternoon and be back in a four-star hotel by evening. It's a plum gig, which is partly why the volume of news seems so out of proportion to the numbers and size of the conflict—also because each story from Israel plays off the big preexisting story, which is the Hebrews, the Promised Land, and everything they told you in church.

Each morning, I had breakfast in the courtyard, where I read the newspapers and watched the correspondents prepare for another day. They spoke the way skiers talk over the free buffet as they gear up for the slopes: "Want to hit the Strip?" "Nah, let's try Nablus." By 9:00 a.m., the hotel was empty. I went for walks through the Old City into West Jerusalem, where the city buses, each aching to burst into flames, groaned up Jaffa Road. Most days, my cousin Anat met me at the hotel. We had lunch, then set off across the country, which is so small you can traverse it in an afternoon. She helped me arrange interviews and, when necessary, interpreted. (I went to Hebrew school for five years and can say only "Thank you," "Be quiet," and "Good for you!") We met settlers, rabbis, activists (Arab and Jew), gurus, historians, soldiers, resisters. I asked about the withdrawal, what it meant, and what would come next.

I met David Sunshine, a young infantry officer, famous (or infamous; it depends whom you ask) for his refusal to serve in Gaza or the West Bank. Sunshine's organization of like-minded officers was considered a threat by the army. He was denounced and jailed. We sat on a balcony with the Mediterranean behind us. "I was better than most," he said. "But serving in the Territories can do something to even the most moral officer. It turns you into an animal."

I met Asa Kasher, the author of the Israeli military's "code of ethics." We talked in his apartment outside Tel Aviv, in a dark, book-filled room with slats closed against the sun. He was gray-haired and spoke in a clipped voice, like a man who holds each word carefully in his hands. When I asked about the withdrawal, he said, "It's necessary, but it's a failure." He told me it was mostly the fault of people like me, American Jews who should have moved to Israel but never did. The Israelis had been, in a sense, holding the Territories for us, and we never came. "It's a shame," he said. "A million Jews from the Western democracies would have changed everything here. Our relationship with the Arabs, our relationship with each other. It would have guaranteed a vast Jewish majority for decades to come. Because you are not afraid, you have forgotten what it means to be a Jew," he told me. "By the time you remember, it will be too late."*

I met Anat Biletski, a founder of B'Tselem, Israel's premier human rights group. She told me that Sharon's plan to leave Gaza was a fake. "Wait and see," she said. "Something will come up. There will be an emergency. The withdrawal will never happen."

I met Pinchas Wallerstein, the leader of the Yesha Council, an umbrella organization that represents the religious settlers on the West Bank and (then) in Gaza. The group's headquarters is in a nondescript building in Jerusalem. The rooms were filled with young people in orange shirts, the "official" color of those opposed to withdrawal. Most had walkie-talkies on their belts. These crackled with voices. The walls were covered with maps—red tacks indicated streets that protesters in-

---

*Here's how Judah Halevi explained the destruction of the Second Temple (this is in a letter to the King of the Khazars): "The Divinity was prepared to come down again as before, if only [the Jews] had all agreed with a joyful heart to return to the land. But only part of them returned; the majority and particularly the outstanding ones remained in Babylon and preferred to live as barely tolerated slaves as long as they were not separated from their homes and businesses."

tended to block—and posters. One showed an Israeli soldier in a cage, over the words THIS IS THE KIND OF CAGE THE IDF WILL USE TO RE-MOVE PEOPLE FROM THEIR HOMES IN GAZA. A JEW DOES NOT DE-PORT A JEW!

A young man in a T-shirt that read IN ERETZ YISRAEL, I BUY ONLY FROM JEWS brought me in to see Wallerstein. He was standing behind his desk, talking on the phone. He was short, stocky, intense. His body was shaped like a fist. He had a kind of energy I can only describe as manic. He had spent time in prison. In the course of a traffic dispute, he had shot an Arab. He looked at me as he talked on the phone. When he hung up, he dropped into his chair, grinned tightly, and said, "So, here is another Jew from America who does not know who he is."

We talked for a few minutes.

I said, "So, what do you think of Sharon?"

He said, "I think he's crazy. I think he's senile. I think he's lost his mind."

I said, "He seems sharp to me."

He said, "He's betraying everything he once believed in."

I said, "I don't agree. I think he's fighting even now for what he believes in: Israel. He was for settlements when he thought they were helping Israel; now that he thinks they're not helping, but hurting, he's against them. The tactics might change, but the goal has stayed the same. Don't you see that?"

"What do you think happens when we leave Gaza?" Wallerstein asked me. "Do you think that's the end of it? That the attacks stop, the rockets stop? No. I will tell you what will happen. Right now, Hamas is firing into our settlements. These are on the fence. When we leave, Hamas will simply move its launchers into the ruins of our towns. Then, instead of hitting the settlements, they will hit towns inside Israel. Sderot. Ashkelon. What will you do then? Pull the people out of those towns too, retreat to Tel Aviv? Then they will start hitting Tel Aviv. What will you do then?"*

*This is, in fact, exactly what happened.

The withdrawal had been scheduled for early August, meaning it would fall in the weeks of mourning preceding the Ninth of Av, the anniversary of the Second Temple's destruction, which Jews mark by visiting the Western Wall, by weeping and praying and singing from the Book of Lamentations, which chronicles the Babylonian exile. The withdrawal was said by settlers to echo that ancient disaster, which made the choice of date unfortunate. It was therefore pushed back to August 15, soon after the anniversary. As a result, the mourning period was especially intense, with weeping for the ancient Temple getting mixed up with weeping for the settlements: what had been lost, what was being lost.

A week before the withdrawal, a settler boarded a bus in the north—it was a route frequented by Israeli Arabs—sat in back with his gun, then, as the bus neared its last stop, stepped into the aisle and opened fire. According to the experts, he did this in hopes of delaying or preventing the withdrawal. Sharon went on TV and called the settler a terrorist. My friends said this was a big deal, as Sharon had never before used that word to describe a Jew. I went to Shefaram, an Arab town in Israel, for the funeral of the people killed on the bus. The crowd was almost entirely Arab. I met an Orthodox rabbi, though: Rabbi Menachem Forman. He lives on the West Bank and says he wants to stay in Judea no matter which government is in control. The caskets were carried on the shoulders of the crowd. Women looked down from the balconies.

I met a student from Tel Aviv who was conducting a study on birds, particularly a species of East Indian finch new to the region. These birds had been imported for display in a park in Tel Aviv, where they were kept in a wire cage beneath a cypress tree. A storm blew through the city one night. In the morning, the cage was broken and the birds gone. Within a year, the birds, which had evolved slowly, somewhere else, and therefore had no natural predators in the region, had multiplied and multiplied. They nested in every tree and foraged for every kind of grub, driving out birds native to the country. The student referred to the finches as "an introduced species," then said, "but, you know, none of the species around here are *truly* native. They all come from somewhere else, they all pushed some other bird out of its habitat."

If this book is working the way it's supposed to, then each individual story will read like the history of Israel, and the history of Israel will read like the life of a single man. I see this most in Ariel Sharon, who traveled the entire journey of his people, from the energy and heroism of youth to the sad, dissipated melancholy of old age—the psychosis of the Jews bracketed between a single pair of ears. As David Grossman said, "His life was biblical," in its sweep and violence and poetry, but also in its rhythms, in its ups and downs. He sinned as Abraham sinned. He sinned as David sinned. He lost the blessing but went on. First a young man on a rocky hill with the day stretched before him. Then hated and old. He was like one of those somber, parable-filled Shakespearean characters who is carried by words but driven by appetite—for conquest, for land, for glory, even for food, the grape of the vine, the first fruit of the harvest—the grand eminence whose face you search for the face of the boy. In him, you saw both the promise of Israel (the face of the boy) and the maddeningly complicated reality it has become (the cannonball-shaped prime minister banging the podium in a roomful of reporters).

At the center of his story is Lebanon, and the tragedy of the Sabra and Shatila refugee camps. It's the stain that can never be made clean. That it was neither unprecedented nor unpredictable made it still more shocking. In some ways, the massacres seemed to follow logically from the Israeli policy that began with the iron wall and the night squads. It seemed inevitable, even, as much a fulfillment of ideology as the glass towers of Tel Aviv. In Lebanon, Sharon made Israelis see themselves as they were seen, as if for the first time, and was therefore hated.

He became a symbol of everything that had gone right and every-thing that had gone wrong—how the early enthusiasm was lost, how the mission was muddied, how the boys went to the front singing songs and came back covered in blood. He was driven from public life. (It's an ancient ritual: the beast is loaded with the sin of the people and sent into the wilderness.) He spent a generation in the outer dark; then, in a moment of terror and fear, was brought back.

Sometimes an old warrior, even a troubled old warrior, is given a moment of grace, a still point in the whirl of events when it seems that another fate is possible if only he can grasp it. This was the case with Yitzhak Rabin at Oslo: the door opened, the hand appeared, he took it. This was even more the case with Ariel Sharon in the wake of the Second Intifada. When the fighting stopped, he paused, looked around, studied the terrain. He was afforded a Moses-like glimpse of the road ahead and quickly saw his mistake: the big one being the set-tlements, an error driven by the belief that Israelis could prevail by force alone, could live in the land as if they were its only inhabitants. In the end, he came to preach against his own earlier preaching. He was, in a sense, fulfilling his story, living the drama through its third act. These final scenes, which played out on TV and in newspapers, were so dra-matic most experts simply dismissed them. ("Wait and see. Something will come up. There will be an emergency. The withdrawal will never happen.") Here was this personification of his people, the New Jew grown old, who had worshipped and feared and killed and been killed and loved, returning to the place where he started to make a final reck-oning. Maybe leadership forces a person to grow up; a prime minister must put away childish things, and make an honest assessment.

Sharon knew what had to be done, and tried to do it, but was run-ning out of time. (His realization, tragically, came too late.) When I think of him in those last months, it's as an old man in a hurry, talk-ing, shouting, giving orders, consoling, explaining. "We must do it," he said. "Israel can no longer rule a hostile and growing population of Arabs. It's bad for them, and it's worse for the Jews."

He wanted to secure Israel as a Jewish nation for generations to come but did not continue long enough in office to see his work to completion. One day, in the summer of 2005—he had already removed the settlements from the Gaza Strip—he complained of a violent headache. He was taken to a hospital, where doctors said he had suffered a minor stroke. They put him on blood thinner (to prevent clotting), then sent him home. A week later, because his blood had been made too thin, he had a brain hemorrhage. He was being driven through the Negev. The wilderness that David crossed in his exile from Jerusalem. He waved at the driver in panic. He could think but could not talk. In his last sensible moment, as the car raced to the hospital, he pointed frantically at his head. For some reason, this image— Sharon pointing at his brain—makes me think of his young son, who shot himself dead with the old Bedouin rifle.

After the old man collapsed, a desolation settled on Israel. A moment had been missed; you could just feel it. Even the manner of his exit seemed symbolic. Sharon did not die but instead lapsed into a living death, kept going by machines, the body alive but the ancient Jewish mind gone. What followed was a parade of dull, gray politicians, pointless actions, and frustrating wars. Everywhere you look, the lines are smudged, the rockets coming in. The people seem spent, exhausted of ideas. It's as if Israel, this tiny high-tech Sparta, has outlived its first identity, has gone through its youth and is still not sure what to make of itself or what it wants to be. Like all revolutionary movements, the question is how to keep the embers glowing after the first fire has burned out. In a sense, every possibility is open to Israel, the best and worst, so its citizens seem to be waiting, worrying, wondering, hoping.

My father tells me my mood is too dark, that somewhere the next Rabin or Sharon, the next warrior or peacemaker, is coming of age, but I wonder if this is just the old Hebrew belief in messiahs and miraculous endings. "You are waiting for a prophet," I tell him, "but the age of prophecy (as in the last books of the Bible) is over." The heroes have gone. Ariel Sharon was the last man to speak to God face-to-face.

Thy glory, O Israel, is slain upon thy high places! How are the mighty fallen!

The mood is manifested in the "separation" wall Israel is building in its territory and in the West Bank. It may be necessary, but it seems like a regression, a retreat from the daring that made the Zionist project possible. The Jews became Israelis only when they heeded Orde Wingate and came out from behind the fence. In a sense, they have now thrown the old fence across the entire country and walled themselves off from the entire world.

What does the Old New Land look like to you now, Dr. Herzl?

I wonder what Israel might have been like had it had a normal history, if it had not been Sparta but Athens, if all the money and blood and ingenuity it put into the military and war had instead been put into the nation.

Every problem flows from this single error: the odd notion that Palestine was without a people, that its history ended when the Jews slipped into the pages of the Book. The Zionist ideology was beautiful, but for the pioneers to fulfill it, the Arabs could not exist. Reinventing that ideology—creating a place in which Jews and Arabs can, in a sense, dream the same dream—is the challenge ahead. Israelis must find a way to detach their nation from their story, and live in the here and now; otherwise the Third Temple may go the way of the other two. This was always the danger of turning the Book back into a temple, even if the Zionists did not realize it. The concept of Israel had, in a sense, been hermetically sealed, stored in shrink-wrap for two thousand years, where it was pickled and preserved and remained pristine. Now the Jews have returned their holy idea to the street, where, as is happening with the Hebrew language, it has been barbarized and filled with slang. In the long run of generations, this will mean a language that is filled with Hebrew but is not exactly Hebrew—not in the old sense—and a state that is filled with Jews but is not exactly Jewish. (You can't really have a Jewish democracy, anyway.) In the end, change may come with some optimistic leader, still unknown to us, who appeals less to the particular ideals of Zionism than to the universal ideals of the Enlightenment. We await him as our great-grandfathers awaited the Messiah. If he does not come, then the structure of this story, as far as the world is concerned, may read less like temple to book to temple than like *Israel is unreal* to *Israel is real* to *Israel is too real.*

I woke early on the morning of August 14, the Ninth of Av. The Yesha Council had called all Jews to gather in the Western Wall Plaza to mourn the loss of the Temple and protest the withdrawal from Gaza. The police expected a hundred thousand people in the Old City. Hoping to avoid conflict, the mayor closed the holy places to Muslims between ages fifteen and forty. I walked to the Damascus Gate. I heard the crowd before I saw it, a thousand men trying to push through an Israeli checkpoint. I waded into the crowd, the way you roll up your pants and wade into a river. A cold river, and you feel the current. People were yelling at the soldiers, who were looking over their heads. I turned to the man next to me. He was dressed in knock-off American casual wear.

"What's this about?" I asked.

"The Jews won't let anybody up to the Mosque."

"Why?"

"Because they're Jews."

He stopped, looked at me, then said, "You're a Jew."

I said, "No, I'm a Christian."

(This made me feel like Peter in the Gospel: "You will deny me three times before the cock cries.")

"No," the man said, "I see you. You're a Jew."

"No," I told him. "I'm a Christian."

I went to the front of the crowd. The soldier said a few words in Hebrew. I looked at him blankly. He waved me away. I went back to the road and walked west. The noise faded. There were just buses, cars, trucks, tourists, the old sandstone walls of the city uncoiling like a ribbon. I walked in the first gate I saw, the New Gate. There was no checkpoint, no crowd. Why don't the men in front of the Damascus Gate do what I did? I wondered. Because they don't want to get in, I decided. Confrontation, protest, shouting—that's what they're after. It's like tennis. A game with a net, a checkpoint or wall, a player on either side. I wandered through the Christian Quarter, then the Armenian Quarter, where each door opens on a garden, a priest in a robe. The street doubled back, climbed. I was in a maze. I came out on a promontory across from the Dome of the Rock, high above the Western Wall. The plaza was crowded with Jews, thousands and thousands, swaying, moaning, praying. From here it seemed clear how the city was organized: vertically, like time, with era heaped on era, kingdom heaped on kingdom.

I went downstairs, through a metal detector. A friend and I had arranged a meeting with an archeologist, a handsome, mild-mannered man who had said he would take us on a tour of the tunnels beneath the Western Wall and the Arab Quarter. These had been water tunnels; some were probably used by men who built the temples. They had long been closed to "protect religious sensitivities." (On a clandestine excavation in the tunnels, Shlomo Goren claimed he saw the Ark of the Covenant reflected in a mirror held at the end of a long pole.) When a few of the tunnels were opened by Benjamin Netanyahu in the 1990s, there were riots across the city in which several people were killed.

I had been in the tunnels before, as part of a tour group, but this archeologist promised to take us to places usually off limits to the public. We crossed the plaza, went into the tunnels. We walked along a broad corridor, then began to descend. The tunnel, illuminated by light fixtures, smelled of wet earth. It felt as if we were going into a mine, the sound of the plaza fading above. The archeologist had a flashlight, which he clicked on and off, pointing at walls, showing us where the stone and masonry work changed, each such change suggesting the rise or fall of a kingdom, which meant another sea of exiles, another ocean of memories. There was a jag in the tunnel—"It's tricky here," warned the archeologist, "Be careful." I could not see my hand in front of my face. He clicked on the light, shone it on the wall: there was an elaborate gate built into the stone, buried as if the Damascus Gate had been buried. It was grand, but the light showed only pieces at a time. The door itself was sealed with stone.

"What's on the other side?" I asked.

"No one knows," the archeologist said. "It was closed over two thousand years ago, when the First Temple was destroyed. Maybe the Jews still had the tablets then."

I asked if someone would excavate the door.

He said, "We're not allowed. It would probably start a world war."

He then said, "I would give anything just to dig five feet. Can you imagine what's inside? Maybe the Ark. Maybe something even more amazing."

We continued, following handrails built in the walls. We were going down and down, through eras and dispensations: from modern Israel, to the British Mandate, to the Ottoman Empire, to the Arab Empire, to the Byzantine Empire, to the Romans, to the Greeks, to the Babylonians, to the Ancient Hebrews, to the Jebusites, to the first nomads who stumbled on this hill, then just a hill among hills, wilderness in a world that was nothing but wilderness. It seemed as if we were going to the basement of Jewish time. I heard a ghostly singing, an echo of an echo, but clearer and more distinct as we went on.

"What's that?" I asked.

"I don't know," the archeologist said.

The voices got louder. We came around a turn and there were three women, Orthodox Jews in head scarves, bowed to the ground, their fingers touching the damp stone, weeping and singing.

I had finally reached the center of this story, the core of Zion, where everything comes together and everything runs apart. Jewish history is rooms and stories and hymns and epics and doors, and when you get through all those rooms and stories and hymns and epics and go through the last door you find these three women, deep in the earth, singing the tragedy of their own terrible past.

We watched them for a minute, then continued.

"Why are they here?" I asked.

"Some believe this spot, the lowest point in the tunnel, is the closest you can get to the holy of holies," the archeologist told me. "It's the navel of the world."

"What were they singing?"

"It's from Lamentations," he said.

He guessed at the chapter and verse, which I looked up later:

Jerusalem remembered in the days of her affliction and of her miseries all her pleasant things that she had in the days of old, when her people fell into the hand of the enemy, and none did help her: the adversaries saw her, and did mock at her sabbaths.

When the sun goes down, I sit on a hill in the German Colony, in Jerusalem, and look at the lights in the east. The wind picks up. It's a desert wind and it makes me think of Israel, both the modern nation and the ancient kingdom that lived for many centuries in the mind of its people. It's a great irony that it was more secure as an idea than it's ever been as a nation with an army. Has Zionism failed? Well, no. It created something real and lasting. It gave Jews a safe harbor. It gave many people faith after the Holocaust. It's impossible to imagine what life would have been like after the Second World War if there had been no answer to Auschwitz. All those exhibits at Yad Vashem but no escalator out.

Will Israel be destroyed? As Hamas and Hezbollah and Al Qaeda and Iran all promise. The optimistic wisemen say no, of course not, it's a strong nation with a strong army, a solution will be found at the negotiating table, in two states, but some with a dark turn of mind think Israel has already missed its moment. The last headland went by in the fog. The ship is out at sea. It must be overrun. By missiles, or a human wave. Judaism survived the destruction of the Second Temple only because a few geniuses turned the temple into a book. But in our time, the Book was turned back into a temple. In the wake of another destruction, would the community dwindle and vanish, or, like a soul freed from its body, would it resume its eternal wandering? In which case, the most quotidian aspects of modern Israeli life—the color of the Number 12 bus, the width of the boardwalk in Tel Aviv, the design of the highway to Eilat—would become a fetish, memorized, contemplated, saturated with meaning. And each of us will wear a chain, and on each chain a replica of an F-16 Tomcat.

Bibliography

Agnon, S. Y. *Only Yesterday.* Princeton, N.J.: Princeton University Press, 1945.

Alter, Robert. *The Art of Biblical Narrative.* New York: Basic Books, 1981; reprint New York: W. W. Norton, 2000.

————. *The Book of Psalms: A Translation with Commentary.* New York: W. W. Norton, 2007.

————. *The David Story: A Translation with Commentary of 1 and 2 Samuel.* New York: W. W. Norton, 1999.

————. *The Five Books of Moses: A Translation with Commentary.* New York: W. W. Norton, 2004.

Amiry, Suad. *Sharon and My Mother-in-Law: Ramallah Diaries.* New York: Pantheon Books, 2003.

Antonius, George. *The Arab Awakening.* Philadelphia: J. B. Lippincott Company, 1939.

Archbold, Norma Parrish. *The Mountains of Israel: The Bible and the West Bank.* Jerusalem: Phoebe's Song, 1993.

Arendt, Hannah. *Eichmann in Jerusalem: A Report on the Banality of Evil.* New York: Viking Penguin, 1963.

Ariel, David S. *What Do Jews Believe?: The Spiritual Foundations of Judaism.* New York: Schocken, 1995.

Armstrong, Karen. *Jerusalem: One City, Three Faiths.* New York: Knopf, 1996.

Babel, Isaac. *1920 Diary.* Trans. H. T. Willets. New Haven and London: Yale University Press, 1995.

————. *Collected Stories.* Trans. David McDuff. New York: Penguin Books, 1994.

Barghouti, Mourid. *I Saw Ramallah.* Trans. Ahdaf Soueif. New York: Anchor Books, 2000.

Baring-Gould, S. *Curious Myths of the Middle Ages.* New York: John B. Alden Publisher, 1884.

Bellow, Saul. *Mr. Sammler's Planet*. New York: Viking Press, 1970.

———. *To Jerusalem and Back: A Personal Account*. New York: Viking Press, 1976.

Berkovits, Eliezer. *Essential Essays on Judaism*. Ed. David Hazony. Jerusalem: The Shalem Center, 2002.

Berlin, Isaiah. *Against the Current: Essays in the History of Ideas*. New York: Viking Press, 1980.

———. *Chaim Weizmann*. New York: Farrar, Straus and Cudahy, 1958.

———. *The Power of Ideas*. Ed. Henry Hardy. Princeton, N.J.: Princeton University Press, 2000.

———. *The Sense of Reality: Studies in Ideas and Their History*. New York: Farrar, Straus and Giroux, 1997.

Berman, Paul. *Terror and Liberalism*. New York: W. W. Norton, 2003.

Bialik, Hayim Nahman. *Songs from Bialik*. Trans. and ed. Atar Hadari. Syracuse, N.Y.: Syracuse University Press, 2000.

Bloch, Ariel, and Chana Bloch, trans. *The Song of Songs*. New York: Random House, 1995.

Buber, Martin. *Israel and Palestine: The History of an Idea*. London: Horovitz Publishing, 1953.

———. *Israel and the World: Essays in a Time of Crisis*. New York: Schocken, 1948.

———. *Moses: The Revelation and the Covenant*. Introduction by Michael Fishbane. Amherst, N.Y.: Humanity Books, 1946.

Carey, Roane, and Jonathan Shainin, eds. *The Other Israel: Voices of Refusal and Dissent*. New York: The New Press, 2002.

Carmi, T., ed. and trans. *The Penguin Book of Hebrew Verse*. New York: Penguin Books, 1981.

Caro, Robert A. *The Years of Lyndon B. Johnson: The Path to Power*. New York: Vintage, 1990.

Chapman, Peter. *Bananas! How the United Fruit Company Shaped the World*. New York: Canongate, 2008.

Daniel, Jean. *The Jewish Prison: A Rebellious Meditation on the State of Judaism*. Brooklyn, N.Y.: Melville House, 2005.

Dayan, Moshe. *Moshe Dayan: Story of My Life*. New York: William Morrow and Company, 1976.

Dosal, Paul J. *Doing Business with Dictators: A Political History of United Fruit in Guatemala, 1899–1944*. Lanham, Md.: Rowman and Littlefield, 1997.

Dyer, John. *Tulane: The Biography of a University, 1834–1965*. New York: Harper and Row, 1966.

Eban, Abba. *Diplomacy for the Next Century*. New Haven, Conn.: Yale University Press, 1998.

Ellis, Marc H. *Toward a Jewish Theology of Liberation: The Challenge of the 21st Century*. Waco, Tex.: Baylor University Press, 2004.

Elon, Amos. *A Blood-Dimmed Tide: Dispatches from the Middle East*. New York: Columbia University Press, 1997.

————. *Herzl.* New York: Holt, Rinehart and Winston, 1975.

————. *The Israelis: Founders and Sons.* New York: Holt, Rinehart and Winston, 1971.

————. *Jerusalem: City of Mirrors.* New York: Little, Brown, 1989.

Freud, Sigmund. *Moses and Monotheism.* New York: Random House, 1961.

Gellman, Rabbi Ezra, ed. *Essays on the Thought and Philosophy of Rabbi Kook.* Cranbury, N.J.: Cornwall Books, 1991.

Gibbon, Edward. *The Decline and Fall of the Roman Empire.* (All volumes.) New York: Peter Fenelon Collier and Son, 1908.

Gilman, Sander L. *Jewish Self-Hatred: Anti-Semitism and the Hidden Language of the Jews.* Baltimore, Md.: Johns Hopkins University Press, 1986.

Goldberg, David J. *To the Promised Land: A History of Zionist Thought from Its Origins to the Modern State of Israel.* New York: Penguin Books, 1996.

Goldhill, Simon. *The Temple of Jerusalem.* Cambridge, Mass.: Harvard University Press, 2005.

Gorenberg, Gershom. *The Accidental Empire: Israel and the Birth of the Settlements, 1967–1977.* New York: Times Books, 2006.

————. *The End of Days: Fundamentalism and the Struggle for the Temple Mount.* New York: The Free Press, 2000.

Grossman, David. *Death as a Way of Life: Ten Years After Oslo.* New York: Farrar, Straus and Giroux, 2003.

————. *The Yellow Wind.* Trans. Haim Watzman. New York: Farrar, Straus and Giroux, 1988.

Haig, Alexander M., Jr. *Caveat: Realism, Reagan, and Foreign Policy.* New York: Scribner, 1984.

Haig, Alexander M., Jr., with Charles McCarry. *Inner Circles: How America Changed the World: A Memoir.* New York: Grand Central Publishing, 1994.

Halevi, Judah. *The Kuzari.* Trans. Hartwig Hirschfeld. London: George Routledge and Sons, 1905.

Hashomer Hatzair. *The Massacre of European Jewry: An Anthology.* Kibbutz Merchavia: World Hashomer Hatzair English Speaking Department, 1963.

Hazony, David, Yoram Hazony, and Michael B. Oren, eds. *New Essays on Zionism.* Jerusalem: The Shalem Center, 2006.

Herzl, Theodor. *Complete Diaries.* Tel Aviv: Herzl Press, 1970.

————. *The Jewish State.* Trans. Sylvia D'Avigdor. New York: American Zionist Emergency Council, 1946.

————. *Old New Land.* Trans. Lotta Levensohn. Jacksonville, Fla.: Bloch Publishing, 1941.

————. *Zionist Writings: Essays and Addresses.* Tel Aviv: Herzl Press, 1973.

Herzog, Chaim, and Shlomo Gazit. *The Arab-Israeli Wars: War and Peace in the Middle East from the War of Independence to the Present.* New York: Random House, 1982.

Heschel, Abraham Joshua. *God in Search of Man: A Philosophy of Judaism.* New York: Farrar, Straus and Giroux, 1955.

————. *Israel: An Echo of Eternity.* Farrar, Straus and Giroux, 1967.

————. *The Prophets.* New York: Harper and Row, 1962.

Hillel, Daniel. *The Natural History of the Bible: An Environmental Exploration of the Hebrew Scriptures.* New York: Columbia University Press, 2006.

Kac, Arthur W. *The Rebirth of the State of Israel: Is It of God or of Men?* Grand Rapids, Mich.: Baker Book House, 1958.

Kahane, Rabbi Meir. *They Must Go.* New York: Grosset and Dunlap, 1981.

Kahvedjian, Kevork. *Jerusalem Through My Father's Eyes* (photographs). Jerusalem: Elia Photo Service, 1998.

Kierkegaard, Søren. *Fear and Trembling.* Trans. Alastair Hannay. New York: Penguin Books, 1985.

King James Bible. New York: Ballantine Books, 1991.

Koeppel, Dan. *Banana: The Fate of the Fruit That Changed the World.* New York: Penguin Group, 2008.

Koestler, Arthur. *The Thirteenth Tribe: The Khazar Empire and Its Heritage.* New York: Random House, 1976.

Kovner, Abba. *A Canopy in the Desert: Selected Poems.* Trans. Shirley Kaufman, with Ruth Adler and Nurit Orchan. Pittsburgh, Pa.: University of Pittsburgh Press, 1973.

————. *Scrolls of Fire: A Nation Fighting for Its Life; Fifty-Two Chapters of Jewish Martyrology.* With drawings by Dan Reisinger. Jerusalem: Kefer Publishing House, 1981.

Jewish Encyclopedia, The. New York: Funk and Wagnalls, 1901, 1906. (See www.jewish encyclopedia.com.)

Josephus, Flavius. *The Jewish War.* Trans. G. A. Williamson. New York: Penguin Books, 1959.

Laqueur, Walter. *A History of Zionism: From the French Revolution to the Establishment of the State of Israel.* New York: Holt, Rinehart and Winston, 1972.

Lawrence, T. E. *Seven Pillars of Wisdom: A Triumph.* New York: Doubleday, 1926.

Lewis, Bernard. *The Middle East: A Brief History of the Last 2,000 Years.* New York: Touchstone, 1995.

————. *Semites and Anti-Semites: An Inquiry into Conflict and Prejudice.* New York: W. W. Norton, 1987.

Lewisohn, Ludwig. *Theodor Herzl: A Portrait for This Age.* Foreword by David Ben-Gurion. New York: World Pub. Co., 1955.

Mazar, Eilat. *The Complete Guide to the Temple Mount Excavations.* Jerusalem: Sjoham Academic Research and Publication, 2002.

Morris, Benny. *The Birth of the Palestinian Refugee Problem, 1947–1949.* Cambridge, UK: Cambridge University Press, 1988.

————. *1948: A History of the First Arab-Israeli War.* New Haven, Conn.: Yale University Press, 2008.

————. *Righteous Victims: A History of the Zionist-Arab Conflict, 1881–2001.* New York: Vintage Books, 2001.

Oren, Michael B. *Six Days of War: June 1967 and the Making of the Modern Middle East.* New York: Oxford University Press, 2002.

Peres, Shimon, and Robert Littell. *For the Future of Israel.* Baltimore, Md.: Johns Hopkins University Press, 1998.

Potok, Chaim. *Wanderings: Chaim Potok's History of the Jews*. New York: Knopf, 1978.

Rabin, Yitzhak. *The Rabin Memoirs*. Berkeley: University of California Press, 1996.

Roth, Joseph. *The Wandering Jews*. Trans. Michael Hofmann. New York: W. W. Norton, 2001.

———. *What I Saw: Reports from Berlin 1920–1933*. Trans. with an introduction by Michael Hofmann. New York: W. W. Norton, 2003.

Roth, Philip. *The Counterlife*. New York: Farrar, Straus and Giroux, 1987.

———. *My Life as a Man*. New York: Farrar, Straus and Giroux, 1970.

———. *Operation Shylock*. New York: Simon & Schuster, 1993.

———. *Zuckerman Bound*. New York: Farrar, Straus and Giroux, 1979.

Said, Edward. *Orientalism*. New York: Pantheon Books, 1978.

———. *The Question of Palestine*. New York: Times Books, 1979.

Sarna, Jonathan D. *American Judaism: A History*. New Haven and London: Yale University Press, 2004.

Scholem, Gershom. *Major Trends in Jewish Mysticism*. New York: Schocken, 1946.

Segev, Tom. *1967: Israel, the War, and the Year That Transformed the Middle East*. New York: Henry Holt/Metropolitan Books, 2007.

———. *One Palestine, Complete: Jews and Arabs Under the British Mandate*. New York: Henry Holt/Metropolitan Books, 2000.

———. *The Seventh Million: The Israelis and the Holocaust*. New York: Hill and Wang, 1993.

Shahak, Israel. *Jewish History, Jewish Religion: The Weight of Three Thousand Years*. Chicago: Pluto Press, 1994.

Shakespeare, William. *The Merchant of Venice*. London: Methuen and Co., 1955.

Shapira, Avraham, ed. *The Seventh Day: Soldiers' Talk About the Six-Day War*. London: Andre Deutsch, 1967.

Sharon, Ariel, with David Chanoff. *Warrior: An Autobiography*. New York: Simon & Schuster, 1989.

Shatz, Adam, ed. *Prophets Outcast: A Century of Dissident Jewish Writing About Zionism and Israel*. New York: Nation Books, 2004.

Shaw, Irwin, and Robert Capa. *Report on Israel*. New York: Simon & Schuster, 1950.

Shimoni, Gideon. *The Zionist Ideology*. Hanover, N.H.: Brandeis University Press, 1995.

Shlaim, Avi. *The Iron Wall: Israel and the Arab World*. New York: W. W. Norton, 1999.

Slezkine, Yuri. *The Jewish Century*. Princeton, N.J.: Princeton University Press, 2004.

Sorel, George. *Reflections on Violence*. Glencoe, Ill.: The Free Press, 1950.

Teveth, Shabtai. *Ben-Gurion: The Burning Ground: 1906–1948*. Boston: Houghton Mifflin, 1987.

Thomas, Hugh. *Rivers of Gold: The Rise of the Spanish Empire from Columbus to Magellan*. New York: Random House, 2003.

Tudela, Benjamin. *The Itinerary of Benjamin of Tudela: Travels in the Middle Ages*. Introduction by Michael A. Singer. Malibu, Calif.: Pangloss Press, 2005. (Original from twelfth century.)

Vidal-Naquet, Pierre. *The Jews: History, Memory, and the Present*. New York: Columbia University Press, 1995.

Weizman, Ezer. *On Eagles' Wings: The Personal Story of the Leading Commander of the Israeli Air Force.* New York: Macmillan, 1977.

————. *The Battle for Peace.* New York: Bantam Books, 1981.

Weizmann, Chaim. *Trial and Error: The Autobiography of Chaim Weizmann.* New York: Harper, 1949.

Yerushalmi, Yosef Hayim. *Zakhor: Jewish History and Jewish Memory.* New York: Schocken, 1989.

Acknowledgments

A long time ago, when he was done dropping objects off a twelve-story tower, David Letterman would look into the camera and say, "It's late, and I'm tired, but it's the good kind of tired." I know exactly what he meant—like a day at the lake when your legs ache, but in that nice, from-over-use kind of way; it's how I felt when I finished this book. So now, in the moment before I fall into a deep, dreamless, end-of-something sleep, I would like to thank the people who helped me exhaust myself. First my Israeli cousins, some on Kibbutz Ein Hahoresh, others scattered across that tiny country, who, as always, took me in, fed me, drove me, introduced me, translated for me, and let me use the pool: Yehuda and Rina Marle, Yonat and Yossi Rotbein, Gadi and Ayelet Marle. Gadi is a historian, and his knowledge and brilliance—there, I said it—in matters of Jewish history were invaluable. Yonat is a leader of Givat Haviva, a foundation and educational center. It started as an archive for the papers Ruzka Marle (Yonat's mother) brought to Palestine from the ruins of the Vilna Ghetto, and has since grown into a powerful force for good. Its primary mission is Jewish and Palestinian coexistence. I spent several days there attending workshops that bring young Jews and Arabs together for the summer, and spoke to experts and fellows who work at the center, including (and special thanks to) Mossi Raz, a founder of Peace Now who helped me understand the predicament and mood of the Israeli Left, and Mohammed Darawshe, who tried to explain the life of Arab citizens in the Jewish state. I would like to thank my friend Michael Kovner, who traveled with me and helped arrange interviews with old-time Israeli officers and military commandos—he was one himself. Michael's mother, Vitka Kempner, one of the few surviving partisans of Vilna (there's a room dedicated to her in Yad Vashem), is always a great inspiration and a great help. I would like to thank my cousin Anat Haffetz and her husband, Bar. I took Anat to see the fireworks on the mall in D.C. when she was seventeen, and she's been taking care of me ever since. Anat is herself a fine young Israeli journalist, and as such was able to get me into places I never would have reached on my own. She helped set up many interviews. I would like to thank Nurit Orchan, an old friend who took me on a tour of the West Bank and the wall or security fence (you choose) that Israel has thrown up. In my house, I have a Michael Kovner painting of the hills and towns east of Jerusalem. Nurit took me to the overlook from which the painting was done, and showed me how the terrain has been remade by the wall. More people to thank in Israel: Yossi Beilin, the crusading politician who, along with Sari Nusseibeh, wrote the unofficial peace treaty that can serve as a model if there is to be hope for normal summer-afternoon life on either side of the line; Boaz Karni, who works at Beilin's Economic Cooperation Foundation, established to make connections between communities after Yitzhak Rabin was assassinated (when I met Karni, he was arranging the purchase and transfer of Gaza Strip greenhouses from the settlers to the Palestinian laborers who worked in the rows; these greenhouses, which were paid for by rich American Jews, were trashed by Hamas within weeks of the withdrawal); Asa Kasher, an Israeli judge and professor who helped write the IDF's Code of Ethics; David Sunshine, a young Israeli army officer who, by refusing to serve in the territories, started a movement and a debate; Amnon Shahak, Israeli general and former IDF chief of staff, the once and future hope of the Israeli political center; Dr. Eilat Mazar, an archeologist who recently discovered (so she claims; there is debate) the remnants of King David's Phoenician-built, cedar-beamed palace; Danny Herman, the archeologist who took me to the Western Wall tunnels; Anat Biletsky, a founder of the Israeli human rights group B'Tselem; Shmuel Ettinger, a fine historian as well as an excellent guide at grown-over battlefields; Pinchas Wallerstein, a leader of the Yesha Council, an umbrella group that represents Israeli settlers—he's a nut, but as Rodney Dangerfield said of Sam Kinison, "I admire his passion"; Richard Pater, from the IDF press office; and Mordechai Kislef, the director of botanical archeology at Bar-Ilan University in Tel Aviv. Kislef told me about the oldest surviving olive trees in the world, which stood in the time of the Second Temple, most of them in the Galilee, as well as a project in which seeds from an extinct species of date are now being grown. He is an extremely religious man, and as I was leaving, he looked at me with sparkly green eyes, so much like the eyes of my father, and said, "I used to be like you."

"Like me? How?"

"I also didn't believe in anything."

I would like to thank the people at the Shalem Center in Jerusalem, because they helped me and because I like them: David Hazony, Stefanie Argamon (and Stefanie's mom, who read *Tough Jews* and then told her daughter, "Yes, help him"), and Yossi Klein Halevi, a model for anyone writing about anything.

I would like to thank the security agent I talked to as I was leaving the country—this is almost always a beautiful woman, as (they think) you are less likely to be impatient or rude with a beautiful woman. Rather than asking the usual questions, she said, "If you can recite the haftorah portion from your Bar Mitzvah, you can go right through." When I started, stammered, then forgot, she said, "What kind of Jew are you?"

I said, "The crying on the inside kind, I guess."

She said, "Oh yes, you mean an American Jew."

I would like to thank, stateside, David Lipsky, who always drops whatever he is doing; Ian Frazier, gosh I love that guy; Jim Albrecht, who traveled with me in Israel, and always made me see old places with new eyes—"Jim eyes" is what I call them; Jean Brown, who not only transcribes tapes but does so with commentary; Michelle Ciaccora, for the fact-checking; Jann Wenner at *Rolling Stone*, my editor and my friend; Robert Alter, who, in the course of an interview I did with him for *The Believer*, helped me see the Torah in new ways—a scary-smart man; Dana Brown, my editor at *Vanity Fair*, and Graydon Carter, who supports the wild flight of fancy; Jeff Posternak and Andrew Wylie at the Wylie Agency; Jeff Seroy, Sarita Varma, and Jesse Coleman at

FSG; and Jonathan Galassi, who I suspect is one of Lamed Vov (you'll have to look that one up, Jonathan).

So now I've reached the inner solar system, the Mercury and the Mars of my life, which is, first and foremost (sun and moon) my parents, Herb and Ellen—see Herbie in the Blue Orb, he nails it; my sister and her husband, Bill and Sharon Levin; my brother and his wife, Steven and Lisa Cohen; my mother-in-law, Dorothy Medoff, and her issue, Jeremy and Stephanie; and my sons—Luca Brasi came to my wedding and said, "May your firstborn child be a masculine child," and the clouds opened and it rained boys— Aaron, Nate, Micah. Also my wife, Jessica, but, you know, the thing is dedicated to her, which isn't enough, but will have to do. And, of course, Francis Albert Sinatra.

Index